"*Silence on the Mountain* has the seductive allure and vivid characters of the finest fiction and the penetration of the most elegant journalism. Mr. Wilkinson's painstaking work has crucial lessons for our government's future role not only in Latin America but in the entire world. Above all, his book serves literature's deepest impulse: to bring forth truth out of silence."
—The 2003 PEN/Martha Albrand Award for First Nonfiction citation

"A young human rights lawyer with an eye for detail and the gumption to ride a rickety motorcycle to get to the bottom of a story until now largely untold, Wilkinson has written a book full of grim details about exploitation of coffee pickers, genocidal massacres, and frustrated leftist organizing."
—Clifford Krauss, *New York Times Book Review*

"[*Silence on the Mountain*] document[s] unthinkable horror, insisting as we try to turn away that attention must be paid, that what happened there must never happen again, that the past isn't past at all."
—Joanne Omang, *Washington Post*

"Wilkinson's quest for information takes him from the upper to the lower to the middle classes, through the different tiers of Guatemala's dependent export economy, all the way to your morning latte."—David Stoll, *New Republic*

"The author's style is taut and precise, but it is the Guatemalans themselves who speak with the greatest eloquence."—*New Yorker*

"Given the recidivist nature of U.S. policy in Latin America, Wilkinson's book [is] a well-timed reminder of the potentially devastating consequences of our successes."—Alex Stone, *Washington Monthly*

"A series of brilliantly recorded encounters with scores of people. . . . a well-told and often suspenseful mystery story."
—Thomas Quigley, *America: National Catholic Weekly*

"A profound book . . . both easy to read and compelling."
—*Publishers Weekly*

"A page-turning work of detective nonfiction."—Diana Nelson Jones, *Pittsburgh Post-Gazette*

AMERICAN ENCOUNTERS / GLOBAL INTERACTIONS

A series edited by Gilbert M. Joseph

and Emily S. Rosenberg

This series aims to stimulate critical perspectives and fresh interpretive frameworks for scholarship on the history of the imposing global presence of the United States. Its primary concerns include the deployment and contestation of power, the construction and deconstruction of cultural and political borders, the fluid meaning of intercultural encounters, and the complex interplay between the global and the local. American Encounters seeks to strengthen dialogue and collaboration between historians of U.S. international relations and area studies specialists.

The series encourages scholarship based on multiarchive historical research. At the same time, it supports a recognition of the representational character of all stories about the past and promotes critical inquiry into issues of subjectivity and narrative. In the process, American Encounters strives to understand the context in which meanings related to nations, cultures, and political economy are continually produced, challenged, and reshaped.

SILENCE
ON THE MOUNTAIN

SILENCE ON THE MOUNTAIN

STORIES OF TERROR, BETRAYAL, AND FORGETTING IN GUATEMALA

Daniel Wilkinson

Duke University Press   Durham & London

2004

Library of Congress Cataloging-in-Publication Data
Wilkinson, Daniel.
Silence on the mountain : stories of terror, betrayal, and forgetting in Guatemala /
Daniel Wilkinson.
p. cm. — (American encounters/global interactions)
Includes bibliographical references and index.
ISBN 0-8223-3368-6 (pbk. : alk. paper)
1. Guerrillas — Guatemala — History. 2. State-sponsored terrorism — Guatemala.
3. Guatemala — History — Civil War, 1960-1996. 4. Guatemala — History — Civil
War, 1960-1996 — Atrocities. I. Title. II. Series.
F1466.7.W55 2004
972.8105'2 — dc22   2004013070

Book design by Victoria Hartman
Frontispiece map by Jacques Chazaud

Illustration credits: pages 31, 43, 58, and 67, courtesy of the author; page 39, "Puerto de San José" courtesy of Margit Lawrence; page 182, courtesy of Francisco Rivera; page 237, courtesy of Mario Robles; page 357, courtesy of Daniel Hernández-Salazar. The following illustrations are reprinted courtesy of the Colección Fototeca Guatemala, Centro de Investigaciones Regionales de Mesoamérica (CIRMA): page 37, "Muelle de Puerto de San José, 1886," anonymous (cropped); page 49, "Volcán Santa Mariá y volcán Santiaguito, Quetzaltenango, ca. 1922," anonymous (cropped); page 99, "Campaña de Juan José Arévalo, 1944," anonymous; page 183, "Campesinos Arbencistas capturados después del derrocamiento de Arbenz, 1954," anonymous; and page 247, "Guerrilla y simpatizantes sobre templo Maya en finca de café, ca. 1981," anonymous.

The excerpt on page 342 from The Cure at Troy: A Version of Sophocles' Philoctetes, by Seamus Heaney, copyright © 1990 by Seamus Heaney, is reprinted by permission of Farrar, Straus and Giroux, LLC, and by permission of Faber and Faber Ltd. The "bit of poetry" on page 340 is an excerpt from W. H. Auden's "Spain."

Para Patricia
quien le dio luz a mi vida

CONTENTS

IV. And They Were the Eruption

AUTHOR'S NOTE

All the characters and places in this book are real. I have used pseudonyms in some cases in order to protect people's identities. I have also slightly altered personal descriptions and shifted the dates of some incidents that took place in the course of my investigation.

I have included a list of names at the back of the book in order to help readers keep track of the characters that appear throughout the text.

As long as there's smoke, we know we're okay.

— Franz Endler

PART I

A HOUSE BURNED

THE OWNER

ALL I KNEW when I began was that a house had burned down. And not just any house. This was the house of the *patrón* — the *casa patronal* — on a coffee plantation named La Patria.

I knew it had been an old house with walls of mahogany and a tin roof painted burgundy red — the same color as the processing plant on the ridge behind it, the color of the berries harvested every year from the surrounding mountainside. While not as large as the houses of *patrones* in some of the neighboring plantations, it had possessed a special charm, a "gracious" and "pretty" design, and a spectacular view of the Pacific coast. Stepping up to the porch on a sunny day, looking in through the front door, down the hallway and through the living room, you could see the glittering blue of the distant ocean out the back window. Time had taken its toll: a half-century of rainy seasons had softened the outer walls; termites had colonized the inner ones. Yet the structure had endured. And for the eighty-year-old *patrón* and his wife, it had still been home, the place where they intended to live out their days.

I knew that it was just after Christmas in 1983 that the fire had consumed the house. And I knew it had been set by a group of guerrillas who called themselves the Revolutionary Organization of the People in Arms — and who were called, by my own government, terrorists.

⬇

I knew all this because I had met the owner of La Patria in one of those chance encounters that begin the detours that become your life. It was

1993. I had just finished college and come to Guatemala with what the people at Harvard called a "traveling fellowship" — money to go see the world and possibly do a little good in it. I had spent some weeks working in a Mayan Indian town and begun research for an article on the community's efforts to reclaim its ancestral lands. On a visit to Guatemala City, the friend of a friend gave me the phone number of an American professor whose published works on Guatemala dated back to the 1950s. I called him one evening to get tips for my research, and before I'd even finished introducing myself he invited me to dinner at his home in an affluent neighborhood in the outskirts of the city.

His wife greeted me at the door. With her hazel eyes, snow-white hair, light complexion, and perfect English, I figured that Sara Endler was also from the United States, an academic spouse who had followed her husband to a foreign land. It was only when we had moved on to dessert and a second bottle of wine that I learned otherwise. I was saying something about the disparities between Guatemala's agricultural elite and the workers who generate their wealth when she cleared her throat and said, "I must confess, I own a farm."

"A farm?" I wasn't sure what she meant.

"A coffee plantation."

She told me then how she had recently inherited La Patria from her aging father, Franz Endler, who had abandoned the plantation after the *casa patronal* was burned down in the 1980s. As she spoke, my mind raced back over the evening's conversation, searching for any comments I'd made about plantation owners that could have offended my host. When she paused, I asked a question, hardly suspecting that it would be the first of thousands: "Why was the house burned down?"

⚜

The war in Guatemala had been one of the most brutal conflicts in the hemisphere in the twentieth century. By the end of 1983, it had been raging for two decades, with a military government allied with the United States battling a guerrilla movement that was backed by Cuba. The burning of the Endler house was just one of countless acts of destruction in a conflict whose history — at the time I met Sara Endler a decade later — remained largely unwritten.

The army had occupied La Patria, she told me, because it suspected that the owners were collaborating with the guerrillas — an absurd suspicion given how much her parents abhorred the guerrillas' "communistic" ideas. What *was* true was that they themselves had never been the target of guerrilla violence. In fact, the one time a small party of guerrillas had visited them in La Patria, the Endlers had been surprised, even touched, by the respectful behavior of their uninvited guests. When Sara's mother offered the group coffee and cookies, one of the guerrillas — a young indigenous woman — put aside her machine gun and politely insisted on serving them herself. Before leaving, this same young guerrilla gently patted Sara's father on his knee and said, "Don't be scared, *patroncito*. We will build the new nation together."

Apparently the army was aware that the guerrillas hadn't bothered the Endlers. And so, in the ensuing months, it chose to bother them itself. Troops occupied the plantation, turning it into a temporary military base, building sentry posts, and digging trenches wherever they thought necessary. They even dug a trench through the garden by the house. The Endlers were not pleased by the intrusion, but there was nothing they could do to stop it. When the shooting began, Sara told me, the couple sat in their living room and watched the bullets fly. They didn't scare very easily, she laughed, they never had.

Then a note arrived at the plantation: "We have suffered great losses here due to your collaborating with the army," it said. "When the army leaves, we will burn you down."

And sure enough, less than two weeks after the army pulled out of the plantation, the guerrillas arrived to fulfill their promise. The Endlers had not waited around to see that happen, and only afterward did they learn — from their plantation administrator — what had occurred that day. The first attempt to burn the plantation had failed, he told them. A group of women workers had begged the guerrillas not to harm La Patria: the plantation was their only job, and the *patrón* was a good man, and he should be left alone. At first, the guerrillas ignored the entreaties, but the women persisted, pleading so insistently that the guerrillas finally gave up and left.

Two weeks later, they were back. This time they entered with a lot of gunfire and went straight to the house, broke open the *patrón*'s liquor cabinet, and passed the booze around to the men who were working in the processing plant. "All the stuff in this house belongs to you," they announced when they had gotten the men good and drunk. "All of it was bought with the sweat off your brows. Have at it!" The workers looted the house, taking pots and pans and other utensils, anything they could make off with. When the cupboards were bare, the fire began.

And when Sara's father heard the news, he swore he would never return to La Patria. He did not want to see his home reduced to ashes.

⁂

As Sara recounted the burning, I wondered about her earlier choice of words: "I must confess, I own a farm." I hadn't detected any guilt in that confession, just the same hesitancy that appeared in her voice when we had discussed Guatemalan politics during dinner. Why the hesitancy? Could be a sign of timidity, I guessed.

I guessed wrong. This was a woman who in her twenties had learned how to fly airplanes and in her sixties was learning how to run a coffee plantation — a woman who, during the intervening years, had figured out how to hold together a family that included a grandfather who was an ardent anticommunist, a daughter who was a leftist intellectual, and a husband who was denounced as a CIA agent by the Guatemalan left and blacklisted by the right. Sara Endler had managed to maintain a home straddling the fault lines of a country at war, and to build her own life shuttling between two worlds — the United States, where she was a liberal Democrat, and Guatemala, where she was a member of an embattled economic and racial elite.

If she hesitated when she spoke, it wasn't because she was unsure of herself, but because she was confronting a minefield of politically charged meanings. The "confession" that evening was, I realized, a tactic to defuse the revelation about who she was. It was really more like a *concession:* she conceded there was reason to be critical of Guatemalan landowners so that her views would not be written off. She was ready to discuss the world she had inherited with her plantation. She was inviting me to do so.

Why? The answer she gave the landowner friends who questioned her judgment was simple: she had nothing to hide.

THE STUDENT

S HE'S GOT PLENTY to hide, even if she doesn't know it." That was
the view of César Sánchez, who had grown up on a plantation two
miles west of La Patria.

I had met César shortly before the dinner at Sara Endler's home. The
journalist who introduced us was enamored of him, and it was easy to see
why. He was our age, handsome, with a dark complexion and curly black
hair. He had a warm smile, which he usually kept hidden behind an ironic
grin, and penetrating eyes, which could turn icy in an instant when he
talked politics. He was as quick with a structural analysis as with a sarcas-
tic crack, and though he was trained to hide uncertainty, he knew the
world still held many secrets from him. He wore glasses and always carried a book or newspaper in one hand, the way the boys where he grew
up carried slingshots and the men carried machetes.

César was the son of the plantation bookkeeper, which meant that he
had a slightly bigger house and ate better than his friends whose families
worked in the fields. It also meant that his parents could afford to send
him to a secondary school in the provincial capital and then to the regional branch of the national university. It was there that he came of
age as a student in agronomy, the program that had a long tradition of
producing political activists. The most celebrated of these was Willy
Miranda, the president of the student association who in 1980 stood on a
chair in the university lecture hall and exhorted his classmates (César
could recite by memory): "We who receive an education paid for by the
people have a debt to the people! We who have the power to analyze have

the responsibility to criticize! An agronomist should carry, in one hand, a machete — and, in the other, a machine gun!"

Within weeks, Miranda was dead. As was the most popular agronomy professor at the university, gunned down as he stood at the blackboard teaching a class. As would be dozens of people in agronomy over the coming years. By the time César joined the student association in 1988, the violence had taken its toll, severing the connection between the university and the guerrillas and eroding the optimism that had inspired risk taking among the students. "We weren't as tough as the ones before us," César told me. "We were scared." Which isn't to say they stopped protesting the government, but only that their activities were tame in comparison with those of their predecessors, who had collaborated directly with the *Volcancitos,* or "Little Volcanoes," as they referred, in code, to the guerrillas who operated in the region. "If I had been just a few years older in, say 1982, the guerrillas would have recruited me, and I would have joined," César mused. "And right now I'd probably be a cadaver — just one more anonymous corpse in the sad history of this country."

Instead, he had applied himself to his studies, doing his coursework and developing a proposal for a thesis on the Agrarian Reform of 1952. The Agrarian Reform had been — students like César would tell you — what provoked the United States to overthrow Guatemala's only democratic government and replace it with the military regime that had ruled the country (in various guises) until the 1990s. And agrarian reform remained — they would also tell you — the only viable solution to Guatemala's problems: peace required greater equality, and greater equality required a redistribution of land in the countryside.

Yet for all its importance, not many people in the university knew much about what actually happened in the 1950s. So César proposed to investigate how the reform had affected the coffee-producing region where he had grown up. It was an unorthodox proposal, and when it was rejected, César grew disillusioned with a faculty that, he felt, had been reduced to mediocrity by the repression. But he retained a stubborn attachment to his project: "To understand the war in this country," he told foreigners like me, "you've got to understand what happened during the Agrarian Reform."

César knew a lot about coffee. He had grown up on a plantation, studied the technical aspects of farming in the university, and spent countless hours thinking about how the plantation system should be reformed. Yet in all these years, he had never spoken to a plantation owner — at least not about anything that had political ramifications, certainly not about the Agrarian Reform or any other controversial aspect of the country's history. Nor had any of his friends from agronomy, not even the ones who had landed jobs on plantations. Such communication was not something they would have even thought to attempt.

"She would never talk to me," he said when I told him about Sara and how she had invited me to visit her plantation and learn more about its history. He was a little bitter that the *gringo* could open doors that were shut to him. But more than that, he was curious to hear what she had told me. He listened attentively as I repeated the story of the burning house. "Of course the guerrillas served the coffee themselves," he interjected. "That's how they make sure the landowners don't poison them!" And later he said, "You don't really believe that the *señoras* in the plantation tried to stop a group of armed guerrillas?" Clearly, he did not.

What he had no trouble believing was that the workers had ransacked the Endlers' house. "Go see the difference between the house of a *patrón* and the houses of his workers, and you'll understand the resentment people feel," he said. "Go find out what happened with their lands after the Agrarian Reform and you'll understand the frustration that fueled the war."

He repeated this challenge whenever I saw him until I realized it was more than a challenge. It was an entreaty. He wanted me to do the study he couldn't do himself.

I had other plans at the time. Yes, I would try writing about Guatemala, but it would be about current events — Mayan communities seeking to reclaim their ancestral lands, young men migrating to the United States — things that mattered to people today. César's war seemed to be yesterday's news; his Agrarian Reform, ancient history. The country's civil war was still going on. But you wouldn't know it from what you saw in the cities or in the tourist spots. There were news reports of peace talks — indefinitely stalled at the time — but no reports of actual fighting. The only guerrillas still around were the aging commanders who wanted to resume negotiations in Mexico City. This war had basically ended — not with a bang, but with a bunch of balding men waiting around for someone to talk to them.

César laughed when I told him this. And then he set about setting me straight. The army had been working for years to minimize reports of guerrilla activity — he explained — covering up its casualties, treating its wounded in hidden hospitals. The aim was to undermine the guerrillas' claim that they were still a force to be reckoned with. "We beat them," the generals insisted, "why should we negotiate?" My own misperception was a testament to the power of their propaganda machine. There was still fighting in the coffee region. And, more important, there were still many people there who cared about the war's outcome.

Then one morning I picked up the paper and found Sara's plantation on the front page. There had actually been a battle. The fighting had begun in the woods outside a municipality named La Igualdad, and spilled over into La Patria and a neighboring plantation named El Progreso. The names on this battlefield — La Igualdad, El Progreso, La Patria — could have come from one of Willy Miranda's speeches: "Equality," "Progress," "Nation." Only here they had lost their meanings, the way that bombed-out houses cease to be homes. La Patria had become a battlefield. Bullets were flying in El Progreso. People were killing each other in La Igualdad. It was as though the propaganda machine had gone haywire.

When I saw César again, we talked more about the violence in the plantations. I had tried to read up on the subject on my own, only to find there was basically nothing to read. There were accounts of the Agrarian Reform (written by foreigners), but these dealt with the rise and fall of the reform government at the national level, not with how the reforms played out in the countryside. And there were accounts of the war in the 1980s, but they focused on how the violence affected Indian communities in the country's highlands to the north. Coffee had been the backbone of the Guatemalan economy, and the plantations had been where millions of people had lived through the major political upheavals of the century. Yet, in the history books, the country's vast coffee region remained a blank space on the map. César insisted I would find remarkable things there. And I figured I shouldn't pass on the opportunity at least to pay a visit.

And so it was that Sara Endler and César Sánchez, two Guatemalans who had never met, together led me to La Igualdad.

THE BATTLEFIELD

L A IGUALDAD WAS A TWO-ROAD TOWN on the side of a mountain in the volcanic chain that ran the length of Guatemala's southern coast. One dirt road climbed up from the coastal city of Coatepeque; the other crawled down from the mountain city of San Marcos. Beginning in very different worlds — the stifling heat of the coast and the cool air of the highlands — the roads plunged into what looked like a tropical forest.

It was a peculiar forest: the canopy had been pruned back and the undergrowth was all of a kind — plants the same size and shape, with the same shiny, dark-green leaves. Beginning at any one plant at the roadside, you could enter the forest and find an identical plant a meter away. Continue in any direction and you would reach another plant, and then another and another. Heading westward, you could travel plant by plant — occasionally hopping a stream or crossing another road, skirting a mill or a cluster of shacks, stopping at the edge of a ravine and continuing where the ground levels off — until you reached Mexico and traveled into the heart of Chiapas. Or you could head eastward — plant by plant — hugging the base of the volcanic chain more or less continuously until you came within sight of the Salvadoran border. And you could pick up again — traveling plant by plant, mile after mile — in large stretches of El Salvador, Honduras, Nicaragua, Costa Rica, and again in Colombia, Venezuela, and Brazil. The plant was coffee, and the beans it produced were, after petroleum, the most valuable commodity on the world market.

The two roads converged on a ridge one thousand meters above sea level. They became paved streets and ran parallel thirty meters apart. Six cross streets connected the two, making five blocks. This was the town of La Igualdad, the urban center of the municipality of the same name.

Entering the town from the highland road, you came upon a bust of Justo Rufino Barrios. In 1871, General Barrios had led a band of insurgents down this route as he crisscrossed the coffee piedmont on his way to the capital. Once in power, Barrios began a political revolution, consisting of legislation and decrees known collectively as the Liberal Reforms, which opened up these lands for cultivation, prompted the migration of peasants from highland communities, and led to the formation of municipalities like La Igualdad throughout the piedmont.

The second street had been paved in 1952 during the second major reform period in modern Guatemalan history. Had the reforms of this era endured, many things might have been different in Guatemala today. For one thing, there might have been a bust of Jacobo Arbenz Guzmán in the entrance to town. Colonel Arbenz was the charismatic army officer who had helped lead the 1944 revolution establishing a democratic government and who had then won the presidential election of 1950. Once in office, Arbenz surrounded himself with Guatemala's best and brightest and set about the task of transforming the world that the Liberal Reforms had created. Four years later, he was stripped of his office, his power, and even his clothes; he left Guatemala in his underwear, exiled to a life of oblivion. He returned four decades later in a casket.

There was no bust of Arbenz in La Igualdad. And no one seemed to remember that the street on the left, as you go uphill, had once been called the Street of the Revolution.

The south end of town began abruptly: the dirt road became a paved street, lined on both sides by wooden and stucco homes, which were painted green, red, and pale blue, and were packed together tightly at odd angles — the adherence to right-angled architecture relaxed so as not to waste space. The street climbed some two hundred yards, passing a bakery, an inn, a mechanic's shop, the cross streets on the right, and a turnoff on the left to a road that dropped into a gully. It continued climbing past several general stores and a pharmacy, and then leveled off at the town's park. The park consisted of a gazebo surrounded by concrete benches. There was an electronics store with video games on the corner: the sound of Mario Brothers echoed through the park all day and well into the night. The street then climbed again, another hundred yards, passing more shops, the municipal hall, the Catholic church, and came to an abrupt halt at the northern edge of the ridge. A dirt path dropped to a line of houses and banana trees on the slope running down to a ravine below.

And there, straight ahead, rising out of the ravine and climbing half a mile up the mountainside and into the clouds, was a plantation. Twelve hundred acres of coffee. On a promontory directly across the ravine was a cluster of large yellow buildings: the processing mill, the offices, and the *casa patronal*. Its name was El Progreso, but the workers in the region called it El Infierno, which means "Hell."

The street continued, veering around La Igualdad's elementary school and then merging with the other street just below the bust of Barrios.

My first trip to La Igualdad was on the road up from the coast. Several weeks had passed since the battle, and Sara assured me that there would be no danger now if I paid the plantation a visit. She arranged for me to meet the plantation's administrator, Carlos Rodríguez, in Coatepeque, and together we rode up the mountain on the back of the plantation's pickup truck. Carlos was a relatively recent arrival in La Patria, hired by Sara after the burning to resuscitate the plantation and turn it into a more productive and profitable operation than it had been in her father's day. Carlos was tall and fit and carried himself with the relaxed and confident air of a corporate executive on vacation. He didn't really look like a farmer. Even when he stood in the fields, his boots caked with mud, he managed to keep his clothes neat and trim, his manner urbane. He didn't wear a sombrero, not even a cap. Like César, he had studied agronomy in the national university. And like him, he had been a student activist in his day. But that day had been back in the 1960s, and those politics had been more a stage of youthful rebelliousness than a lifelong commitment. "The university student who's not a Marxist is a fool," he liked to say. "The adult who remains a Marxist is even more of a fool." Carlos spent two or three days a week in La Patria and the rest running a consulting business in the capital and managing his own property.

After two hours, we reached the town, turning off below the park onto a dirt road that dipped into a gully and then climbed for another twenty minutes up into La Patria. We unloaded in front of the processing plant and carried our bags to the *casa patronal*. The house was a no-frills replacement for what had been destroyed: a concrete floor supporting four adjacent rooms that opened onto a porch. Like all the buildings on the plantation, its walls were painted white, and the roof burgundy red. Carlos handed me a beer from the refrigerator and headed over to the plantation office.

Out on the porch, I sipped the beer and took in the view of Guatemala's Pacific coast, four thousand feet below. Squinting, I could make out the faint outline of the water's edge fifty kilometers southward and, above it, a blurred horizon where ocean blue melded into sky blue. To my left, some hundred kilometers eastward, it was the dark blue of dusk. Westward, the ocean-sky brightened and gave way to a reddish haze where the sun was beginning its descent over Mexico. The view was much too large to take in with one glance. My eyes wandered about the coastal plain: over there, a plume of smoke rose from a sugar refinery; over there, a patch of darkness, a rain shower, made its way inland; over there, a ray of sunlight glinted from a car or truck moving near the border.

Down below, the foothills cast long shadows. In Spanish, they call these hills *la falda*, "the skirt," of the mountain. To me they looked more like long bony fingers clawing at the coastal plain — a death grip frozen in some moment of geo-continental violence long ago and left buckled and broken by centuries of seismic aftershock.

⁂

Over dinner, Carlos told me about the battle that had made the news. He had not been in the plantation at the time, but he recounted what his employees had told him. How several hundred troops marched up past the house one morning. How land mines planted in the upper reaches of El Progreso prevented them from attacking the guerrillas who had dug into the mountainside there. How bleeding soldiers were carried back down the hill. How the military set up a mortar that night in La Patria and shelled the guerrilla encampment until dawn. How the soldiers marched up again, this time over a thousand strong, and flushed the guerrillas out. How some of the guerrillas fled down through La Patria and had a gun battle near the house before disappearing into the community where the workers live at the foot of the hill. How the administrator of El Progreso decided not to risk harvesting the coffee in the plantation's upper corner where the land mines were discovered, and how a peasant who decided to risk collecting the berries for himself had his leg blown off.

I awoke the next morning and watched the sunrise on the porch and tried to imagine the events Carlos had described. But there was something about the place — the crisp mountain air, the spirited singing of the birds, the sumptuous colors of the surrounding fields — infusing the hillside with a beauty so intense that it saturated my senses, dulled my imagination. Try as I might, I could not populate the meadow below with soldiers, or fill the air with bullets and screams. Last night's story seemed as fantastic by daylight as something I might have dreamed in my sleep.

Carlos joined me on the porch and — as if reading my thoughts — pointed out a hole that a bullet had blown out of the wall of the processing plant twenty meters away.

⚜

After breakfast, Carlos introduced me to the plantation's field master and asked him to show me around the property. The field master was a slight man with a nervous smile and a deferential manner that made me uncomfortable. Our tour began with the processing mill, where he showed me the machines that clean, dry, and sort the coffee beans during the harvest season. Then we mounted horses and set off on a path that climbed through the coffee groves up the hill above the plantation buildings.

When I asked the field master why there were no workers about, he explained that the plantation had to wait for the first rains before starting the next task in the annual cycle. The rains were several weeks late.

As we approached the upper reaches of the plantation, I asked him if this was where the battle occurred. "The battle?" He looked as though he didn't know what I was talking about.

"Yeah, the battle that was in the news, didn't it take place around here?"

"That was in El Progreso."

"But I thought it was here too."

"No. Nothing happened here."

"But Carlos told me . . ." I started to say but decided to let it go.

After an hour making our way through the groves, we came to the cemetery, a clearing on a ridge a few hundred meters below the plantation buildings, a colorful oasis in the sea of green, with a line of palm trees running the perimeter. At the entrance stood a cement cross and below it, inscribed in stone, were the words:

HIER RUHT
FRIEDRICH ENDLER
GEB AM 5 OKTOBER 1869
IN LEHIN
GEST IS 15 MAI 1941

Behind this tombstone was a field of crosses with names like Fuentes, Yoc, Tojil, and Bautista.

As we climbed the ridge above the cemetery, I said to the field master, "I heard that the *casa patronal* was burned down."

"*Sí pues,*" he answered.

"The house did burn down, didn't it?"

"*Sí pues.*"

"And it was the guerrillas who did the burning?"

"*Pues,* that's what they say."

Leading questions wouldn't get me far with this man. "Why was it burned?"

He shrugged and said, "*Saber.*"

Saber is a favorite Guatemalan expression, one that I was to hear time and time again in the coming weeks. It is the infinitive of the verb "to know," but works like the rhetorical question in English "Who knows?"

"Has there been a lot of fighting here in La Igualdad?"

"No." He shook his head and, putting a bit more distance between our horses, added over his shoulder, "Not much happened around here."

⚓

Later, I talked with the cook in the *casa patronal.* I was sitting on the porch when she came out to sweep. She wore a colorless skirt and blouse, had her hair pulled back in a single braid, and showed no sign of adornment, not even the gold-starred front tooth that seemed to be the fashion among women in La Igualdad. When she smiled, I saw she had no front teeth at all. (Carlos would later tell me why so many of the women had the same star on the same tooth. It was common for breastfeeding and poorly nourished mothers to lose front teeth; the "dentist" in La Igualdad only stocked four-tooth prosthetics, with a star on one; when a woman came to him with a tooth missing, he knocked out the others so the prosthetic would fit.)

I tried to strike up a conversation: "Is that the ocean I'm seeing out there?" I pointed to the blue horizon.

She stopped sweeping, looked out at the coast, and shrugged. "It could be."

"Do you go to the beach much?"

"Just once we went." She smiled at the memory. "That was years ago."

We talked a little about the weather, about the rains being late, and then she asked what I was doing here in the plantation. I took the question as my cue. "Well, I was hoping to find out about the history of this place," I explained. "Maybe you could help me a little?"

She didn't speak.

"I was wondering, for example, what happened here during the Agrarian Reform?"

She looked blankly at her broom and said: "*Pues,* I don't know anything about that."

"But was there ever some kind of dispute here over the land in the plantation?"

She shrugged and began sweeping again: "*Pues,* I don't think anything happened here."

Maybe she really didn't know. Maybe she was younger than her toothless face made her look. I changed to a more recent topic, the battle in the news. Again, the blank expression: "*Pues,* everything has been pretty calm here." Her sweeping became more vigorous. My eyes found the bullet hole in the wall.

"But isn't it true the house was burned down?"

"*Pues,* that was a long time ago."

"Why was it burned?"

"*Saber.*"

⚜

Later I wandered into the plantation garage and struck up a conversation with the driver who had driven us up from Coatepeque and another employee who was helping him tinker with the car engine. They were talk-ative — about the car's problems, about the rain being late. But when I asked them about the war, they had no more to say than the field master and the cook: the house was burned down, but otherwise the war had not had much impact in the area, neither the army nor the guerrillas both-ered people very much.

Later still, when the sun was setting — an orange fireball over Chiapas — I heard singing coming from somewhere down below. I found the cook in the kitchen and asked her what it was. "A procession," she said. "They're praying for rain."

Together we climbed down the mountainside and joined the line of two dozen peasants, mostly women, with candles in hand, as it wound its way on a path through the coffee groves. A man with a megaphone prayed to *el Señor* that he send rain so that the *patrones* could give the people work. His entreaty was backed by a mumbled chorus of Hail Marys from the women. When he finished praying, five men strummed guitars and the women sang:

> *Te ofrezco este canto,*
> *mezclado con llanto,*
> *y mi corazón. . . .*

The following day I left La Patria with Carlos. He agreed to drop me off in La Soledad, the plantation where César's family lived. We drove into La Igualdad and took the road that headed north toward San Marcos, passing the bust of General Barrios as we left town. We came to a planta-tion named La Independencia — "Independence" — and there, for the first time, I saw soldiers. They were marching in a line at the side of the road, one soldier every twenty feet. They were very young and looked very serious, with machine guns ready in their hands. They were headed in the direction of El Progreso.

EXHUMATION

THE HOUSES in the plantation La Soledad lined a stretch of road that climbed the spine of a ridge two miles to the west of La Igualdad. We stopped first at the workers' quarters, a row of dismal wooden sheds with chipped and faded white paint. Carlos asked a young man standing in one of the doorways if he knew where César Sánchez lived. The man shook his head and said nothing. We continued. The gravel road became cobblestone as it approached the coffee patio. Carlos asked some men who stood there, dressed in faded green soccer jerseys. They didn't know who he was talking about. We continued past the patio and the processing plant and came to the *casa patronal:* a two-story house, white with green latticed shutters, glass windows, and French door, built to dimensions so much larger than the workers' homes that it seemed designed for a different species. Farther up the ridge was another row of houses, more modest than the *patrón's,* but not so derelict as the others. Standing in one of the doorways was César.

"So what did you find out?" César asked as soon as the pickup from La Patria disappeared down the road.

"Well," I answered, following him into the house, "seems nothing much happened there. At least, that's what the people told me."

The front part of the front room was a *tienda,* a small store with snacks, soap, toothpaste, and drinks displayed on a shelf behind a counter. The back part of the room had a large bed and an old wooden dresser. César had me drop my bag on the bed. "Do you believe them?"

"No, not entirely. I mean, Sara told me there had been fighting. But she wasn't actually around the plantation in the years leading up to the burning. Her administrator showed me a bullet hole from a recent battle, but he hadn't witnessed the fighting himself. Everyone who had been there said nothing happened."

César brought me into the back room to meet his parents, who smiled shyly and exchanged amused glances — the sort that might accompany a question like, *What will our son bring home next?* César then suggested we look for a friend of his who could tell me something about the war. We headed out the door, and as we walked down the road toward the coffee patio, he said, "So nothing happened, eh?"

"That's right. And it seems no one has heard of your Agrarian Reform. They seemed evasive when I asked them about the war, but when it came to the Agrarian Reform I really don't think they knew what the hell I was talking about."

César nodded. "Well it's possible La Patria was one of the plantations that wasn't affected by the reform. But there definitely was a lot of fighting up there above La Patria and El Progreso in the early eighties. We used to watch it from over here."

I followed his gaze across the patio, over the line of trees at the other end, to the mountain above La Igualdad. When I had seen it on the way up from Coatepeque, the summit had appeared to have the conical shape of a volcano. From this angle, however, I wasn't so sure: it looked like just another mountain. I wondered how much César was exaggerating.

"If you don't believe me, you know the house burned down. The guerrillas wouldn't have done that without a reason."

We passed the men who hadn't known who César was. "Are you playing today, César?" one of them asked.

Down by the workers' quarters, we climbed the embankment and approached a house where an old man was sitting, his back against the wall, methodically banging a stone tool against the bottom of a pot. "*Buenos días*," César greeted him. "Is the owner of that pot around?"

The man looked up from his work. "No, *joven*. He went to play football."

We turned back up to the road. "There's a man who could tell you some stories," César said when we were out of earshot. "He comes through once a year to fix the pots. He's been doing that for as long as I can remember. He travels all over San Marcos fixing pots. I bet he's repaired every pot and pan in every plantation in the area. But," he grinned, *"saber* if he'll talk to you."

"Saber if anyone will talk to me. Maybe it's just too soon to try to find out what happened during the war."

César disagreed. "What about the forensic team? They're doing it." He was referring to the team of forensic anthropologists that had begun digging up the clandestine cemeteries that the army had left throughout the highlands during the 1980s.

"That's different," I said.

"Why?"

"Corpses don't lie."

"Neither do memories," he said. "You just have to get people to tell them."

I shook my head. Of course memories lie. People repress and distort things, or simply forget them. "Well, even if I could find some people in La Igualdad who would talk, I doubt I'd ever get the full story."

He thought a moment. "The forensics never get the full corpse, do they?" He had a point. What they got was decayed. Sometimes, it had even been mutilated beyond recognition. "But it still tells them something, right?"

We had caught up with the soccer players and walked with them to the soccer field.

Plantation men take soccer seriously, or at least they used to. The game I saw that afternoon wasn't much: graceless hustle, hard tackles, missed shots. But the talk I heard later was of greatness. A group of players gathered in front of the Sánchez house after the game and, with César's prodding, told me about a glorious past. A time when people had cared about their teams. When plantations had hired coaches, provided their men with uniforms and cleats, and given light work to the key players the week before the important games. Some even put professionals on the payroll to beef up the roster. La Soledad had boasted some great teams, and there were plenty of trophies in the *casa patronal* to prove it. When a truck carrying the team back from a tournament in La Igualdad rolled off a bridge, killing two players and crippling several others, the *patrón* visited his men in the hospital and wept at the sight of their broken bodies.

But things had changed since, they told me. Players had aged; some had succumbed to alcohol; some had joined Evangelical churches that prohibited alcohol and sports. The pool of new talent had shrunk as young people moved to the city. And the *patrones* just didn't care what went on in the plantation the way they once had.

Jorge Fuentes was a veteran of that era. As evening settled on the mountainside, we continued the talk of soccer with him, until we were alone and César, lowering his voice a notch, changed the topic. "*Vos,* Jorge," he said. "I was hoping you could tell Daniel a little about the war and what it's been like around here."

Jorge's voice also dropped. "What does he want to know?"

César looked at me. What *did* I want to know? *Whether it was real,* I thought. *Not just the bullets and the burning house, but the popular sentiment that the guerrillas claimed to represent.* "Well, for starters," I said, "I'm curious if there's been much support for the guerrillas in these parts."

Jorge thought a moment. "*Pues,* right now, direct support, not so much. But sympathy, yes. I mean, before, a few years ago, there was a lot of support. When the *cuates* came through, *a la gran puta,* it was a party! Everybody was happy to see them. You remember, César?"

"*Sí pues.* There were a lot of them back then. I remember sitting in my parents' store and counting the *cuates* as they went by up the road. There were more than eighty, and that's counting just the ones we could see."

"What did they do when they came?" I asked.

"They would hold a meeting on the patio, and everyone would come out. They'd talk about the revolution and the Agrarian Reform. They'd find out how the plantation was treating people. Invite people to join them."

"They'd also stock up on food from the stores here," César added. "I remember the first time they came to my parents' store. It was that commander, Chano."

"Ah, that Chano was one tough bastard!" Jorge shook his head with admiration.

"He was my idol growing up. You'd always hear stories about him. He was like our own Che Guevara."

Jorge nodded in agreement but said nothing. Someone was approaching up the road. It was a young boy. We watched him pass, and when we were alone again, I asked Jorge about the house burning in La Patria. He didn't know much about what had happened, but he had heard that the owners had been collaborating with the army, and so the guerrillas punished them.

"The people I talked to in La Patria said there was never much fighting around there."

Jorge chuckled. "They're lying. There was lots of fighting in that part of La Igualdad. Those plantations are closer to the woods where the guerrillas had their camps. The army went after them many times."

"Was there fighting around here too?"

"Not as much. Some shootouts now and then. There was one in the plantation San Miguel where a commander got killed."

"It wasn't Chano, was it?" César asked.

"No, Chano fell somewhere else. This was somebody else, a doctor, they say, from Xela." I detected another change in Jorge's voice, as if he were shifting gears back into the story-telling mode he had used when we talked about the soccer teams. "The *tío* arrived in the plantation one day with three others, two of them women. They say one of them was his *compañera.* So they arrived, and two of them went to the office and made the bookkeeper show them the books —"

César interjected: "The guerrillas used to visit all plantations to check the books and make sure the workers were being paid."

"The other two went to scout out the plantation. They walked out of the office and turned the corner to the patio and, *puta 'mano,* the patio was full of soldiers! Seems they'd arrived at the same time as the guerrillas, but from the other direction. So the *canches* ran back and told the others and they took off. The commander told the bookkeeper not to say anything till they got away. But the bastard got scared, and he immediately went and told the soldiers. The *cuates* got down the ravine and were climbing the other side when the soldiers arrived and started firing on them. The commander's woman was hit. So he ordered the others to carry her, and he stayed to hold off the soldiers while they got away. He held them off for a few minutes. Just him against the whole platoon of soldiers."

Jorge held an imaginary machine gun in his hands and fired.

"But while he was firing, some of the soldiers got around behind him. They got closer and closer and then — pow! — they nailed him in the back. The captain ordered the rest to stop shooting. He wanted the commander alive. But before they could capture him, the *cuate* took a pill from his pocket — they always carried pills so they wouldn't be captured — and he swallowed it. The captain grabbed him, 'Don't die, you piece of shit!' But it was too late. So they carried the corpse up to the patio and made all the workers come look at it. The captain yelled at them: 'This is what happens to communists!' Real abusive, that bastard. And then he had the soldiers line up and walk past the corpse. Each one cursed it and kicked it and hacked at it with their machete until it was all cut to pieces."

Jorge paused, letting the image sink in. "The captain was going to burn the body. But the administrator begged him not to. 'Why do you care?' the captain said to him. 'Are you a communist too?' 'No,' the administrator said. 'It's just that we don't want the guerrillas to come back and punish us after you leave.' The captain finally agreed, and when the army left, the administrator had the body buried in the plantation cemetery."

"Did the guerrillas come back?"

"Yes, or at least one of them did. Every year, on the anniversary of his death, flowers appeared on the grave. Not flowers like you find around here, but those nice flowers they sell in the market in Xela."

It was dark now. A starless night. Clouds must have rolled in while we were talking. There was no movement on the street, but a lantern across the way revealed that the air was full of life: insects of all shapes and sizes fluttered about, and occasionally a bat darted into the light.

"If the guerrillas had so much support, why didn't they win?"

"Things changed," Jorge said. "When the army did what it did in Sacuchum, everything changed."

"Sacuchum Dolores is a community up on top of the mountain," César explained. "Tell him what happened there."

"The army showed up one day and found the women washing green uniforms. And none of the men were home. So the soldiers had the families go inside their houses. They closed the doors and they set the houses on fire. The women and the children and the old people were inside, and they burned with the houses. That was the new law of the land. If the government hadn't done that, the guerrillas would have kept growing. But that was too much. You come home and find nothing — no family, no house — just ashes. That was too much."

⚛

That night I had a strange dream: I was out on the soccer field with a group of workers who turned out to be guerrillas. They selected me to be on their team. I was flattered, though I tried not to show it. Then there was some commotion. "Helicopter!" Everyone started running off the field, seeking cover, and I woke up. It took me a moment to remember where I was — on a bed in the front room of the Sánchez house. Somewhere outside, there was a mechanical thumping sound, like a helicopter in the distance.

When I awoke again, the thumping noise was still there. And now there was another sound: a metallic clink like a muffled bell. I got up, found the front door ajar, and stepped outside. It was just before daybreak. The sky was luminescent, but the world below remained in shadows. The pot-fixer sat on the stoop of the neighbor's house, tapping a pot between his knees. That accounted for one sound. The thumping, which seemed to come from a house farther down the ridge, remained a mystery.

Someone approached on the street, a woman with a pot balanced on her head. *"Buenos días."* It was César's mother. *"Cómo amaneció?"* she asked, stopping in front of the door: how did you wake up?

"Good, thanks, and you?"

"Algo regularcito, gracias a Dios," she said smiling: *not bad, thank the Lord.* She entered the house and returned a moment later with a cup of coffee, then disappeared again inside.

I sat on the bench, sipped the coffee, and thought about what I had learned in La Igualdad. My notes from several interviews consisted of just a few lines, many of which said simply: "Nothing happened." Sara and her administrator told a very different sort of story from César and his friend, but they all agreed that a house had burned down. In light of that single fact, the notes that said nothing seemed to speak volumes.

César was right. A mutilated body could tell a story — one in which the mutilation was a central part. Even obliterated bodies have been known to speak. Like the hollows in the rock of Pompeii, pockets of nothingness, which, when filled with plaster, revealed human figures that the volcano there had buried. Or the silhouettes found on the walls of Hiroshima, pale shadows that had outlasted their human source, revealing the darkness that the atomic bomb had cast upon the surrounding world. Memories, like corpses, can be exhumed. If they come fragmented or incomplete, that is part of their story.

Emptying the sugary remains of the coffee, I came to a decision. I would return to La Patria. I would find out what had caused the house to be burned. Maybe it *was* yesterday's news. But that news had never been told — at least not in public. And I wanted to find out why not.

I got up from the bench and entered the house to get more coffee. For a moment, the darkness inside reduced the world to its sounds — the metallic tapping, the mechanical thumping. Once my eyes adjusted, I moved slowly past the shadows of the room, opened the door at the other end, and stepped into the kitchen and the warm glow of daylight. The morning sun had just risen above the mountains to the east, and its light streamed in through an open window, catching the curls of smoke that rose from the hearth stove at the center of the room. César's mother stood by the fire, her hands at work in the pot she had carried up the street. Now I knew the source of the thumping sound: an electric mill grinding maize into a golden pulp. The thump-thump was echoed here by the clap-clap of her hands slapping the gold into tortillas. The work, like the day and the year, had a rhythm: deliberate, unhurried, unre-lenting.

The open window framed the southern face of the highlands, the chain of volcanoes stretching out of sight to the east. The highest, Santa María, climbed abruptly from the piedmont just a few miles away and culminated in a perfect cone. The symmetry of the peak left no doubt about the mountain's origins. At its base was the dark outline of an im-mense crater where, not so long ago, the earth had blown open. A col-umn of gray smoke emerged from the crater. As it cleared the shoulder of the volcano, it caught the morning sun and turned red.

PART II

ASHES FELL

I can turn but little light on the darkness; too little is known of the country, beyond its trade and political relations to the rest of the world. Volcanoes, earthquakes, and revolutions have popularly been associated with the whole region, and public taste has turned away from such unpleasant outbreaks of subterranean fires or human passions.

— William T. Brigham, *Guatemala: The Land of the Quetzal* (an 1887 travelogue)

RUMOR

SOMETHING STRANGE HAPPENED in Guatemala in the weeks that followed. Somewhere, someone told someone else that foreigners were abducting children and removing their internal organs. The rumor, once started, spread through the countryside like an epidemic, replicating itself as it went. The version I heard in one place went like this: "They say that over in [a nearby town] they found a boy's body. His organs were missing, and his chest was stuffed with cotton." In a version I heard elsewhere, "they said" the chest was filled with dollar bills, and in another there was a note that read, "Thank you for your cooperation."

Violence followed. The first publicized casualty was an American tourist who made the mistake of photographing the children of strangers in a highland village. Villagers accused her of being a *robachicos* — a "children-stealer" — and beat her into a coma. In another highland community a German woman tried to say "I like your children" — but was understood as saying "I *want* your children" — and a terrified mother reportedly hacked her to death with a machete.

I call it a rumor, but many Guatemalans had no doubt the story must be true. They had sufficient evidence — all hearsay, of course — in the numerous accounts of abductions. And they could see an obvious motive: money. The country's largest newspaper ran a front-page story listing the going rates for human organs in the United States.

Meanwhile a counterpart to the rumor circulated within the ex-pat circles in Guatemala City: the army had intentionally manufactured the *robachicos* scare. This counter-rumor was also backed by evidence (hearsay as well): video footage of the lynching of the American woman apparently revealed that the mob's leaders were military intelligence agents. And there seemed to be an obvious motive: the army was worried about foreigners documenting the abuses it had committed in the countryside.

They had reason to be worried. In recent years, an increasing number of foreigners had been drawn to Guatemala by the stories that Mayan Indian leaders were telling about the violence the army had inflicted upon their communities. The most prominent of these stories was the testimony of a K'iche' woman named Rigoberta Menchú, which had been turned into a book by a foreign anthropologist and had reached a wide readership in the United States and Europe. In 1992, Menchú had been awarded the Nobel Peace Prize, and the subsequent media coverage had brought increased international pressure on the Guatemalan government to rein in its military.

The generals were not keen on having more stories like Menchú's reach international audiences. For years, they had promoted the idea that the guerrillas were led by foreign agitators by referring to them as *canches* — which means "blonds" (and, in a land of black-haired people, "foreigners"). Talking with foreigners was tantamount to talking with the *canches*. The *robachicos* scare would be just the latest ploy to sow seeds of distrust in the countryside and confound efforts to document the violence.

Whatever the cause, the effect was undeniable — as I discovered firsthand when I traveled one weekend with César and two German friends to a small island on the Pacific Coast. In the narrow launch that took us there, we met a soldier on leave and, after a friendly chat, accepted his invitation to spend the night in a bamboo beach hut belonging to his mother-in-law. In the morning, an angry mob from a nearby village marched out to the family's house and demanded to know why they had brought *gringo robachicos* to the island. Before the mob could move on to us, the soldier yelled at them: "These are not *robachicos*. They're my friends. And I warn you: if any of you lay a hand on them, I *will* find you . . ." The crowd dispersed.

As we waited for a launch to take us off the island, I began to wonder about the risks I might face when I went back to La Igualdad. What if a dangerous rumor were spread about me? Best to play it safe, I thought, at

least until people knew me well enough to disregard it. For the time being I would avoid politically sensitive topics, asking only about things that had taken place long before the fighting began: how the Endlers came to occupy the *casa patronal*, how the workers came to pick their coffee, and how these two groups of people, born in very different worlds, came to be buried together on the mountain ridge where La Patria had its cemetery.

TRAVELOGUE

WHEN THE TWENTY-THREE-YEAR-OLD Friedrich Endler
left Germany for Central America in 1892, it wasn't the first time
he had been overseas. Five years earlier he had gone to live in
England because — he would later tell his son — he wanted to escape
the militarism of Germany: he saw no sense in "white men killing white
men." He also wanted to escape the "tyranny" of his father, a doctor of
noble lineage in a small town in northern Prussia.

Friedrich apprenticed for three years in the Liverpool shipyards and
then secured the job of mechanic on a British steamer headed for Australia. It was the most difficult job he would ever take.

The ship's engine room was an inferno. It was so hot that the stokers
who shoveled coal into the flames often lost their senses as they worked.
When a four-hour shift was over and the hatch unlocked, the stoker
would stumble up onto the deck and into the hands of his shipmates, who
waited ready to subdue him lest he, in his heat-crazed condition, attack
someone or try to jump overboard. Often they tied the stoker to the deck
until he cooled off and regained his senses.

As mechanic, Friedrich also worked in the heat of the engine room,
though never long enough to lose the wits he needed to do his job. That
job was to make sure that the inferno generated the steam that turned
the turbines that propelled the ship full of English manufactured goods
around the globe and then back, several months later, with a comparable
tonnage of Australian wheat. As long as he kept the engine running,
through periodic maintenance and repairs, Friedrich could avoid the
steam room and, from the deck, enjoy such sights as the Suez Canal —

the engineering wonder that had halved the distance between Europe and the East. But a mechanical failure in, say, the middle of the Red Sea would condemn him to time in the hell below.

Friedrich liked Australia so much that upon returning to Germany, he announced that he was abandoning the fatherland and heading back to the British colony, this time for good. As he was preparing his departure, an old friend, Heinrich Schmidt, introduced him to a Guatemalan named José María Solórzano. Over beer one afternoon, Schmidt and Solórzano told Friedrich about Central America. They urged him to hold off on Australia until he had seen the possibilities that awaited industrious Germans across the Atlantic. Solórzano even offered to write Friedrich a letter of introduction to the president of Guatemala, a personal friend.

Friedrich took the letter and set out in July 1892 on a steamer bound for the Caribbean. He crossed Panama by train, passing the ruins of the original Panama Canal, the colossal failure of the same French entrepreneur who had built the Suez. He headed up the western coast of Central America on another steamship. In Guatemala City, he presented the letter of introduction to President Manuel Lisandro Barillas.

"What do you do?" the president asked him.

"I'm a machinist," said the young German. "I work with steam engines."

"You're hired." President Barillas added him to the staff of his coffee plantation, La Libertad.

That's the story of how the future *patrón* of La Patria came to Guatemala — a story, honed through a century of retelling, which I heard from his son one hundred and two years later. From Sara, his granddaughter, I obtained a translated copy of a letter he wrote home two weeks after his arrival.

"Dear Parents," the letter began, "I hope you are now in possession of my telegram. Only now am I able to tell you the details. I long very much for some from you. . . . I wrote a birthday letter to you, dear Mama, from Saint Thomas and the continuation of the travelogue followed from Haiti. . . . Now I want to continue my travelogue from Colón. You shouldn't be angry with me about the bad writing because I am already sufficiently annoyed with these hard quills with which I am forced to write."

Over the next twenty pages, Friedrich described the new world to his parents. If what he saw was alien to him, the act of describing it must have been very familiar. The European imagination had long been captivated by the tropical world their nations were colonizing; description of unknown, "uncivilized" peoples was flourishing as both scholarly inquiry and amateur pastime. When Friedrich set those hard quills to paper, he was engaging in a favorite genre of his day.

"The trip that followed is hard to describe," he wrote. The "description" of the unfamiliar that followed relied on references to what was already known at home. "All the tropical plants that are grown with difficulty in the hothouses in Europe grow here in great profusion. The loveliest fan palms, coconut palms, breadfruit trees, bananas, all kinds of bushes and trees the names of which I unfortunately don't know." He offered a few more botanical observations and marveled at the "splendor" of the "beautiful jungle."

The young German's first encounter with human specimens was in the Colón harbor, on the Caribbean coast of Panama, as he hurried to transport his luggage to the railway station. "My traveling companion and I hired two Negroes who hang around the harbor for that reason. The [train] station is about ten minutes from the harbour. After long bargaining we settled with the Negroes and $1.00 was the price, but after we had gone half the way the rogues stopped and demanded another dollar. I swore in English and my traveling companion in Spanish, no police in sight and groups of Negroes with ugly faces gathered around us so we were forced to yield." Once on the train he could observe the "Negroes" from a safer distance: "Our journey took us through about six stations called by names such as Negro Murder, Holy Paul and so on, lovely names for dirty Negro huts which beggar description . . . some piles, a palm leaf roof, a fire underneath, a hammock surrounded by a cactus hedge. Half a dozen naked children scuffle around with pigs and chickens in the swamp in front of the house. Father concerns himself mostly with hunting and mother sleeps."

Heading by steamship up the Pacific Coast from Panama he encountered new human varieties: "You hardly see Negroes in Central America further north than Colombia. The color of the native's skin varies between yellow and brown." In one port of call these lighter-skinned natives paddled up to the side of the anchored steamship in hollowed-out tree trunks to sell fruits and parrots. "One can find lovely girls and women among them, mostly dressed in white and with amply low cut dresses."

Fruits, parrots, and hollowed tree trunks; hunting, sleeping, scuffling with the pigs, and naked: Friedrich described the natives living in a state of nature. He made no mention of civil authorities: there were no police officers, soldiers, custom officials, public servants. The single reference to political institutions was oblique: the passengers did not go ashore in one harbor because "there was a comfortable little revolution going on there."

The physical infrastructure of these societies did catch the young machinist's eye: Colón, for instance, was "a real awful Negro hole" which had burned down a few years earlier. "Nobody has deigned to rebuild it, or even to remove all the rubble. One has to wade through knee-high marsh and meter-high grass and could easily be found dead there some day either from a fever or a bullet. . . . The few respectable huts which still exist are built on piles surrounded by the ubiquitous morass. I would advise everyone to bring stilts along if he would want to see Colón."

Here and elsewhere, the letter depicted human technology succumbing to the voracious vegetation of the tropics. Grass grew over a foot high between the railroad tracks, and outside Colón "everything is covered with vines." Occasional clearings "revealed humans living in the most primitive conditions." They also revealed one of the most extravagant failures of European technology: "Sometimes we pass, quickly, by the debris of the Panama Canal. There are machines, many millions of dollars worth of machines, which were stolen one after another or just left to rust. The Canal is a giant's task, there are almost depthless swamps to conquer, extremely big rock masses which rise out of seven-hundred-foot depths to crush and excavate. The climate eliminates the larger part of the foreign labor, and the natives are too lazy to work."

Only as he reached the shores of El Salvador did Friedrich encounter a landscape dominated by human technology. "Up until now the coast had consisted of woods and bare rocks, but now my eyes can see nothing but coffee plantations." Yet here too, nature threatened: "In Acajutla, which we reached on the 9th, the mountains, which sometimes smoked, were planted with coffee. During the daytime we sometimes saw a cloud of smoke rising but at night it turned into a pillar of fire."

On August 11, 1892, Friedrich Endler's steamer arrived at the port of San José, its first stop in Guatemala. Friedrich remained on the ship. Although his letter didn't describe the view from the deck, I imagine it looked very similar to the image I found in a collection of photos taken by a European traveler who had been there several years earlier. With one difference: the volcanoes in the distance would have appeared smaller to Friedrich than the ones in the photo, which had been doctored to enhance their size (a common technique used by foreign photographers visiting Guatemala in those years).

On August 13, the steamer reached the port of Champerico, which is today a small town several miles from the fishing village where César and I were mistaken for *robachicos*. It was here that Friedrich disembarked and, in his letter, recorded his first observation of Guatemala: "In Champerico there were four houses along the front, and everything behind is evil, mud holes, huts, filth."

But despite the town's sinister appearance, Friedrich reassured his parents that "the dear father country is always very close and present: German pictures, frames included, for 150 marks hanging in every pub. Munich beer can be bought everywhere for two Marks a bottle, and even in the poorest village one can find a beloved countryman."

An English businessman guided him inland to Retalhuleu, which was "not at all a nice town with its narrow badly paved streets" and, running through the center, a "little creek, which is also the gutter." There he met his Guatemalan contact, a man named Cárdenas. "When I arrived at the Cárdenas house (which is very pleasantly furnished inside), the nice Spanish speech I had crammed suddenly deserted me, and there I stood mute, dumb in the fullest sense of the word. I handed him my letter."

Fortunately the encounter was salvaged by Cárdenas, who was "as good-natured a man" as he had ever met. "He looks like an old Spaniard, his wife like a German, and so do the children. In order to better understand one another, we went across the street to a little German shop where the employee could interpret for us."

Friedrich spent a few days in Caballo Blanco, Cárdenas's plantation. He marveled at the administrator: "certainly a German, a broken giant who is very well able to keep a half a hundred Indians in hand." And he described the Indians: "The women bake the tortillas, and the children sunbathe with the pigs."

After a few days, he headed to his final destination: La Libertad, the coffee plantation "which is one of the biggest and loveliest in Guatemala," owned by Barillas, "a former president of Guatemala and General of the Republic." He found employment immediately as the plantation's mechanic. (Unlike the story passed down by the family, the letter made no mention of meeting in Guatemala City with President Barillas, whose term in office had in fact already ended.)

Friedrich concluded the letter with a description of the country's social hierarchy — framed by his own relation to it, both present and future: "The patios, the drying places for the coffee, are electrically lighted during the night, and this electricity-producing machine is presently puzzling me a lot. Recently, there have been six nights of Indians dancing on the patios to the dull sounds of the marimba. . . . It is a wonderful sight to see these savage, ragged creatures performing their fantastic dances under the electric light. The inhabitants of Guatemala are Indians, the native people, who belong to different tribes and speak different languages. They are small, dumpy figures who occupy the lowest rung on the plantation, the so-called *mozo*, or worker, and eke out an existence on one mark a day. The second kind are the *mestizos*, mixed breed people who are tradesmen or servants and tend to the cattle and horses. The descendants of the Spaniards are the owners of the plantations, and most of the trading houses are owned by Germans. An enormous disadvantage for this country is that the Indians won't work more than just enough to fill their basic needs, and these are very few. The only way to make [an Indian] work is to advance him money, then he can be forced to work. Very often, they run off, but they are caught and punished very severely. The owners of the land have a very different viewpoint, if they don't earn 120 percent on something, they don't consider it worth the trouble to plant it or build it. . . . One could earn 25 percent easily. A person with just a little ability but who is willing to work and begin in a small way can make a very good life here, but he does have to say good-bye to even the slightest amount of European comfort."

⬇

A week later, Friedrich wrote another letter, which he attached to the first: "During the last week such a spectacle has developed that I would like to share it with you. I had to fight for my position here, and I would rather have preferred to fight with wild animals than with these people here. It is a custom to try to chase every foreigner from the place. If I hadn't had so many friends who gave me such good advice I would have had to find my way out of here."

The administrator, "a Spaniard [who] is a so-called Germanophobe, a glutton," had rallied several Guatemalan foremen against him, and they had been sabotaging the electrical machines. Friedrich complained to the son of a British minister who was visiting Barillas. The administrator was fired. "Since then my electric lights are burning better than ever before, and the foreman will have to be shown what German fists are for."

He ended this letter with a brief anecdote that contained a key insight into the nature of Guatemala's economy: "Last night I woke up with the thought that somebody was having fun by throwing my bed around, it was an earthquake which are very common here. Wooden buildings are for this reason very practical!" Then he made a simple observation that unwittingly foreshadowed a great disaster to come: "From here one can see a 14,000 foot high volcanic mountain which hasn't smoked now for 5 years."

Friedrich's "German fists" and German know-how served him quite well in the coming years. After a brief stay in La Libertad, he secured a job as the manager of a lumber mill in Caballo Blanco. There he worked until 1899, when an indigenous woman bore him a son. Friedrich would later tell his family that after taking one look at that dark-skinned child he declared, "Friedrich Endler, you get your ass back to Germany and get yourself a white wife. There aren't going to be any brown babies in the Endler family."

In 1900, he returned from Germany with a German bride, Elsa Sauer, an amateur artist who, in lieu of a travelogue, sketched some of the landscapes she encountered, including the port of San José, her first stop in Guatemala. Friedrich quickly found a job as administrator of the

San José, Guatemala. F. J. 1901.

plantation Mundo Nuevo — "New World" — a large coffee plantation owned by a German exporting company. In August 1902, Elsa gave birth in Mundo Nuevo to a son, the first Endler born in Guatemala.

Two months later, the side of the Santa María volcano — which hadn't smoked since Friedrich described it in 1892 — blew skyward, giving birth to Guatemala's thirty-seventh volcano. It was named Santiaguito, after the patron saint of the Conquest.

⚜

The third letter I obtained from Sara had been written by Elsa Endler just days after the eruption. "On Saturday morning," she told her parents, "we were sitting down to drink coffee on the verandah, and wondered why the sun had not risen. The air was curiously still and cold, and all of nature was eerily quiet. We expected a strong earthquake. As Mrs. Heinrich Schmidt went to her room, which was located in a coffee warehouse close by, she stopped and exclaimed 'Look! Look! It's snowing!' The two husbands ran over to her and found that the fine white flakes were ashes and pumice. Everyone felt great dismay, and all eyes turned toward an immense cloud which grew darker by the moment and came from the direction of Quetzaltenango. The steady fall increased, and soon all the earth, every leaf and every head was powdered white and gray. It grew darker and darker, and with hearts pounding we took all kinds of precautions."

Her description of those precautions gives some sense of the authority Friedrich had come to wield in the plantation world. "In the early morning hours, the workers had refused to go to work, but nevertheless they had been sent out to work, and now they were returning in mass. My husband ordered the mayor to bring the people of the plantation (about 150 families) together and keep them in one place, in the large machine house. He then ordered the plantation police to put ladders against the roof of the machine house, and to collect brooms, shovels, kindling wood, and kerosene and to put out the oil lamps."

When Friedrich had recorded his first impressions of the new world ten years earlier, he had described its dangers with the excitement of a young man having the adventure of a lifetime. Elsa Endler's tone was quite different: her letter conveyed the awe and fear they felt before the overwhelming forces of nature: "Now we were surrounded by pitch-black darkness and the stench of sulfur and ashes. Sand and ashes were falling faster and faster. . . . The possibility of a fall of hot ashes was our greatest fear. . . . All day long, we looked for the sight of sunlight, but the darkness remained absolute. . . . On the third night, we were terribly frightened. From anxiety and exertion I had fallen asleep, and when I awoke the windows were tinged with red. I jumped out of bed and looked in the direction from which the ashes had come. The sky was tinged with red. The air was quivering, lightning flashed behind the clouds of ashes. My immediate thought was that burning ashes were coming. My brave husband tried to make believe that it was the sun trying to pierce the clouds of ash. I struck a match and saw that it was 1:15 in the morning. 'Then,' he said, 'it's the clearing of the air that permits us to see the fire of the volcano, and instead of losing hope you should be thankful that the rain of ashes has stopped.' He was right. Shortly after six o'clock the day dawned leaden gray, but at least we could distinguish things again. Oh, God, what a sight! As far as one could see everything was gray and dead, like an enormous cemetery. Trees and bushes loomed ghostlike. . . ."

NATURAL HISTORY

THEY SAY it was a punishment from God himself," the old peasant worker told me as he sat on the tomb of Friedrich Endler in the plantation cemetery. "There were tremors, and earth began to drop from the sky. Night fell, and it stayed night — a long, hot night. And what heat, *señor!* Even though there was no sun — because the sun stayed away for three days — the heat was awful. And the ash! There was ash up to here. . . ." He stood up and held out his hand at the level of his chest, about four feet from the ground. "And they had to sweep the roofs so they didn't fall in on them. But some did fall and killed the people."

No travelogues, no letters, nothing written. When I asked the workers why their families had come to La Patria, they had only tales, like this one, passed down from the parents and grandparents who had made the trip.

"The ash destroyed everything," another man sitting on the tomb picked up where the first had left off. "All the crops and all the wild plants too. And the animals from the woods came into town. There were deer and snakes and coyotes and cats. And they made their way through the streets, looking for food. But there wasn't any. And all the water was dirty too. So the animals died because they didn't have any way to live. And the people also died because they didn't have anything to eat."

The first man concluded the story: "And later on came the illnesses. Ay, dios! People got sick and just dropped dead. You could bury me in the morning and they would be burying you that same afternoon! That's how it was — a punishment from God himself. So the people left and came to the coast to look for work. And here is where they lived out their days."

⇊

It was the Day of the Dead, and these men had come to the cemetery to visit their deceased relatives. On the ridge behind them, dozens of people were relaxing in the sun, mostly women and children sitting by gravesites, which they had adorned with colorful plastic ribbons, candles, and flowers. Several radios blared *ranchera* music from Mexico.

The mood was festive, but it was nothing like the celebration taking place that day in cemeteries throughout the highlands, where whole communities joined in solemn prayer — mostly to a Christian God, though some, discreetly, to Mayan deities — and made offerings to their ancestors: burning candles; elaborate flower wreaths on the family tombstones; food spread out on the grave as for a picnic; and drinks (a soda, a beer, a swig of rum) poured into holes in the ground.

Julia López may have been the only person in the plantation cemetery who had seen the Day of the Dead celebration in the highlands. I learned this after her daughter saw my camera and asked me to take a photo of

her family. The eighty-year-old Julia wore the wrap-around skirt (called a *corte*) that indigenous women use in the highlands, and the button-down blouse that women wear on the coast. The daughter's outfit was entirely that of a coastal woman. The great-grandson who posed with them could have been a schoolboy from the city.

When I asked about the family's past, Julia told me that her parents came from a village in the highlands "when the ash fell." Their crops had been destroyed, and they had needed to look elsewhere for a source of food. They had made the journey by foot — one day to the town of San Marcos and another day up through the mountain pass to Sacuchum Dolores and down the other side on a mule path, which brought them to La Patria. It had been November or December, the peak of the harvest season, and they had gone to work picking coffee.

⁂

"That would have to be the 1902 eruption," a historian in Guatemala City would later tell me. "But I never heard of a volcano being the primary cause of the migration. There were forced labor drafts where the *jefe político,* or governor, of a department would round up a work gang in an Indian community and send them to work on the plantation. And there was also a system of debt-peonage. The historical record is full of violence."

He offered some examples. An 1884 letter from the mayor of one highland town complained that troops had twice arrived "to arrest and tie up the unlucky workers, they hit them and abused them as if they were beasts. . . . They committed the worst abuses, robbing corn, poultry, food, and money, raping our wives and daughters. . . ." Villagers in another community recalled hiding from the labor draft. "The survivors were those who hid from the persecution, only coming to their houses at night and slipping out again to hide at daybreak; they were like lizards hidden among the rocks, only raising their heads to spy the danger that came in search of more workers for forced labor." In another village, the people described how they were drafted into the system of debt-peonage. "When I was twelve," said one man, "the official and a number of policemen arrived at my house, forced my mother to accept 60 *reales,* and stuck my name in his black book, and I was sentenced." And in another: "When a poor man would arrive home [from forced labor], he received the awful news from his wife that the officials had left another sixty *reales* with orders to work again, perhaps this time in an even less hospitable area."

⇓

I made repeated visits to La Patria but found the workers there had nothing to say about labor drafts or debts, nothing of being forced by other people to seek work on the plantations. The only violence in their story was nature's violence — the erupting volcano.

This omission wasn't unique to people in La Patria. With the help of one of César's friends, I interviewed some older workers in La Soledad and heard the same story: people knew where their families had come from, but they didn't know — or didn't care to recall — much more about what had brought them to the plantations.

César wasn't surprised. "Looking back now," he said the next time we talked, "when I was growing up, we had very little connection with that past. My grandparents had family in the highlands but they were born on the coast. When they talked about the past, it was stories about hunting, or about droughts and plagues, but always about life there in the plantations. They cut their ties with the highlands. It was only when I went to the university that I learned about the labor drafts and those things. But if you talk to my friends who stayed there in the plantation, they have no idea. They don't know their history."

⇓

Looking elsewhere for clues, I came across a copy of the national census of 1921. It said that 85 percent of La Igualdad's population was Indian. When I later compared it with the 1994 census, I found the number had dropped to just 5 percent.

What happened to all the Indians? They didn't leave. They didn't die off. They weren't displaced by new immigrants. Judging by the census data, they simply stopped being Indians.

How do you stop being an Indian? In Guatemala, you become a *Ladino*. An 1894 census report had divided the people of Guatemala into two groups: "the Ladinos and the Indians, the former being descendants of the white race and of a mixture of European and Indians." What really set the two groups apart, however, was not the presence of European blood — for, in fact, there were many Ladinos who possessed none. The difference lay, rather, in traits of an entirely different sort.

"Indian," a term coined by non-Indians, meant the bottom of the social ladder — as Friedrich Endler observed in his travelogue, describing
the Indian workers as "savage, ragged creatures" who "occupy the lowest
rung on the plantation." Just how low their rung was is conveyed in another travelogue written a few years earlier by a visitor from the United
States: "People regard [the Indians] as little better than animals and fit
only for cargo carrying, almost always addressing them as *'chucho,'* a
word used for a dog."

"Indian" also represented the past in a timeline — the timeline of historical progress. The 1894 census report put it this way: "The Ladinos
and Indians are two distinct classes; the former march ahead with hope
and energy through the paths that have been laid out by progress; the lat-
ter, immovable, do not take any part in the political and intellectual life,
adhering tenaciously to their old habits and customs. The Indians do not
cooperate actively in the progress of civilization."

Implicit in this definition of Indian was the possibility of movement —
up the ladder and forward on the timeline — the possibility, that is, of
becoming Ladino. Such movement was encouraged by the Ladino elite.
Justo Rufino Barrios had once bestowed, by presidential decree, the status of Ladino upon an entire town of Indians in the highlands above La
Igualdad. And according to the 1894 census, the government was constantly striving "to instill into the Indians new customs, showing them
new paths to success."

In Guatemala, in other words, people could stop being Indians by
abandoning old habits and customs, by leaving their past behind.

⚜

Very few of the families that migrated to La Igualdad maintained ties
with their ancestral communities. There were some like Julia and her sisters who visited their parents' village in the highlands. But their own children grew up in the plantations speaking Spanish. Within a generation or
two, the region's workers had abandoned their ancestral language and
dress. They stopped being Indians.

At least that's how it looked to the government officials who carried
out the censuses. Prior to 1994, census workers determined whether a
family was "indigenous" (*indio* had been replaced by *indígena* in official
discourse during the course of the century) by visiting the home and see-

ing for themselves whether the inhabitants talked or dressed like Indians. For the 1994 census, the government chose a new approach: they let the people identify themselves by answering a yes-or-no question: "Are you *indígena?*" In La Igualdad, 95 percent said no.

But did saying no to this question make them Ladinos?

In order to find out, I went around posing the question in a different way: "Some people call themselves *indígenas,* and some other people call themselves Ladinos — what do the people here call themselves?"

"Natural" was the answer I heard most often. "We're *naturales,*" one sixty-year-old man told me. "But now we have some among us who are more educated. My son for example. He is of the same race, but he can defend us." He explained that his son had finished high school and the equivalent of junior college and now taught at the local elementary school.

Later I asked César about the use of the term *natural,* and he offered an explanation: "People here know they're from the indigenous race. But they also know that they're different from the people in the highlands. And they're pretty racist — they consider themselves superior to 'those *indios.*' So they don't like to call themselves *indígenas. Natural* seems more neutral."

I had also posed the question to one sixty-eight-year-old like this: "Where are the people here from?" His answer: "Now, more than anything, we're from right here."

⬇

"My dad always said this is not my land," a plantation worker told a Guatemalan writer in the 1940s. "This is not where my deceased and their spirits are. Here we don't have contact with the ancestors."

Half a century later, Mayan families scattered throughout the coast and packed into the slums of the capital still journeyed to the highlands on the Day of the Dead to celebrate with their deceased ancestors. But the workers in La Igualdad stayed put on the piedmont, celebrating in the plantations where their parents or grandparents had come to pick coffee. Some of the elders among them, like Julia, remembered relatives buried in the highland cemeteries. But their own dead were buried in the plantation. The plantation was their home.

BILDUNGSROMAN

PANAJACHEL HAD ONCE been a small Indian town. Now it was a major tourist attraction. Every day scores of foreigners strolled down the main street from the town center to the shore of Lake Atitlán, searching out souvenirs in the scores of shops and curbside stalls. Dollars, marks, francs — exchanged for quetzals — purchased the exotic patterns and sumptuous earthy colors of "traditional" Mayan textiles, masks, sandals, and hacky sacks.

Away from this cosmopolitan bustle, on a side street, behind a thick hedge, was a large white house with a glassed-in verandah. And on the verandah, in a reclining chair, there sat an old man. His legs, which were bowed from countless hours on horseback, were propped up in front of him. His large hands, spotted from years in the sun, hung over the arm-rests at his side. His sky-blue eyes gazed through thick glasses out the window toward the hedge. For hours he would sit in silence and gaze. Sometimes he turned his head, very slowly, to watch the two dachshunds playing at his feet. Sometimes he lifted a mug of beer to his mouth, took a slow sip, put the mug back down, licked the foam from his lip, and re-turned his gaze to the hedge. Mounted on the wall behind his chair was an enormous map of Guatemala. Its place names were out of date, and its topographical colors had faded to a uniform yellow.

My eyes explored the map as I sat in a chair brought to the man's side and told him of my recent travels. Speaking slowly and loudly — as in-structed by Sara — I shared some impressions of La Igualdad, the coffee plantations, the cemetery in La Patria. It was over a decade since the old man had abandoned the plantation, saying he would never go back. The family had later convinced him to visit two or three times; but those visits had been brief, and years ago. In recent months he had not even ventured beyond the hedge.

He seemed to enjoy hearing me describe the places he knew so well. When I spoke of the view from La Patria — where every morning you see the puffs of smoke blown up by Santiaguito twenty miles to the east — he laughed: "Well, as long there's smoke, we know we're okay." When a live volcano stops smoking, he explained, the build-up of pressure inside will eventually lead to an eruption. "I was two months old when Santiaguito was born. That's why I call him my little brother. It looks like he'll outlive me yet!"

He took another slow sip of beer, returned the mug, licked the foam off his lip, and recalled the stories of destruction he had heard from his parents. "We had it easy, you know. There were plantations just below Santa María that were completely destroyed. And in some places all the people were buried alive. The Germans who had land there, friends of my father, they had to force their workers to leave. The workers didn't want to abandon their homes. So the Germans said, 'If you don't leave, we'll shoot you!' That's how they saved those poor people's lives."

His gaze had come in from the hedge and focused on me, on the dogs playing at his feet, on his own hands. Speaking in English, with bits of Spanish and an occasional word of German (which he paused to translate), he told me how the Endlers had come to occupy the *casa patronal* in La Patria.

In Mundo Nuevo, Friedrich Endler had befriended a Frenchman who owned the neighboring plantation, San Ignacio. When the Frenchman died, his widow, an American woman, asked Friedrich to manage the plantation for her. If he did it for seven years, she promised, she would give him half the land. He agreed, the widow moved to California, and the Endlers moved into San Ignacio.

"When I was a youngster, our diet was very limited. We ate black beans and corn, and once in a while we would butcher an animal. One time my mother killed a pig in the morning and that night, at around ten o'clock, our dog started barking furiously, and we heard people coming. A man got off of his mule and asked for a place to stay. His name was Herbert Wilson. He was a coffee buyer from San Francisco. Mom brought out many different kinds of meat, and that man sat there and ate and ate. The next day he talked with Dad about buying and selling coffee and asked if he could make his headquarters there in San Ignacio. This was very welcome, because in those times, guests didn't come around the house much and people got very lonesome.

"So Herbert Wilson would come back every year and do his buying. One time he asked Dad to buy coffee from another farm. Dad got the coffee for him. And when Wilson left, he gave Dad a check for $2400. He said it was his commission. Dad couldn't understand that, he was not a businessman, and he didn't think it was right. He thought that money ought to go to the farmer who produced the coffee.

"Another time Herbert Wilson came and said, 'Don Federico, you look very distressed. What's happening?' What had happened was that, after seven years, the widow had come and turned over half of San Ignacio to the Endlers and then offered to sell the rest. Friedrich had agreed to buy it, mortgaging his half in order to make the payment. The following year, the coffee market dropped, and he found himself deeply in debt. 'I am going to be foreclosed,' he told Herbert Wilson. 'I owe $25,000, and there is not the slightest chance of me ever getting out of that hole.'

"Herbert Wilson did his rounds, and on the day he left, he had already mounted his mule, he called Dad over and said, 'God-a-mighty, I damn near forgot something!' He reached into his pocket and gave Dad a sealed envelope. He spurred his mule and left. When Dad opened the envelope, he found a check which read: 'Pay to the order of Friedrich Endler $25,000.' Dad raced down a footpath and caught up with Wilson and said, how could he give a man that was broke $25,000, when he knew perfectly well he would never get it back? Wilson just laughed, and said, 'Don Federico, coffee prices go up, coffee prices go down. I haven't the slightest doubt about your ability to pay, if you have the time.'"

Franz paused a moment, remembering. "I still get tears in my eyes after so many years thinking of that good, honest man."

He sipped the beer and continued. "Well, Dad was ready to tear the check into pieces, because he knew that that was all wrong. But instead he took it back to the house to show my mother. Mom told him to put it in a safety box, and someday he would use it."

And he did use it, less than a year later, to pay off his debt to the widow. The following year coffee prices went up, and within another two years, he had paid off his debt to Wilson. Three years later, he pooled his resources with a German friend and bought Mundo Nuevo.

After spending his early childhood in San Ignacio, Franz was sent off to study at the German School in Quetzaltenango. When his parents moved back to Mundo Nuevo, he and his younger sister went to Germany to continue their education. The outbreak of the world war prevented transatlantic travel, so the children did not see their parents again until 1919. Franz returned to Guatemala with his father and went to learn the coffee trade, working as an apprentice in El Porvenir.

He began in the blacksmith shop making machetes, then horseshoes, then chisels, and finally, cutting steel. Each new task required greater skill and precision. The most demanding of all was maintenance of the water wheel that provided the plantation's power. When a part of the giant wheel cracked — the shaft, the spokes, the chassis — it had to be replaced as soon as possible. The replacement had to be precise: the slightest wriggle could break the entire machine and bring the processing facilities to a halt. So they would make the part a fraction of a millimeter larger than the original, tempering the steel until it was just the right color, dipping it in water for a second, and hammering it into place.

After several weeks of metalwork, Franz moved on to work in the machine house, tending the machines that removed the pulp of the berries, the machines that dried the beans, and then the machines that removed the husks. Once he had mastered the machine house, he spent several weeks in the coffee groves, and after that he worked tending the plantation livestock.

Upon finishing the apprenticeship, Franz was ready to work. His first job was on the plantation that his uncle, recently arrived from Germany, had just purchased with the help of Friedrich Endler: La Patria.

By the time his story reached La Patria, the ninety-two-year-old Endler was tired. His energy had already ebbed at points during the interview, his words slowing down, his gaze drifting out toward the hedge. Yet each time I thought the interview would end, the old man returned to life, his imagination rekindled by certain memories — memories of powerful machines, of precocious and faithful animals, of jobs that had tested his strength and ingenuity — memories of the things that had made the Endlers who they were.

"Now, *that* was a water wheel!" he said about the machine that had generated so much energy and demanded so much of its caretakers. And, as he said it, he clenched his fists in the air and jerked them in a downward motion, as if he were hammering Spanish exclamation marks on either side of his sentence. "Now, ¡*that* was a job!" he said with the same motion, referring to his father's work in the ship's steam room. "Now, ¡*that* was a horse!" he said, referring to the animal that he trained in El Porvenir and that would carry him around the piedmont for the next twenty years.

But arriving at La Patria, he was overcome by weariness. He stopped talking and stared out the window.

"Maybe we should continue another time," I suggested. He didn't respond. I sat quietly and glanced back through my notes.

"La Patria," he broke the silence, "that's where I first lived with my wife."

I looked up and saw that his eyes had returned from the hedge and were focused again on me. "Oh, really?" I flipped to a new page. "Where did you meet her?"

"Now, ¡*that's* another story!"

In 1924, after working in La Patria and doing brief stints at other plantations in the area, Franz decided to travel to the United States with a cousin. They went to Los Angeles and stayed several months, working in a glass factory and doing odd jobs such as loading bricks. One day a friend invited them to visit the home of a German immigrant couple who had five "lovely" daughters. When Franz laid eyes on Laurie, the second youngest, he said to his cousin, "That girl's going to be my wife." The cousin laughed: "You don't even speak English!" But before long Laurie, who worked as a real estate agent, was giving Franz English lessons, and within a few months they were engaged.

The engagement carried a condition: Laurie would first spend some time in Guatemala and see if she could stand living there. So in 1926, Laurie and her sister arrived in Champerico ("the only passengers on a ship that was full of dynamite!" Franz said gleefully). They stayed in La Patria while Franz lived in a neighboring plantation where he was working.

"Did she like it? Oh, she loved it!"

It took only a few weeks to decide. She married Franz there in La Igualdad and lived in Guatemala until her death sixty-five years later.

The honeymoon was spent in La Patria, riding horses and hunting. "Laurie was a city girl, but boy could she handle horses!" Franz beamed with pride. "And she was a great shot, much better than me, I tell you." He paused and lifted his fists in the air: "Yes, ¡*that* was a woman! That was a woman . . ." His voice trailed off. His arms slumped to his side. Tears gathered in his eyes.

The silence was broken when his servant, a plump and energetic indigenous woman, marched out from the kitchen. "*Bueno*, Don Franz. It's time for your rest!" The old man emerged from his reverie, feigning annoyance as she helped him out of the seat. Once standing, he turned to me: "When will we talk again?"

"Well, I could come by tomorrow, if you're not busy."

"Busy? An old man like me? Hah! I'm on my way out. The only thing I've got left to do is drink my beer and wait to die."

"Don't talk like that, Don Franz!" the servant scolded him.

"She doesn't like me to talk like that," he said with a playful smile. "But it's true." I watched as she led him slowly down the verandah to his room.

⚓

When I arrived the next day, Franz was in the same seat — dogs, cane, mug of beer at his side. He was in good spirits. "Hello, young man!" he greeted me affectionately. "What did you say your name was again? At my age you don't remember names."

I told him my name and took my seat next to him.

"Well, Daniel, I have a story for you."

I opened my notebook, and he began. "The first job my wife and I did together was drive a car up to La Patria. No one had ever brought a car to La Igualdad. The roads weren't made for them. Now, ¡that was a job!"

They picked up the car in Coatepeque, and their first challenge was getting it started, since the engine "was almost rusted through." After some effort, they got it going and drove it north, out of Coatepeque, down the ravine to the Naranjo River. "There was a bridge over the Naranjo River, but the approaches of the bridge weren't finished at the time. We had to get the car on to the bridge somehow. So we tied some ropes to the car and about forty men were on the ramp and bridge while another twenty were on the sides, pulling and pushing."

When the newlyweds and their sixty helpers finally got the car onto the bridge, the drive continued. But it didn't get far. Above the river, the road became too narrow for them to pass. On one side was a wall of solid rock, on the other a cliff that dropped down to the water. The Endlers parked the car and called it a day. They returned in the morning with chisels, hammers, pick-axes, and a team of workers from La Patria, and set about widening the road.

Six weeks later, they had removed a twenty-meter strip — six inches deep — of rock from the mountain, enough for the car to squeeze through. Laurie Endler got behind the wheel, while Franz, "two Indians and a Swiss chap" used a long pole to prevent the car from sliding off the road. "It would have tumbled down the cliff! As we were just married, I wanted to keep that young girl next to me as long as I could."

They got through, and, where the road widened, the drive continued again. After two days of "traveling with every known trick," the drivers arrived at last in La Igualdad. "As we approached town, the people came out of their houses. They didn't know what was making all the noise. They had never seen a car before, and when they saw it they got scared. Some crawled through the barbed wire fences at the side of the road to escape. At last we reached La Patria. We were exhausted! And everything was boiling over in that car. The people came and gathered around. We told them not to be scared. But they didn't know what to make of this thing. And some of the braver ones reached out to touch it, and . . ."

Once again he lifted his arms as if to hammer exclamation points — only this time the hands were extended to touch the car that stood before him in his memory. They came down and just as quickly jerked back up: "¡The engine burned their hands!"

REVELATION

THE ROADS in La Igualdad had improved since the Endlers drove the first car in — but not all that much. The buses that climbed up from Coatepeque every day took anywhere from two and a half hours when the road was dry to five or more hours when the rains had turned it to mud. Sometimes, after particularly heavy rains, the buses stopped running for days. If I were going to travel in and out and around La Igualdad on my own, I would need my own transportation. So César activated a network of uncles in Coatepeque who found me a used motorcycle that was tall and fast and built for mountain roads. I paid $300 cash, and we christened it *La Poderosa* — the Powerful One.

When I arrived in La Patria on the motorcycle, a six-foot-two foreigner with a black helmet and goggles, the children who saw me fled in terror. One little boy arrived at his house out of breath and weeping. "Why are you crying, my son?" his father asked. The child, who was mute, responded with three hand gestures: fists held out revving the handlebars of an imaginary motorcycle, a hand raised high in the air indicating a large person, a finger drawn across his throat expressing what was on everyone's mind: *robachicos.*

That's the story I heard when, several weeks later, I ventured alone into Las Cruces, the community where most of La Patria's workers lived. I had by then made a half dozen trips to La Igualdad, staying a few days each time in Sara's house and interviewing anyone I could in the center of the plantation, where the processing plant, the office, and the mechanic's shop were. From them I had learned more about coffee farming, but made little headway with the history I was after. It was time to try talking to the people who worked the fields. But that required finding them in Las Cruces, a half-hour walk down the mountainside, and the plantation field master insisted that it would be unwise for me to go there alone. I heeded his warning and instead went one afternoon with one of the plantation drivers, who introduced me to several elderly men who he thought could "talk about times past." The interviews produced little more than what I'd heard above — if anything, these men seemed more reluctant to talk to me.

It was possible, I realized, that people simply didn't know the history of the plantation's earlier years. But even when I asked about recent events I encountered the same silence. At first, I stuck to my plan of holding off on such questions, but my curiosity soon overcame my caution. Wasn't there anyone who would acknowledge that plantation life hadn't always been entirely harmonious and uneventful? Supposedly there had been a war around here. Supposedly there were still guerrillas in the woods above La Patria. But none of these workers would give me any clue as to what the fighting was about.

Whatever they were hiding about the plantation, it couldn't help that they saw me staying in the house of the owner or showing up at their homes in her truck. I needed to find a way to encounter people on my own. The visit to the cemetery on the Day of the Dead had given me a chance to meet a few. Now the photos I'd developed from that day provided a pretext for visiting them on my own.

Following directions from the cook, I found Julia López's house in Las Cruces, where the road from town began its climb toward La Patria. Julia wasn't home so I gave the photo to her son Huicho, a youthful-looking man in his forties with a friendly and self-assured smile. Huicho offered me a warm Coke and a seat in the shade of his front porch. He sat on a stool, and a group of children gathered around him to peer at the photo. After chatting about the weather, about this year's crop, about where I was from, he told me the story of the mute boy. The way he imitated the child's terror was quite funny, and all the children laughed.

I smiled too. I had finally found a worker of La Patria who did not seem reluctant to talk to me. Rather than question him in front of the children, I returned later and found him alone with his wife. This time he invited me into the front room of his house. It wasn't as decrepit as the homes I'd seen in La Soledad: the floor was concrete; the walls were cement block for the bottom third, and wood planks rose the rest of the way to the corrugated tin roof. There were three beds — thin mattresses on wooden frames. Two light bulbs hung from the ceiling and on one wall was a colorful mural: a yellow river cascading through a green countryside, orange fish in the waters, red and blue birds in the trees, and white doves flying above the light switch and through the blue sky toward the words "And God blessed them saying Be fruitful and multiply and fill the waters of the seas and multiply the birds on the land."

Huicho was as talkative as before, at least until I asked him about the history of the war. Then, like all the other workers before him, he became evasive. Unlike others, though, he didn't seem uncomfortable; he merely changed the topic to something else.

His topic of choice was religion. He talked of his Evangelical church, one of dozens that had sprung up in the region in recent years. I listened for a few minutes and then tried changing the topic back, posing what I figured was a relatively innocuous question. "What do you think of the peace negotiations going on between the government and the guerrillas?"

"*Pues.*" He paused, considering the question. "I say that this war will never end."

"Oh, really?" I felt encouraged that he was at last offering an opinion on a political subject. "Why not?"

"Because that's what the Bible says."

Our conversation became a gentle tug of war. I pulled toward the region's political history. He pulled toward the teachings of *el señor Jesucristo.* I wasn't winning. So after a while I changed tack. If he didn't want to discuss history, perhaps he could introduce me to other people in the community who would.

Sure, he told me, only right then he was late for a *culto* — as evangelical Christians referred to their religious services. I declined the invitation to attend, and we agreed to meet another day.

Huicho's wife, Lidia, greeted me at the door.

"Is Huicho here?" I asked.

"He'll be here any minute. Come on in."

I followed her through the front of the house and into a back room — the kitchen — where their poverty was more apparent than in the front: the floor was dirt; light filtered through walls made of weathered wooden boards; the underside of the corrugated metal roof was soot black from the smoke of the hearth-fire. I sat down at the table and Lidia brought me a cup of brownish water that smelled of coffee but tasted only of sugar. She then turned to a hen that had jumped onto the table and, yanking a cloth rag from her waist, shooed it to the ground.

Soon I heard someone approaching from outside. It wasn't Huicho, but rather his mother. "*Buenas tardes, Doña Julia.*" I stood up and greeted her. "Sit down, sit down," she insisted and, seeing my camera on the table, asked, "Taking more photos?"

"No, just asking more questions. Maybe I could ask you a few, if you have a moment?"

"*Está bueno.*" She sat down at the table. I pulled out my notebook.

"What I wanted to know is . . ." I glanced at the assortment of questions I had jotted down there and chose one. "What did the people eat in the old days?"

⇓

The main food, she told me, was maize. Some days they served it as tortillas, others as *tamales* — which are small cakes of dough wrapped in corn husks. In some plantations the workers were given plots of land to farm. In others, the plantation provided them with maize at reduced prices. In La Patria, workers also planted banana trees at the edges of the coffee fields. They ate roots, herbs, and other wild plants that grew in the uncultivated parts of the plantation, in ravines, or in the woods higher up in the hills. There was often hunger. Some years it was due to drought: the corn would dry out and produce little. And if the coffee trees produced little, the *patrones* wouldn't be able to pay them. One time the summer lasted two whole years. Only after months of prayers and processions did the dry spell break.

I would hear similar stories from other coffee workers her age, including one who told me about the years of the locusts, when the swarms descended on the corn fields and destroyed the crops. Once there was no maize for two whole years. Food prices soared above what people could afford, so they supplemented their meager maize supply with banana, mixing banana pulp in with the maize to make *tamales.* When the maize ran out, they ate *tamales* made entirely of banana pulp. For months they lived on bananas and wild herbs. In an effort to control the plague, the people dug ditches near their crops, swept the locusts in and buried them. But as soon as the ditches were filled, more would descend from the sky. Again there were processions. The prayers for divine reprieve weren't answered until someone invented airplanes, which came and sprayed poison over the land, killing the locusts and ending the plague.

⇓

The hen had jumped onto the table again, and both women shooed it off. Lidia pulled a handful of corn from a bag by the wall and scattered it on the floor. Half a dozen birds raced to the spot and began pecking away.

"Who was the owner of La Patria in those days?" I asked Julia.

"There was Don Federico. And after that was Don Franz. They were good *patrones.*"

"Were there ever any problems between the workers and the *patrones*?"

"No. They were good people. Good people."

"They say there was an agrarian reform back in the days of President Arbenz, and in lots of plantations there were disagreements between the workers and the *patrón*. Was there any disagreement in La Patria?"

"I don't know much about all that. *Pues,* here everything was peaceful. And you," she changed the topic. "Are you related to the family?"

"What family?"

"Doña Sara's."

"No. I'm just a friend."

⬇

Julia had chores to do, she told me, and left the kitchen. Lidia followed her, assuring me that her husband would show up any time now. I sat and waited, watching the chickens make their way across the floor.

These are foraging creatures. They spend the daylight hours wandering the kitchen in search of food. With every step, their heads bob — forward, back, forward — like metronomes in perpetual motion, occasionally pecking at a speck on the ground without interrupting the jerky rhythm. The pace picks up when humans let crumbs fall; it dissolves into a pecking frenzy when someone throws scraps. Occasionally a larger bird will dart at a smaller one — the old pecking order. When the rooster struts in from outside, watch out! A flurry of wings, a moment of panic, and then only a few feet away, the persecuted bird will return to the perpetual motion, the strut, the bobbing head, as if nothing had happened.

The direction of movement seems random, but like balls ricocheting around a pool table, the birds will eventually cover all the exposed surfaces in the room. The result is a spotless kitchen. Although the family may need to sweep away the gathering dust and bird droppings, all edible matter is taken care of by the birds. It's not merely removed; it's recycled. Over the course of weeks, the birds put on weight, until eventually they are large enough to provide a meal (or two or three) for the family. It's an elegantly efficient system: little is wasted. What scraps and crumbs of food make it to the kitchen floor are converted into something the family can consume: meat. The bones will make a tasty broth, and whatever the humans can't consume will go to the skinny dogs who keep intruders away with their bark and, in some cases, help hunt wild game in the woods.

When Huicho finally arrived, we headed out together, climbing the dirt road that led into the center of Las Cruces, turning off onto a narrow path that ran between the banana trees and wooden shacks, which were fenced into tiny family compounds.

We reached the first home on our tour just as the man who lived there was arriving with a large bundle of firewood strapped on his back. He had a small, wiry body, and the way he carried the load — doubled over with his face to the ground, the tumpline pulling at his forehead, his long arms dangling below his chest — made him look like a beast of burden, especially when he tilted his head sideways to look at us through the corner of one eye. His feet were bare.

Inside the house, sitting on a wooden stool, which wobbled on the uneven surface of the dirt floor, the man looked as old as Franz Endler, though he was probably younger by a decade or more.

The interview was short. He told a variant of the volcano story; he said that Don Federico and Don Franz were good *patrones;* he said that nothing happened here during the time of Arbenz. He was now retired, he told me, and received scanty social security payments. It was very difficult to live off what they gave him, but he trusted in the goodness of *el Señor,* who would provide for all who believed in him.

We visited two more homes and got more or less the same story — the story of a world in which the principal actors were either natural — volcano, rain, insects — or supernatural — *el Señor.*

Our tour was cut short by the rain — a torrential downpour, which pounded the corrugated metal roofs, creating such a din that it was impossible to communicate without shouting. Huicho and I ran the hundred meters back to his house and arrived drenched. By the time the storm let up, the sun had set. The family insisted that I stay the night rather than venture out in the darkness on muddy roads.

As we waited for dinner, Huicho began to tell me about a *culto* that would be taking place in their home. He asked me about my own church affiliation, and I answered that my family was Catholic. Then he pulled out his tattered Bible and opened to a passage that, he explained with a smile, teaches us that Catholic priests are in union with the devil. I nodded — I'd heard this before from other Evangelical Christians in Guatemala — and braced myself for the proselytizing onslaught that would follow.

He began to read the passage, but then stopped suddenly, in mid-sentence, and looked up. "Listen . . ."

I heard dogs barking nearby . . . a radio blaring from a neighbor's house . . . a preacher singing through a megaphone somewhere up the hill . . . and then in the distance: *Pop-pop-pop.* It sounded like firecrackers, a common sound in these parts at night. But the precise rhythm suggested something else. Again: *Pop. Pop.* Lidia came in from the kitchen and stood in the doorway listening: *Pop-pop-pop.*

"They're in El Progreso," she said, almost whispering, "shooting at La Independencia."

No explanation was needed: the guerrillas had come down from the mountain to a ridge in the plantation El Progreso and were shooting down at the army encampment on an adjacent but lower ridge in the plantation La Independencia.

Then a new sound: *Pa-pa-pa-pa.* Rapid fire. That had to be the army shooting back. The guerrillas were precision fighters; they didn't waste bullets; they knew their target. The soldiers were shooting blindly, with fear, up into the darkness: *Pa-pa-pa-pa-pa-pa.*

The exchange intensified and then abruptly stopped. The dogs continued barking, the preacher singing. I held my breath and listened for more.

Pop-pop: it started up again. I looked at Huicho. The tattered Bible lay forgotten on his knees. His eyes caught the light of the electric bulb, and in that brightness I saw my own excitement reflected back at me. This was my chance — I could feel it — the moment of truth had come at last — no one could deny now that something was happening here, something political, something violent. The bullets had shredded the evangelical veneer of the hereafter and exposed the harsher reality of the here-and-now.

"What will happen?" I asked.

Huicho didn't answer. Instead, to my surprise, he returned his attention to his Bible. He flipped pages, stopped to read — lips moving silently — and then continued flipping. Finally, he looked up at me. "Listen, it explains it here," and looking back down, he read slowly: *"There shall be wars, and rumors of war. . . ."*

Again he showed me that self-assured smile. He didn't seem to notice my own look of dismay. "Right? *Wars and rumors of war.*" He pointed his index finger in the air over his shoulder, not to God, but to the gun battle that continued nearby. "You see, it's all here in the Book." He continued reading: *". . . see that you are not alarmed. Such things are bound to happen; but the end is still to come. For nation will make war upon nation, kingdom upon kingdom. . . ."* He looked up: "Right? Isn't it true they say there's a war over there, in Europe, right?"

"That's right. A place called Bosnia."

". . . there will be famines and earthquakes in many places. . . . Wasn't there just something in the news about an earthquake?"

"In Asia."

". . . With all these things, the birth pangs of the new age begin."

DECREE

S O WHAT ABOUT THE BIRTH PANGS of *this* age? How did there come to be a coffee plantation on this mountainside, with Germans living in the patronal house and "natural" people working the surrounding fields?

In the history the Endlers recorded, the family's property and position in Guatemala resulted from hard work, perseverance, courage, and luck. Theirs was a story of men struggling to dominate the natural world — to harness its energy while escaping its destructive force. It was a story of individual achievement. What they had, they got through their own effort, with the support of their wives and the occasional help of good friends along the way.

In the history the workers told me, the main protagonist was nature. When pressed to discuss the political aspects of plantation life, these storytellers jumped instead from the *natural* to the *supernatural*.

For all their differences, the histories of *patrón* and worker did have two striking similarities. One was what stood at the center: a volcano. The other was what was missing: the government.

I decided to go looking for that missing piece in the library of a historian. I knew I would find that a government had played some role in the early life of the plantations. But I never could have expected what I found: an official account that flipped the volcano stories on their heads. As it turned out, not only had a powerful government *existed* back in 1902, but — in one of the more bizarre episodes of the century — this government had decreed that the erupting volcano *did not*.

OCTOBER 24, 1902

As the ashes were burying the Endlers in Mundo Nuevo and the Lópezes in their highland village, a town crier took his place in the central plaza of Quetzaltenango, just four miles north of the volcano that had blown skyward that morning. Churning black clouds had blotted out the midday sun, blanketing the city in darkness. Lightning flashes now revealed a gray emptiness where there should have been a colorful Saturday market. The town crier held up a lantern and watched as a military band struggled with drums and bugles to overcome the deafening roar of the volcano and summon the townspeople to the plaza. Ash fell steadily around them. Rocks crashed against rooftops and shattered stucco walls. And as the ground shook below his feet, the town crier read the proclamation sent from the capital, letting it be known to all who would listen that there were no volcanoes erupting in Guatemala, that any disturbances taking place were, in fact, far away in Mexico, and that the Republic of Guatemala remained in a state of peace and tranquillity under the protection of its illustrious president, Manuel Estrada Cabrera.

After years of silence, Santa María had blown at a most awkward moment: the eve of the Feast of the Goddess Minerva. During his four years at the country's helm, Estrada Cabrera had made Minerva the patron saint of the nation's progress — a progress consisting of the cultural and intellectual development of his people. This notion of progress dated back to the Liberal Revolution of 1871: the first president of the new regime had made public education his "top priority"; the second had declared that education was "the cement and base that must sustain the new edifice begun by the revolution." Now Estrada Cabrera had raised the tribute to education to its most dramatic expression. Assuming the title of "Educator and Protector of the Youth," the century's first Education President led his people in annual tribute to the Roman goddess of wisdom.

This year was to be the grandest Feast of Minerva yet, celebrated with special flourish in the capital, where the president would welcome diplomats and businessmen from around the world. His representatives abroad had obtained letters from heads of state — including President Theodore Roosevelt — honoring the Guatemalan Republic and lauding Estrada Cabrera's commitment to progress through education. The president was not about to let the Santa María volcano interfere with the festivities.

Needless to say, Estrada Cabrera's commitment to education was about as credible as his claim that there was no eruption. When the government of Chile actually sent a delegation to study Guatemala's new school system, they found "nothing," according to one Guatemalan observer: "No teachers, no equipment, no students, not even buildings." Instead of constructing schools, Estrada Cabrera had built replicas of the Parthenon throughout the country — like the one that still stands just north of the Santa María volcano. Instead of funding the national agronomy school, he had opened a national opera. Estrada Cabrera's education program entailed little more than the conspicuous celebration of European culture, even as the vast majority of his people remained unschooled and illiterate.

Years later, Guatemala's Nobel laureate Miguel Angel Asturias would immortalize Estrada Cabrera as *el Señor Presidente,* the quintessential Latin American dictator whose vaulting ego and despotic pretensions went unchecked by democratic institutions. Another renowned writer, Eduardo Galeano, would recount the denial of the Santa María eruption in the opening of his history of Latin America's twentieth century. He titled the passage "The Government Decides That Reality Doesn't Exist."

Yet as I pieced together the events leading up to the eruption, I began to see the volcano decree as much more than the conceit of a megalomaniac. The dictator's effort to suppress reality was in fact entirely consistent with the very *real* agenda of the Liberals in Guatemala: progress they sought, not through education of course, but through coffee.

BIRTH OF THE COFFEE NATION

It was in the 1860s that Guatemala's well-to-do realized that their future lay in coffee. The beans could bring unprecedented profits on an emerging world market. Yet landowners soon found that setting up coffee plantations was not an easy business, and many began to feel that the Conservative regime governing the country at the time was not doing enough to make it easier.

In 1871, these frustrated landowners threw their support behind a rebel army as it made its way eastward from San Marcos, crisscrossing the piedmont, confounding government troops in the highlands and on the coast. After several weeks of fighting, the rebels marched triumphantly into Guatemala City and established the Liberal regime that would rule the country for the next half century. During their first decades in power, the Liberals would enact sweeping reforms that addressed the needs of coffee production.

What was needed to produce coffee?

First, land. The volcanic soils of the piedmont were ideal for growing coffee. And much of the piedmont, especially to the west in Quetzaltenango and San Marcos, was virgin forest. The problem for the aspiring coffee growers was that most of it belonged to Indian communities located at the edge of the highlands. Growers complained bitterly: how was it possible that lands ideal for coffee were being "wasted" by the Indians on subsistence farming or, even worse, not being farmed at all? Once in power, the Liberals took care of the problem by carrying out a massive land redistribution. The government decreed that most of the piedmont was "uncultivated" and put it up for public auction. (Although some of these lands were already being farmed by Indian communities, the decree defined "utilized lands" as only those planted with coffee, sugar, cocoa, or cattle feed — lands used for subsistence agriculture were therefore considered "uncultivated.") A land rush followed. And within a decade the piedmont was transformed into an archipelago of large coffee plantations.

Second, capital. Obtaining capital to finance farming had always been extremely difficult in Guatemala. So once in power, the Liberals did all they could to make it easier. They created two national banks that would make long-term, low-interest loans to landowners. They also created a land registry to keep track of titles, transactions, and mortgages, and so make private lending to landowners more secure, and therefore more available. But the government banks failed, and the private banks operated with very limited success.

The Liberal regime quickly found that it could not secure capital for the plantations as easily as it had secured land. Land was a national resource; capital was not. Or rather land could be turned into a national resource by dispossessing indigenous communities; capital could only come from abroad.

THE INTERNATIONAL PARTNERSHIP

The people best situated to bring capital to Guatemala were those who had access to foreign banks, which is why the coffee business would be built through partnerships between men like José María Solórzano and Heinrich Schmidt, the two who convinced Friedrich Endler that his future lay in Central America.

What compelled the two men in the Bremen beer house that day to steer this young German engineer to Guatemala? Solórzano was a personal friend of the coffee baron and ex-president Manuel Lisandro Barillas, and it's likely he shared the Liberals' vision for the future of Guatemala. Central to this was the hope that European immigration would contribute to economic growth by bringing capital and skilled labor. To that end, the government established an Immigration Society that recruited European immigrants and created incentives for them, including assistance in obtaining lands and exemptions from taxes and import duties.

Schmidt, meanwhile, most likely shared the concerns of the German business community, which had become increasingly involved in Guatemala in the previous twenty years. The growth of German industry, business leaders believed, would depend on foreign trade. Germany would need markets for its manufactured goods, as well as suppliers of raw materials. The presence of German citizens abroad was central to this project. Emigrants would establish businesses that would import German goods and send local agricultural products back to Germany.

When the Liberals took power in 1871, a small German community already existed in Guatemala. It welcomed the revolution and provided the new regime with a loan as a token of support. German migration grew steadily in the coming years, bringing with it increased investment of German capital. In 1876, the German government assigned a consul to Guatemala City to keep business leaders informed about developments affecting their investments and to alert them to possibilities for new ones. In 1887, Guatemala and Germany signed a treaty that conferred upon one another "most-favored-nation" status, removing restrictions to trade and travel between the two countries.

Coffee prices rose the following year, and the flow of German capital to Guatemala increased. In addition to financing the plantations, it financed the development of the country's infrastructure. German capital underwrote the electric companies, built the ports, and laid railway lines throughout the country.

When Friedrich Endler set out for Guatemala, coffee prices had been high for five years, and the demand for coffee was increasing steadily throughout the industrialized world. The partnership between Guatemalan plantation owners and the German capitalists who financed and bought their coffee was reaping sizable profits on both sides of the Atlantic. Prospects looked good for men like Friedrich: "A person with just a little ability," he wrote home, "who is willing to work and begin in a small way can make a very good life here." And that's exactly what he did: beginning in a small way and forgoing "European comfort," Friedrich was able to work his way into the landowning elite.

Yet, by Franz Endler's own account, the family's rise required more than sacrifice and hard work. His father became a landowner only because a friend's widow made a special deal to sell him her property. And he was only able to complete the deal because, when he became so overwhelmed with debt and on the verge of foreclosure, the North American exporter Herbert Wilson chose to bail him out. "Don Federico, coffee prices go up, coffee prices go down," Wilson had explained, articulating a cardinal rule of the coffee trade. "I haven't the slightest doubt about your ability to pay, if you have the time."

Ninety years later, Franz Endler was visibly moved as he recounted Wilson's words to his father. Wilson may indeed have been a generous friend. But lending money to friends was also a central part of his business. Wilson needed growers he could trust to supply him with coffee, and there were two things that could guarantee that trust: friendship and debt.

It took money to get into coffee, and it took even more money to stay in. Most planters were deeply in debt by their first crop. Some never got out of it. When prices dropped (as they did periodically), landowners went bankrupt. Franz Endler would himself come close to losing his first plantation in the 1930s. After sinking in debt for several years, he traveled to Guatemala City and spoke with his creditor, a German exporter named Baumgartner. "I can't do it," Franz told him. "I'll never be able to pay you. Take the plantation." The exporter would have none of it: "Listen, Mr. Endler, you get back to your family. I wouldn't think of taking the plantation away from you. You're the best administrator we have."

Not every landowner fared as well. When world coffee prices plummeted in 1897, plantations throughout Guatemala were driven into bankruptcy and, over the next few years, were foreclosed on by creditors, who were often German merchants. Most of the original Guatemalan coffee elite would lose its property. By the turn of the century, over a third of Guatemalan coffee production was in German hands, and much of the rest was owned by foreigners from other countries.

Merchant houses did not necessarily *want* to foreclose on their debtors. And as in the case of Franz Endler, they sometimes made it possible for landowners to keep their plantation until prices went back up. But here the confidence of the creditor was key: the Endlers survived the bad years because Wilson trusted Friedrich, and because Baumgartner trusted Franz. Without that trust, who knows what would have happened to the Endlers?

THE CONFIDENCE GAME

As with the individual plantation, the prosperity of the coffee nation depended on the inflow of outside capital. It depended therefore on the confidence of international creditors. And this confidence depended largely on the country's public image abroad.

So the Liberals set about trying to improve that image. The 1894 census report is just one example of their efforts. Published in English, it assured foreign readers that Guatemalans were not savages: "The prepondering race possesses all the aptitude necessary to acquire science, the arts and industries, and are not foreign to the ways that form modern culture. In all the different branches of knowledge they reveal education, and taste for arts, and in many instances an extraordinary facility for skillful labor. Refinement, good manners and sound practical sense place Guatemala amongst the most cultured countries of the new world."

And it depicted Guatemala as an investor's paradise: "Good faith is the predominant point in business transactions, there being but few cases of deliberate failure or swindle. Wealth inspires respect and no individual or party wishes to change the actual state of affairs. Capital and labor disputes which agitate in other countries do not exist there; neither do ill feelings or spite form a feature of the inhibitants [sic]. Property can be easily acquired and by perseverance in the different branches of agriculture, industry, etc., etc., one is sure of success."

Of course, words alone couldn't win the confidence of international capital. Appearances were also important. So the Liberal regimes set about giving Guatemala City the look and feel of a modern capital, with broad tree-lined avenues, cultural institutions like the national opera, statues, monuments, and, of course, temples of Minerva.

But these P.R. efforts would never be enough to overcome Guatemala's basic problem: investment depended ultimately on the profitability of coffee, and profitability depended on prices in the world market, over which Guatemala had no control. The country was only one tributary in the vast flow of coffee beans from the tropics to the industrialized world.

The 1890s had been prosperous years for Guatemalan coffee growers because the abolition of slavery in Brazil in 1888 had reduced the production of the world's largest coffee supplier. But when Brazilian production recovered, the Brazilians put the squeeze on their competitors by lowering prices again.

During the boom years, the Guatemalan government had worked to facilitate coffee production, but in the process it had itself become increasingly dependent on coffee revenue. The successor of Barillas, President José María Reina Barrios, had borrowed large sums from banks to finance public works projects, using as collateral "exportation bonds" that would be paid off with export taxes on coffee. But when coffee prices dropped, he was forced to lower those taxes and promise the government's creditors that he would find another means of paying the debt.

He never got the chance. A political crisis followed the financial one. Disgruntled landowners in San Marcos took up arms against the government. The government managed to put down the uprising. But several weeks later, the employee of one executed rebel avenged his boss by assassinating the president.

Manuel Estrada Cabrera now took over a country in crisis. The government was broke. Its public works projects were stalled. The state bureaucrats and, worse yet, the soldiers hadn't been paid in weeks. The president could find no one willing to lend the government the money it needed to keep going. So he issued six million pesos in paper money to pay the back wages and cancel some of the debt. This action may have eased the political situation, but it did not help the financial one, producing instead massive inflation.

Coffee prices stayed low for over a decade. As one plantation after another went under, Estrada Cabrera searched desperately for foreign investors who could bail out the government and allow it to renew the infrastructure projects that, once completed, would lower the cost of export. He also hoped to create a bank with foreign capital, which would facilitate commercial transactions in the cash-starved country.

Thirty-five million dollars is what he wanted, and he sent envoys to Germany hoping to get it. But the same businessmen who had eagerly invested in Guatemala during the boom years had grown wary of their Central American partner.

Estrada Cabrera offered concessions: the investors would have substantial control over the bank; they would have the authority to issue paper money; they would be free of all taxes. The Germans declined the offer. Estrada Cabrera persisted, asking the German consul to help promote his idea in Germany. He also tried to interest the diplomatic representatives of England and the United States. But to no avail: there were still no takers.

So as 1902 rolled around, Estrada Cabrera found himself facing what would be the development dilemma of the twentieth century: in order to resolve the country's economic and political crises, he needed foreign capital; but given the instability produced by the crises, no one was willing to invest in his country.

THE PRESIDENT'S DILEMMA

The Feast of Minerva was Estrada Cabrera's presentation of Guatemala before the world. A diplomatic liaison of the president in Europe described the press coverage of the event. From France: "such ceremonies in honor of education, are . . . a wise example for the rest of Latin America." From Germany: "Guatemala deserves the enviable name of Athens of the New World." From England: "An enthusiastic 'hurrah!' for the crowning of science below the Hellenic porticos."

A leader who placed such importance on the symbolic representation of European cultural ideals would surely be sensitive to the symbols and stereotypes of Central American savagery. "Volcanoes, earthquakes, and revolutions have popularly been associated with the whole region," wrote one foreign traveler in the 1870s, and just about every travel writer visiting Guatemala since has made a great deal of these associations — which is significant since what a traveler sees, and especially what a traveler *writes,* often has as much to do with prior expectations as with the sights themselves. Friedrich Endler filled his travelogue with images of technology succumbing to the forces of nature, and he ended with an earthquake — *"very common here"* — which prompted him to see a rationale for the primitive dwellings that he had been describing throughout the letter — *"Wooden buildings are for this reason very practical!"*

The destructive force of geological violence was not merely symbolic. Already, in March of 1902, earthquakes had severely damaged the docking facility in the port used to export the coffee of San Marcos. In September, a tidal wave washed away another portion of the same docks. In the weeks following the eruption, the ash-filled river would overflow and wreck what remained of the port, preventing many landowners in San Marcos from exporting the year's harvest. The eruption would destroy plantations below the volcano in Quetzaltenango and damage others as far away as Mundo Nuevo.

Consider now Estrada Cabrera's dilemma: the guests gathered for the Minerva celebration in Guatemala City on October 24 may have felt the tremors, but since the fire and ash were many miles away, they wouldn't know that yet another natural disaster was taking its toll on the year's coffee production. To acknowledge the disaster and then proceed with the festivities surely wouldn't look good for the president. But to cancel the celebration because of a volcano would confirm the worst stereotype of the Central American republic: a land inherently unstable, unfit for "the crowning of science" after all. Wooden buildings are very practical on shaky ground, but who will invest in modern railroads and processing plants?

The festivities went forward.

But Estrada Cabrera wasn't delusional. As soon as the guests had gone home, the government newspaper (which had, until then, reported that there was no volcanic eruption in Guatemala) conceded that in fact Santa María had exploded (though it maintained that the damage was far less than rumor would have it). The government set up a special office in Quetzaltenango to draft workers from the surrounding highland communities in order to replenish the labor supply throughout the western piedmont and make sure that the year's coffee crop would be harvested.

This was the most the president could do. He couldn't control nature. He couldn't control international capital. The only thing he could control was the Guatemalan people. And *that* control was the basis of the coffee nation.

THE HANDS THAT BUILT THE COFFEE NATION

Guatemala's only natural source of wealth was its fertile soil. But the land was of little value without its other principal resource: the labor of the Indian population. The 1894 census report was matter of fact: "The Indians do not cooperate actively in the progress of civilization, neither do they resist it. Notwithstanding, they furnish all the necessary work to make the soil productive, and this alone creates the national wealth."

But there was a problem — a problem that Friedrich Endler described after a week on the former president's plantation: "The Indians won't work more than just enough to fill their basic needs, and these are very few. The only way to make him work is to advance him money, then he can be forced to work. Very often they run off but they are caught and punished very severely."

Two years earlier, Barillas's minister of development had articulated the official rationale for such coerced labor: "It is necessary to make the Indian work for his own good, for the good of business and for the country because as a result of his apathetic and stationary character and his few needs, he is satisfied with practically nothing." Another prominent Liberal explained the Indians' lack of interest in wage labor as a lack of the "civilized needs" that would make them want to work.

Progress — coffee production — depended on finding ways to make the Indians choose to exchange their labor for cash. So the plantations sent labor contractors to visit highland towns at the times of the year when Indians did have "needs" that cash could help satisfy: during June and July when corn supplies started to dwindle or during festival days when heavy drinking required money and, once drunk, men and women were more likely to sign away their future. A foreigner described the festival in one highland town: "Above all, [there is] an unceasing coming and going of labour contractors and plantation agents getting out gangs of Indians for the Pacific coast. And there is rum. The place stinks of it. The Indians are drunk from morning till night. . . . The rum business and the coffee business work together in this country, automatically."

Yet even with labor contractors exploiting these limited "needs" for cash, the majority of the Indian population could have subsisted well into the twentieth century without working in the coffee plantations. Left to their own preferences, they probably would not have descended to work in the plantations in sufficient number to harvest all the trees that were planted during these years.

What made them go? The labor drafts. Upon the request of a plantation owner, the governors of each department would round up a work gang of fifty to one hundred Indians and send them to work on the plantation. An 1894 law provided Indians with one way to escape this form of forced recruitment: become an indebted worker for a plantation. By the turn of the century, most highland Indians had done so. Yet the labor drafts still played a crucial role in the coffee economy. They dissuaded workers from trying to pay off their debts. And they supplemented the indebted labor force in times of emergency — like the Santa María eruption of 1902.

THE GREAT DICTATOR

Capital always seeks a return. In the coffee economy, this return was guaranteed by a chain of debt: the worker was indebted to the landowner, the landowner to the exporter, the exporter to the importer. When coffee prices dropped, the importers squeezed the exporters, the exporters squeezed the landowners, and the landowners squeezed the workers. The old pecking order.

In order to guarantee capital's return, the debts had to be enforced. And in Guatemala the enforcer was the state. It militarized the countryside, posting militia units throughout the highlands, where they could make sure workers went to the plantations to fulfill their labor obligations.

The plantations clearly benefited from the state's growing military muscle. But because they were so dependent on coerced labor, the owners were often forced to indulge the conceits of the officials who made it available to them. And that indulgence included, above all, *el Señor Presidente* himself. When Estrada Cabrera said that the erupting volcano didn't exist, who would dare to disagree? So long as he got workers to the piedmont in time for the harvest, their plantations would stay in business.

Later the landowners could retell what had happened their own way — having the president disappear instead of the volcano. It didn't surprise me that they would omit the government (and its procurement of forced labor) from the stories they told of their past. They were merely doing what most prosperous people do when explaining their prosperity: highlight personal effort and downplay privilege. We had done the same in the United States, especially during the 1990s when mainstream politicians and pundits embraced a worldview that depicted markets as inherently good and government as basically bad. According to these opponents of "big government," wealth was created when the entrepreneurial effort of individuals was rewarded by the invisible hand of the free market. Omitted from the story were the many ways the government intervened in the economy to help industries, companies, and even wealthy individuals turn a profit. Like most ideological creation myths, this one was all immaculate conception and no original sin.

What I found more surprising was how the plantation workers had left the state's intervention in their lives out of the stories they told. Forgetting about forced labor at the turn of the century was one thing — but forgetting the Agrarian Reform and the war? Obviously they were holding things back. And, of course, given how little they knew about me, they had reason to be somewhat distrustful — if I wasn't a *robachicos*, I could be a spy of the plantation or maybe even the government. In the United States we had also had our moments of fear and silence. At the height of the Red Scare, for instance, many Americans would have thought twice about discussing parts of their history with a stranger. Yet the silence in La Igualdad was something else. It was as if everyone in a small town in 1950s America had told you — with a straight face — that nothing had happened during the New Deal and that World War II had been a nonevent. It made no sense to me. No harm would come to the people in La Igualdad if they told me about the Agrarian Reform — César and his friends were as convinced of this as I was. The fear, I concluded, was a product of ignorance. Once these people knew me better, understood my intentions, it would subside. They would open up. They might even appreciate the opportunity to recount their history. Knowing what I know now, I can see that my confidence was itself the product of ignorance — the misjudgment of a person who had never known real terror and had not yet learned how to listen to silence.

There was one other aspect of the events of 1902 that surprised me: the part that had been left out of the stories that we in the United States told ourselves about Latin America. *Lots* had been left out, of course. We had never been terribly interested in the history of our southern neighbors. Still, the depictions we did have of Latin America in movies and novels and occasional news articles had prepared me to recognize President Estrada Cabrera right away. He was a familiar figure: the tropical dictator — exotic, brutal, and absurd. It was a stereotype that helped us explain the backwardness of countries like Guatemala as the result of unenlightened leadership. And it contributed to the belief that increased interaction with democracies like ours — what today we call "globalization" — would salvage them from their backward ways.

What further surprised me was finding out that the great dictator had himself been, in large part, a creature of globalization. His exotic behavior had actually been an effort to make his country look more like ours. His absurd decree denying the volcano's existence turned out, upon closer inspection, to be a rational response to the behavior of international investors. And the brutality of his regime was part and parcel of his country's participation in the world economy; it was what sustained the chain of debt linking Guatemalans to people in Europe and the United States, what allowed our capital to be sown into their mountainsides with the assurance that their coffee would reach our kitchen counters.

PART III

A FUTURE WAS BURIED

A DANGEROUS QUESTION

I

LONG BEFORE ANY HOUSES BURNED, there had been a law that could have made a difference in Guatemala. Or rather there had been a law that, for a brief two years, did make a difference — such a difference that even after it was revoked and its authors were in exile or unmarked graves, it continued to shape the way Guatemalans understood their place in the world. The law was Decree 900, the 1952 "Law of Agrarian Reform." Its overarching aim, set forth in its opening paragraph, was to "overcome the economic backwardness" of the country and "improve the quality of life of the great masses." Whether it could have achieved these ambitious ends will never be known. In 1954, the CIA toppled Guatemala's reform government. A military regime took power. The reformers were driven underground. And the country began its long, terrifying descent into a state of lawlessness, cruelty, and despair.

The United States celebrated the coup as a triumph for democracy. For years to come, the cold warriors in Washington held it up as a model for what covert operations could accomplish overseas. Yet few Americans really knew what had taken place in Guatemala in 1954. The press coverage had been carefully choreographed by the CIA. Even the *New York Times* had complied with the agency's request to keep its correspondent from the country so that he could not give a firsthand account of the coup and its aftermath.

The *Times* would eventually cover the story more fully. But only forty years later. In 1997, access to once classified documents (obtained through the Freedom of Information Act) would provide the *Times* and the U.S. public with a more reliable account of the 1954 operation. Among these documents was a history commissioned by the Agency and published for internal consumption in 1994. Unfortunately, this declassified history was riddled with holes — names, facts, and descriptions that the Agency had excised on the grounds that, even after forty years, there were some things that the public should not know.

The biggest hole left in the story was how the coup affected the countryside, where the process of agrarian reform — which had been gathering momentum for two years — was brought to a sudden halt. This omission was the product of ignorance as much as secrecy. According to the Agency's internal history, the men who orchestrated the coup had done so with "only a dim idea" of Guatemalan history. And the Agency had later recycled its own misinformation into an authoritative account of events that would serve as a model for future intelligence officers, including the ones who would shape and implement U.S. policy in the region for years to come.

In Guatemala, official history also omitted the agrarian reform. But what had taken place in the countryside would remain a central part of the stories people told about their past. The plantation owners remembered the reform as a time of chaos, corruption, and communism. To mix words like "land" and "inequality" and "reform" was, to their ears, to conjure up the specter of that time. And since so many Guatemalans still dared to do so, the landowners forged a pact with the military: the generals could govern as they pleased, provided they kept the specter at bay.

The country's leftists remembered the agrarian reform differently: it had been a moment of democratic effervescence, a step toward a more humane and productive society, an oasis of hope in a century of oppression. And many among them pointed to the reformers' demise as proof of the need for armed struggle, arguing that only a revolution that was prepared to defend itself against U.S. aggression would be able to succeed in Guatemala.

As the violence escalated in the coming years, both sides looked to this part of their past to justify the war they waged for the country's future. César's advice made sense then: in order to understand the war, examine the agrarian reform that preceded it. Gaze into the hole where the U.S. government had not bothered to look. Find the source of Guatemala's conflicting memories. And imagine, as people there had done, things could have been different.

⬇

Since my first visit to La Igualdad, I had steered clear of controversial subjects, asking people to recall only what were, I figured, the safer memories of an earlier era. I'd had a chance now to familiarize myself with the region — getting to know the lay of the land and enough of the people who inhabited it to feel more comfortable venturing out on my own. The time had come to start asking César's question: what happened in the plantation during the agrarian reform?

Before heading back to La Igualdad, I contacted the U.S. embassy. It wasn't the first time I had done so. The university officials who administered my fellowship had insisted that I check in with the U.S. authorities when I first arrived in the country.

Riding across town the morning of that first visit, I had been as curious as any tourist going to see a famous historical site. The U.S. embassy had occupied a central place in this country's history — most notoriously in 1954, when the ambassador stood on the roof and directed bombing raids by the mercenary force sent by the CIA. (In the following weeks, he would direct the formation of a military regime from his office downstairs.) The cab dropped me in front of a massive concrete structure with an American flag. Clearly, this bunker of a building had been constructed after the glory days of the Monroe Doctrine, when U.S. officials had become targets of local discontent. I passed a line of people that stretched half a block — Guatemalans seeking permission to travel north — and entered the front door. A Guatemalan employee from the cultural attaché's office escorted me past the security desk and left me in a room where, she told me, an embassy officer would give me a security briefing. The room contained the familiar framed photos of our president and vice, a large outdated map of Guatemala, and what I thought was a photocopy machine until someone came along with a stack of documents and fed them into it. Instead of copies, paper shreds came out the backside.

A little later the security officer arrived. He was a young man with an athletic build and a friendly grin. When I explained where I was going and why, the grin faded. He nodded slowly as I pointed to my anticipated destination on the map. "So," he said in a subdued tone, his gaze lost somewhere in the highlands, "you're going up there." The way he said "up there" sounded ominous, and I almost expected him to continue, "In the interior you will no doubt meet Mr. Kurtz . . ." But he didn't seem to have any idea of what I might meet in the interior. He and his colleagues rarely ventured out far beyond the city limits, he conceded, except to visit popular tourist attractions.

The briefing was brief and concluded with a warning: "There's a lot of stuff going down in this country, and we can't really control it. You're basically on your own." He gave me two embassy numbers to call in case I had any problems, but then cautioned me once again that there wasn't much "our people" could do if I got into trouble.

On another occasion I would attend an official "security briefing" given to several men with large biceps and college rings who had come to fight the war on drugs. I thought I might learn more about the country than I had in my individual briefing. Instead I found myself listening to a lengthy discussion of paperwork — who could see what documents and what measures would be taken to make sure no one else did. The officer explained that the primary responsibility of the embassy's marine detachment was not to protect the building (though it helped out there too) but rather to enforce the rules regarding classified documents. As he talked, it dawned on me that this concrete box called an embassy was actually a giant data processor that sorted, filtered, and channeled information in and out (mostly out) of the country. Yet unlike other processors, its main function seemed to be to limit rather than to increase the flow of knowledge.

It hadn't take long for me to forget all about that dark, dangerous world I had expected to find when I traveled up into the highlands. My initial sense of foreboding lasted barely longer than the four-hour bus ride that took me to the city of Quetzaltenango, where I spent my first weeks in the country brushing up on my Spanish. Quetzaltenango was a cozy provincial capital, with some hundred thousand residents, located just north of the Santa María volcano, at the center of a broad valley blanketed with fields of wheat and corn. The city took its name from the Quetzal bird that — according to local legend — had risen from the chest of the K'iche' prince, Tecún Uman, after he was slain in 1524 by the conquistador Pedro de Alvarado in a battle that turned the nearby river red with Indian blood and brought these mountains under Spanish rule. Over four and a half centuries later, a majority of the residents were still

K'iche', and almost everyone still referred to the city as "Xela" (pro-nounced SHEY-la), an abbreviation of its preconquest name, Xelajú.

In addition to the university where César studied, Xela was home to a dozen language schools that taught Spanish to foreigners, and the city's center had adapted to service the needs of the hundreds of Europeans and Americans who came to study in them every year. César taught in one. I studied in another. It was a comfortable life for all involved: morn-ings in the classrooms, afternoons in the cafés, evenings in the bars and discos. It was not a place of danger. At least not anymore. It wasn't un-common for teachers to try to impress (or seduce) starry-eyed foreigners with tales of political persecution. Yet the reality was that political vio-lence had become largely a thing of the past here — so much so, in fact, that it was easy to forget, or come to doubt, that it still existed in other parts of the country.

It was only after I heard gunfire in La Igualdad a year later that I re-membered the phone numbers given to me in the embassy. Now that I planned to delve into more sensitive topics, I figured I ought to give them a call. It might help to have an official letter of introduction from the em-bassy — something I would be able to show to any Guatemalan authori-ties who might have doubts about who I was and what I was doing.

"I'm sorry, Mr. Wilkinson," the embassy officer who took my call told me. "We don't normally provide such letters. I mean, after all, we don't really know who you are. We don't know what you're doing."

Her response surprised me. "But I can tell you what I'm doing. And I can give you a letter of introduction from my university and a phone number if you want to contact someone there."

She wasn't interested. "Look, we just can't go around supporting any-one who says they're doing research."

"I'm not anyone," I insisted. "I'm a U.S. citizen. You're my embassy."

That gave her a moment's pause. A very brief moment. "Yes, well, if you were affiliated with one of our programs, it would be another mat-ter."

"All I'm asking for is a letter saying who I am and what I'm doing . . ."

The conversation continued back and forth until finally she put me on hold and, after a long minute, returned. "Okay, I'll write a letter, you can pick it up tomorrow."

The letter said only that U.S. citizen Daniel Wilkinson "has informed this Embassy that he came to Guatemala with a fellowship" and "has plans to visit the plantations and people in San Marcos." As for the bit I was hoping for about respecting my human rights, I'd have to pencil that in myself.

II

On the way to La Igualdad, I dropped by Panajachel and visited Sara Endler in the small house she has just around the corner from where her father lived. I was hoping to get another letter — this one on her business stationery — that could explain my presence in La Igualdad to anyone who asked. And I figured I'd begin this phase of the investigation with her account of how the agrarian reform had affected La Patria.

The letter was no problem. As for the history, it turned out that she wasn't around the plantation during those years and could tell me only a little about what had happened. The land was never expropriated, and while there was a labor union, she didn't think it "amounted to much."

But she did have lots to say about the world that the revolutionary government had sought to reform — the world she had grown up in — a world that had been, she recalled now, "a disaster waiting to happen."

Sara's earliest memories were from the 1930s in a plantation named La Gavia in the southeastern part of the country.

"La Gavia was completely isolated. The only way in and out of that farm was four hours on mule back. There were no roads, and absolutely nothing there — I mean, nothing. I had no friends except the kids on the plantation. And they weren't allowed to come into our house. I'd play on the porch with them. But I wasn't allowed to go into their houses. So I really didn't have any friends.

"And yet I felt totally happy — a very solidly busy, happy little girl. I had horses and cows and chickens and dogs and cats — everything imaginable. And they were mine to take care of. And I had lots of books. I just didn't lack for anything. Everybody on the farm was looking out for me. I could take a horseback ride by myself and be gone all day long, knowing

that if I fell off the horse or got hungry or something I could find someone who could help me. I just thought the world was my oyster."

⬇

Franz Endler had purchased La Gavia, his first plantation, with help
from his father. After a few years, Friedrich's other son came to La
Gavia, and Franz allowed him to live with the family in their new *casa
patronal.*

Sara would eventually learn how this man was related to her family. "It
was clearly a racist attitude on the part of my grandfather. He was living
with this indigenous woman, and she got pregnant, and a baby was born,
and he took one look at the baby in the crib and said — she now repeated what her father had told me her grandfather had said — 'Friedrich Endler, you get your ass back to Germany and get yourself a white
wife.'" He would not abandon this first family entirely, though. He gave
his former mistress a small farm on the Mexican border. "He gave it to
her in his son's name, but he never gave the son the Endler name. He
didn't recognize him as his son. His name was Rafael Zamora.

"I don't know how the contact was maintained. I imagine it was the
woman who maintained contact with my grandfather. And when I was little, Rafael came to live with us. Dad gave him a job as a foreman. My
mother treated him very much like family. So he lived in one of the bed-
rooms in the house and ate with us at the table and was rather close to
us. My father felt like he owed it to him. Like he was his brother. He
didn't resent him or anything. And as long as Rafael behaved himself and
worked that was okay."

She paused. "Not quite like a brother, like a brother who's an employee. When Mom and Dad sat out on the porch in the evening, that
was their time together. Rafael was not there. He would go out to the
kitchen and talk to the servants or go to the office area and hang out with
the employees."

⬇

Despite their isolation, events in the outside world eventually caught up
with them. "The Germans invaded Poland," Sara recalled, "and we didn't
find out about it until the following week." She remembers one of the
workers telling her mother when he heard the news that he would pack

his belongings and head home to his ancestral village in the highlands where he would be safer from trouble. Her mother had to explain to him that this fighting was happening in a place called Europe, which was another continent far away, and so there was nothing for him to worry about.

But the conflict in Europe did in fact find its way into Guatemala's plantation world. The first sign of change came to the Endler family when German men arrived in La Gavia and explained they were there to hunt alligators. There were no alligators anywhere near La Gavia. Sara's father had no doubt what they were really looking for: fellow Nazis. There had been an active Nazi presence within Guatemala's German community ever since 1936, when the National Socialist Party invited Germans throughout Guatemala to attend a grand celebration on a ship docked in the country's Caribbean coast. There they would enjoy beer and music from the fatherland and have the opportunity to vote, in absentia, for the Nazis in the upcoming election.

Then, the Guatemalan president, Jorge Ubico, siding with the Allies, declared war on Germany and began to treat Germans in Guatemala as enemies of the state. He got hold of the guest list for the Nazis' boat party and used it as a blacklist to target Germans for arrest and deportation to detention camps in Texas. In addition to the arrests, Ubico began expropriating German properties, including many of the best coffee lands in the country.

The Endlers had never been fond of the Nazis themselves. In fact, word later reached them that local Gestapo agents had placed them on a list of "unpatriotic" Germans to be executed once Germany took over Guatemala. But the family's political views would not save them from Ubico's anti-German measures. Friedrich Endler lost Mundo Nuevo to expropriation. In order to save La Patria, he turned it over to Franz, who, by right of birth, was a Guatemalan citizen. After a protracted struggle with government officials, Sara's father managed to save his property from expropriation. And in 1940, he took the family to live on their new plantation.

⬇

"La Patria was a little bit more on the map. There were neighbors — kids — that I didn't have before. That was the first time I got socialized as a young woman. We'd have dances just about every Sunday at one plantation or another. We'd all run around on horseback and meet in La Igualdad and go in a great cavalcade of horses to one farm or another and play ping-pong or dance or whatever. It was always with the owners and the employees, like bookkeepers, who were allowed into our social group. They were mostly Germans or middle-class Guatemalans. And every year we had a big dance in La Igualdad, and there that level of people — shopkeepers and all that — we could consort with them. But no workers ever came to those parties.

"I don't think we ever had any friends in La Patria, in the workers' quarters. There was a lot of watchfulness over us when we were becoming adolescents, teenage girls. And we weren't supposed to consort with people very much. I guess it must have been the fear that we'd fall in love with the wrong guy or sleep with someone, I suppose.

"I remember one guy in La Gavia who was helping me onto a chair when I was a little girl. And either he did it deliberately or not, but his hand got down below on my butt, and I was upset by it. And I was about six. So the next day he was gone. He was just plain out gone. And I said, 'What happened to him?' Dad said, 'I told him to go join the army. I didn't want him around here anymore.'

"That kind of reaction was common. The worker couldn't answer for himself. Nobody would listen to him. If he told my father that it was a mistake or that it just hadn't happened, that wasn't enough. It was my six-year-old word against whatever he would have to say.

"I remember another guy on the plantation named Arturo. Arturo felt a little bit above the other people because he had a German grandfather or father maybe. He was light-skinned, and he was quite nice looking. And he would sort of flirt with both my sister and myself. And he didn't last long. I don't know what happened to him but he was gone very quickly."

She laughed.

"I remember a couple of times Dad had problems with people who answered him back — because answering back was considered appalling. And if you said: 'Do it quickly,' and the guy didn't do it quickly, that was also considered insubordination. People really had to run. If you said to a worker, 'Go bring me such and such,' they would always run to do it. They wouldn't walk. I remember a story about my father's aunt who lived in La Patria when my parents were first married. She would send a man to La Igualdad from La Patria. And she'd spit on the floor, and she'd say, 'Before that dries, I want you to be back here.'

"By the time we moved to La Patria, the attitude wasn't quite like that. But still, if there was some insubordination, the guy would just be fired outright. Like: 'Out! Out you go. Go now! Now! Now! Now!'"

Was there ever any fear that the workers might rise up?

"No. It didn't seem like [this treatment of the workers] was really done out of fear. It always seemed to me like it was done out of power. And also a tremendous lack of consideration for them as people. Really they didn't care if the guy had ten kids and was starving to death or not. If he was insubordinate, he was out. To hell with his wife and ten kids."

The interaction wasn't always hostile, though. "My mother was constantly giving presents. I don't think there was a trip made to the city where my mother wouldn't bring back mounds of candies for the kids, and cookies. And for the people in the kitchen, ribbons and materials to make aprons and that kind of stuff."

Gift giving was common in all the plantations in those days. Some plantations celebrated the end of a good harvest by slaughtering a cow and distributing its meat among their workers. Some sponsored fairs, hiring marimba orchestras and dance troupes. In one plantation near La Patria, the *patrón*'s wife would sit under a certain tree every Sunday, and workers would line up to tell her their problems — a sick child, a leaky roof, no money for clothes, and so on. She would dispense advice and sometimes even cash.

Gift giving was the cement that held the plantation together. After all, candies and ribbons were not the only gifts — just about everything the workers had was given to them by the *patrón*. That is because, instead of paying even subsistence-level salaries, the plantations gave their workers what they needed. "Truckloads of corn would come up every Monday to give out rations. You paid for the medicines. You paid for the clinic. You paid for the school."

But perhaps "gift" isn't the right word. For the plantations never really let go of what they "gave." So, for example, when the plantation gave the worker a house, the house would belong to the worker — but the worker, in turn, would then belong to the plantation. Sara recalled, "My mother used to walk into people's homes, and they couldn't say anything. It always seemed like she was saying, 'This is my house because it's on my plantation, and I can do whatever I want to with it.'"

As Sara got older, she became increasingly uncomfortable with the arrangement. "The dependency wasn't good for anybody. It was a disaster waiting to happen."

Why would it be a disaster?

"The workers weren't allowed to grow up and be responsible human beings."

What kind of human beings were they then?

"They were very unworldly. Tremendously isolated. They didn't know anything about the world at all. If you told them the simplest story, maybe just a story about buying a dress in the city, they would be in awe. Tell them about cars, or about how many cars there were in the city, they'd get awed and be afraid to go to the city. When we installed a toilet in the *casa patronal* and one of the house servants was shown how to use it, he thought it was a miracle. 'Look, it's eternal water!'"

Sara laughed and then continued seriously: "Almost none of them knew how to read and write. They were all barefoot. None of the houses had any kind of floors in them. They were all dirt floors. None of the houses had electricity. The sidings were boards."

She paused.

"I remember one thing — something I'll never forget — something which had an effect on my later life. We had very nice horses in La Patria, very nice horses. And we had a very pretty barn. And the mares that were about to foal, we had them in a very large room and a lot of nice fresh hay on the floor and, you know, well fed with corn and all that, which I always did myself. And I remember one night a mare was giving birth, and Dad and I went up with our flashlights, and the lights were on, and we watched this birth process, and this young colt was born. And he was given to me, and I was very thrilled.

"And just the same week the field master's wife gave birth. And their house was right near the stables, just across the little river. And she was having a very hard time, and Dad asked me if I would go with him. And we went in. And I realized . . ."

She paused again.

"I remember the bed was boards, and she was lying on these thick old dirty boards with some rags and a piece of material crumpled up for her head and a kerosene lamp in a very dark corner of this dirty floor. And I just remembered the difference between the way the mare had given birth and the way she was giving birth. That really did just sort of stamp something in my head. I can still see it and . . . and smell it.

"I thought there was something wrong then. This woman, you know, is the field master's wife. His name was Benedicto and he was illiterate but he was a man of great responsibility. And yet at that level, to be living like that. In comparison with the horse, they didn't do very well.

"I never talked to my father about it. He probably would have just said something like, 'Well, they could live better if they wanted to. They didn't have to live like pigs unless they wanted to.'"

⚜

One day, a few years later, Sara was in the barn in La Patria when an indigenous man arrived on a mule. "Can I help you?" Sara asked the stranger.

The man dismounted from his mule, removed his sombrero, and made a formal bow: *"Buenos días, señorita.* Maybe you don't remember me, but I'm a relative of yours. I have come to speak to your father. I have something important to tell him."

Sara had never seen the man. But he looked perfectly harmless, and she took him to the *casa patronal.* Her father greeted him warmly and acknowledged the family relation. He was the son of Friedrich Endler's brother, who had spent a few years in Guatemala in the 1920s and had himself fathered a child with an indigenous woman.

Inside the plantation office, the man unrolled a large document that he had been carrying under his arm. "I have developed something that could change the course of the war," he announced as he spread the document out before them, revealing a crudely drawn blueprint. "It is a special car. A car that not only drives on land, but also can drive in the water! I believe that something like this could help the good side win the war. But it needs to be in the right hands. Now, I don't know much about the affairs of the world. But you do. And so I would like to present it to you so that you may decide what to do with it."

Sara's father was dumbfounded. "That's, uh, very interesting," he said. "But, um, you see, they actually already have cars like these."

The visitor looked surprised. "They do?"

"That's right. They call them amphibious vehicles. 'Amphibious' means they can go on land and in water."

"Oh."

Sara's father felt embarrassed for the man and invited him to join the family for lunch. "No," the man said, bowing his head. "I've already taken enough of your time."

He rolled up the document and set off on his mule. Sara never saw him again.

III

Ceferino González was one of the men who now drove the cars in La Patria. He was all bones and a smile — a skinny man somewhere in his fifties who wore an ingratiating grin on his face whenever I was around him. I knew from Sara that he suffered from tuberculosis. I guessed the skinniness might have something to do with his deteriorated lungs, and the smile with the fact that he depended on the plantation for their treatment. One of Ceferino's responsibilities was to bring the children of the overseer and the cook down to La Igualdad for school each morning. One day I joined them for the ride.

The car was an old Toyota jeep that looked as dilapidated as its driver. There was no key for the ignition. Instead Ceferino released the emergency break and let the car roll down the gravel drive. When it had picked up enough speed, he shifted abruptly into second and released the clutch. The old vehicle lurched forward, its engine turning over, and then settled into a crawl, coughing and wheezing as it went.

As we began the slow descent from the plantation center, Ceferino told me the story — told to him by his mother — of the first car in La Igualdad. "When they heard the noise of the car, people got scared. Some even hid under their beds. Others watched from their doorways, but as the car came close, they shut the doors. These people weren't scared of horses. They weren't scared of wild animals. But that car, boy did it scare them! When the car had passed, the braver ones said, 'Let's go see that thing. It's in the plantation.' But some others said, 'No, we're not going. It could eat us!'"

The children in the back seat laughed at Ceferino's mock terror, and he looked pleased with his story. A few minutes later he recalled another one. "When they brought the first radio to La Igualdad, all the people gathered around. They had never seen anything like it. And someone asked if there were little dolls inside the box singing!"

⤋

Just when I thought I might never find a worker in La Patria willing to tell me about the war and its causes, Ceferino gave me a glimpse of hope. One afternoon, as I parked my motorcycle in the plantation garage, I found him alone tinkering with the engine of the Toyota. We had talked before, but always in the presence of others, and I was curious to find out what lay behind that smile of his — if anything. Sure enough, as we talked about the car and the motorcycle, his face relaxed and took on a more dignified expression. And when I told him I was investigating the history of La Igualdad, he said, "If you're going to find out anything, you have to talk to the right people."

Ceferino was himself just a child during the Arbenz years and didn't know what was going on. But he knew who were some of the labor leaders in those years, because when he was growing up, people would point them out and say: "Look at what happened to them!"

"What did happen to them?" I asked.

"Lost everything they had."

Ceferino couldn't tell me what exactly it was that they lost and why they lost it — or maybe he just didn't want to. I didn't press him then because another driver had entered the garage within earshot of where we were talking. But now the first thing I did upon returning to the plantation was ask if he could bring me to the "right people."

We told the other drivers that I was getting a lift to town. But after dropping off the children, Ceferino took me on a dirt path down the hill behind the school to the home of his uncle, Julio Ortega.

⤋

"They had us living like slaves," Ortega said when I asked him to tell me about life in the old days. "They used debts to keep us there, so we couldn't go to other plantations."

Ortega was a sprightly man, nearing ninety, with bright eyes bulging from a head shaped like a light bulb: close-cropped white hair on a scalp that rounded down to prominent cheekbones, protruding over sunken cheeks and a narrow, angular jawbone. As I scribbled in my notebook, he described how the debt system worked. "In those days, the government made everyone pay taxes. And what the plantations did was to pay these taxes for the worker and that way put him in debt for the year. They didn't even talk to the worker. They just went to the government and paid. Then they could imprison the workers on their property."

Ortega had come of age indebted to El Progreso. After several years working there, he realized that conditions were better in other plantations and began working on Sundays in neighboring La Independencia to earn the cash necessary to pay off his debt to El Progreso. When he had enough, he went to the administration of El Progreso with the money. "'Keep your money,' they told me. 'Enjoy it, eat well, let your kids eat well.' But I told them, 'No, thank you. I don't want to be in debt anymore.'"

Ortega was packing his belongings when the plantation had him arrested on the grounds that he was absconding with an unpaid debt. After three days in jail, he managed to communicate with the administrator of La Independencia, who visited the jail and lent him three pesos. The administrator then went to the local justice of the peace and demanded that Ortega be freed to work off this new three-peso debt. The official obliged on the grounds that La Independencia had more claim to Ortega's work than El Progreso did since he now owed more money there.

"And that's how I became a worker in La Independencia."

⁂

"We were slaves because of the law of Ubico," recalled the next elderly peasant we talked to. He was referring to President Jorge Ubico, who had governed the country from 1930 to 1944, and the "slavery" he described was not debt peonage but the vagrancy laws that had replaced it. "We had to carry a booklet, like an identity card, which showed what plantation we worked in and how many hours we had worked that year. If you didn't carry it, the government could jail you and make you work without pay."

Another man on our tour recalled, "Because of the law of Ubico, workers always had to be humble. The field masters used to hit them. And the plantation had stockades where they'd put you if you didn't work."

And then there was the roadwork — the most memorable aspect of the Ubico years for Guatemalan peasants of that generation. All able-bodied men who could not afford to pay a road tax (which meant all plantation workers) had been required to labor without pay, opening roads through the mountainside. Often they were sent to work far from home. They would have to bring a week's worth of food and sleep by the side of the road. The work was arduous, and the overseers were often brutal. "If the overseer saw you standing upright too long, he'd hit you with a cane," one veteran worker recalled. Another said, "If you talked back to the overseer, or didn't work hard enough, you'd be thrown in jail, and you'd have to work again the following week."

Early in the Ubico era, workers had been required to do one week of roadwork a year. Later it became two weeks. And rumor had it that it was going to become three. But then one day news arrived from the capital that President Ubico had been toppled. The workers of La Igualdad celebrated in the streets, setting off firecrackers and dancing to the marimba.

Ubico was succeeded by Juan José Arévalo, a man whom the peasants remember with great affection. One of them said, "Juan José Arévalo, may his soul rest in glory, came to remove the yoke from all of Guatemala." Ortega explained. "There was freedom where before there'd been none. Because of Arévalo, there was an eight-hour workday, and there was a seventh day, and there was half-salary for workers when they got sick. With Ubico, the worker always had to humble himself. Now with Arévalo, the owner also had to humble himself before the law. Because this president came along to help the peasants."

⚜

I felt as if I was finally making some progress. Ceferino had found me five elderly men who were willing to talk about the coerced labor they had grown up with. What they told me about life in La Igualdad was consistent with what the history books said had been taking place then at the national level — at least up through the Arévalo years.

Jorge Ubico had been this century's second great dictator in Guatemala. Like Estrada Cabrera three decades earlier, he had come to power after plummeting coffee prices had sent the country into a deep economic crisis. It was the stock market crash of 1929 that had provoked this one, and while the ensuing depression prompted other Latin American countries to diversify their economies, Ubico responded in the same way

Estrada Cabrera had earlier, trying to salvage the coffee economy by giving new incentives to international capital investment and tightening the
screws on the increasingly impoverished working population. He abol-
ished the system of debt-peonage and replaced it with vagrancy laws
that accomplished the same end — securing a cheap labor pool for the
plantations — only more efficiently. He also launched the massive road-
building program that depended on the forced labor of peasants.

Ubico emulated the European fascists in his dress, his mannerisms,
and his pretensions — ruling the country as a populist dictator and using
repressive measures to generate evidence of his popularity. But when
World War II rolled around, he dressed down his fascist sympathies and
cast his lot with the United States. Despite the makeover, he would himself become a casualty of the war. The Allies' wartime rhetoric of freedom
and democracy flooded the country and helped undermine the legiti-
macy of his dictatorial rule. In 1944, a popular revolt broke out in the
capital, led by students and the urban middle class, and then joined by
members of the economic elite who had also grown to resent Ubico's
heavy-handed interference in their affairs. Ubico resigned in June, and
his successor lasted only until October, when a second uprising brought
to power a pair of reform-minded army officers who immediately called
for democratic elections. So began what would be called the October
Revolution.

The presidential election was won handily by Juan José Arévalo, a charismatic young professor who ran a campaign promising a "new Guatemala." Once in office, Arévalo set about making Guatemala's labor system more humane, outlawing the various forms of forced labor that Ubico had established and then, in 1947, signing into law a labor code that outlawed corporal punishment in the plantations, established a minimum wage, an eight-hour workday, and a six-day workweek, and protected the right to unionize.

Arévalo's new labor code was only the beginning of the decade-long October Revolution. The most radical changes would occur after 1950 when Jacobo Arbenz was elected to succeed Arévalo as president. The centerpiece of Arbenz's political platform was the promise of agrarian reform, and when he made good on it in 1952, the pace of the revolution accelerated — or so the history books said.

*

"So what happened after Arévalo?" I asked Ortega.

"Well, then there was Arbenz. They say Arbenz was becoming a communist, giving out lands and all. The rich people didn't like it. I didn't takes sides for or against it. Anyway, then Castillo Armas brought back the law of the past."

Where history accelerated, the memories of it seemed to fade. After telling me about Ubico and Arévalo, these veteran workers had little to say about Arbenz. When my questions led them to the subject of the Agrarian Reform, they moved deftly on to another one. The sentence beginning with Arbenz ended with the man who had overthrown him, Castillo Armas. Yes, Arbenz did this, but that all came to an end with Castillo Armas. It seems that what occurred during the Arbenz era was less significant than the fact that it had ended.

IV

It was time to try a new strategy: talk to people *outside* the plantation about what had taken place inside it. Maybe those outside would be less reticent about the Arbenz years. I checked into a pension in town and went directly to Ceferino's house to see if he knew anyone who fit the bill. He did.

Alberto Chavez was the principal of La Igualdad's elementary school, which meant he was largely responsible for what little schooling the children in the area received. Chavez's father had been a leader of the Revolutionary Party in the 1950s and mayor of La Igualdad when the Agrarian Reform was carried out. He was, Ceferino said, one of many revolutionaries thrown in jail when Arbenz fell.

I headed up the street from Ceferino's home and entered the school. The noise in the courtyard was deafening. Some two hundred primary students in blue and white uniforms were playing basketball, soccer, and tag, several overlapping games in the same small space. It took a few moments to find an adult, and when I did, she pointed me to the principal's office. The door was open, and inside a small tidy man sat behind a small tidy desk, reading a newspaper. "Excuse me, are you Señor Chavez?"

"Para servirle," he said without looking up: *at your service.* He eased out of his seat and was on the way to the door before his eyes lifted from the paper. He had a bland face and blank eyes that seemed to register nothing unusual about seeing a large foreigner in his office. He greeted me with a limp handshake, closed the door against the noise of the courtyard, and invited me to sit down across from his desk. "What can I do for you?"

I introduced myself, telling him I was from a university in the United States and writing about the history of the region's coffee plantations. He nodded slowly as I spoke, gazing toward me without quite making eye contact. "They told me your father was a leader of the Revolutionary Party, and I thought that from him you might know something of the history."

He was silent for a moment, waiting for me to continue. When I didn't, he spoke: "Yes, my father was the mayor." His voice was as dull as his appearance, and so soft that I had to lean forward to hear him. "I was too young at the time to know what was going on. But from my father, I know a few things."

He recounted these with the monotone of a spent schoolteacher reciting a lesson long gone stale: there had been unions in many of the plantations; the Agrarian Reform expropriated some plantation lands and redistributed them among the workers; the workers who received lands also received credit from the government; the government didn't plan adequately, and the reform failed; things got out of control, and the workers began invading plantation lands; it all ended with the fall of Arbenz.

I scribbled in my notebook, excited by what seemed a promising start. It turned out, though, that this was all I was going to get. When I tried some questions, he answered them all the same way: *No sé.* He didn't know who had organized the unions; he didn't know which private plantations had been expropriated; he didn't know if there had been a union in La Patria or if La Patria had been one of those expropriated or invaded.

I tried a different sort of question. "Is it true they threw your father in jail?"

"Yes." He looked bored.

"What did they do to him?"

"Nothing really." He looked like he had said all he was going to say.

"Do you think it would it be possible for me to interview your father?"

"You could," he answered without enthusiasm. "But my father is old now and won't remember much."

We were both silent. I closed my notebook and looked out through the office window at the kids in the courtyard. I thought I saw one of the girls from La Patria wrestling a basketball from the hands of a younger girl. I turned back to Chavez. "Look, you must know a lot of people in the community. You've taught their children, I'm sure. Is there anyone who could help me?"

He paused, considering the request, and then shrugged. "Well, my father wrote a book that might help you."

"A book?"

He stood up and went to the filing cabinet, opened a drawer, removed a thick bound volume and handed it to me. It was a history of La Igualdad, he explained, written for the celebration of the municipality's centennial in 1988. I opened to a table of contents, written out longhand, and started to read. He interrupted me: "You can borrow it if you like."

His tone now had a slight edge to it, a hint of impatience. He stood waiting in the middle of the room. I got the point: it was time to leave.

"I'll get it back to you as soon as possible," I promised as I headed to the door. He nodded as if he didn't care and gave me another limp handshake.

I made my way through the courtyard clutching the book in both hands as if it were a treasure. It *was* a treasure. After weeks of hearing nothing happened, here was a history book written by a local historian! A local historian who had been the leader of the Revolutionary Party during the height of the Revolution! The several histories written by professional historians said little about how the Agrarian Reform had played out at the local level, but they said enough for me to deduce a few things: that as local head of the Revolutionary Party, Rodulfo Chavez had been a key figure in promoting the transformation of power relations in the region; that as mayor during the Arbenz administration, he had probably been the most powerful politician the town ever had; that if anyone would know the history of the reform years in La Igualdad, it would be he.

I hurried back to the pension, sat down on the rickety bed in the tiny windowless room they'd given me, opened the book, and began to read.

⬇

I began at the beginning. Each entry was brief — a paragraph or two — and had a heading: *Founding and founders and other facts . . . First electrical installations . . . Electricity 1960.*

I read through these quickly, anxious to get to the political history: *First radio . . . First bicycle . . . First mill . . . Telegraph co-founders . . .*

Okay, where is it?

Private School 1940 . . . First marimba . . . Second cemetery . . .

Finally on page 27, I found something political. *Municipal accords* was the heading. The first one recorded was from August 1939, the appointment of a municipal secretary. There followed two or more accords each year up to 1948, where it stopped and picked up again in 1956. The key years of the Revolution were missing!

A few pages later, I came to the heading *Acts and accords.* It began in 1944 and ran through 1948 and then, inexplicably, moved on to the next topic: *The Inauguration of the first fair of La Igualdad* in 1931.

And so it went for over three hundred pages, a collection of facts that was occasionally chronological, though more often not: *Data from the 1981 census . . . Beauty pageants . . . Earthquake . . . The first parish . . . Fauna and flora. . . .*

I began to skim and then to skip pages, searching for any mention of the reform years. I grew dizzy as I read. Exasperated, I put the book down and took some deep breaths. Then I picked it up and tried again. Only after several attempts did I find the name Chavez. On page 90, the historian included himself in the entry that listed all the mayors from 1945 to 1988. But several pages later, he was absent from the list of "most outstanding mayors between 1945 and 1958." Modesty perhaps. He did include the mayor who had succeeded him (the one who, I would later learn, had thrown him in jail in 1954).

There was no mention of the Revolutionary Party or the Agrarian Reform or the Labor Code. This local historian recorded La Igualdad's first car, its first bicycle, its first soccer team — but nothing of the first political rally, the first labor union, the first land expropriation. He did not even mention what was perhaps his only enduring legacy: paving La Igualdad's second street, the Street of the Revolution.

V

Sara didn't know what happened in La Patria during the reform because she wasn't around the plantation then. Her parents had also absented themselves from the plantation during those years, she told me, going to live in Panajachel, where her father had devoted the better part of his time to sport fishing. Although he had maintained contact with the plantation, he chose to tell the family very little about what was taking place.

I would have liked to ask Franz Endler to tell me what he hadn't told them. But it was a topic he would rather stay away from, Sara had told me, and given his frail condition, I had felt I should respect this preference. Fortunately, Sara had another suggestion of where to go for information.

⬇

Erich Becker now managed the processing plants of one of Guatemala's largest coffee export houses. After a few phone calls, I arranged to meet with him at the company's headquarters in Guatemala City.

Arriving at the arranged hour, I was led by an employee in coat and tie past the uniformed guards armed with shotguns at the front gate, past the elegant secretaries at computer terminals in the front office, and into an immaculate conference room adorned with photos of coffee groves and volcanoes. It was one of those small rooms where big decisions get made, ones regarding the fate of hundreds of plantations and millions of coffee beans. They weren't always happy decisions. This was reputed to be among the most successful export houses in the country, and that success was attributed to unusually aggressive business practices. "They're making lots of money," I had been told by the frowning CEO of another export house who disapproved of his rival's methods. Their disregard for the clients' well-being was somehow unethical, he insisted, and foolhardy as well: "You foreclose on one plantation owner too many in this country, and you'll wind up with a bullet in your head."

I was greeted by a booming voice and a firm handshake. "Erich Becker, at your service!" Becker was a tall man with the build of an aged athlete, still quite fit considering his sixty-four years. His red hair and freckles had faded into an otherwise pale complexion. His eyes were blue. He wore jeans and an old summer shirt. Unlike the rest of the people in the building, he was not one to bother with a tie. Nor with formalities. In less than a minute we were sitting at the conference table and he was telling me the history of Guatemala, answering my questions without hesitation, speaking his mind with straightforwardness I had rarely encountered here. When I realized he was a talker, I asked if I could tape the interview.

"Sure, why not?" he answered, his tone making it clear he couldn't give a damn what people thought of what he might say.

As the tape rolled, Becker began telling me of his childhood.

"In those days, there were three Franzes in La Patria — Franz Haekel, Franz Endler, and my father, Franz Becker Endler. The only one who kept his name was Franz Endler, since he was the son of one of the owners. My father changed to Manuel.

"My father was Federico's nephew. He came from Germany in 1921 and worked in La Patria until 1936. I studied in the German School in Xela in 1938–9 and then in the German School in Guatemala City in '40 to '41. The teachers were all Germans. In 1942, my father was taken prisoner and sent to Texas. I had to go to work selling fish in the Guatemala City market to take care of our family. Then I went to Germany and studied agriculture in school. When the currency changed [after the war], we were left totally broke. That's when Franz Endler showed up in Germany and offered me work to get started in Guatemala."

Becker traveled to Guatemala and spent several years working in La Gavia, and in 1952 Franz made him administrator of La Patria.

"In those days all the workers had as their papa, you could say, the owner of the plantation, or the administrator of the plantation. Because there in the plantation is where they were born, it's where they studied, where they ate, where they died. They worked and they died. Everything was taken care of in the plantation. They were like slaves of the plantation, in a manner of speaking, no? Even though they could say, 'I'm leaving.' But where could they go?

"With the union, things began to change. When I arrived in La Igualdad, the majority of the plantations already had unions formed. They were advised by the party of Arbenz in Guatemala City, which meant that generally, if there was a conflict, the *patrón* lost. The government dictated what the salaries would be. The salaries increased in part because the workers were liberated from the plantations. In the sense that [the plantations] stopped giving them rations, right? They didn't give them maize, they didn't give them beans, or meat or salt. So that they'd be less like children of the plantation, no? So they'd live instead by their own means.

"Many times they would come and say to me, '*Miiiire, patrón.*'" He imitated a worker speaking in a singsong manner. "'We're not going to do this work.'"

He returned to his own voice: "'But you are going to do it. Because you've always done it, and you're going to continue doing it for me.'

"'Aaah! Then we're going to fight!' With their machetes in my face. So I'd grab a wrench and say, 'All right, then. We're going to fight here or in the courts.'

"With just about every change in work, I'd have a conflict with the union. Why? Because they wanted to do less and earn more. They'd be fighting for the workload. The majority of times they wouldn't want to do the work that I ordered done. Or I'd get rid of someone, tell that person to go to hell. Then they'd stop working: '*He stays, or we're all going to strike.*' I'd catch a thief, I wouldn't be able to fire him. Because the union would defend him.

"When the union said 'Work,' they worked. When they said 'Don't work,' they didn't work, those bastards! So I had to fight with the union. Every day, there'd be some discussion with them. It was rare that there wasn't some dispute. And I had some disputes where they wanted to hit me. I remember in 1954, I was in the nursery, below the cemetery. I was carrying bags of compost when they said they weren't going to keep working. They weren't in agreement with the job. Why not? Because I was hanging around near them, so they had to work harder. So they all surrounded me, because they didn't like it that they had to work so much. So it was a rebellion. This wasn't the first time. But it was the most dangerous one I had. Fifty of them, wanting to really fuck me up, to go at me with their machetes. So I called out the three leaders of the union. They stood in front of me. Now that I had them right there, I pulled out my knife, which was the only weapon I carried. I flipped it open and waved it at the three. I said, 'All right boys, you're going to kill me. You're more than fifty here. Go ahead, kill me. But you three leaders are going to be responsible. I'm going to kill you three before anything. If you're going to kill me, go ahead and kill me. But I'll kill these three first.'

"'Ahh, no!'" He imitated them in a whiney voice. "'We're not going to kill anyone!' So I began to yell at them: 'Boys, we're going to work! Because they're paying you to work, not to be bums!'"

When I asked Becker where all this hostility came from, he explained, "There was resentment against the Germans. There still is today — that you're a gringo and you're only here to exploit the people. I explained it this way to the people: 'What's the difference between a Ladino from here and someone from Europe?'

"And my explanation to the workers went like this: 'Look here, Don Franz and everyone didn't come here with big amounts of money. But they're thrifty. You people aren't thrifty. And I'm not going to blame you entirely. Because you never learned to be.'

"And I explained it to them like this: When the cold season came in Europe, the ancestor of our people had to dress. He had to save for the winter, put his things in a cave during the summer. In other words, he began to save. Why? Because of the wretched climate with four seasons a year.

"But the Ladino? Here a fruit, there another fruit. There was no need for clothing — the climate is always hot. I have lots of fruit just hanging there. Why the hell do I need to save? So you see, because of the natural environment, the guy from here was never trained. He didn't have the ability to save. He had everything at his fingertips. That's why the European here was able to save and rise above the rest."

⬇

Arbenz's effort to reverse this evolutionary process had been, according to Becker, a complete disaster.

"When they parceled up the plantations, the government gave each of [the workers] Q200 or Q300. So, what did they do with the first advances given to them? Some went drinking. Others bought refrigerators. Others radios. And they didn't even have electricity for these things in their huts! They didn't know they needed electricity to work!"

The problem, as Becker saw it, wasn't just that they hadn't understood electricity. They also hadn't understood the labor regime and what they had been giving up with the reform. "They saw one quetzal in the other plantation. And they saw the 60 cents [which they received]. But for that difference of 40 cents, the plantation was providing medical care, it was providing medicine, it was providing school, giving rations, everything up to the casket to bury them, right?

"The people were misled. Looking at it in hindsight, the people really were good. What happened was — well, it's the same as if you say to a child: 'Go knock over that table, and I'll give you a box of candies.' So what can you say about the worker? He thinks that they're going to give him the lands, that they're going to be the owners. What they do is ruin the plantation. What they were basically doing was bringing down the production. Because they didn't plant, they didn't work and they had a higher salary."

Who was it that had misled them?

"It was Arbenz's people, the communists, who told them to do all that stuff. And in La Patria, the one who played dirty with Franz was that half-brother of his."

"The half-brother . . . you mean Rafael Zamora?"

"That's right. Rafael."

⬇

"That's how I came to La Patria in the first place," Becker explained. "Franz made him the administrator. Why? Because Franz's wife liked him a lot. But then they called me to La Patria because there was a big uproar. Rafael had been messing with the women of the workers. He was taking the workers' women to bed, or worse yet, in the coffee fields, he'd rape them. That was the reason. I was a bachelor. If I grabbed me a girl, you know, it was another matter. But him, a married man grabbing the workers' women, that's ugly. If he had grabbed a girl who wanted him to grab her, perfect. But grabbing the workers' women — uh huh, no way! So the workers wanted to hang him. And all hell broke loose. So the workers requested me as administrator. And that's how I began my life as administrator of the plantation.

"I didn't have problems with Rafael. I treated him with respect. For me, he was still a dignified person. Even though he messed around with the women, for me he was a fellow worker. But then later on is when he got involved with the union, and that's when I said, 'Good-bye.'

"He spoke badly because Franz had dropped him. And I was using him as a driver. And driver is below his category. No? A young guy like me ordering around an old man. So he sent the town police against the plantation, telling them that I had weapons on the plantation, which was true.

"Now, in those times there was the agrarian law. Which means that they wanted to redistribute the plantation among [the workers]. And that's where Rafael Zamora got involved, helping advise them on how to parcel up the plantation. You see, he wanted them to parcel the plantation and set up a cooperative. He was going to take over the processing plant and become the head of the cooperative. That was the idea of Rafael — he wanted to take control of the plantation."

⬇

Before Rafael Zamora could take over La Patria, Becker recalled, Castillo Armas overthrew Arbenz, and the Agrarian Reform came to an end. Franz Endler arrived at the plantation and told his half-brother and the dozens of unionized workers to get out and never come back.

When I saw Sara a few days later, she told me she had never heard most of what Erich Becker told me. She hadn't known that the union had been so active, or that the workers had hoped to divide up the plantation, or that Rafael had aimed to take La Patria away from his younger half-brother. All she had learned about Rafael from her father was that he had become involved in some mischief and that her father had expelled him from their lives.

And there was one story of his mischief that had stuck in her mind. Rafael had gotten the workers in La Patria to cut off the stud bull's penis. The animal had bled to death.

VI

Again I was in La Igualdad. And thanks to Erich Becker, I now had some evidence that the history I was looking for existed. There *had* been a union in La Patria. The agrarian reform *had* affected the plantation. At least that was what Becker said, though I didn't know how reliable his account was. The way Becker told it, the workers had acted like unruly children and had been misled by the *patrón's* resentful half-caste half-brother. But I wondered why these workers would have followed the man who had been raping their wives.

One morning I set off after another of Ceferino's leads. I rode the motorcycle down the Coatepeque route into the warm air that was just beginning to rise off the coastal plain. I was still on the piedmont when I turned onto another road traveling west between two sprawling coffee plantations. After a short distance, the road dropped into a ravine, the coffee groves disappeared, and I found myself surrounded by the wild vegetation of another era. There were leaves larger than a human torso and moss thick as an animal's pelt. Slowing at a bend, I saw wild orchids climbing from the fierce tangle of roots, branches, and vines with a tenacity long ago forgotten by those domesticated dandies in the hothouses up north. I felt as though I had been transported back centuries to the world that existed before these hills had been invaded by the frail red-berried bush whose survival required clearing out the native species. At the bottom of the ravine, I came upon a single, magnificent ceiba — Guatemala's national tree — that towered above its neighbors. Its elegant, outstretched boughs were hung with blossoming vines, the regal trappings of the forest's undisputed queen. Yet the fact that the ceiba stood alone revealed just how diminished this forest kingdom really was. When I stopped to admire the impressive thickness of the ancient trunk, I found fresh graffiti carved into its wooden flesh.

The road itself was like something Friedrich Endler had described a century ago, back when the struggle to dominate the New World tropics was well under way, but not yet triumphant. Grass grew tall between tire tracks that, in many places, had dissolved into muddy troughs. There were occasional stretches littered with stones, which must have been cobbled together by forced labor in Ubico's day, but had long since come loose and now made for treacherous riding. The absence of any signs of human life made me uncomfortable — if something should happen, who would find me, and when?

After what seemed an interminable journey, I arrived at a hamlet that was as decrepit as anything I had seen in a year of traveling Guatemala's back roads. The half-dozen houses that lined the main street — the only street — were in various states of decay. The roofs sagged. The walls leaned precariously, waiting for one powerful tremor to bring them to the ground. I cut the engine, removed my helmet, and wiped the sweat from my brow. I gazed down the desolate street. A deathly stillness hung in the air, broken only by a sickly-looking dog that rolled about in the dust, snapping angrily at its own haunches. In the shadow of an open doorway, I made out human forms — half-naked children peering at me with wide eyes. I looked away, not wanting to show undue interest in any children, and my eyes were drawn to the only unfaded, unchipped paint in town — two colorful signs hung over opposing doorways. One said COCA-COLA, the other PEPSI. Had any corner of the world escaped the cola wars? Did the world even have "corners" anymore?

I bought a Coke. Unlike the children, the señora behind the store counter regarded me with striking indifference, as if gringos on motorcycles stopped by her store every day.

"Is this La Estrella?" I asked her.

"*Sí pues.*" She didn't look at me.

"I'm trying to find Armando Tojil. Is he around here?"

Silence.

I added: "His friends from La Patria sent me here to talk to him."

She pondered this a moment, then reluctantly pointed across the street with her chin. "Take that path. You'll come to his house."

I paid for my drink and headed out. The path plunged into the cool shade of coffee groves packed densely with banana trees. The groves seemed better tended than the buildings back on the street. Every thirty yards or so there was a small clearing with a small house and no one at home. Or at least no one answered when I called out at the first few houses. But then I came to one with a young girl standing in the clearing. She looked up at me with awe and mustered enough courage to say that Armando Tojil was her grandfather and this was his home. Then she disappeared into the coffee grove. Moments later, a man emerged from where she disappeared and came directly over to me. He had a machete in his hand and a stern look on his face.

"*Buenos días, don.* How can I be of service to you?"

"Are you Armando Tojil?"

"*Para servirle.*"

He didn't look like he was about to serve me. He didn't ask me to sit down or offer something to drink — the customary treatment of visitors in the Guatemalan countryside. He just stood with his machete in hand, looking me straight in the eyes.

"My name is Daniel. I'm from the United States, and I'm writing a little about the history of the region. I was hoping we could talk some about the old days."

"How is it that you know about me?"

The directness of the question took me off guard. "Well, uh, I spoke with a few people in La Igualdad who used to be workers in La Patria. And they told me a little about the history of the plantation. And they said you also were a leader of the workers in the Arbenz years."

He nodded, keeping his eyes fixed on mine. "And what do you want to know?"

"Well, how did the union work? What did it do?"

"If the workers were given too much work, the union went to Don Franz. And if a worker wasn't working, Don Franz went to the union. And in that way, they solved any problems they had."

"But sometimes there were conflicts, right?"

"No."

"What about work stoppages?"

"There were no work stoppages."

"Okay . . ." Should I tell him what Erich Becker told me? I decided to be less direct. "And Erich Becker, what was he like?"

"Don Erich was a good man. He knew how to run a plantation. Is this something political?"

"Something political?"

"What you're doing, with all these questions."

"No," I assured him. "I'm just writing a history. How about Rafael?"

"Rafael?"

"Rafael Zamora. Don Franz's half-brother."

"He was a good person also."

"Is it true what they say about the bull — that he had it castrated."

His expression hardened. "Look here, *señor,* I'm an Evangelical. So I don't get involved in political things. According to the Bible, we have to respect the laws, whatever they may be."

I closed my notebook. Clearly he didn't want to talk. Maybe it had been a mistake to come here. I gazed at the coffee plants that surround the clearing. "Is all this coffee yours?"

"That's right."

"How's this year's crop looking?"

"Not too bad, thank the Lord."

He took his eyes off me for the first time and gazed at the coffee plants. "Unfortunately, I abandoned it a few years ago." The edge was gone from his voice. "Back then I used to drink. When my son died, I abandoned the coffee completely . . ."

He paused, and then his expression hardened again. "But then I put myself right with *el Señor,* and now the crop is coming back, thanks to him. God wants us to suffer so that we become good. He wants us to respect the law. So that's what I do. I don't get involved in politics. *El Señor* teaches us not to preoccupy ourselves with the things of this world."

I braced myself for another attempted conversion. But Tojil was not interested in my salvation. He just wanted me to leave. "Okay, we've talked," he said. "Now I have work to do."

Back in the town that evening, I had dinner at the home of a health worker named Mario Montes. I had met Mario one morning when I had parked my motorcycle in front of the government health center in La Igualdad. Mario was an effusive, chubby Ladino man, with bright eyes that brightened further when he was talking politics. Mario liked to talk politics, and by the third time I passed by the health center, he was saying things like: "As long as the land is in the hands of only a few, we're going to have a civil war. Only next time it won't just be in the mountains, and it won't be ideological. It will be pure violence." And: "It's not in the interests of the landowners to let the workers have a good education. When they go to the university they come to see the reality, and that's when they get rebellious."

I took these comments as overtures, inviting me to share my own views. But I was reluctant to accept the invitation. Guatemalans generally distrust strangers who talk revolution, and this distrust had rubbed off on me. I chose my words carefully, presenting myself as a curious but detached observer who was skeptical of the propaganda put forth by both sides.

Over a dinner of eggs and beans, Mario told me about the battle of the previous year — about how the health center had overflowed with bleeding soldiers and the school had served as a second hospital. He was describing the progression of the battle when his wife suddenly rushed in from outside, wide-eyed, and interrupted him with a frantic whisper: "Mario, they can hear everything you're saying next door!"

"Really?" he said, his voice lowered.

"Yeah, I was just there. Your voice travels right through the wall!"

He looked at me and for a moment seemed to be doing some calculation in his head. Then he smiled. "Don't worry about it. It's okay."

Keeping his voice low, he explained: "The women next door cook for the soldiers in the camp in La Independencia. My wife's scared they'll tell them about our conversation. But don't worry, we won't have any trouble."

I said nothing. He opened his mouth, hesitated, then said, "Look, Daniel, I used to be in the army. So I can always make them believe I'm one of them."

As we finished dinner, we talked in hushed voices, not about the battle in La Igualdad, but about his military background. Mario had fought in the Ixcan region of the northern highlands in the early 1980s. The Ixcan had been the site of one of the most brutal counterinsurgency campaigns in Guatemala. Scores of villages had been massacred. Mario had been a soldier there at the time.

And only now he was telling me.

⬇

An ex-soldier who talked revolution in a war zone in Guatemala was not someone you wanted to hang out with. Maybe Mario was telling the truth when he said he no longer worked with the military, that he had become a "revolutionary" in recent years. But there was no way of knowing for sure. The fact that his wife had been scared suggested that she didn't see him as a friend of the army. But it also suggested that there was reason to be scared.

As I headed back to the *pension,* I chewed over what Mario had told me. I should probably keep talking to him, I thought, whatever the case may be. If the military had taken an interest in what I was doing, I would be better off dispelling their doubts than letting them fester. Surely by now they knew that there was a gringo showing up regularly in La Igualdad and talking to workers. And surely someone would be wondering what I was doing. Better to let them know myself.

The next morning, I took the San Marcos road north out of town, past the bust of Barrios, into the plantation La Fortaleza. Soon I began passing bunkers that had been dug in at regular intervals between the coffee plants on the embankments above me. The camouflaged men manning them sat so still they looked like permanent fixtures of the coffee grove: the chalum trees protected the coffee from excessive sunlight; the izote plants protected it against erosion; the soldiers protected it against subversion. Living scarecrows, they sat with their machine guns and watched me go past.

I came to the camp, an old wooden plantation that had been fortified with rows of sandbags. There was a roadblock and a sentry post with three soldiers. I slowed to a stop in front of the building and cut the engine. One of the sentries swung his gun off his shoulder and, clutching it in both hands, walked toward me. I eased off the bike and slowly removed my helmet, making an effort to look as relaxed as possible. *"Buenos días,"* I greeted the soldier with a smile.

"Buenos días." He didn't smile.

"I was hoping I could speak with the officer in charge here."

He led me back to the sentry post, where another soldier made me repeat what I had come for and then sent the first to consult with the captain inside the building. We waited in silence. The soldiers were dark-skinned, small, and very young. They might have looked like kids if they hadn't been armed to kill. One held a composition book with cartoon figures on the cover, the kind used by primary school students. He flipped through its blank pages until he came to one with writing. The script was that of a child — large, awkward letters, upper and lower cases mixed together. It looked like a poem. I read through the corner of my eye:

> If I advance, follow me.
> If I hesitate, push me forward.
> If I retreat, kill me.

I had seen these words before. It was the anthem of the Kaibil, Guatemala's elite combat troops. The Kaibil had been modeled on (and initially trained by) the U.S. Green Berets and had played a prominent role in the massacres of civilians during the 1980s. According to lore, to become a Kaibil, a soldier had to pass through a grueling and exceedingly abusive training program. One version had it that each prospective Kaibil was given a puppy at the beginning of the training session and was responsible for feeding it and taking care of it as it grew. At graduation time, the soldier was required to kill the puppy with his bare hands. It was also said that the true initiation of a Kaibil came only when he drank human blood. The signature of the Kaibil uniform was a burgundy beret. None of these boys was wearing one; they were mere soldiers.

The other sentry returned and told me to follow him. As we headed down a sandbag corridor that led into the building, I felt my gut tightening. If I looked nervous, I'd look suspicious, and if I looked suspicious, I could be in deep trouble. I took a deep breath to calm my nerves and entered the building.

The soldier directed me through a door into the captain's office. The captain sat behind a desk in a bare room. He was older than the soldiers, with lighter skin and a much larger build — a muscular torso, a thick neck, and a wide-set jaw. He remained seated as I entered, greeting me with an icy stare and pointing to the bench in front of the desk. "Have a seat. What can we do for you?"

"Thank you," I said and sat on the bench. "Sorry to bother you. I'm from the United States and I'm doing a study about the history of the coffee plantations." I felt my throat constricting as I talked. "I'm working with the permission of the plantation owners. And I just thought I should stop by and introduce myself because, well, because as you probably know, when a foreigner enters a community like this, there's often a lot of fear and mistrust."

He remained silent, staring, entirely still but for a peculiar twitch of his jaw muscles, which reminded me somehow of a reptile.

"I have my documents here if you want to see them." I pulled out my passport and the letters from the embassy and the plantation. He held out a hand to take them and, without a word, opened the passport, picked up a pen, and began to write in a notebook.

As he wrote, I took several deep breaths to relax my throat. I looked around the room. There were no weapons in sight, nor any other military paraphernalia — just a dictionary standing alone on a bare bookshelf behind the desk. The room's only adornment was a word — KAIBIL — mounted in wooden letters on the wall above the captain's head, printed across the chest of his olive green T-shirt, and stenciled into a name plate on the desk — "Kaibil Instructor."

He put down his pen, read the two letters, then looked up and handed them back to me without saying anything. Instinct told me to keep talking: "The truth is I don't think I'll have any problems. But you know with all this talk about gringo *robachicos*, it can be dangerous."

At last, he opened his mouth. "It's serious stuff. You have to be careful."

"I know . . ." I then told him the story of the island where the villagers had thought we were *robachicos*. *"They're my friends."* I impersonated the soldier. *"If any one of you lays a hand on them, I will find you . . ."*

The captain seemed to enjoy the story. "It's incredible the ignorance of some of these people," he said, amused. His expression had relaxed. His jaw muscles had stopped twitching.

Encouraged, I took a gamble. "You and your troops, you're from the 1715, right?" The 1715 was the military base in Quetzaltenango. I knew the number because I had seen it on the uniforms worn by the base's marimba orchestra when they performed in Xela's central park.

"Well, yes," he said slowly, distrust flickering again in his eyes.

"You've got a great marimba!" I said and watched the distrust give way to surprise. "I love hearing them in the park on Sundays."

For the first time, a smile spread across his face. "You like it?" he asked. I was no longer looking at a Kaibil, but a proud Guatemalan. He then asked me how long I had been in the country. How I liked Xela. The climate was nice, wasn't it? Then he told me he had relatives in the United States. He wanted to go there someday.

I told him a bit more about my research, emphasizing that I was talking to people with all different viewpoints — workers as well as landowners — about things that had happened a long time ago. He offered an opinion: "The landowners around here are largely to blame for this war. If they treated their workers decently, we wouldn't have to be here."

After we chatted some more, he invited me to an awards ceremony that the soldiers would be holding two weeks later for the students in La Igualdad's school. We shook hands and I left. Emerging from the sandbags, I looked up and down the road to see if anyone from town had witnessed the visit.

VII

The school principal had said his father wouldn't remember much, but I decided to try my luck anyway. Maybe the son was wrong. Maybe I'd be able to get Rodulfo Chavez to tell me a little of the history he hadn't written in his history book. I dropped a coin in a pay phone in Xela's central park and dialed the number I had brought from La Igualdad. The voice that answered was an old man's, formal and friendly. I explained who had given me his number and why, and he invited me to visit his home in the capital.

Back in my apartment, I threw some clothes in a knapsack and headed out to the highway to wait for a bus. Four hours later, I was in the heart of Guatemala City, in the *18 calle* where the buses from the western highlands dropped their fares before returning to the safety of depots a neighborhood away. The *18 calle* was Guatemala's version of 42nd Street (without Times Square to attract the tourists, without Disney to clean it up). The traffic was constant and noisy. The sidewalks were crowded with hurrying pedestrians, commuters in line for buses, street vendors hawking watches, wallets, umbrellas, jewelry. Behind them were the display windows of shoddy retail stores and the narrow doorways of strip joints and sinister-looking hotels. In the evening, the *18 calle* filled with shadows, and if you dared to peer closely, you could see the doped-up street kids who inhabited them, a sight that would tear at your heart even as it made you quicken your pace. The *18 calle* had the ambiance of a border town: not a place where you wanted to linger, especially not if you happened to look like a walking dollar sign.

And that was on a normal night. Tonight was not normal, as I sensed the moment I stepped off the bus. The traffic was backed up and honking furiously, and down the block I saw black smoke billowing up past a street lamp. Curiosity led me toward the smoke. I noticed a glow in the air and then caught sight of flames that leaped ten, fifteen feet off the pavement. I smelled rubber and then saw the tires that were burning in the middle of the next intersection. The blaze transformed the night, casting a reddish light on the pedestrians' faces and creating a host of new shadows on the walls behind them. The smoke, the flickering light, the dancing shadows made the intersection look even more menacing than usual, like a circus in a horror movie.

I paused a moment to stare at the fire, then glanced around for some clue of its purpose. Seeing none, I hurried away down the adjoining avenue. Several blocks later, I stopped at a pay phone and tried the numbers of friends who might offer one of two things: a place to spend the night or an explanation of why there was a fire in the *18 calle*. No one answered, so I walked a few more blocks to the hotel where I stayed whenever I had to stay in a hotel.

At the front desk, the security guard was showing off his new electric cattle prod to the clerk. Both were young men, both were jokers, and both were in the habit of joking with me. "Some cows check in tonight or something?" I asked.

"It's to protect the hotel," said the guard proudly.

"It's to protect him from his girlfriend." The clerk corrected him.

As the two discussed where the guard could stick his new toy, I tried to imagine what the management had had in mind when they had given it to him. All I could think of were the street kids who often made this street their home. When the two stopped snickering, I asked them about the fire I had seen on the *18 calle*. "There are protests against the government," said the guard, now looking very serious.

"Who's protesting?"

"Mostly it's university students," he answered.

"Why?"

"Because the government has raised the bus fares."

"So the students are burning tires?"

"Not just tires — whole buses!"

"It's serious, man." The clerk joined in. "The increase will affect everyone."

"So why is it just the students protesting?"

"They're the only ones who can afford to."

Back out in the street, I found a pay phone and again had no luck. I grabbed a bite to eat and returned to the hotel to get some sleep. When I closed my eyes, the image of the flaming tires came back to me with startling vividness, like a flash of light seared on my retina.

Over breakfast, I read the morning paper to find out what had motivated whom to set fire to what. Earlier in the week, the government had allowed the city's bus companies to raise their fares. For several days, university students had led demonstrations protesting the decision, claiming it would have grave economic consequences on the students and working people who commuted daily. The government refused to budge. So the protesters set out to shut down bus service, hijacking and burning the buses that dared to go out.

When I stepped out of the hotel to head to the Chavez home, I saw the fire had done its job. The streets were completely rid of the noisy, fuming, recklessly speeding buses that normally dominated the cityscape. It was a sight as surreal as Manhattan without yellow cabs. Now I had to find some other transportation. And so did tens of thousands of city residents, which was why every enterprising man with a vehicle and some spare time was out on the road providing substitute bus service. Cattle cars and pickup trucks, crammed with passengers, raced to pick up more. These substitutes made the real thing look safe. After seeing a few careen by, passengers dangling over the sides, I signaled a taxi.

Twenty minutes later, the cab dropped me at the address Rodulfo Chavez had given me. It was a modest middle class neighborhood — "modest" because the middle class of a poor country like Guatemala lives like the poor of a wealthy country. (Guatemala's wealthy neighborhoods, by contrast, looked like wealthy neighborhoods in the United States, except for the armed guards and barbed wire required to maintain such communities in a country this poor.)

Rodulfo Chavez greeted me at the door and invited me inside. I followed him through a tidy family room and into a smaller, windowless space that was a combination of workshop and study. Old newspapers and books and household tools cluttered a bookcase and a small desk. Framed diplomas and family photos hung on the wall.

Chavez offered me the sturdier of two chairs and eased slowly into the other. He bore a physical resemblance to his son, but little more. He was alert and warm and had the dignified, grandfatherly demeanor of a professor emeritus. If he had lived in another climate and had had more money, he might have worn tweed. Instead he wore the simple colorless combination of shirt and slacks that had been the fashion for middle-class, middle-aged men in Guatemala for decades.

I repeated the introduction I had made over the phone and told him I had some questions about his monograph. He was clearly pleased by my interest in his hometown and in his work. He seemed to have a good memory. He seemed to enjoy remembering. And he didn't seem to mind when I told him that I had heard accounts of the first car and the first radio that differed from his. "There are so many stories," he said with a contented sigh.

Time to ask the question, I thought. "I've also heard a lot of stories about what happened during the Arévalo and Arbenz years." He didn't respond to that, so I continued: "They say you were mayor when Arbenz signed the Agrarian Reform law. I was wondering if you could tell me a little about what happened."

I waited for a response. He sighed again, though this one sounded a bit forced, and when he spoke, the pleasure was gone from his voice. "I don't know. What is it exactly that you want to know?"

I tried some specific questions — about the Revolutionary Party, about the labor unions, about the expropriation of the plantations. His answers were vague: "It was active for a few years and then went away." "There were some unions but I'm not sure what they did." "Expropriations? Well, maybe there was something like that, but that was a long time ago." With each answer, the light in his eyes grew dimmer, his face assuming the bored expression that had been a permanent fixture on his son's. His gaze drifted around the room and finally settled on the floor.

I tried to shake him back to life with a blunt, leading question: "As a leader of the Revolutionary Party, you must have played an active role in the reform process, right?"

His shaking head suggested a flicker of life, but his eyes remained glued to the floor. "*Mire usted,*" he said quietly. "I don't remember those things anymore."

I tried some questions about the Arévalo years, remembering that the workers in La Igualdad seemed to find them less threatening than questions about Arbenz. But that didn't work either. *"Mire usted,"* he said. "I don't remember those things," he repeated, only this time his eyes were off the floor and looking into mine, the bored expression replaced by an imploring one.

I felt like a bully. And yet I couldn't seem to let go of my hope that he would tell me what he knew. So instead of asking more questions, I started talking to him. Maybe I could inspire his cooperation by explaining why I bothered tracking down people like him. "So little is written about the history of the coffee region," I said. "You all have lived through so much history, some of it dramatic, some of it painful, and people outside don't know anything about it. And young people in the schools today don't learn anything about it. It really seems tragic that all that history should be forgotten."

My words had some kind of effect. The life returned to his eyes. He nodded with growing enthusiasm and then exclaimed, "Yes, it's true. History is very important!" Now it was me who was nodding as he began talking about the importance of history. I was still nodding when I realized that he had changed the topic to tell me about his new project. It was more ambitious than his monograph on La Igualdad, he conceded. He was writing a history of the world.

From the shelf behind him he gathered a bundle of papers and handed them to me. It was the work in progress. I glanced at the first few headings: *The Founding of Rome . . . Sports in 1896 . . . Volcanoes. . . .*

Now it was my turn to sigh.

⁂

Taxis didn't circulate in this part of town. After fifteen minutes of waiting in vain, I tried to figure out which of the substitute "buses" passing by was headed my way. When I heard a kid on the side of a cattle truck yell, *"18 calle!"* I signaled the driver to stop. I hurried around to the back and found myself facing a solid human wall, the outer edge of a condensed mass of commuters which also happened to be the outer edge of the truck. My first impulse was to turn away, but when two arms reached down, I accepted their help, feeling somehow compelled by solidarity to join the suicidal venture. I nestled my way into the mass of bodies and managed to grab hold of the truck's siding with one hand. That hand would be the only thing that could save me if a sudden lurch sent the wall of people spilling out the back. I held tight and watched the pavement rush past my feet.

Safely back in the hotel, I lay down on my bed and stared at the ceiling. Normally, this would be the time to write up my notes from the interview, but this interview hadn't produced any notes. I recalled the vacant expression on Chavez's face when I had asked him about the revolution, and for a moment I felt myself getting angry: the man had let me travel all this way only to forget everything! Then I remembered the imploring look that had come later, and I felt a twinge of guilt. Why was I harassing these people? Maybe they really didn't have anything to tell me. Maybe it had all happened just the way Erich Becker told it. And even if it hadn't, what was it to me anyway?

Too depressed to answer these questions, I forced myself up and out of the hotel to look for a phone. I got through to a journalist friend, and she invited me to a party at the apartment of another ex-pat.

It was dark when I set out for the party. The evening traffic had dwindled. Two blocks down, a flickering light caught my eye. Turning, I saw flames four or five blocks away. Even at this distance, the sight was unsettling. Just some old tires burning, nothing more. Yet there is something about fire in the street that seems to portend a violence much greater, a subterranean force rending the city apart at its seams.

The ex-pat's second-floor apartment was filled with the usual mix of journalists and human rights workers, alcohol, and world music. The main topic of conversation was the latest in the bus fare standoff: several *maras* — gangs of adolescent boys — from the poor neighborhoods on the city perimeter had appeared earlier in the day in various parts of downtown and gone on pillaging sprees, smashing windows and attacking pedestrians. I grabbed a *mojito* and joined the group that was gathered around a prominent Guatemalan human rights lawyer, listening to him interpret the day's events. "How is it that all these gangs struck in several parts of the city at the exact same time?" He paused dramatically, and then provided the answer: "Clearly all this was orchestrated by someone who wanted to sow chaos and distract from the social content of the protests. The army is just waiting for an excuse to force a state of emergency . . ."

Later, I found a chance to introduce myself to the lawyer and told him about my research in La Igualdad. "Very interesting, very important," he told me in a very earnest tone. Along with the encouragement, he offered a contact — a labor activist in the city who had grown up in La Igualdad. I jotted down the man's name and the address of an office where I would be able to find him.

By midnight, my spirits had been lifted by the music, the *mojitos*, and the company of people who shared my commitment to digging up Guatemala's past. My journalist friend saw me making ready to leave and offered me a ride to the hotel. I told her I preferred to walk. But as I headed down the stairs to the street door, someone in the apartment suddenly yelled, *"Una mara!"*

I rushed back up and joined the others at the window just in time to see a gang of adolescent boys march down the middle of the avenue directly below us. There were about twenty of them, and they all carried clubs. As they neared the intersection, a young man turned the corner directly in their path. Without a moment's pause, the youths swarmed him like a school of piranhas, their clubs flailing. "Oh my god!" someone next to me gasped. Everyone else remained silent, and, with the Gypsy Kings playing in the background, we watched the man's futile effort to ward off the clubs with his arms. A solid blow to his head sent him to the ground.

"What do we do?" someone asked in a whisper.

"Call the police!" someone answered, also whispering — as if the gang could hear us.

The party's host crossed the room to the phone. The rest of us stayed glued to the window. After a few parting kicks to the gut, the gang moved on. Two kids lingered to remove the man's sneakers and then catch up with the rest, leaving their prey barefoot in a widening puddle of blood.

"Should we go down there and help him?"

"They could come back and do the same to us," someone said. But this wasn't really an answer, at least not for a group of foreigners who liked to think they were in Guatemala to help the Guatemalan people. And so we stood there, staring, speechless, until a police car showed up at the corner, followed shortly by an ambulance. Turning away from the window, I found myself wondering about the sneakers. Had those kids actually wanted them or was that a final gesture of violence?

I told my friend I would accept the ride after all.

⚜

The name the lawyer gave me was Juan Guillén, and the next morning, I dropped by the union office where he worked. I had been in offices like this before, and I usually found them depressing — activists in varying states of inactivity sitting below the posters of other people's struggles and complaining about the overwhelming onslaught of privatization. Unfortunately, Guatemala's wealthy privatizers told the truth when they claimed that the state employees' unions were grossly incompetent and corrupt. But it wasn't the whole truth they told — they never mentioned just who had corrupted the unions, assassinating their most promising leaders and buying off the rest.

This office was more alive than others, though today's excitement was due to the bus-fare demonstrations rather than anything related to their union. As I waited for a secretary to find Guillén, I listened to the people in the room discuss the latest rumors that the government's resolve was wavering.

After a few minutes, I was shown through to the office Guillén shared with several others. He was an amiable man in his thirties with a chubby face and a potbelly in its second trimester. I told him who had sent me and why, and he suggested I talk with his father, who had been in La Igualdad in those years.

Guillén made a call, and a little later I was sitting with his father in a café on a busy avenue several blocks away. Guillén senior was in his late fifties and had the demeanor I had encountered before in veteran revolutionaries — sharp men softened by age, in the process of growing detached, trading in their street wisdom for the more humbling wisdom of life. With him was another son, Hugo, who, unlike his half-brother Juan, had continued to keep a home in La Igualdad.

We ordered coffees. "My son says you're interested in what happened in La Igualdad during the Arbenz years. What is it you want to know?"

"Well, at this point, anything you can tell me."

Guillén pulled a cigarette from his shirt pocket and stuck it in his mouth. "The person who really could have helped you was my father."

He fumbled for a match, lit the cigarette, and exhaled. "Unfortunately, he passed away. He was the head of the Revolutionary Party in another municipality of San Marcos. I lived with my mother in La Igualdad and was just a youngster at the time. But I'll tell you what I remember."

✦

The first political rallies in La Igualdad had been held in 1949, Guillén recalled. Although the October Revolution had begun five years earlier, it took some time for revolutionary politics to gather momentum in the region. The Revolutionary Action Party, which people called simply the "Revolutionary Party," or the PAR, had appeared first in the nationalized plantations and the urban centers, and then spread to the rest of the plantations. Once begun, the rallies quickly grew in size until, on the eve of the national election of 1950, workers from the surrounding plantations filled the town square to support the Revolutionary Party and its candidate, Colonel Jacobo Arbenz. The party leaders gave speeches calling for an end to "salaries of feudalism" and trumpeting the centerpiece of the Arbenz platform — agrarian reform.

"The land to those who work it!" the crowd chanted. "*Que viva el compañero Arbenz!* Soldier of the people!"

On election day, the "people with money" (the plantation owners, their upper-level employees, and some merchants in town) voted for Arbenz's opponent, and the workers for Arbenz, which meant that Arbenz and the Revolutionary Party won an overwhelming majority in municipalities like La Igualdad throughout the country. La Igualdad would have a revolutionary mayor; San Marcos would have revolutionary representatives in the national congress; the country would have a revolutionary president.

The labor unions grew with the Revolutionary Party. They formed first in the nationalized plantations, where workers were able to pressure the government-appointed administrators to comply with the labor code and allow them to unionize. The new union leaders then taught workers in the neighboring private plantations to organize and make demands on their employers.

Then, in 1952, after two years of anticipation, Arbenz signed the Law of Agrarian Reform. In La Igualdad, the law had its greatest impact in the nationalized plantations whose lands were divided up among their workers. Some of the private plantations also had parts expropriated — though Guillén couldn't recall whether La Patria was one of them.

With the fall of Arbenz, the workers lost their land. Rodulfo Chavez and the other leaders were thrown in jail, and the union leaders were thrown out of the plantations. Revolutionary politics came to a quick end in La Igualdad.

🔻

"Why didn't Chavez write any of this in his book?" I asked when he finished.

"He's scared," Hugo told me.

"But you don't think anything would actually happen to him now?" I looked from son to father. "I mean these are things that took place almost half a century ago."

"You're right. Nothing would happen to him now," said the son.

"But he's still scared," added the father.

"You see," the son continued, glancing at a man sitting alone at the adjacent table, then leaning toward me and lowering his voice, "his son had problems with the military some years ago."

"His son?" I asked. "You mean the school principal?"

"Yeah, Alberto."

One night in the early 1980s, he told me, Alberto Chavez had been abducted by soldiers and brought to the military base in Coatepeque. There he had been beaten and interrogated, then left overnight in a tank of water. He had been able to breathe only by standing on his tiptoes until morning, struggling against fatigue and fending off the bloated corpses that floated in the water around him. Fortunately for Alberto, the Chavez family had a relative who was an army colonel and was able to get him released alive. "That experience left the family traumatized. You can see why they don't talk."

I nodded and remained silent.

"Who else have you spoken with?" he asked.

"Well, there's the health worker. I was wondering about him."

"Mario?

I nodded.

"They say that Mario works for the G-2," he said, referring to Guatemala's military intelligence. "You better be careful with him."

I chewed on this a moment, then asked, "What about Armando Tojil?"
"Did you talk to him?"

"Well, I tried to interview him, and he said he was an Evangelical Christian and didn't want to talk about political things."

"Maybe he is an Evangelical. But you should also know that the G-2 killed his son. It was just a few years ago, maybe three or four. The son had been driving a pickup truck from Coatepeque, loaded with supplies for the guerrillas, when they pulled him over. They left his body on the side of the road."

I remembered Tojil telling me about abandoning his coffee groves after he had lost a son. "So, is there anyone who was involved who would want to talk about what happened?"

"Definitely," Hugo answered. "But not if they don't know who you are. What we should do is travel there together sometime."

"Great idea. How about this weekend?"

"I'll see if I can. Call me the day after tomorrow."

⟱

On my way back to the hotel, I walked up Sixth Avenue. La Sexta, as it was known, was the central artery of downtown Guatemala, bustling, bright, colorful, with fast-food restaurants and modish but not too expensive retail stores. It was not as cosmopolitan as the places where the wealthy did their shopping and dining. But for everyone else, it was the heart of town.

I stopped in front of one of La Sexta's movie theaters and was reading the day's listings when I suddenly realized that the people around me on the sidewalk were running. I looked down the avenue to find out why, but saw only merchants scrambling to pull metal shutters down over their storefronts and everyone else speeding my way, spilling off the sidewalk into the street as they came. I didn't wait to see more but turned and joined in the flight.

When the crowd slowed on the next block, I turned to a woman who was panting next to me and asked what was going on. "A gang!" she said and, oddly enough, began laughing. It was a nervous laugh, and looking around, I noticed that most of the people catching their breath had nervous smiles on their faces.

⟱

I returned to the theater an hour later to see a movie with a Guatemalan friend. It was after eight o'clock when we left the restaurant and headed up the avenue toward the *18 calle,* where a cattle car would take her home across town.

"Look," she said when we were across from the police headquarters, a towering stone fortress that occupied a whole block between 13th and 14th Streets. I followed her gaze across the small parking lot to the entrance of the station. In front of it was a line of riot police, outfitted with helmets, shields and clubs, frowns, and silent stares.

Just then, someone sprinted past us on the sidewalk. My eyes returned to the street and saw that once again there were people running down it. It wasn't quite the stampede of this afternoon. There were fewer people, and they didn't seem entirely sure of whether or not they should be running. Some slowed down, looking over their shoulders. Others stopped, turned, and waited.

"Can you see what it is?" my friend asked.

I saw there was another fire up on 18th Street, and two blocks closer, I made out a large group of people marching down the middle of the avenue. "It looks like a demonstration," I told her. "They're wearing *capuchas,* so they must be students." A *capucha* was a type of pointy hood that covered the face and looked a bit like a clownish version of what the Ku Klux Klan wears. Student protesters often used them to conceal their identity.

"You can't be sure," my friend said. "They could be delinquents dressed up like students."

The half-dozen people ahead of us on the sidewalk seemed to share her uncertainty. None were fleeing, but they all looked anxious. I suggested we wait where we were. "If it's a *mara,* they won't do anything to us here in front of those police."

The closer the crowd came, the more it looked like a student demonstration. There were over a hundred people, mostly young men, many wearing *capuchas.* One carried a bullhorn, and the rest chanted slogans after him. When they were right in front of us, they stopped and faced the station. The chanting became louder and more aggressive. Someone began yelling insults at the policemen. Another threw a tire on the pavement, poured gasoline on it, dropped a match, and jumped back as flames shot into the air. Seen this close, it seemed like a dangerously provocative gesture. But it was nothing compared to what happened next.

One of the hooded protesters reached into a knapsack, pulled out an empty bottle, took aim and hurled it at the police line. *"Puta!"* my friend exclaimed as the bottle smashed on the pavement at the policemen's feet. "Let's get out of here!"

Two more bottles crashed against the pavement; a third hit the wall behind them. I saw the policemen raise their shields to protect their faces and I felt my friend tugging at my arm. I thought I saw a hand move to the butt of a gun. I didn't wait to see more.

"Incredible," I said when we were safely down on the next avenue. "Throwing bottles at armed policemen! Those students are crazy!"

"Maybe they weren't really students," she said wisely. Guatemalan wisdom tends to be cynical.

⬇

When I closed my eyes to sleep, the image of the fire came back again, brighter than before. And now other images danced within the flames: glass bottles crashing on Plexiglas shields; wooden clubs beating bloodied arms; a blank face bobbing in a pool of corpses.

⬇

I woke in the middle of the night wondering what I had gotten myself into. Why was I doing research in a war zone? By now, the people who had killed Armando Tojil's son would know who I was. Even if Mario wasn't with military intelligence, the captain would have reported my presence. He had probably already done so before I visited him. What if his superiors didn't buy my story? What if they thought it was a cover for something else? It would be so easy to knock me off on one of those dirt roads in La Igualdad. They could even make it look like a motorcycle accident or a mugging.

I turned on the light, stared at the ceiling, and tried to think clearly. *Okay, Daniel, why would they bother going after you?* The Guatemalan army was not looking for an international scandal right now. And even if it were, there were plenty of other foreigners doing human rights work that was much more threatening to it — like digging up the corpses of massacre victims. None of these other foreigners had been touched. Why would they start with me? *Well . . . they could use you to scare the others . . . But then they couldn't make it look like an accident, could they? . . .*

And if it wasn't an accident, they would have the international scandal they can't afford . . .

I tried to think through the possible scenarios. But I couldn't think clearly. I was disoriented, nervous. Something in the atmosphere of the last few days had rubbed off on me. A city where demonstrating students might actually be violent gang members — where violent gang members might actually be military operatives — where vicious beatings might await you around any corner, even on the busiest street in town. It could change the way you looked at things, make you a bit paranoid.

I got out of bed, opened the room's one window, and breathed in the cool night air. A plane passed overhead. I watched it disappear and thought: *You could always just leave.*

Why didn't I? I had fulfilled the obligations of my fellowship a long time ago. I had used up its money and had been living ever since off a mounting credit card debt. No one in La Igualdad was asking me to tell their history. In fact, it seemed like Tojil and Chavez would prefer I left it alone. Yet it was precisely their silence that had turned my curiosity into something of an obsession. Important things had happened, and now no one would talk about them — at least not to an outsider. Why not? There could be many reasons. But what the Guilléns had told me about the children of Tojil and Chavez seemed to confirm my suspicion: the silence was the work of intimidation. There had been a vast cover-up. Other Guatemalans who had not been subject to the same intimidation shared this view: César, the Guilléns, the human rights lawyer I met at the ex-pat party. They had all encouraged me to keep going. They believed the cover-up needed to be exposed. Only they were not in a position to do it. Unlike me, they couldn't just leave.

It's because you can leave, that you should stay, I thought. *With your U.S. passport you can go places and ask questions without facing the risks a Guatemalan would face.*

As I repeated this justification to myself, I felt I'd stumbled back onto solid ground. The anxiety began to recede behind me. I closed the window and climbed back into bed. *Your U.S. passport,* I thought, *and your Harvard resources.* The embassy officer had said they wouldn't be able to help me much, but now I remembered the Harvard officials saying they would be ready to bail out any of their fellows who got into trouble.

And as I considered that possibility, I thought of someone else I might turn to for help. It was a crazy idea, perhaps. But it just might prove to be worth a shot.

In the morning, I called my journalist friend to get the telephone number of General Héctor Gramajo Morales. Gramajo had been Guatemala's defense minister for much of the 1980s and, after retiring, had received a fellowship to study at Harvard.

The idea of calling him had originally come from some wealthy Guatemalan businessmen who were also Harvard graduates. "You know it was a dirty war," one of them had told me. "And they — the army — did what they had to do to win. Which isn't to say I support everything they did. But you have to give Gramajo credit. For a soldier, he's a pretty sophisticated man. That doesn't mean he'd be my choice for dinner company, but you know what I mean."

Yeah, I knew what he meant. Not choice dinner company, but still a Harvard man. The name Harvard had already gotten me into the offices of some of the most powerful people in Guatemala. It meant I existed in their world. Its significance was all the more grotesquely inflated among the status-conscious cosmopolitans in a small country like this. Gramajo was a member of the club and would surely know that a Harvard life counted for more in any public relations calculus, that harming it would be more likely to bring bad press.

I called Gramajo's number and told the woman who answered the phone that I was from Harvard and would like to speak to the general. After a minute, Gramajo's husky voice came on the phone. I introduced myself, explaining that I was in the country doing research and that I was hoping he might be able to help me with my project.

"*Con mucho gusto*, Don Daniel!" the general boomed with evident gusto. "Come by my office."

With his tie loosened and his sleeves rolled up, the fifty-five-year-old Gramajo barely resembled the double-chinned bull of a man who had appeared on military review stands throughout the 1980s — the stern, frowning face of authority behind the civilian president. Now he smiled easily. And though he still spoke with the syntax of a drill sergeant, he displayed a worldliness and sense of humor that made me think he'd do just fine at a Harvard dinner. On the wall next to his desk were framed photographs of his alma maters: the Guatemalan military academy where he had begun his professional education; the Kennedy School of Government where he had completed it. On the shelf behind him was a photo of the former general in cap and gown receiving his latest degree, and another of him posing with a big grin under a street sign that pointed to Harvard Square.

We chatted first about life in Cambridge, and then I told him about my research on the history of the coffee plantations in San Marcos. The general offered a piece of advice: "You have to understand that there are some things that do not seem normal in one place, but are normal somewhere else."

I nodded and said, "Well that's sort of why I'm here." I explained that as part of my research, I was interviewing plantation workers, and that though I had permission from the landowners to enter their plantations, I was still a bit worried that someone would misinterpret my presence. "I mean, it's not normal to see a gringo going around asking questions in a place like La Igualdad. So I was wondering if you could put a word in to the military people there so there's no misunderstanding."

He laughed. "Well, why don't I give my friends a call right now." He went to his desk and buzzed his secretary. "Call the colonel in the military base of Coatepeque." A moment later, the phone rang, and he picked it up: "Hello, Colonel? What's up, man? Listen, I'm here with a friend of mine from Haar-vard," he said, drawing out the vowels nicely. "He's doing some research down your way. That's right, in La Igualdad. Mm-hmm, exactly. Talking to people about the history of the plantations. And you know how these historians-anthropologists-scientists are always so . . . well, let's say, so inquisitive . . ." He let out a hearty laugh. "But don't worry about this one. He's not mixed up in anything. He's a gringo . . . That's right! Ha, ha, ha!"

After he hung up, we talked some more. I listened to the general's account of how he brought "democracy" to his country. When I left, he gave me a card on his personal letterhead, which he signed, then added his telephone number. "Call me if you have any problems."

Over breakfast the next day, I read the paper and learned that police had shot a student and he had bled to death on the pavement. There was more talk that the government might give in to the protestors and rescind its new bus fare policy. But there was also more talk that the government would stand firm and impose a state of emergency, which would mean suspending basic civil liberties.

I called Hugo Guillén, and he told me that we were on for the weekend. I headed across town to the office of one of the bus lines. I was two doors from the office when I heard a shout and saw the employees scrambling to pull down a steel shutter. I managed to get through the door before it came down. As I did, I caught a glimpse of the first few boys rounding the corner with clubs in their hands.

VIII

A change had taken place in La Igualdad, though I didn't notice it when I first arrived, exhausted from a trip on roads turned to mud by the heavy rains of recent weeks. I checked into the pension and, leaving the bike, headed up the street to the house where Hugo had said we would meet. The two men standing in the doorway looked at me askance. No, Hugo hadn't shown up. No, they didn't know he was planning to. No, they didn't really want to give me the time of day. I wasn't sure what to make of their coldness, so I just said I would try again later.

On my way back to the pension, I passed a woman I knew from La Patria in the street. Or rather she passed me. When I stopped to greet her, she only nodded and kept on her way — which surprised me, since she had been more friendly in the past. After a few more outings from the pension I realized that it wasn't just that woman who was acting differently. Other people didn't acknowledge me as they usually would; or when a greeting was unavoidable, they made it quick and didn't linger. I began to feel uncomfortable. The *robachicos* scare taught me that when people here don't talk to you — and especially when they don't look at you — it's very likely that you are what's on their mind.

I sat in the park with my notebook and watched the town. The more I saw, the more I was convinced: people were scared. They kept their voices low. They didn't smile when they usually would. They went about their business with unusual concentration. Those who ventured out onto the street looked straight ahead as if they had blinders on. As if they didn't want to see anything they didn't have to. As if they didn't want to be noticed, and they especially didn't want to be noticed noticing.

I used to think of fear as something private, one individual's reaction to danger. People who said others shared your fear were using a figure of speech. People who wrote things like "fear was in the air" were just being poetic. You might be afraid at the same time and for the same reason as someone else, but ultimately fear, like physical pain, was something you experienced alone.

Guatemala had taught me otherwise. Here I encountered a fear that was larger than the individual, a fear that pervaded an entire community, flooding the channels of human interaction like the charge of an electrical storm. There are some storms that generate a charge so strong that it can make a person's hair stand on end — or so I've read. With others, you detect the charge only indirectly. You sense an eerie silence when the birds fall silent, for example — though, perhaps if you're a city dweller, insulated from nature's exigencies, you won't even notice the silence.

The first time I felt it for sure was during the bus fare protests in Guatemala City. My memory associates the feeling with certain details — the smell of burning tires, the sound of running feet, the sight of boys wielding clubs. But these details were just the physical manifestations of the danger. The charge itself came from the people around me. It was the current of nervous energy generated by the political storm that was brewing. It was the collective anticipation of disaster.

Not just disaster, though. After all, storms can also be exciting: the danger quickens the senses and provides a break from the oppressive inertia of everyday existence. Hope may accompany the fear. Pressure is building. Something has to give. The charge portends change — and since change is something people both fear and crave, it creates an innervating cyclone of emotions. To galvanize this emotional energy — to channel the fear into hope, and the hope into action — that is the work of revolutionaries.

In Guatemala City, the fear was tinged with hope. The people fleeing down Sixth Avenue that day were grinning, some even laughing. The people I encountered — friends, acquaintances, strangers — spoke of danger, but they also spoke of possibility. Would those hooded youths coming down the street beat you up — or champion your rights — or do something altogether unpredictable? Would the military crack down on the protesters — or would the students actually force a government concession?

The atmosphere in La Igualdad had been charged all this time I had been visiting. The silences I had encountered bespoke a current of fear that lingered in the air after years of violence. I had suspected this from the beginning, but I couldn't be sure. By now I knew there was a lot of history the people here were not telling. And I had spent enough time in the community to notice the change in behavior when the current of fear had been jacked up a few volts.

There was a crucial difference between the mood here and what I had witnessed in Guatemala City. Here there was no excitement, no nervous laughter, no glimmer of hope. There was just fear. Experience seemed to have taught the people of La Igualdad that if something was going to happen, it could only be bad.

⬇

When the last bus from Coatepeque rumbled into town that evening, Hugo wasn't on it. So I decided to call his home in the capital. I walked over to the bakery that housed the public phone. The baker's wife was not a native of La Igualdad, which might have been one reason she was less reticent than her neighbors. When I had entered the bakery on my first visit to the region, she looked me up and down and asked the question that so many others had never dared to ask: "You're not a *robachicos*, are you?" As I answered no, the family cat had jumped on the counter between us. "But watch out," I added with a straight face. "I could be a *robagatos*." Weeks later she would still laugh remembering that response, and from then on I was known in the bakery as "the cat-stealer."

This evening, the señora looked more serious than usual, but she didn't try to ignore me. As soon as the customers before me had left, she asked, "Have you had any problem with the military? Did they stop you?"

"No, why?"

"They've been stopping people a lot." As she said this, two women came in from the street. She didn't say any more, and I knew not to ask her.

I placed my call. When Hugo came to the phone, he told me he couldn't travel this weekend. He gave some excuse, but his voice was slurred, and I couldn't tell what it was. All I could tell was that he was very drunk. I said I'd call him in the morning and hung up.

⬇

When I called Hugo again in the morning, a woman answered, his wife perhaps. No, he wasn't around. No, he wasn't on his way to La Igualdad. No, she didn't know when he would be back. I didn't bother leaving a message.

The bakery was full, so there was no chance of asking the señora for more information. But as I crossed the park, I saw another possible source — Ceferino the driver standing in front of his house.

Ceferino didn't ignore me. No, he told me, the charged atmosphere wasn't my imagination. "Come inside, and I'll tell you what I know."

Inside, away from the street, he told me that two guerrilla combatants had been captured by the army a few days earlier. They had passed through La Igualdad, dressed as civilians, and then headed down the road toward La Patria. Someone in town thought they looked suspicious and hurried to La Independencia to inform the military. A detachment of soldiers caught up with the two men at a roadside store. They were buying drinks when the soldiers surrounded them and forced a surrender.

"Since then, the army has been getting serious," he told me. They had been patrolling more in the town and in the plantations. They had been stopping everyone who passed the encampment and checking papers. The captain had called a meeting of field masters and administrators where he announced, "We're going to do here what we did in the Ixcan." What exactly he meant by this ominous reference wasn't clear. The meeting's clear message was that all the plantations had to take a more active role in reporting all suspicious movements on their property to the army camp.

⬇

I called Guatemala City a few more times that morning, but never got through to Hugo. Finally around noon I gave up. I didn't have anything else to do in La Igualdad. So I decided to return to Xela.

On my way back to the pension I ran into Mario on the street and, keeping with my strategy of conspicuous engagement, I stopped for a chat. His effusive character seemed unaltered by the general mood of the community — although he did lower his voice slightly when a group of soldiers made its way down the other side of the street. He was telling me, once again, about how poverty led to political unrest, when his face suddenly lit up. "You want to know what real poverty looks like?" He told me that the worst cases were hidden behind closed doors, invisible to the outside eye. Years of health surveys and house calls had taught him where they were, and now he offered to show me a few.

Why not? I thought. At this point I had nothing else to do, and seeing some such families might give me new perspective on this world I was trying to understand. We agreed to meet for a short tour at three o'clock when he got off work.

⬇

Our tour began with a visit to a family with a malnourished child. We headed off on a dirt path down the hill from the town center. Only when we arrived at the home did it occur to me to ask Mario how he would explain my presence. "I've already thought of that," he said with a mischievous smile. "When I become mayor of La Igualdad, you'll see how well I handle things like this."

I hadn't realized he had such political aspirations. But there was no time to find out about them now. I followed Mario through the narrow opening in the yucca plants that lined the path, into a small dirt clearing beside a house that, from the outside, didn't look any worse than its neighbors.

Mario gave a loud whistle — Guatemalan for "anybody home?" There was no response. Again he whistled. Again no response. The third whistle, accompanied this time by a rap of knuckles on the wall, brought a man to the door who clearly was not expecting company. Feet bare, hair disheveled, shirt unevenly buttoned, he squinted against the sunlight with the confused look of someone yanked out of a nap.

"*Qué tal, vos?*" Mario greeted him informally, though it was soon clear that they were not intimates. He offered no handshake, no names, no apologies — just an explanation, and an untruthful one at that. "This *señor* here is from the International Program of Nutrition." He winked at me and ignored my frown. "Where's your child?"

"Inside," said the man, pointing inside the house.

"*El señor* would like to see him," Mario said, moving toward the door.

"*Pase adelante,*" the man said to Mario, who had already begun to do so. I had a bad feeling about this, but I followed. My eyes adjusted to the darkness in time to see the young woman standing up from a bed and hastily fastening the top button of her blouse. She walked toward us, bowing her head slightly. "*Buenos días.*" She looked even more flustered than her husband.

"*Buenos días, señora,*" Mario said. "*El señor* here wants to take a look at the child."

She glanced back at the bed, and I now saw the baby lying there on top of the rumpled covers. Mario walked over to it and gestured for me to follow him. I stayed where I was. He lifted the child, a hand under each armpit, and held it up away from him as if he were weighing a sack of coffee beans. The child wore a tattered T-shirt and stained pants. Something gooey stuck to its chin.

"How old is he?" Mario asked, looking over his shoulder at the mother. I would have guessed less than a year, but the mother answered that he was going on two. "See how small he is," Mario said. "That's the first thing you look at in a case of malnutrition."

The child started crying. Mario placed it back on the bed and continued talking in a professional tone, his back to the parents. "Another thing is the hair." He stroked the child's scalp, grabbed a clump of its thin hair, rubbed it between his fingers, and then slowly pulled away. "See how it comes out." His outstretched hand was full of loose hairs. The child's crying grew louder.

Mario turned to the parents. "How many meals do you give him a day?"

"Two," the mother answered nervously, as if this were a pop quiz and she a struggling student.

"What do you feed him?" The child's sobs grew louder.

"*Pues,* what we can. Tortillas, and when there's time, we collect herbs from the river."

"And *atol?*"

"Yes, *atol,* yes." She pointed to the other side of the room. As I followed her gaze, I took in the extent of their worldly belongings: one bed, one table, a large plastic bucket in one corner, two machetes and some rope in another, some tattered clothes hanging from nails stuck in the wall. The table was what she was pointing at. It was cluttered with a few bowls, spoons, cups, and two cans with lids ajar. This was their kitchen. One of the cans was condensed milk; the other, which had yellow powder spilling out of it onto the table, would be *polenta,* the vitamin-fortified cornmeal, which, mixed with the milk, made an *atol.* Cans like these were donated by the Catholic Church to rural health posts to distribute among lactating mothers. The women were usually eligible only until a child reached six months — this one must have gotten a special break.

I looked back at the mother and saw her gazing anxiously past Mario at the sobbing baby. Why didn't she just go pick him up?

"Where do you work?" Mario asked the man.

The man looked down at the floor. "Well, the truth is right now I'm not working. I haven't been able to work for weeks, because I'm bad in the head."

"Bad in the head?"

The man explained that he had been suffering from headaches that became unbearable when he tried to work. One of the nurses at the health post had given him some pills (health posts distribute aspirin free of charge), but these hadn't helped. So she told him to go to the national hospital in Coatepeque. There the doctor told him to take other pills, but these were too expensive, so he stopped taking them.

"So you're not taking anything?"

"*Pues,* the pharmacist here in town sold me other pills that are cheaper."

"What kind of pills?"

"He says they're pills for cancer."

"Who said you had cancer?"

"*Pues,* the pharmacist said maybe that's what it is."

Mario shook his head. "Don't listen to the pharmacist. You need to do what the doctor told you. You don't have IGSS to pay for the medicine?"

"No."

"Where do you work?"

"Wherever I can find something." He explained he usually worked at El Progreso, but it only gave work by the *quincena* — two-week stretches. The plantation hired him for four *quincenas* and then gave him a *quincena* "rest." It was a practice that had become standard among La

Igualdad's plantations in recent years. It saved them money by depriving the workers of legal status as "permanent employees," which would entitle them to benefits such as the social security and workers compensation provided by the IGSS (which stood for Guatemalan Social Security Institute in Spanish). Until he got better, the family would have to survive on the mother's wages, assuming she was able to find temporary work in a plantation.

The child's sobs were growing more desperate. The mother looked distressed. Clearly she wanted to move past Mario to the bed, but she didn't. I couldn't stand watching this anymore. "Mario," I said. "Maybe we should get going."

He signaled with his hand to wait. "This is your only child, right?"

"The only one," the woman answered. *"Pues,* there was another one, but it died."

"Are you planning to have more?"

"No, not now."

"And you're taking precautions to make sure you don't get pregnant?"

"Yes."

"What precautions?"

He might as well have asked her to strip for an examination in front of me. "We went to the clinic," she said, blushing. "They said I had to have an operation."

"You had an operation?" Now Mario looked surprised.

"Well, yes."

"Do you know if it's permanent?"

"Pues . . ." She looked confused.

"Mario, let's go."

"Did they say whether you'll ever be able to have children again?"

"Mario . . ."

"Pues, we're not exactly sure."

". . . let's go."

The child wailed. The mother fidgeted. The father stared at the ground. And Mario analyzed the situation: "A big problem in families like this is the lack of education . . ."

Just then a little girl, about ten years old, appeared in the doorway and, reading the room in an instant, walked past me, past the parents, and, completely ignoring Mario, picked up the sobbing child and began to rock him gently in her arms. I didn't know if she was a sister or a cousin or what, but at that moment she seemed like an angel.

⇊

The tour was over. I got away from Mario as soon as I could, grabbed the motorcycle from the pension, and rode up to La Patria. Sara had said I could use her *casa patronal* when I needed to, and right now I needed to. After a half hour racing uphill, I arrived at the heart of the plantation and found an employee to let me into the house. Once inside, I threw off my clothes and jumped in the shower.

This was what I had really come for. I could sleep anywhere, and I preferred sleeping in town. But only a *casa patronal* had a hot shower. And right now I felt an overwhelming need to get clean. Yesterday's muddy ride up from Coatepeque had been enough to make me filthy. The squalid *pension* hadn't had any running water to clean with, and last night's sleep on stained sheets in a bug-infested room hadn't made me feel any cleaner. In the past, I had endured days, even weeks, living like this. But not today.

The steaming hot water washed away the sweat and the dust and the odor, but it didn't get rid of the dirty feeling. If anything, it made it worse. I dressed, grabbed a beer from the refrigerator, sat on the porch, and stared absently at the millions of acres of productive farmland on the plain below.

Well, Mario, you showed me what it means to be poor all right. Poverty is when your kid's hair falls out because you can't give him enough food — because your husband can't work, because he has a problem in his head which he can't treat, because he can't afford the medicine the doctor prescribed, and even if he could afford it, maybe that's not what he needs, but he doesn't know for sure.

Poverty is when your family has to survive for who knows how long on your wife's wages — which in almost every plantation in the region is half what a man receives — and what a man receives is already below the legal minimum wage — and the legal minimum wage isn't anywhere near what it would take to give your kid a truly healthy diet and a decent education.

Poverty is the first child dead, the second one ailing, and perhaps no chance of a having a third. Poverty is no medical attention — or on rare occasions too much, but never fully understanding what's happening and rarely having much control.

That's the crux: poverty is not having control. Not controlling your diet, your work, your health, not even who enters your home. That's right, Mario, poverty is when your kid's hair comes loose — but more than that, it's when strangers can walk into your home and pull it out.

Why so bitter? Enjoy the beer. Enjoy the view. The distant glitter of the late afternoon sun on the big blue Pacific. . . . Whoever thought up that name must have been looking at it from this distance. The last time I had been down there, I had almost been lynched; the time before that a friend had almost drowned, carried away by an undertow that is so violent that the U.S. embassy tells its employees never to swim on the country's southern coast. Our hosts in the fishing village (after saving us from their neighbors) had informed us that most of their men will meet death at sea, and the reason so many of the huts had black ribbons over their doors was that a fleet of twenty men in canoes had gone out to fish a month before and never come back.

Or I suppose the person who christened those waters inadvertently anticipated the doublespeak of this century, when "pacification" would become a euphemism for bombing villages.

Poverty also pacifies. Someone from another plantation once told me why coffee workers don't talk to strangers: "If something happens, they have nowhere to go." I had assumed he was referring to their vulnerability to violent repression. I hadn't considered the specter of sudden destitution — all the more terrifying in a world where the only safety net to catch you was the charity of poor neighbors and the herbs that grow by the river, since the net put in place by Arévalo in the 1940s had been cast aside by plantations in La Igualdad that save money by denying their workers health benefits and steady work.

There's a nice name: *La Igualdad*. There were few more dramatic displays of the world's inequality than a Guatemalan coffee plantation. Ask plantation owners here why they paid women half what they pay men and they would explain that women were only capable of half the work that men did. Probe a little and you would find that "half the work" referred to half the heavy labor — like carrying sacks of coffee — and that what the women were paid half for was a full day's work at tasks that men wouldn't have been able to do any faster — like sorting coffee beans by hand. Guatemalan landowners were much more creative at justifying ways to pay workers less than imagining ways to pay more.

Criticize them, and they would call you a hypocrite. They were no different from people in Europe and the United States who preferred to buy coffee from the countries that provided the cheapest labor. And they were no different from employers in those affluent countries who also minimized their labor costs in order to maximize their profits. But there *was* a difference. Here in Guatemala's coffee fields, employers met practically no resistance, no organized labor, few legal restraints. They had complete control of life in the plantation; their workers had almost none.

There had been one brief period of time when the coffee workers of La Igualdad had gained some share of control over plantation life. That had been forty years ago. Now they had so little that they didn't dare recall what it had been like.

⚓

"Are you sad?"

The cook's question startled me out of my reverie. She had just come out on the porch with the broom in hand. She was looking down at me, smiling. "Oh, *hola!*" I said, recovering from the start. "Uh, no. I was just, uh, watching the sun go down."

She laughed and began sweeping. I sipped the beer and watched her. My staying meant she would have to prepare a meal for me. I considered telling her that I would take care of my own dinner, but I realized that breaking protocol would only complicate her life. After a moment, she rested the broom and looked out toward the Pacific horizon. I followed her gaze. The sun had begun its fiery plunge to the horizon, exiting the day like a shameless diva, her golden red boa stretching across the sky behind her.

"Do you know where the sun hides when it goes down?" the cook asked.

"Actually, it doesn't go anywhere . . ." For the next few minutes, I tried to explain the rotation of the earth. It was nice to be able to answer questions, rather than be asking them. I picked up a rock from the path below to help illustrate my lesson. I wasn't sure how much she followed. It didn't help that the rock wasn't very round. It didn't help that she had probably never seen a globe before.

She began sweeping again when she saw the field master approaching from the plantation office. I tossed the rock into the weeds below and greeted him. He looked as nervous as ever. "You haven't had problems with the military?" he asked, smiling as if he thought problems with the military were a laughing matter.

I told him no, that in fact I had visited the base on an earlier trip, so they would know who I was.

"Yeah," he nodded. "They told me."

I considered asking him which "they" he meant, but instead told him that the captain had invited me to a ceremony with the students. "I don't think I'll go though," I said.

"You wouldn't be the only one going," he said and explained that the administrators and field masters of all the surrounding plantations had also been invited.

"Oh, really? Are you going to go?"

"I don't think so." He shrugged. "What for?"

A little later, the cook came out to the porch to tell me that my dinner was on the table. As I ate, she stood in the doorway of the kitchen watching me. Other times I had stayed here, I would use these moments to bombard her with questions about anything and everything to do with the plantation. There would be no questions tonight. I was tired of asking them. I had watched Mario ask enough for one day.

Tonight, though, she needed no prompting. "The guerrillas have been passing here a lot lately," she told me. "And when it's not them, it's the army that comes by patrolling. You never know who will come next. I always keep my door open so anyone can see in, but I don't look around. The other night the guerrillas came to my door, and they asked me about the plantation. 'If there's one good plantation in La Igualdad,' I told them, 'if there's one good plantation in Guatemala, it's La Patria.'

"So they said, 'Why are you defending the rich people, *vos?*'

"'I'm not defending anybody,' I told them. 'Without the rich, we're nothing. Without them, we couldn't be here. And without us, they couldn't be here either. That's all there is to say.'"

I didn't suggest otherwise. I just kept eating the food she had cooked for me. After a long pause, she said, "According to the Bible, the work of the rich is more gentle on the body, but it's their minds that get worked harder."

"It's not the same," I started to say but stopped myself. A working mind grows throughout a lifetime; a working body just gets worn out. Did the Bible say that anywhere?

I cleared my place, carried the dishes to the kitchen sink, and thanked her for the meal.

"You still going around with all those questions?" she asked.

"Yeah. But it's hard to find anyone who wants to answer them."

She ran water over the frying pan and began to scrub. "You know, one person you might talk to is Pedro Díaz. He lives down in Punta Arenas. I think he was involved in all that stuff with the union."

Before going to bed, I returned to the porch and stared out at the night sky. It was one of those skies you could only see at the planetarium back home. I tried to pick out familiar stars and, by connecting the dots, form the constellations I had memorized as a kid. I tried the same game with the earthbound lights below, connecting the flickering yellow beams of cars and trucks and mapping out the network of asphalt that traversed the coastal plain. Most of these lights were converging on the Mexican border, making their way — I imagined — north to the United States.

There was no visible movement on the dirt roads that climbed the piedmont, just the small clusters of light that seemed to be floating up like spores from the electrical efflorescence of Coatepeque. Hidden from view, just down the hill below, were Las Cruces and the town of La Igualdad. Muffled sounds of human life echoed up through the coffee groves. The ecstatic wail of Evangelicals at a *culto* filled the night.

Somewhere on the mountainside above was a band of guerrillas. I imagined them sitting silently in the darkness taking in the same view. Perhaps they were wishing they could inspire the same devotion as the preacher below. Maybe they once had. Maybe, among some people, they still did.

I thought of the cook at home with her door thrown open for any uninvited guests who might come by. She knew, as everyone here must, that she could not prevent people from coming into her home and asking her questions. All she could do was find ways to answer without saying anything. This obfuscation was an art. A final line of defense. The only way, perhaps, to salvage her dignity.

⁂

It was dark when I got up in the morning. A thick fog had settled in the night, reducing the whole world outside to just the narrow width of the porch and a short stretch of lawn below. I sat in the usual place and stared into the gray nothingness. The only evidence that yesterday's world still existed were the disembodied voices of people passing below on their way to work.

The first rays of the sun reached over the volcanoes to my left and began to melt away the fog. Within a half hour, the piedmont air had cleared, but for the smoke rising from Santiaguito. As long as there's smoke, we're okay, said Franz Endler. Today's threat lay elsewhere. A dark mass of clouds was brewing out over the ocean, gathering force for an inland march.

The field master trudged down the path in front of me and stopped. "There's a storm coming," he said. "You should get going early if you want to miss the rain."

I rode down from La Patria and arrived late to the ceremony in La Independencia. The sentries escorted me around to the back of the building to a clearing where a dozen students sat on benches in front of two lines of soldiers. At the podium before them, a girl recited a poem about the flag. The captain stood behind her with his Kaibil beret, his jaw muscles twitching. When the girl finished, he handed her a diploma and awkwardly bent down to give her a kiss on the cheek.

The only other person I recognized there was the school principal, Alberto Chavez. He stood directly across from me next to the row of students. He had the same inscrutable expression on his face as always. He didn't look at me.

I stayed only through two more performances and then quietly found my way around to the front of the building. As I reached the entrance, I ran into the field master from La Patria climbing the embankment. He smiled sheepishly and, with the soldiers looking on, shook my hand.

⁂

I found Pedro Díaz in a tiny hamlet tucked into a ravine just below La Patria. It wasn't easy getting there — the path running down from the roadside was overgrown with coffee branches, which forced me to walk doubled over, but also gave me something to hold on to so that I wouldn't slide down the muddy slope. I made my way downhill like a hunchbacked Tarzan, moving from one branch to the next. Toward the bottom, the path forked repeatedly, and I lost my way several times. I was about ready to give up when I stumbled upon the home of Pedro's daughter, a middle-aged *señora*, who showed me to the small house, behind her own, where her father lived.

The inside was dark and damp and felt like a tomb. Pedro sat on a narrow cot, a gray blanket wrapped about him like a cocoon, his bare feet dangling out one end, his head jutting out the other. His hair was white, his skin had blanched a yellowish-brown, and he had a ghostly air about him that I had encountered before in elderly peasants. Coffee workers seem to age differently from other people. Their faces don't sag and wrinkle, but rather sharpen and shrink, the coarse skin tautening like the head of a drum, until the outline of the skull becomes clearly visible beneath — the mask of death asserting itself before its time.

Pedro's daughter passed me a stool and then uncovered a window, allowing fresh air and the light of day into the room. She sat on the bed beside her father and as we talked, acted as something of a translator, yelling into the old man's ear an abbreviated version of everything I said.

"I want to ask some questions about the history of plantation La Patria and what life was like there in the past."

Translation: "The *señor* says, 'What was life like in the old days?'"

Pedro smiled. He spoke slowly, almost shouting, and paused to catch his breath between sentences. Talking was an effort for him, but one he seemed to enjoy. It took about fifteen minutes to cover his early life — essentially that he had been born in 1909 in a highland village where the people spoke Mam, and that when it had come time to divide the family land among his siblings, his inheritance proved so small that he decided to look for work on the coast, ending up in La Patria. Then he told me about life as a coffee worker — the road work under Ubico, the reforms of Arévalo — stories that I had heard so often now that they had become rote for me. After about twenty minutes, we came to the point where the interviews always ended: Arbenz.

When, weeks before, I had first encountered the resistance to discussing the Arbenz years, I had tried to get around it by approaching the issue from different angles. The interviews had come to resemble a game I had played with magnets as a child, finding the sides that repelled each other and trying to figure out a way to push them together. In the game, I would use all my ingenuity, testing different angles and speeds of approach, hoping to outwit or outquick the polarizing force. But the efforts had been futile — the closer I came, the harder I pressed, the greater the resistance became.

My interviews with the coffee workers had been no more successful. They had refused to tell me how the agrarian reform had affected lives in their plantations. And by now I had grown tired of trying to make them. Not that I'd lost interest — my curiosity had only grown, becoming almost obsessive. But the day before, when I saw Mario tugging at that kid's hair, it had occurred to me that my tugging at people's memories was not so different. Maybe I should just leave them to their silence.

I decided I would broach the topic directly with Pedro and let him do whatever he wanted with it. Then I would be on my way to Xela.

"I wanted to ask you about what happened during the Arbenz years — if there were unions, if there was an agrarian reform. I know most people here don't like to talk about those years. So if you don't want to, that's fine, I don't want to bother you."

Maybe Pedro was closer to death than the others I had interviewed, or maybe it was that he had lived more freely, escaping the worst extremes of poverty and repression. Whatever the reason was, this time, to my great surprise, the magnet stuck. *"Mire, usted,"* he said. "I'm going to tell you the truth. Yes, we did have a union in La Patria . . ."

"It all began with the Revolutionary Party. They formed the party in all the plantations. Then permission came from the capital to form unions. We held a meeting, the workers in the plantation, and chose a *señor* named Felipe Arreaga to go to the capital to get instructions. When he returned, there was another meeting, and we elected the leaders. Felipe Arreaga and Armando Tojil were the principal leaders in La Patria. And they got instructions from the leaders of the party in La Igualdad."

"Who were the leaders of the party?"

He named a few, including Rodulfo Chavez.

"How many of the workers joined the union?"

"Ayy, everybody!" he said with a big grin. "*Pues,* there were some one hundred twenty members of the union of La Patria. Maybe twenty people didn't join. Only twenty!"

"And what did the union do?"

"Well, the union drew up a list of demands they would make to the *patrón.* Like for example, when the minimum wage was raised, we refused to work until it was paid. The plantation wouldn't pay. So we said, 'We're not going to beg, we're not going to grovel.' We did strikes so that they would pay. It was the strike that got us what we wanted — raises to sixty cents, then eighty cents, then one quetzal. We also got the task loads reduced. And with the union, we didn't let them hit us . . ."

"They used to hit you?"

"They treated us without mercy, as if we were animals. The administrator, Don Erich, was strict about punctuality. If a worker arrived five minutes late, Don Erich cursed at him. 'Go to hell!' he'd yell."

He paused, catching his breath.

"But with the union, we wouldn't let them do that. I said to that Erich, 'Don Erich,' I said, 'I don't know how your people came to be in charge here. But I'm from here. I'm Guatemalan. And I'm not going to let you push me around!'"

As he said this, a shaking fist emerged from the blanket cocoon, and the trace of an ancient fire flickered in his eyes, then faded. He readjusted the blanket and continued.

"It was not all fighting, though. With the union, everything worked according to the laws. We'd try to reach an agreement, and if we couldn't we'd go to Xela, to the labor judge, and the *patrón* would go to Xela. The inspectors came from the government and made sure the laws were applied."

"And what happened with the Agrarian Reform?" I asked.

"Well, everything was worked out to give us lands in the plantation. But they never let us."

"Is it true that you were going to take the whole plantation from the *patrón?*"

"Ay, no! Just what the agrarian law said was for us. The rest stayed with the *patrón.* In that time, the laws applied as much to the *patrón* as to the worker. There was equality in the plantation — the workers humble and the *patrones* humble."

He paused again.

"Then Arbenz fell, and all that ended. They threw us out of the plantation. They threw us out without giving us so much as a penny."

⬇

In La Igualdad, you can usually see the storms before they hit. From the top of a ridge, you can watch the rain clouds roll up from the coast like a white tsunami, swallowing the green hills as they advance. Inside Pedro's home, I wasn't aware of the approaching storm until the room suddenly dimmed — the sunlight disappearing from the window — and I knew the clouds had enveloped us.

I had so much to ask this man — about the Agrarian Reform, about Rafael Zamora, about the union — but I knew this interview was coming to a close. The excitement had drained from Pedro's voice, and he seemed ready to disappear inside his cocoon. I heard the first drops of rain on the corrugated metal of the roof. Talking was already difficult because of his poor hearing; shouting over the deafening noise of the imminent downpour would be close to impossible.

I threw out another question — what had he done after being evicted from La Patria? — and jotted down his answer absently, thinking of the other questions I would like to ask, realizing I would have to save them for another time. I decided to come back to La Igualdad as soon as I could arrange another visit with Hugo Guillén. Right now, though, I'd better get going before the storm hit.

When I emerged from Pedro's house, the rain had tapered off, but I knew it was only a temporary reprieve. I hurried up the path out of the hamlet and through the coffee groves to the road where I had left the motorcycle.

Only much later would I appreciate the tragic weight of Pedro's last story.

⬇

Riding toward town I faced the decision of how to leave La Igualdad. Did I head down the piedmont to Coatepeque or up over the shoulder of the mountain to San Marcos? Either route required crossing the waters of the Río Naranjo — fording one of the tributary streams that cascaded down from the upper reaches of the mountain, or taking one of the

bridges in the deep ravine the river had carved at the base of the piedmont.

Fording a stream on a motorcycle can be tricky. Though this one was
only two feet deep, the water flowed rapidly across the road and then
dropped over a precipice — not a very far drop, but enough to destroy a
motorcycle and do grave harm to its driver. If you went straight through
without stopping you would be fine. The problem was that the water was
so muddy that you couldn't see the bottom; a loose rock or log, unseen,
could throw a bike, or at least force it to stop. And if you got stuck mid-
stream, you would be in trouble — the current was strong enough to
knock you off balance as you tried to restart a stalled engine; and if the
engine flooded, there would be no restarting it.

I had forded the stream once several months earlier and had decided
then never to do it again, opting instead to take one of the bridges above
Coatepeque (usually the one the Endlers had crossed with the "first car"
in the 1920s). Today, though, the downhill route would lead me right into
the heart of the advancing storm. Going uphill, there was a chance I
would escape it.

Uphill it was then. When I reached town, I turned north, riding into
La Independencia, past the military station, through several more plantations, and then began the climb up the mountainside. The image of the
stream came back, menacing, and I wondered for a moment if I had
made the wrong decision, but there was no time to think about that now.
The road deteriorated after leaving the plantations and navigating it demanded my full attention.

It was an exhilarating ride, dodging loose rocks, weaving in and out of
the troughs carved by past rains. It was a bit like downhill skiing — the
speed, the danger, the intense physical exertion necessary to stay balanced. Eyes focus on the road ten to twenty feet ahead; body manages
what's immediately underneath; mind makes the split-second calcula-
tions of how to get into the troughs when it's necessary, and how to get
out while it's still possible. Disaster is often a blink away. Only here there
was no snow to cushion a fall.

Propelling me up the mountainside was a 175-horsepower engine. It
was a capricious little machine, sensitive to small changes in altitude and
climate; but it was built for speed and, when handled just right, speed it
delivered. Handling it involved another whole set of movements — shift-

ing gears, applying brakes, and finely tuning an explosive throttle. The changes had to be quick and precise, and required that the hands and feet performing them stayed nimble and calm, even as the arms and legs were struggling violently to keep the motorcycle balanced. It had taken me a long time to be able to coordinate the two types of movement; now I felt like a virtuoso, and I tackled tough roads with the joy of a musician improvising a difficult chord progression.

Adding to the thrill of the ride was the immense beauty of the world I was traversing. After several miles of coffee groves, the road swung out to the edge of a massive canyon. The mountain climbed sharply to my left — alternating between steep green pastures, bursting with yellow and violet flowers, and sheer cliff-face with an occasional waterfall. To my right the ground dropped into oblivion, only to rise as dramatically a quarter of a mile away. A nice spot for a hike, I thought. But I knew full well that no nature walk could give me the same rush I got charging through on my bike, reducing the continent's roughest terrain to a joy ride. It was a feeling Friedrich Endler would surely have appreciated. Just the man and his machine against the mountain. It was the thrill of . . . well . . . conquest.

Adding further to the excitement was the competition — the storm that was racing up the coast behind me. I didn't turn to look at it, but I knew it was there, gaining ground. Faster, faster, I pushed my speed, hoping to escape it yet.

And there was something more — the reason for the smile that flickered occasionally below my helmet — I felt as though I were fleeing with a treasure, a priceless bit of buried history, salvaged from that little hamlet hidden in the ravine below La Patria.

⇊

I was a third of the way up the mountainside when the storm clouds overtook me. I felt the first heavy drops of water and then, as if a floodgate had suddenly opened above, the downpour began. The road changed color, the grayish brown turning quickly into a dark red that spelled danger, a wet surface as slippery as melting ice. I had no choice but to slow down — and, despite the precaution, in less than a minute the wheels of the bike shot out from under me and I crashed to the ground.

Picking myself out of a puddle, I hobbled over to the motorcycle, which lay on its side, the engine snarling, the spinning back wheel spewing mud. If the tire caught solid ground, the bike would begin thrashing about violently, like an animal in agony. I approached it carefully and then darted in to cut the engine. Then I looked myself over. My clothes were covered with mud. My waterproof boots and jacket were soaked through. My jeans were ripped at the left knee, and I felt a throb of pain below. I couldn't tell if the dark spot by the rip was earth or blood. And this far away from any medical help, I wasn't sure I wanted to find out. I bent my knee a few times and then tried putting weight on it. Felt all right. Then I glanced through the rip: yes, there was blood, but it didn't seem like enough to worry over.

It took me two tries to right the bike. I mounted it, started the engine, and continued the journey. My nerves were a bit shaken; my reflexes off. So I went even more slowly than before, alternating between first and second gears. The downpour continued relentlessly. Streamlets of muddy water formed in the middle of the road. The cold began to gnaw at my fingers. My knee throbbed.

Again the bike slid out from under me. This time I managed to remain standing. I righted the bike, mounted it, and sat still a moment to catch my breath. The canyon to my right had filled with clouds. They seemed to cling more closely to the mountain across the way. There were peaks and rocky protrusions visible through the whiteness, like shoals in the cloudy sea, some above me, others below, creating a multilayered image like something I'd seen in Chinese landscape painting. I was vaguely aware of the beauty of the scene, but the pain from my knee left no room for aesthetic pleasure. The thrill I had felt twenty minutes ago had been washed away by the downpour. Nothing mattered now but the road ahead.

I continued the climb. I could feel the engine heating up between my legs and soon my wet jeans began to steam. Making a motorcycle race this long in first and second gears was like making a man run upstairs on his knees. But I couldn't go fast enough to shift into third. And I couldn't stop now. Occasionally, I passed a house built on the side of the road. I could ask for shelter. But it wasn't a good idea to drop in on strangers around here. And waiting out the storm would probably require spending the night.

The rivulets in the road were running wider and deeper. It dawned on me now that the stream above would also have swelled, making it all the more difficult to cross. What could I do? There was no turning back now. *Just have to cross that bridge when I come to it.* The cliché struck my weary mind as funny, and I laughed aloud. *Cross that bridge!* The mountain didn't laugh with me. It just loomed large — much larger now than before the storm. I was no longer confident my machine was up to the task of climbing it. I didn't dwell on the odds, though, but plowed ahead, chanting, mindlessly, at the top of my lungs: *Cross that bridge! Cross that bridge!* My lonely voice was swallowed by the thunderous downpour.

When I reached the stream, I found what I had feared: the water was running faster and deeper than the last time. But the same rain and cold and pain that had sapped the joy of the ride seemed to have done in my fear as well. I didn't have the energy to be scared. My single option was to go forward. I paused only long enough to see if the current would give any clues as to what lay underneath. It didn't. I plowed into the water.

A moment later, I was up the other side.

I didn't feel relieved. I didn't feel anything. Just cold. And I still had a long way to go. And the storm would only get worse. The motorcycle managed to make it over the shoulder of the mountain, but as I began the descent into the San Marcos Valley and I was finally able to shift into third, I noticed a new, ominous clicking sound, coming from the engine. Eventually I reached the highway and began the journey east toward Xela. Even the paved road had succumbed to the storm: at one point the rain gave way to hail, which pelted my shoulders and thighs and covered the asphalt with ice; at another place, the fields on either side had flooded and were running over the road, hiding the pavement below a brown river.

It was dark when I arrived in Xela. My teeth were chattering. So was the engine. I left the bike steaming in the street and climbed the stairs to my third-floor apartment. With each step, I felt the pain in my bruised knee. My whole body ached. Once inside, I peeled off my waterlogged clothes, took a hot shower, scrubbed the dirt from my cut knee and put myself to bed.

When I awoke the next day, I listened to the radio news and learned the extent of the storm's damage. The stream running through La Patria had swelled into a river that triggered a mudslide that washed away twenty-four homes in Las Cruces. Three people had been buried alive. Farther down the piedmont, where these streams joined into a river, the water had swelled so high it had swamped the bridge I would have taken to Coatepeque, carrying with it a bus full of workers and merchants. Miraculously, all the passengers were rescued but two. The bodies of these had not yet turned up.

I wouldn't make it back to La Igualdad that year. When I brought my bike to a mechanic to check the chattering noise, I found that the overheated piston had worn out its socket during the ride. Now it was loose, and a loose piston could only get looser, until the engine seized up (which, if it happened at high speed, would send me flying). Replacing the piston and chassis would require tracking down parts, which could take several weeks.

I called the bakery in La Igualdad and found out that the roads there had been so damaged by the storm that the buses were not passing and probably wouldn't be for some time to come. So there was no chance now of rescheduling the trip with Hugo Guillén. And in any case, he seemed to have disappeared. I couldn't seem track him down by phone at home or at work.

I could have waited a few weeks. But I decided not to. My fellowship money was gone, and my credit card debt was getting out of control. More than anything, I was exhausted. I had probably been exhausted before the storm. I had just not let myself know it, determined as I had been to unearth the history of the agrarian reform. The fear I had encountered had reinforced my resolve, but it had also worn me down. The storm had pushed me over the edge. It was time to head home.

Before leaving, I met with César and told him that it looked like he was right: something big had happened in La Patria during the Arbenz years. I told him that, even though I had only just begun to unearth the buried history of that time, I was too worn out right now to dig anymore.

"You'll just have to come back," he said.

"Yeah, I'll just have to come back," I agreed, though at that moment, I wasn't so sure I would.

THE LAW THAT WOULD
CHANGE THE WORLD

I

I WAS STANDING on a broad avenue near the Guatemala City
airport. There were no cars in sight, no pedestrians, not even a sidewalk
— just walls and hedges hiding unnamed, unnumbered buildings from
the street. Fifteen minutes of knocking on doors and ringing bells had
narrowed the possibilities down to this: an open gate leading into a parking lot surrounded by what looked like warehouses. Yellow weeds pushed
through cracks in the pavement. An old school bus sat rusting on bare
axles.

It was the summer of 1995 and, after five months in the United States,
I was back in Guatemala. Back to write a magazine piece on the upcoming presidential elections — not to continue with my research in the coffee plantations. After a sobering tally of my findings of the last year (so little to show for so much effort), I had just about convinced myself to give
up that project.

Just about. The curiosity-turned-obsession wouldn't die so easily, and
within a week of my return, it had gotten the better of me. I borrowed
La Poderosa from César (he had bought it from me and fixed the motor)
and traveled to La Igualdad with the idea of continuing the interview
with Pedro Díaz and getting suggestions from him of people who might
corroborate his story. But it turned out he had passed away several
weeks earlier. And since I had no other leads, and was determined not to
harass any more strangers, I returned to the capital to continue work
on the article.

Then an e-mail message arrived from a Canadian historian who had recently published a history of the Arbenz years, using a national archive to examine how the Arbenz government had implemented the agrarian reform. He was responding to a query I had sent him months earlier. No, he had never come across documents dealing with plantations in La Igualdad. Yes, he knew where I might find some. His tip — and a week of dealing with a bureaucracy no worse than the worst of them — had brought me to this street with a letter from the president of the National Institute for Agrarian Transformation, granting permission to look at the government archives from the Agrarian Reform years.

I stepped through the gate. A security guard lounging in a shaded doorway righted himself and stepped reluctantly into the sunlight. "*Sí, señor*," he said after studying the letter, "this is the place you're looking for." I followed him past the abandoned bus and into one of the buildings, into a room where two workers sat at desks cluttered with old documents. Seeing me, their eyes lit up with recognition — they recognized an excuse to take a break from the tedium piled before them. They gave me a tour of the archive, past rows upon rows — floor to ceiling — of old inventory books coated with a dusty film that had probably settled in the decade before I was born. I was only the third researcher to visit the archive, my guides told me, *ever*.

The tour ended with what I was after. "All the paperwork from the Agrarian Reform," one of them announced as we stopped in front of a wall of ten-foot-high filing cabinets. My eyes scanned the drawers until I found the two labeled "San Marcos" on the top row. "Perhaps I'll begin up there," I told the archivists. They brought me a ladder and returned to their desks.

By now I was used to disappointments, and as I climbed upward, I mumbled the refrain I'd heard so often in La Igualdad, *nothing ever happened, nothing ever happened* . . . Balancing on the top step, I pulled at the drawer handle. It didn't budge. I tugged gently, then not so gently, and then gave it a violent yank. The drawer came unstuck and with a loud sigh rolled open, revealing a dense mass of paper crammed so tightly that I had to pry the files apart to see their labels. Each had the name of a plantation and, beginning at the front, I worked my way into the drawer. Almost two feet in, I came to El Progreso, then passed several other plantations from La Igualdad, and finally, toward the back, I came upon the file labeled La Patria. I pulled it out.

The folder was an inch thick. The first pages were mimeographed memos, office communiqués that told me nothing. Skipping these, I came to a letter. It was dated Plantation La Patria, December 25, 1952, addressed to the president of the Local Agrarian Committee of La Igualdad, and signed by four men on behalf of the Agrarian Committee of La Patria. I skimmed past the formalities and came to a line that said: "We are certain that the plantation . . . will prove to be subject to the Law of Agrarian Reform and for this reason we denounce it."

This is it. I reread to be sure. *Yes, this is it. Written proof that something happened.* And the next letter was proof it had been something big: two pages, typed single-space, addressed to Jacobo Arbenz Guzmán, president of the Republic. I climbed down the ladder, sat on the bottom step, and read.

Plantation La Patria
1 January, 1953

Señor Presidente:

The undersigned, who endorse the present petition, every one Guatemalans, Unionized Workers of this plantation, adults, fit and in full enjoyment of our civil rights to act in conformity with Article 30 of the Constitution of the Republic, before you, with expressions of our highest respect, hereby bring to your attention . . . the deceitful acts being carried out by the Owners of this Plantation, Señor Franz Endler and Señora Laurie B. de Endler, the first a Guatemalan citizen in conformity with the Inciso 2 of Article 5 of the Constitution of the Republic, and the second a foreigner of American Citizenship. . . . Mocking the Decree 900 Law of Agrarian Reform . . . they have undertaken to parcel up the plantation, as soon as the coffee harvest finishes, which will be at the end of the present month, or the beginning of February. [W]hat offends us most *Señor Presidente* is that after so many years of work, expending our youth, exploiting us, and taking up to the last drop of sweat on our forehead, they don't give us, the peasant workers, this gift . . . but rather [are giving it] to anticommunist reactionaries, who are . . . openly opposed to our Constituent Government. . . .

Señor Presidente, we workers, genuinely poor, request that this case be studied [and that] the parcels be adjudicated to us, the needy, in order to work the land, respecting of course the discretion of the highest Agrarian Tribunals, in view [of the fact] that said proprietors do not have a right to [engage in] these tricks, much less that they come to suspend our work, because they are not complying with the intent of clause "b" of Art. 85 of the Labor Code. . . .

Sr. Endler, during the second world war was named in the black list as a German, and this plantation was expropriated by order of the Supreme Government for a short period of time, and if it were not for the Agrarian Law, he would not think of giving even one inch of land, siding with the enemies of the Government and the impoverished working class.

The bottom of the second page was filled with signatures. And when I turned it over I found the back covered with them — mostly thumbprints with a name written underneath identifying the illiterate signatories. Here were Armando Tojil and Julia López, and just about all the former workers of La Patria I had interviewed the year before, 107 signatures in all. Seventy-nine of them were thumbprints.

II

Before reaching President Arbenz, the workers' petition would have to pass through a series of committees that Decree 900 had set up to administer the reform. The first was the "Local Agrarian Committee" of La Igualdad.

A few pages further into the file, I came across a report drawn up by the committee president, Francisco Morales, in which he recounted visiting La Patria's administrator, Erich Becker, who had told him that the plantation had already divided up all its uncultivated lands and intended to give them away to "'whomever solicits it with the exception of the workers of La Patria.'" By saying this, Becker was confirming the charge the workers had made in their petition — that the plantation was trying to get around Decree 900 by deeding its uncultivated lands to nonworkers.

Under Decree 900, the government could only expropriate "uncultivated" lands — defined as lands not farmed directly by the owners. In other words, workers could not expect the government to expropriate the plantation's coffee groves, but they could ask to be granted ownership over the lands they used for their own subsistence crops. There was an exception, though: owners who attempted to "subvert the law" could be punished by having their entire plantations expropriated, which was precisely what La Patria's workers were asking President Arbenz to do in their letter.

But when Morales met with Becker again, this time with the rest of the agrarian committee present, Becker changed his story, insisting now that there were no uncultivated lands in the plantation, period. When asked for proof, he produced survey figures that (Morales pointed out) were different from what the plantation had reported to the government two years earlier.

The committee concluded that, given the disparity between the two sets of figures, a new survey of the plantation would be needed.

⬇

Four decades later, Francisco Morales did not remember that meeting, nor any of the people who were present, nor even whether La Patria was affected by the agrarian reform or not. At least he said he didn't.

I had tracked him down in a Guatemala City neighborhood similar to the one where I had found Rodulfo Chavez. Unlike the would-be historian, Morales was willing to recall the history of the Agrarian Reform — though he said he couldn't remember the names of the people or specific plantations involved. "It was a good law," he insisted repeatedly. "Implemented right, it would have saved this country. In La Igualdad, we did it right."

Morales had arrived in La Igualdad in 1950, a young man with a degree in agronomy and several years of work experience, first on a German-owned plantation and then on a national plantation elsewhere in San Marcos. Those jobs had introduced him to a world governed by cruelty and corruption: the living and working conditions of the workers were cruel, he recalled, and the managers and the union leaders regularly colluded to rob the plantations at the expense of the workers.

Morales had found that the government managers in La Igualdad were as corrupt as those he had known before. But the unions were cleaner — a fact he attributed to the secretary general of the labor confederation in the area. "Adrián Bautista," he said (remembering a name, after all), "now, that man was a true leader."

Morales got along well with the unionized workers in his new plantation. So well that when the agrarian reform began in 1952, La Igualdad's labor leaders nominated him to serve as president of the Local Agrarian Committee. This job entailed meeting with the committee members regularly to identify potential leaders in the plantations and to explain the expropriation process to them. Morales also attempted to discuss the reform with the landowners and administrators, hoping to convince them that it was good for the country. The only one who was willing to hear him out, he recalls, was the owner of the plantation La Asunción, who had become a personal friend since he had begun working in La Igualdad. This owner was a devout Catholic who treated his workers better than his neighbors did. But he was also a passionate anticommunist (head of the local anticommunist committee, in fact) and wouldn't be budged from his conviction that the labor movement was a menace to the country. The other landowners and administrators simply refused to talk to Morales because they were convinced he was a communist.

Had he been a communist? "No! Never!" Morales insisted. "They thought I was because they saw the revolutionary leaders come visit me all the time. And, well, it's true that many of them in the capital were communists. But I didn't get involved in that stuff."

What he had involved himself in actively was the cooperative that the workers set up in the plantation where he had been administrator. "We produced more than ever before, and this time the profit from the harvest was divided among the workers. These people had never seen so much money."

They would not see a second harvest, however. The berries were still green when Arbenz was toppled, and Morales was carted off to jail in San Marcos. "When I got out of jail, I stayed away from La Igualdad. I never went back, not even to collect my things. And I never got involved in politics again. If I had stayed involved in politics, I wouldn't be here today. But I tell you, politics aside, those cooperatives *worked.* If they had been allowed to continue, this country would be producing a hundred times more than it is now, and our people wouldn't be so poor."

III

The petition next went to the "Departmental Agrarian Committee" in San Marcos. The committee president summoned Franz Endler to San Marcos so that he could defend his lands. Endler told the committee that he had no problem with allowing his workers to farm the lands that they had "utilized for their crops for a long time," provided that they did so "in the customary form, that is within the limits that have been recognized up to this date." But he insisted that "there is no way there is land available" for expropriation. And he "emphatically" denied the charge that he had tried to give away part of the land to nonworkers.

After reviewing the case further, the departmental committee ruled that Endler had not proven that his plantation was exempt from expropriation. But neither had the workers proven that the owners had tried to get around the reform by giving land away to people outside the plantation. Therefore, the lands already being cultivated by the workers — and only these — could be expropriated.

⇊

José Maldonado had been one of the agrarian inspectors who worked with the San Marcos committee. Maldonado was now a man in his seventies with a humorless face, grayish white eyebrows, and dubiously dark hair. The walls in his Guatemala City home displayed photos from his years as a government functionary under a military regime in the late 1970s. Once he gleaned where my interests lay, another collection of photos came out of a drawer, and the self-important air of the successful career bureaucrat gave way to the subterranean passion of the long-repressed revolutionary. These other photos were from the Arbenz years. They showed gatherings of the Revolutionary Party. There he was with the general secretary and other national figures at a meeting. There was the delegation from San Marcos, where he had been secretary of organizing. "The PAR was so well organized in San Marcos!" he told me. "We had so much support that we won all the elections — all five spots in Congress and all twenty-nine mayors in the department were ours!"

Like Morales, Maldonado remembered Decree 900 as the law that could have made the revolution but ultimately helped break it. It was a good law, if applied right — and he had worked for two years trying to make sure it was. "My job was to resolve confusions and prevent land invasions. Sometimes I would show up in a plantation and find that the workers had dug up the *patrón*'s crop or pastures to make it look like the lands were uncultivated. Of course they couldn't fool anyone who knew anything about agriculture. The problem was that some of the inspectors collaborated with them. 'Take it,' they would say, 'and we'll legalize it later.'

"In San Marcos? Yes, there were invasions. In La Igualdad? Possibly, though I remember La Igualdad was one of the places where the leadership was good. The main leader there was a *señor* named Bautista, an honorable man, a responsible leader, who wouldn't stand for invasions.

"The invasions helped bring down Arbenz. The rich people already hated him, but this was their excuse to conspire with the CIA to bring down the government. Today we're all suffering the consequences of the so-called Liberation. We had a chance to improve this country. Instead we're stuck living with poverty and violence and crime so much worse than we ever imagined."

IV

The petition had gone next to the National Agrarian Department in Guatemala City. There it joined the backlog of hundreds of petitions from around the country, waiting to be processed. It took a full year, but a ruling finally came: those lands in La Patria that were already cultivated by the workers could be expropriated.

José Manuel Fortuny was an irascible old man with sharp eyes and a sharper tongue. A chain smoker in his seventies, he coughed and fumed and looked back at history with bitterness. How could he not be bitter? As a young man, he had masterminded the transformation of his homeland, only to spend the next four decades in exile, watching it plunge into the abyss of civil war. Fortuny had been the founder of the communist Guatemalan Labor Party (known as the PGT, for Partido Guatemalteco de Trabajo), the principal adviser of President Arbenz, and the chief architect of the Law of Agrarian Reform. His wife, María Jerez de Fortuny, had been secretary of the National Agrarian Department and signed the department papers in the file on La Patria.

In their Mexico City apartment, she served me coffee and cookies as he vented about the arrogance and stupidity of the U.S. officials ("your government," he kept saying) who had orchestrated the 1954 coup. "It was a bourgeois law, do you understand? A bourgeois law!" he said of Decree 900, explaining that both its aims and its methods had ultimately reinforced the principle of private property.

When he paused to catch his breath and light another cigarette, she spoke up, sounding more wistful than bitter as she remembered the great hope and frustration that had accompanied the Agrarian Reform. "What we lacked was time," she said, recalling the many meetings where Arbenz had implored the Agrarian Department staff to hurry with the case documents so he could authorize expropriations. "But at the same time, he always insisted that everything we do be completely legal. The basic criterion of our work was that we not damage private property."

When complaints arrived about land invasions, Arbenz had intervened directly. She recalled one time he had upbraided the head of a national labor confederation for telling workers to occupy lands before they were officially expropriated. "We could hear Jacobo shouting from the next room: 'You irresponsible fool!' The man defended himself: 'It's just that you all work so slowly and our people need to start farming to have a crop this year . . .' 'I don't care! You have to do things right! We're doing everything we can to make it go more quickly.'"

She shook her head sadly.

"The problem was that we couldn't process the petitions more quickly if we were going to make sure the plantations weren't expropriated unfairly. So in the end, we respected private property, but the reform took too long to carry out. Maybe if there had been fewer legal restrictions, it would have worked."

⁂

Why would a revolutionary government put legal restrictions on its revolution?

One reason was that this "bourgeois" reform aimed not only to help plantation workers, but also to modernize the country's entire economy. The reformers' reasoning had gone something like this: industrialization required domestic markets for industrial goods; domestic markets required a population with money to spend; for the rural population to have spending money, they would have to earn more than subsistence-level wages; and plantation workers would never receive higher wages as long as they were dependent on specific plantations. The reformers, in short, aimed to develop a capitalist economy. And they understood that secure property would be key to its success.

Another reason was the political aims of the reformers themselves. The PGT was still very small and unable to win a national election. Its decisive influence within the Arbenz government was largely due to Fortuny's close relationship with Arbenz. Yet Arbenz's term would end in 1956, and the party did not expect to retain its influence in the next administration. They would have to find another way to secure their political future.

The agrarian reform was their way. More than a redistribution of land, it was a redistribution of power. Plantation workers would, in many cases, own no more than what they had always used. But their lives would change in a basic way. The threat of dispossession would be gone. They would be able to engage in union activism and party politics, and still have a home at the end of the day and a crop at the end of the year.

Had the agrarian reform done only this, it would have alienated the plantation elite. But it went further. In order to obtain land, workers had to take the initiative. They had to submit a petition to the government. And to submit a petition, they had to form an agrarian committee and elect their peers to lead it. In this way the reform would not only make it possible for workers to act independently of the plantation, it would engage them right away as independent actors. It would mobilize them as a political force that would be capable of dominating elections for years to come.

And that is precisely what worried the U.S. government — not the reform's impact on the economy, but its impact on national politics. American aid officials considered it "constructive and democratic in its aims." And in fact, the CIA was actually encouraging other countries to implement similar reforms at the time. But in Guatemala, U.S. officials feared that the reform's success would benefit the communists who had designed it. The State Department reported to the National Security Council that the communists were using land reform to gain control of the country. "Communist strength grows, while opposition forces are disintegrating. . . . Ultimate Communist control of the country and elimination of American economic interests is the logical outcome, and unless the trend is reversed, is merely a question of time." The agrarian reform, therefore, had to be stopped.

The petition from La Patria's workers reached Jacobo Arbenz on February 18, 1954, and the president signed an order to expropriate. What I couldn't figure out from the file, however, was whether the workers had ever gotten a chance to claim their land before the invasion began.

BETRAYAL

I

OF COURSE CÉSAR felt vindicated. The file proved him right: the agrarian reform *had* reached La Patria. But César's interest in my investigation went beyond merely proving himself right. I reported back to him regularly on my interviews with plantation owners and people like General Gramajo and José Manuel Fortuny who had been central figures in his country's history. He had never heard these people talk in the way they talked to me, and he listened to the stories they told with such rapt attention that I began to think that he had something else at stake besides his political views — something more personal.

César was particularly intrigued by the stories of the German administrator, Erich Becker. He sat in my apartment one afternoon and listened to the whole interview on tape. When he heard Becker's explanation of Guatemala's racial stratification — of how the thriftiness of Europeans had allowed them to rise above the locals — he let out a bitter laugh. Later, though, he told me that he had heard that same account from people in his own family. He remembered his own grandmother telling him about the virtues of the German race. He also remembered how she, like other people in the plantation, looked down on the Indians from the highlands. Just recently, there had been a big scandal in the plantation when a young woman wanted to marry a man whom her family considered to be "too Indian."

César was neither European nor Indian. He was "Ladino." That meant, as the 1894 census had put it, he was the product of a "mixture of the European and Indians." The term was more than a racial category, however. During the early years of Spanish rule in the region, it had been used to describe Indians who learned enough Latin to participate in the Catholic mass. Over the years, it had come to refer to Indians who learned enough Spanish to interact with the Spaniards on Spanish terms. And it had evolved the corollary meanings that appear in standard Spanish dictionaries today: "smart," "astute." Other meanings you'll find there include "cunning," "wily," "smooth-tongued," "smarmy." Like many educated Guatemalans, César had heard that Ladino derived from the word *ladrón,* which means "thief." While this popular etymology may be incorrect, it was nonetheless revealing.

In Guatemala's racially stratified society, Ladinos had generally occupied the positions of political authority and, from there, mediated the relationship between the European elite and the Indian peasantry. During the Arbenz regime, for instance, the government officials who implemented the agrarian reform had been, for the most part, Ladino. During the war, the generals and the guerrilla commanders had been, for the most part, Ladino. But despite whatever political power these individuals acquired, they could never obtain full acceptance within the elite world of the European descendants — nor, for that matter, within the world of the Indian communities. Their place would be, forever, somewhere in between.

Perhaps that explains César's reaction to Erich Becker. What most intrigued him about Becker's account was the figure of Rafael Zamora. The brown baby. The brother-employee. The administrator-driver. The man who had occupied that "somewhere in between," at once intimate with, and distrusted by, both the *patrón* and the workers — at least as Becker told the story.

⩗

It was 1996, and my own curiosity about Ochaeta was one reason I was back in La Igualdad, asking again about the Agrarian Reform. The other was that I wanted to know if the workers in La Patria had ever gotten their land.

I was confident I would be able to collect more information than I had the previous year. I now had documents and the documents had names.

From these I had put together a list of people to interview. I would no longer be groping around in the dark.

But more important, the war seemed to be coming to an end at long last. The government and the guerrillas were in the final round of peace talks. A cease-fire had been in place for six months. Less violence should mean less fear. And from what I could see walking around La Igualdad, there seemed to be less of both now. There was still a military camp in La Independencia, but the soldiers were not the scowling sort I was used to seeing. Those others had looked like armed men despite their boyish faces; these ones looked like boys, despite their guns. They came to town to enjoy themselves — to play soccer, to call home, to flirt with school-girls.

People in town remembered me — how could they forget the big gringo on the motorcycle? — and they weren't afraid to show it with bright smiles and loud greetings: "Don Daniel! I thought you'd never come back." "It's the *robagatos!*" "And *La Poderosa?*" The climate of fear seemed to have gone. Though, of course, you could never be sure.

Mario, the revolution-talking ex-military health worker, hadn't changed a bit — other than that he was now a leftist officially. When I ran into him, he greeted me excitedly and told me he was heading the local branch of a new leftist political party. He insisted I drop by his house so he could tell me about the party's activities in the municipality.

He wasn't home when I did, but a teenage daughter said he would be back and invited me to wait inside. There was another man already there waiting, sitting on one end of a sofa, holding his sombrero between his knees. I nodded to him and took a seat at the other end.

"What brings you to La Igualdad?"

The voice was friendly. I glanced over. The man sat stiffly upright, not leaning back into the cushions, as if he would rather not make himself too comfortable. I said, "I'm trying to find out what happened in the planta-tions during the Arbenz years. And you?"

"I came to see if I could help with the new party in some way," he said.

We sat in silence for another minute. Then he spoke up again: "You want to know why the revolution happened? I'll tell you." He didn't say it the way Mario would have, throwing out dangerous words like a kid showing off with firecrackers. His tone was more . . . well, I wasn't sure what it was, so I glanced at him again, looking for a clue. What I saw were tired eyes on a tired face, a gray mustache and thinning gray hair, a solid frame and strong hands, which were fiddling with the brim of an old but clean sombrero. His manner suggested shyness — yet he was the one taking the initiative here. There was no edge in his voice as he talked, which was why I didn't immediately notice the edge in his words.

"In the time of Ubico, when the *patrones* celebrated the annual festival, they had it in the hall in the center of town . . ."

Yes, I thought, *Sara told me about those parties.*

"They would send a group of workers to San Marcos to carry the marimba. You know how much a marimba weighs?"

I nodded. Marimbas are giant wooden xylophones that must weigh several hundred pounds.

"And since the road to San Marcos was so bad then, they would have to carry it walking. All the way from San Marcos to La Igualdad. When the marimba arrived, the plantation owners would have their party in the municipal salon. The only people who were invited were the owners and their staff. They would have their guards surround the building so no one could enter — so no one could even look in the window."

"No workers ever came to those parties," Sara had told me. *"We weren't supposed to consort with them. . . ."*

"That is why there was a revolution."

My notebook came out and the questions began. Name: Gabino Romero. Grew up in plantation El Recuerdo, which lay at the lower edge of La Patria. Came of working age during the Arbenz years. His older brother had been one of the union leaders in the plantation.

"Most Germans were good people," he told me. "As long as a man didn't talk back, they treated him well. They saw the workers as their family. They gave them presents. For instance, if there was a festival or celebration, the *patrón* would give a worker a cup of whiskey or some quetzals to buy drinks. 'Here, take these and go have some fun.' But when the political parties and unions came along, they began to get tough with the workers. They no longer trusted them. They wouldn't give the workers a penny."

"Did you know the owners of La Patria, the Endlers?"

"Not really."

"How about Erich Becker, the administrator?"

"Oh yeah. Don Erich treated workers in a very severe way."

"What about Rafael Zamora, the half-brother of Endler?"

"Rafael was a good man. He was on the side of the working class."

"I once interviewed Erich, and he told me that Rafael had gotten into trouble because he had been taking advantage of the women on the plantation. Is that true?"

"That's a lie!" He shook his head vehemently, as if he were personally offended by the accusation. "Rafael was a very decent man, an upright man."

I jotted down his words and then asked him how the Revolutionary Party came to dominate local politics. "It's like I told you," he said. "It was the attitude of the owners, the way they never reached into their conscience. That's why the Revolutionary Party won the elections. Its leaders were very popular."

"And the unions?"

"The unions were formed by the leaders of the party. Pamphlets of the constitution arrived with instructions for the workers. 'Be punctual. Behave well. Communicate with the *patrón*.' And I remember they said: 'The Labor Code is like an orange to be shared — one half for the worker, one half for the *patrón*. You shouldn't abuse it, or take more than what's yours.' Some people tried to, and that was a problem. That's what caused it all to fail. And another problem was that the leaders of the unions weren't educated. They didn't know how to talk. And most didn't know how to read. I think that's why the whole thing was lost in the end."

"What about the leaders in La Patria — were they educated?"

"They knew how to read more or less."

"Enough to write petitions to the government?"

"Well, that's where Rafael helped them out."

Gabino's tone — I had figured out — was that of someone who had nothing to lose, not much to gain, just something to say. He seemed like a straight talker — just the sort who might help me. I pulled out the list of names I had taken from the file in the archive and asked if he could help me track them down. He looked over the list. About half of the people had died, he told me, and many of the others weren't likely to talk, because they were scared.

"But hasn't the violence stopped?" I asked.

"Right now things are quieter, but you never know when it will start again."

"So are there any people who would want to tell me what happened here during the agrarian reform?"

"Of course."

He agreed to help me track them down. And I left without seeing Mario.

II

Chepe Santos had served with Gabino's brother as one of the leaders of the union in plantation El Recuerdo. He had also been a member of the Local Agrarian Committee and attended the meeting with Erich Becker that I had read about in the archive.

Gabino directed me to Santos's home two blocks down the slope from the town center. I entered the front room — an immaculate and well-stocked *tienda* — and was greeted by an energetic old man with a joker's grin — the sort of grin that told you that something was funny but *you* weren't going to find out what. And whatever it was, it didn't stop him from answering my questions — about how he had become a union leader and then a member of the Local Agrarian Committee. When I asked if he recalled the meeting that the committee held in La Patria, he nodded. "What happened was that Erich said, 'We'll give the land out all right, but not to these bastards here!'"

"What sort of person was Erich?" I asked.

"He was good, and he was bad. He was good because the plantation was always in good shape. It was the best plantation with the most work. He was bad because he was real tough with the workers."

"And what was Rafael Zamora like?"

"Rafael got along with the workers."

"But is it true that he took advantage of the women? I heard that's why he was demoted from administrator."

Santos burst out laughing. "That's a lie! No, they wanted to get rid of him because he was helping the workers. The truth is that he helped the union."

The joker grin had been flickering on and off throughout the interview, and when I told him I had no more questions, his eyes lit up as if this were the moment of the punch line. As I closed my notebook, he pulled out his wallet and showed me the photo he had in the sleeve where most people display their loved ones.

"You know who this is?" he asked. I did. It was General Efraín Ríos Montt, who had led the military regime that governed the country during the worst years of violence in the 1980s. "This is who I support now."

He removed the photo from the wallet and handed it to me. It was a card for the Guatemalan Republican Front, Ríos Montt's political party, whose candidate had been runner-up in the 1995 presidential election. As he handed it to me, I caught a glimpse of another card hidden in the wallet behind this one — a card for the PAN, the party that *had* won those elections.

"So why do you also have a PAN card?"

He laughed aloud, as if I had outwitted him. "That I keep just in case."

"Just in case what?"

He didn't answer.

⬇

Humberto Yoc, a former worker of La Patria, welcomed Gabino and me into his home with a friendly smile and asked, "You're the one who talked to Pedro Díaz, aren't you?"

"Yes, I did. How did you know?"

"*Pues*, that's what they told me."

He offered wooden stools to Gabino and me while he remained standing. In the corner behind him was a table with candles surrounding a framed portrait of the Virgin Mary.

"I was working on the road above Coatepeque, doing the road work, when Adrián Bautista came up the road and told us to stop working, that there had been a revolution. Bautista had pamphlets with him, and he read them to us: 'A good law is on the way — the law of liberty!'

"Bautista became secretary general of the first union in the region. And he helped us organize our union in La Patria. At first the people didn't want to join because they were scared. So we organized secretly. We held meetings in the woods, three or four times a week, where we read the pamphlets that came from the central. Adrián Bautista showed us which parts of the Labor Code we should read, and we discussed these.

"The first confrontation with the plantation took place over the *caja*."

(The *caja*, or "box," was the unit of measurement for berries collected during the harvest. Workers were paid per *caja* collected.) "We told the *patrón* that the *caja* was supposed to be one hundred pounds. 'We don't have any problem with you,' we told him. 'We have the Labor Code. Let's apply it here.' Don Franz said no, that it wasn't in the law. So we showed him the Labor Code. Still Don Franz said no. So then we told him, 'We're going to have to do a strike.' An hour later we were called to the plantation office. Don Franz told us, 'Listen boys, forget about all this. I was wrong. Let's keep working.' They adjusted the *caja* to one hundred pounds. But after that, the plantation stopped giving us things. For example, the plantation had a pasture and cows, and before it used to sell milk to the workers at a low price and give it free to the children who were sick. Don Franz got rid of that."

"Is it true all the workers were going to divide up the plantation?"

"Just the land that had no coffee. It was the land that Don Federico had given us, where we were allowed to plant our own crops — maize, yucca, and plantains. My family had twenty *cuerdas*." A *cuerda* was roughly a third of an acre. "Some others had thirty *cuerdas*. And some didn't have any."

"When you divided it up, how much were you going to get?"

"Each family would get ten *cuerdas*."

"So you were going to have less land than before?"

"Well, yes, but the difference is that it would be *our* land."

"So what happened?"

"After doing the petition, we waited. But nothing happened. And after a while we realized that Felipe Arreaga wasn't doing his job. And then Arreaga and his people switched parties — from the Revolutionary Party to the party of the *patrones*. That's when we realized that Don Franz had bought them off. So three of us — Pedro Díaz, Vicente Hernández, and I — went to the labor federation in the capital and got permission to form a new union."

"And then did you divide up the land?"

"Yes, we divided it up. But we never planted a crop because the political situation was getting hot. It wasn't clear how things were going to turn out. Then Arbenz fell, and Don Franz kicked us all out."

"And what about Rafael Zamora?"

"Don Franz got rid of him too."

"Why?"

"Because he was with us. Rafael helped us from the beginning. He came to the meetings. It was because of the union that they got rid of Rafael. They said he was getting into communism."

I asked Yoc to tell me more about Rafael's role in mobilizing the workers. But he didn't have much more to say. Rafael had helped them throughout, but he didn't seem to have been the mastermind that Erich Becker had made him out to be. In Yoc's account, there was no such mastermind. Instead, there was a series of people who had provided the workers with the guidance and encouragement they needed to change their world — Rafael in the plantation, Bautista and Morales in the town, the national leaders in the capital.

So perhaps Rafael had betrayed his half-family. But he hadn't acted alone. Rather, his betrayal had been part of a broader shift of allegiances on the part of the country's small, mostly Ladino middle class — a shift that, during those few years, had begun to reshape Guatemalan society.

There was only one person left on Gabino's list who was a veteran of La Patria. This was Vicente Hernández, one of the four men who had signed the original petition, and one of the three who had formed a new union after the other leaders had been "bought off." He lived in Coatepeque. He would be our last interview.

Gabino and I met in the morning and rode the bus down the piedmont. After two hours, we got off on a dusty avenue that dead-ended at the outskirts of town.

"Vicente's an old friend of my brother, and I think he'll talk," Gabino told me as we approached the house. "But to get things started, we can say we wanted to interview him because he was a soldier. He served in the militia back in the time of Ubico."

We knocked on the door. A boy opened it a crack and looked out at us. Gabino asked, "Is Vicente in?"

"Who's looking for him?" the boy asked back.

"Tell him it's the brother of Rodrigo Romero."

The boy disappeared from sight, leaving the door open just far enough to see a dead mouse on the cement floor, a horde of ants devouring its gut. Then the door yanked open, and a wiry man with unkempt white hair and intense eyes jutted his head out. "What do you want?"

"Buenas tardes!" Gabino greeted him warmly. *"Qué tal usted?"*

Hernández looked at him blankly. Gabino continued to smile and introduced himself as if it was just a matter of jogging the man's memory: "I'm Gabino Romero, you know, Rodrigo's brother."

Hernández showed no sign of recognition. He glanced down at the dead mouse and flicked it out of sight with his foot, then turned and yelled into the house for the boy to come remove it. He looked back out the door: "And him?" He pointed his chin in my direction but kept his eyes on Gabino.

"He's a historian from the United States, and he and I have been talking to people from around here about the old days." Gabino's smile dissolved under Hernández's hard stare. He fumbled with his words. "We thought, *pues*, we thought maybe you'd be a good person to interview because, *pues*, because you were a soldier . . ."

Hernández cut him short: "Right now I'm eating lunch. You have to wait until I'm finished." He shut the door.

We found a patch of shade on the sidewalk across the street and sat down. Gabino looked worried. "He should have recognized me. He definitely knows my brother." He explained that after being evicted from La Patria in 1954, Hernández had gone several years without being able to secure a job. None of the plantations would take him. He had been growing desperate when Gabino's older brother had helped him get a job in Coatepeque.

Only a few minutes had passed when Hernández opened the door. We crossed the street, and he let us in, motioning for us to sit in chairs right next to the entrance. On the walls were framed photographs of the family. Other than chairs and a stereo system on a bookcase, there was no furniture. It looked like the home of a poor man with children who were better off — his might be in Guatemala City, though judging by the size of the speakers, they were probably in Los Angeles.

"What do you want to know?"

Gabino cleared his throat. "He's looking for information about past times, about the time of Ubico and Arévalo and also Arbenz. And since you were a soldier, he thought you might remember how things were in the army."

Hernández looked very alert, his mind moving faster than Gabino's words, trying to figure where they were headed. Suddenly it clicked. He interrupted Gabino and looked directly at me for the first time.

"Look, *señor.*" His voice was low but intense. "It's not easy to talk about these things. You know that around here words are dangerous. Very dangerous."

"I understand," I tried to reassure him. "I've done many interviews, all over the country. And there have never been any problems. The interviews are confidential. I won't publish the names of people who tell me things."

I paused a moment, considering how to proceed. My gut told me to go straight to the matter. He had been blunt. I should be too. "I've spoken with a lot of people in La Igualdad about the era of Arbenz and the unions and the agrarian reform, and I was hoping you could tell me a little more about what happened during those years."

He spoke: "The leaders got us involved, and then they sold out. Now they're gone and we're screwed. I lost thirty-five years' worth of severance pay. I couldn't get work. I went to La Asunción, to La Serena." He named a few more plantations. "Everywhere I went they asked me where I was from. 'I come from La Patria,' I said. 'Why did they kick you out?' they asked. And then they wouldn't give me work. What else do you want to know?"

Gabino answered before I could. "He wants to know about how the unions worked. I've told him a bit about what my brother did with the union in El Recuerdo. And he's talked to Pedro Díaz, before he died, and Humberto Yoc and Armando Tojil . . ."

Don't mention names! I almost blurted out. But it was Hernández who interrupted him, standing up abruptly and saying, "Wait a minute. I'll be right back." He left the room. Gabino and I traded glances. I saw the dismay on Gabino's face and felt bad for having placed him in this situation. Soon Hernández was back with a notebook in his hand. I continued with my effort to explain my project. But Hernández did not seem to be listening. The moment I paused, he said, "What was your name again?" And as he wrote it, he added: "Just in case."

I didn't ask him "just in case what?" Instead, I asked if he could tell me a little about La Patria. He ignored the question and asked me where I was from. When he finished writing, he turned to Gabino. "And what is your name?"

Gabino looked stunned. But he didn't protest. He gave his full name. He didn't bother repeating who his brother was.

"Well, I believe that will be all." Hernández closed the notebook and opened the door wider for us to leave.

Back out in the sun we headed slowly up the street. I didn't know what to say. Gabino broke the silence: "He got scared." But it looked to me like Gabino was the one who was scared.

BURIALS

I

ON JUNE 18, 1954, after many months of preparation by the CIA, a rebel force led by the former army officer Carlos Castillo Armas began the invasion that would topple Arbenz and end a decade of democratic rule in Guatemala.

This "Liberation Army" was, by the CIA's own estimation, "extremely small and ill-trained" and "no match for the 5,000-strong Guatemalan Army." It would win only one small battle on its way to victory — taking a town just over the Honduran border. But it would not need to win any more. For it was really intended to serve "a psychological rather than a military function."

The CIA aimed to overthrow the Arbenz government through "psychological warfare" rather than military confrontation. The "psy-war" operation, known as PBSUCCESS, had several components. One was to isolate the Arbenz regime internationally by pressuring other Latin American countries to denounce its communist tendencies. Another was to convince the American public that U.S. national security was threatened by communist penetration in Guatemala — which was not a difficult task, according to the CIA internal history, given the "uncritical acceptance by the American press of the assumptions behind United States policy." In addition to getting the *New York Times* to keep its correspondent off the story, Ambassador John Peurifoy met with the remaining American reporters in Guatemala and got them to agree to "drop words such as 'invasion'" in their coverage of the coup.

And finally, most important, the operation entailed "using contacts within the press, radio, church, army, and other organized elements susceptible to rumor" to convince the Arbenz regime that their defeat was inevitable, and, as one CIA field officer put it, "create dissension, confusion, and FEAR in the enemy camp." These "psy-war" efforts focused largely on army officers, trying to impress upon them certain "facts of life," such as that "If they think that a people of 3,000,000 is going to win in a showdown with 160,000,000 they need psychiatric help," and that "if they are unhappy about being in the U.S. sphere of influence, they might be reminded that the U.S. is the most generous and tolerant taskmaster going, that cooperation with it is studded with material reward." Other forms of persuasion included denouncing these officers to their superiors with accusations ranging "from treason to tax evasion," as well as telephoning them, "preferably between 2 and 5 A.M.," with ominous warnings about their impending doom.

In case the "psy-war" tactics fell short, the Agency prepared a backup plan. It drew up a list of fifty-eight Guatemalan leaders to be assassinated and sent the list along with instructions to the camp in Honduras where Castillo Armas's troops were being trained. The instructions included a handwritten diagram showing "an effective technique . . . by which a room containing as many as a dozen subjects can be 'purified' in about 20 seconds" by two assassins using automatic weapons. It also included a nineteen-page "Handbook on Assassination" that explored the pros and cons of other killing techniques. "The simplest local tools" could often be "the most efficient means of assassination," it noted. "A hammer, axe, wrench, screw driver, fire poker, kitchen knife, lamp stand, or anything hard, heavy and handy will suffice." When using "edge weapons," it would be important to keep in mind that "puncture wounds of a body cavity may not be reliable unless the heart is reached." It also warned practitioners that "assassination can seldom be employed with a clear conscience," and therefore, "persons who are morally squeamish should not attempt it." And it stressed the importance of maintaining deniability by never leaving a paper trail.

As rumors of the pending invasion spread inside Guatemala, the PGT, the PAR, and the labor confederations attempted to form popular militias to defend the government. But their efforts were too little, too late. The army, thoroughly intimidated by the prospect of having to defend their country against the United States, pressured President Arbenz not to provide the militias with weapons, and abandoned him soon after the invasion began. Arbenz resigned and sought asylum in the Mexican embassy along with hundreds of other leaders from the October Revolution. It would be over a month before he was allowed to leave the country. Before boarding his plane, he was forced to strip to his underwear in front of a jeering crowd of Castillo Armas supporters. It was the last thing he would ever do in Guatemala. He would die in Mexico in 1971, at the age of fifty-eight, a broken figure still in exile.

Months before the coup, the U.S. ambassador to Guatemala, John Peurifoy, testified before a congressional committee that "Communism is directed by the Kremlin all over the world, and anyone who thinks differently doesn't know what he is talking about." Now, with Operation PBSUCCESS concluded successfully, a new operation was launched. It was named PBHISTORY and entailed gathering all the documents left behind by the deposed government and disbanded labor unions, with the hope that these "would conclusively prove the Communist nature of the Arbenz regime."

With the help of the Guatemalan army, the CIA was able to gather over 150,000 documents. But they were disappointed to find that most of the material had only "local significance." While they did dig up evidence of "pro-Communist" sentiment within the Arbenz regime (including the First Lady's copy of Stalin's biography), they "found no traces of Soviet control and substantial evidence that Guatemalan Communists acted alone, without support or guidance from outside the country."

II

"A defense committee was formed in La Igualdad," the elder Guillén in Guatemala City recalled. "Three hundred people volunteered and were ready to go — eager, determined, but unarmed. They were told they would be armed in the capital. But before they got there, the government fell.

"Three or four days after the fall, soldiers came to La Igualdad to arrest people. They had a long list of people who were communists — the mayor, the municipal officers, the union leaders. They took them to the San Marcos jail. They were going to shoot them, but a counter-order came to stop the executions. That was the end of unions in the plantations. Afterwards, no one dared try to unionize again."

"We were ready to fight," a former worker of El Progreso recalled. "We gathered in town, three hundred of us with machetes and clubs. We set out in trucks for San Marcos, but when we got there, they told us it was all over. So we returned to La Igualdad.

"Two days later they rounded us up, sixty or seventy prisoners. They put us in the back of a truck with armed soldiers at each corner. And they took us to San Marcos. They told us they were going to kill us all as soon as we got there.

"When we got there, the governor, who was an army captain, intervened. 'These are workers,' he said to the soldiers. 'These men aren't the guilty ones. The guilty ones, the ones responsible for there being unions in all the plantations, are Adrián Bautista and Francisco Morales. Those ones deserve to go to the penitentiary. But these poor men don't.'

"Then the governor told us, 'You will all go free today. And you'll go present yourselves before the *patrón*. And if he gives you work, you're going to behave yourself well. You're going to work well. You're not going to get involved in anything political. And if the *patrón* doesn't give you work, you have the right to lodging for thirty days. But after the thirty days are up, you're going to look for somewhere else to work. You will move out of the plantation.'

"'*Bueno,*' we told him. 'We understand.'"

⬇

"When the change to Castillo Armas happened," Erich Becker recalled, "from there on there would be no union. It stopped dead. Franz came to the plantation and said to Rafael: 'Out!' Because now he'd found out which side he was on. And he ordered me to throw out all the people. 'I don't want to see any of them here again, ever!'

"If I had paid attention, I would have had one big fight with the people there. So I said to him: 'Look, that's not democracy. That's not helping. That's just fomenting communism. The people were right, after all. All you do is screw them instead of helping. What should be done here is see that the people progress and have a future here on the plantation.'"

⬇

"Not long afterward," a former worker of La Independencia recalled, "people from the new government came and told us that there would no longer be a cooperative, there would no longer be any unions. And they made us return all the equipment and livestock of the plantation that had been divided up among the workers. Not only that, they made us give up all the things we'd bought with the money we'd earned in the cooperative — sewing machines, motorcycles, radios. 'These things belong to the *patrón*,' they said.

"A worker protested, 'This plantation is nationalized and expropriated legally. Here we don't have a *patrón*.' So one of the men pulled out a gun and pointed it at the worker's head: 'This is your *patrón*, you communist!'"

⬇

"Don Franz came to the plantation, and he said, 'You're all communists!'" recalled Humberto Yoc. "I said to him, 'I'm not communist. I'm pure Guatemalan.'

"He kicked us out of the plantation — all the union people, even the ones who had sold out. No one got severance pay. We all went to look for work. I showed up at various plantations. But they didn't want to give me work. In one plantation, the administrator came out with a rifle: 'You can go to hell!' Afterward, things returned to the way they had been before the revolution. If one worker stood up for another, they would kick him off the plantation.

"When they took us to jail, they took all our papers. A lot of people burned them before the police arrived. My father got scared, and he gave them over to the soldiers. The only thing I saved from back then was my identification card. I've kept it with me all these years."

He reached in his bag, removed a card, and handed it to me. His name was printed on it below the words "Union of Workers, Plantation La Patria."

III

The Castillo Armas regime dismantled a decade of reform in a matter of weeks. It outlawed most of the labor unions and the leftist political parties. It revoked the laws that allowed plantation workers to organize. And it gutted the Agrarian Reform.

Among the documents in the file I found in the Guatemala City archive, there was a petition from Franz Endler, dated October 1955, in which he requested that the new government nullify the 1954 expropriation, pointing out that there had been a "manifest injustice on the part of the agrarian authorities of that era."

In response to his petition, the San Marcos governor summoned the four workers who had signed the original 1952 petition in La Patria. One of the four was Vicente Hernández, the man I visited in Coatepeque on my last day with Gabino. Hernández signed a statement testifying "that if indeed it is true that he signed the petition, it was because the Secretary of the Plantation Union, Felipe Arreaga, obliged him to do so, . . . that they gave him a plot of ten *cuerdas*, that he received it but that he never farmed it, and that . . . he does not even recall that Plot, that it only caused him misfortune and that he does not think about it anymore, that he only busies himself now with his daily chores in the new Plantation where he is working."

An agrarian inspector then traveled to La Patria and reported back that "[a]t a simple glance it is possible to prove that by having decreed the applicability [of the Agrarian Reform law,] the *señores* of the previous regime only sought to foment disorder and so demonstrate to the peasants that they could do whatever they wanted to." A few weeks later, the general director of agrarian affairs in Guatemala City concluded that the workers in La Patria had been coerced into filing their petition, and that the prior government had broken the law when it ordered the expropriation. The expropriation was therefore nullified.

Another agrarian inspector traveled to La Patria and had the workers who remained there sign a document that said that "all the former parcel holders are working in the plantation as permanent workers, receiving all the benefits that the law prescribes and free land for their crops, and therefore at the present time there are no foreseeable agrarian problems."

IV

Many years after Rafael Zamora was expelled from La Patria, Sara Endler would see him working as a security guard at the Nicaraguan embassy. Later she learned that he had died of cirrhosis of the liver.

In 1987, the year she inherited the plantation, she received a visit from Rafael's daughter. "Rafael's daughter came one time to visit my father. She was a beautician in Miami, and she brought her twin sons. One was about five-five and the other about six-two and the six-two one had just come out of the Marines, and the five-five one was a poet. Really wonderful twins. Neither of them spoke Spanish. And they had been born and raised in Florida. And she wanted them to see Guatemala, to see where she came from. So she left her husband behind and came with them and wanted them to visit my father. And my father told his servant to tell her to go to hell. That he didn't want to have anything to do with Rafael ever again. The servant didn't say that, she just said that Don Franz couldn't receive them.

"So she came over here. And she introduced herself, and she said, 'You don't remember me. But I lived in La Patria at the same time you were living there. And I used to see you often. And we played together occasionally. And I used to see you often' — she said a number of times. And she gave me her name, which I've forgotten — again!" Sara laughed, "— and asked me if I could intercede for her with Dad so that her sons could meet my father. She said she knew that there had been bad blood between her father and my father, but that she wanted very much for her sons to meet Dad. So I went over, leaving them outside and went in and I said, 'Daddy, this woman is really very nice, and it's not her fault that Rafael was a bastard.' I didn't say: 'It was your father's fault.'" She laughed again. "I just said, 'She came a long way. Why don't you just say hello.' So Dad said, 'Sure, tell them to come in.'

"They were very polite. And Dad told them stories about their grandfather. He told them quite a lot of stories. And they were very impressed, and she was very happy. And we invited them to lunch, but they said no thank you.

"Later that afternoon, I took out some old photographs of the family to show them. Their grandfather, Rafael, looked almost exactly like my grandfather. I mean they could be confused. Except for that they had different color skin. Rafael had snow-white hair, and he wore it just like my grandfather did. And he had the same round face. My grandfather had pale blue eyes and blond hair, and this guy had brown eyes and black hair, but when he got older it was snow-white.

"So they came back here, and one of the sons asked his mother, 'Why is Franz Endler so rich, and why was my grandfather so poor?' And she said: 'Because your grandfather was a drunk. And Sara's father worked hard.' And she left it at that.

"From there she took them up to see her mother's family, an indigenous family in the highlands."

V

Every year at Christmastime, in every town and city in the Guatemalan highlands, solemn processions of indigenous men and women wind their way through the streets at dusk, filling the evening air with candlelight and incense. The processions, inspired by the biblical account of Mary and Joseph searching for a place to stay in Bethlehem, are called *posadas*.

I didn't realize what *posada* meant until I heard the word again from the workers in La Igualdad as they described what happened to them after the fall of Arbenz. Evicted from their homes, they went in search of *posada*. Lodging.

Now when I read accounts of the cold warriors in Washington celebrating the success of their intervention in Guatemala, an image comes to me of another procession: the families of La Patria and a hundred other plantations, winding their way through the piedmont, in search of a new home.

The first to tell me about this search was Pedro Díaz. As the raindrops of the advancing storm began to sound on the roof above, he had recounted his exodus from La Patria. His family had eventually found a home on a plantation down on the coast, where they stayed twelve years, until his mother fell ill and insisted on returning to La Igualdad. She wanted to be sure she would be buried with her family when the time came. Of the fourteen children she had brought into the world, twelve were buried in La Patria. So Díaz found work again in La Igualdad and built a home in the hamlet just below the plantation.

I had closed my notebook, eager to be on my way before the storm hit. But Don Pedro wasn't finished. "Look," he said, the rancor gone from his voice. "I have the seal of La Patria."

He let the blanket slip from one bony shoulder and held out his arm. I looked, my gaze falling first on the thick artery which wound down the withered limb, like the root of a tree exposed by the erosion of the ground where it grew. Then I saw the scar. It began at the back of his wrist and ran between his thumb and forefinger. It must have been a horrible wound when it happened, but after three-quarters of a century it had blended with the creases of his dark skin. He held it up proudly, like a veteran showing off a war wound.

"I did this with a machete when I was a youngster. I almost lost my thumb. I haven't been able to use it since. I remember it was up where the road goes to Sacuchum. Back then it was all forest. I did this while we were clearing away that forest. That's why I call it the seal of La Patria."

He then folded his arm back under the blanket and said, "When I die, I want to be buried in La Patria with my family and my *patrón,* Don Federico." He repeated Friedrich Endler's name with affection. "Don Federico. Now, *he* was my patrón!"

He paused again and shrugged. "That is, if the plantation gives me *posada.*"

PART IV

AND THEY WERE THE ERUPTION

Señores vamos al volcán
A ver qué dicen los dioses
Porque he escuchado sus voces
Mas no sé lo que dirán.

Señores, let's go to the volcano
To see what say the gods
Because I have heard their voices
But I don't know what they could be saying.

— The Ajis (Dance of the Conquest)

THE SAVAGES

A S FRIEDRICH ENDLER was crossing the Atlantic in 1892, preparations were under way on a patch of marshland just south of Chicago to commemorate the crossing that Columbus had made four hundred years earlier. The marsh was to be cleared and, above it, a spectacular "White City" erected, filled with statues and fountains and colonnades in a display of neoclassical grandeur that would make even Estrada Cabrera's parthenons seem understated. Some twenty million visitors were expected to pass through the White City's portals and, once inside, marvel at the latest technological triumphs in transportation, mining, and modern industry, as well as the many exotic natural resources that abounded in faraway lands. The theme of this "World's Columbian Exposition" was the progress of civilization, and above all it celebrated American know-how. It was this know-how that discovered new continents, created new technologies, and made the riches of the earth available for consumption.

Adjoining the White City would be a sideshow organized by the Smithsonian Institution. Its theme would be "the evolution of man" — or, as one observer would put it, "the sliding scale of humanity." Entering from the White City, visitors would come first upon live exhibits of the Teutonic and Celtic peoples, then pass the Asians and Arabs, and finally "descend to the savage races": the Africans and Indians. "What an opportunity," the *Chicago Tribune* would later write, "was here afforded to the scientific mind to descend the spiral of evolution, tracing humanity in its highest phases down almost to its animalistic origins."

After a ride on the giant metallic wheel invented for the occasion by George W. G. Ferris, visitors could experience another sort of thrill — the opportunity to contribute to the advancement of science — by having their crania measured by a team of experts who could determine where a person belonged on that sliding scale that ran from the savages at the far end of the fairground to the two nearby statues — apparently the pinnacle of human evolution — of students from Harvard and Radcliffe.

Word went out to governments around the world that they were welcome to mount their own exhibits at the exposition. And while they surely knew they would be upstaged by their host, they nonetheless scrambled at the opportunity to show what their countries had to offer civilization — and, in particular, what they had to offer the men who managed its capital.

When Endler arrived in Guatemala, the government there was busy gathering material for an exhibit in which visitors would be able to sample the "best coffee in the world," peruse a map of the country's extensive network of roads and railways — those already built, those being built, and those projected to be built — and read a pamphlet describing the opportunities for making money in a land of abundant untapped resources where "Nature . . . always brings forth with interest that which is entrusted to her care."

The Columbian Exposition, mounted long before the days of radio and TV, would be one of the first P.R. events to involve the active participation of people around the globe.

Not everyone in Guatemala was so eager to participate, however. That's the impression I got when I came upon a relic from this era, buried in a four-foot heap of documents in a musty closet of the government building in Quetzaltenango. It was a letter, dated July 11, 1892, sent by the mayor of an Indian town named Cajolá to the *jefe político* of the department. It read: "With respect to your very attentive note, wherein you instructed me to have samples collected of every mineral known to exist here, and to deliver them to the *Jefatura* so that the special appointee of the Department of Mines of the Chicago Exposition could fulfill his charge, I have the honor of informing the *Señor Jefe*, that in this entire jurisdiction, which is quite small, there are no minerals to be found, nor is there anyone who could provide information about them; therefore I must forgo the honor of delivering to you samples of minerals, or of useful clays, or colorful ones, of which there are also none. Writing with all due subordination your absolute and true servant, Toribio Gómez, Mayor."

The tone of the letter seemed familiar. Not only did the mayor not know anything, he didn't know of anyone who *would* know anything. It seemed like a formal, nineteenth-century way of saying something I had heard time and time again in La Igualdad: *saber.*

⚓

Saber. "Who knows?" The expression captured one of the traits the Guatemalan government would use at the Columbian Exposition to describe its Indians — people who "do not take any part in the political and intellectual life" of the nation, nor "cooperate actively in the progress of civilization." Their *who-knows* was the antithesis of the *know-how* celebrated in Chicago — that combination of knowledge and ambition that brought Friedrich Endler across the Atlantic, landed him a job in La Libertad, and allowed him to fix the plantation's faulty generator in time to watch the "savage ragged creatures performing their fantastic dances under the electric light."

Digging deeper in the century-old archive, it became obvious to me why the people of Cajolá would say *saber* when the government asked them about their land. A decade earlier, President Justo Rufino Barrios had given the better part of what they farmed to a group of Ladino militiamen. At the time, the mayor of Cajolá had written to Barillas, who was then the *jefe político* of Quetzaltenango, beseeching him to intervene on their behalf. The community had farmed these lands since "time immemorial," the mayor pointed out, and it had obtained legal title to them from both the Spanish Crown (when Guatemala was a colony) and later the national government (after it won its independence). His claim was confirmed by a surveyor sent by Barillas to measure the lands: "It is clear that those from Cajolá are the owners, with legitimate title, to these lands, with perfect right to reclaim them," the surveyor reported back, adding that the lands were "an indispensable element for the necessities of life."

But Barillas ignored the petition. Cajolá lost its land. And President Barrios had the mayor executed in the town square.

A few years later, after Barrios died and Barillas became president, a new mayor made a new appeal, requesting this time that Cajolá be compensated for the lands it had lost. "The *Señor Jefe Político* knows full well," he wrote, "as does the *Señor Presidente,* that the indigenous class and especially that of Cajolá is most abject and miserable and, working always and always working, cannot acquire any more comfort than the frugal and modest satisfaction of our basic needs; and at death, we leave our children just a piece of land, irrigated by the sweat of our brow, and the example of our work."

The letter then used the president's own words to make Cajolá's case: "We are under the understanding that upon inaugurating the new government, the *Señor General Presidente* Manuel Lisandro Barillas, promised in his speech that there will be justice and the law will be upheld, with respect for the rights of men and the protection of property."

It was the same language that Guatemala would use to describe itself in Chicago. But it apparently wasn't meant for use by the people of Cajolá. Their petition was ignored. And, as a result, they would have to seek work in the plantations on the piedmont. Coincidentally — or maybe *not* — one of the plantations where they found it was Barillas's own, La Libertad.

And that is how they came to be dancing under the electric lights that the industrious young Endler had just gotten to work.

The Columbian Exposition would leave physical traces around the planet, the way some geological events, such as a meteor crashing into earth, spread their debris across faraway continents. The document in the Quetzaltenango archive was one bit of Columbian debris. And part of the reason it caught my attention was that I had grown up with another: a coin with a detailed engraving of the explorer's ship, the *Santa María,* sailing above two half-globes, under the banner "World's Columbian Exposition." This Columbian half dollar had been passed down through my family, along with a collection of Indian head cents (pennies with the word "Liberty" emblazoned on the brow of a Native American man), and it would become a talisman of sorts for me in the years when I was first discovering the appetite for exploration that would later help lead me to my own encounter with the people of Cajolá — a century after Friedrich Endler had had his.

Some things had changed during that century. Harvard students were no longer put on pedestals. And even if some of them still saw themselves as pinnacles of evolution, the racist worldview displayed in Chicago in 1892 had fallen out of fashion. What *did* remain strong among young Americans from expensive schools, however, was a faith in knowledge — that it was attainable and that attaining it was good — that a person could go anywhere, get to know the people there, document their situation, and so help improve it. Multiculturalism had taught us that multiple perspectives might coexist, but it also insisted that we could — and should — know them all.

This was the sort of *know-how* that I brought with me to Guatemala. Just as Friedrich Endler drew satisfaction from figuring out a plantation's generator, I drew it from my ability to figure out a plantation's history — to see past the *saber,* past the accounts of natural and supernatural events, and uncover the history of revolt and repression that was buried in the shadows of the past.

This faith would be put to the test in Guatemala. The more I learned there, the less confident I would become. And the closer I got to what I'd thought would be the bottom of things, the more I felt I was only scratching the surface.

⩔

Several weeks after finding Cajolá's petitions in the archives, I stumbled upon another account of the community reacting to intrusive outsiders. It was in an obscure collection of oral histories told in the local Mam language to a researcher who was himself a native Mam speaker. It was a story unlike any I'd heard before, and it gave me my first inkling that *who-knows* might sometimes be delivered more like a punch than a shrug.

"The foreigners came along with an idea," an elder had recounted in his native tongue. "They climbed each hill to find out where there was gold, where there were mines. Here in our pueblo Cajolá, they found the hill Twi Saq'b'aqun. They said, 'Give us this hill. Because from there, in your pueblo, a great fortune will be made.' So word went out to the whole community. The people of Cajolá met and talked. 'This isn't going to turn out well, because they're going to ruin our pueblo. Because they will build a big road. But we'll never stop the foreigners with our words alone. Better we think like our ancestors. Let's stand up and protect ourselves so they forget about this. So the hill itself stops them. If it's true the thing is in there, it's there because we're poor people. We don't have machinery. If we were foreigners, we would be working there. In other towns they have broken the hills and taken the riches for their own people. And we just serve as peons for them. But now we won't give it up. Let's look for the *ajyox* so that they do a ceremony in our pueblo.'"

I looked up *ajyox* in the book's glossary and found the translation: "Mayan priest." The term was the Mam equivalent of the K'iche' *ajis*, which foreign academics had sometimes referred to as a "shaman" and Ladino Guatemalans generally referred to simply as a witch.

"And so they prayed on the hills for nine whole days. Our *ajyox* were able to enter the shadow of God and make the foreigners go away. The foreigners went to look at the hill. They wanted to break it open. But the car they brought turned over and left them dead there on the hill. The foreigners forgot and left. That's how Cajolá kept the hill from being opened."

SACUCHUM

I

WHEN LA PATRIA BURNED DOWN, Sara Endler was living in the United States, where her husband was a university professor and where she had raised her three children. During her years there, she had visited her parents regularly. She hadn't lost touch with Guatemala, but as the civil war developed during the 1960s, she had come to feel increasingly isolated in the middle of a polarized society. She did not share the extreme anticommunism of people like her father. Nor did she identify with their critics on the left. "I was very much aware of the fact that workers were misused, mistreated, poorly educated, and suffered from poor health. And that allowed me to be responsive to the ideals of the left. I was with the revolution in 1944. I was for that. But by 1954, I had serious doubts. I personally found Arbenz very appealing — an upright, imaginative man. But I think he was misled, badly used. When they started talking about expropriation, giving a piece of land to everyone, it just freaked me out. I saw personal property as the basis of any sane government. I never regained confidence in the left."

Then the assassinations began. In the late 1960s, leftist guerrillas killed several U.S. officials. Perhaps the most disturbing incident for Sara was the 1970 abduction and murder of a German ambassador. She was in Argentina at the time and saw the story on the front page of the newspapers there. "There was a photo of him in a street in Guatemala City, on his knees, pleading that they spare him. And they shot him. It was grotesque." The Argentine press denounced the act, she recalled, saying that "'only savages in Central America could kill a man in cold blood like that.'" (The Argentines would, of course, discover their own capacity for savagery a few years later.) "All sympathy I had for the left was wiped away by those assassinations." And as the levels of violence escalated in the following decade, her aversion to the left only intensified. By 1980, bodies were appearing on the roadsides regularly. And like the rest of her Guatemalan friends, she "believed that the left was doing all the killing."

But then she had a revelation. It was 1982, and she was crossing Lake Atitlán in a motorboat driven by a man who had worked for the family for many years. In the middle of the lake, the man suddenly slowed the boat and turned to her. "Doña Sara," he said, "there's something that I think you should know." He then told her that the army had massacred an entire village. He explained what had happened, and, when he finished, he continued their trip to the other side of the lake.

At first Sara wasn't sure what to make of this news. She confided with a Guatemalan friend, who said that she too had heard about the military killing large numbers of civilians. They wondered if it was really possible. "It was difficult for us to believe. You see, many people in the capital were sheltered from the massacres." And they continued to doubt the mounting evidence that the army was killing civilians, until it became too overwhelming to ignore.

This knowledge did not change Sara's views of the left, however. "It was a really dirty war on every level. I think the army was horrible. But the guerrillas were also responsible. Those people killed by the army were giving aid to the guerrillas. They had been warned not to."

"Why did they aid the guerrillas?"

"As far as I know, everybody who gave the guerrillas anything did so because they were forced to by the guerrillas. I don't know who was really supporting them."

II

Who *was* really supporting the guerrillas? Two years after I began asking questions, I still didn't know for sure. According to César and his friend Jorge Fuentes, everyone in the plantations supported them until "what happened in Sacuchum." I had heard a similar account from the

Guilléns in Guatemala City. And in La Igualdad — where I had ᵦ only vague answers and then had stopped asking — the stories also revolved around this place: Sacuchum.

I had often gazed up at the mountain above La Igualdad and wondered whether or not it was a volcano. Now I began staring up and wondering about this place Sacuchum. Sacuchum de los Dolores was its full name. Sacuchum of the Pains. Something awful had happened there that had changed the course of the war. Sacuchum of the Sorrows. It seemed to be the black hole of history, sucking everything around it into its darkness.

From below in La Igualdad, you couldn't see any kind of clearing, no lights at night, no smoke rising, no movement except that of the clouds that drifted by and occasionally gathered around the peak. I knew that there was a path that left from the top of La Patria, climbed through the forest, and supposedly reached Sacuchum. It would be a beautiful hike. But the war was still going on, and that woods was one of its battlefields. I also knew that there was a road that climbed to Sacuchum from the San Marcos plateau on the other side of the mountain. And I often thought about taking the motorcycle up that way. It would be tough going — far worse than on the roads in La Igualdad, which were kept passable by the plantations. It would probably take hours. And once I got there, what would I do? Who would talk with me?

So all I could do was stare up and imagine and wait until I found someone who knew people there. I found that someone in an unexpected place.

⚜

I was in Cajolá, interviewing a group of old men about the history of the community's lands. They were speaking Mam punctuated by words of Spanish — an unusual combination, like someone playing two different instruments simultaneously: Spanish consonants formed at the very front of the mouth, while the guttural clicks and rasps of Mam came from back in the throat. A younger man was translating for me. Or rather he was interrupting the men's stories every now and then, condensing what had been spoken in Mam, and pushing it into Spanish syllables at the front of his mouth — and in the process, it seemed, passing the stories through a sieve that yielded only fragments of the original.

They were talking about a man who, in times long gone by, had petitioned the government to protect the community's lands. His name was Pe't Chum, and it was said that he had possessed special powers. One of these was the ability to travel long distances in little time — so, for instance, the trip from Cajolá to the capital, a walk that took others several days, he could do in just a few hours. These powers were somehow linked to the fact that although he was human, he had a tail like an animal.

I asked if his name meant something in Mam. He was "Chum," they answered, because his family was originally from a place called Sacuchum.

"The Sacuchum in San Marcos?" I asked.

"That's right."

⁂

My translator was Pascual Huinil. I had known him for over a year, since before traveling to La Igualdad, when I had lived in Cajolá for a few weeks. After I left Cajolá, we had continued working together in an effort to obtain international funds for a sewage system in the community. He put me up at his house numerous times and had stayed in my Xela apartment more than once.

After we left the old men, I asked Pascual if there was much contact between people in Cajolá and Sacuchum. "No," he answered. "Pretty much none."

And then after a moment he added, "But I've been there."

"Oh, really? Why did you go?"

"I was just passing through."

Passing through? The road up from San Marcos came to a dead end at the town. "Where to?" I asked.

"Just around there."

Just around the top of a mountain? I didn't press for an explanation, and only much later would Pascual offer one. Now he told me that he had stayed with a family there and had heard about the massacre a few weeks later. He had never gone back. But he did know some people from Sacuchum, and he could arrange for me to meet one of them.

⁂

The meeting took place in Guatemala City, in the office of a national indigenous rights organization to which people from both Cajolá and Sacuchum belonged. The man from Sacuchum was named Fabián Ramos. He was working on a campaign to obtain land for the community. He said he could tell me about the massacre, but he thought it would be even better if I went with him to Sacuchum and talked with some of the survivors there. I immediately agreed. Here was my chance to finally see the summit of the mountain — and find out what had happened there.

III

"Why dig up the past?" the wife of one plantation owner had once asked me as we drove across town in her Mercedes-Benz. Her husband's coffee plantation was to the east of La Igualdad, on the other side of the Sacuchum mountain. "Americans come here, and they just write about all the negative things we've been through. Why doesn't anyone write something good about this country?" She was not denying that there were ugly things to dig up. "Those were terrible years," she recalled. "You never knew if your husband was going to make it home from the office without being kidnapped. A lot of ugly stuff happened, but we need to move ahead, to get beyond all that."

Later I rode with her husband. "Democracy doesn't work here," he told me. "This is the paternalist culture — you know, *el señor presidente*." He was referring to the novel about Estrada Cabrera by Miguel Angel Asturias, Guatemala's Nobel laureate in literature. "The paternalism hasn't been all bad, you know. In some ways it has helped the workers. Even if the plantations paid them as little as they possibly could."

"Why didn't they pay more?" I asked.

"It's the same as why the importers in the United States pay us as little as they can. They've said, 'Let the Mexican' — you know, the folks south of the border — 'suffer a little so I can lead the good life, buy my car, etc.' And the landowner here has done the same thing: 'Let the Indian suffer a little, so I can lead the good life. I want to live well, to let my family live well, have a good car.' It's sort of a chain."

His car was a Land Rover. The kind that I'd seen crowding up the Long Island Expressway as wealthy New Yorkers headed out to the Hamptons for the weekend. Unlike them, he actually drove regularly on the kinds of rugged roads its safari features were designed for. The CD player was an accessory.

As for benign paternalism, he offered his wife as an example. She had recently insisted that for their wedding anniversary, instead of giving her a present, he would fix up the workers' quarters on the plantation. He would install electricity and running water in their homes.

I asked, "Would you ever consider giving them lands the way the government did during the Agrarian Reform?"

He shook his head. "I use all my land. There's not an inch unused. And I tell you frankly I'm not going to give up any of it. I want more, in fact. You have some, and you want more." In this respect, he pointed out, Guatemalan landowners were no different from people in other countries. And that was why they so deeply resented "the human rights" always singling them out for mistreating people.

The human rights. Like other wealthy Guatemalans, he used the term to refer not to a set of moral or legal principles, but rather an interest group intent on besmirching their country's image abroad. "What's screwed us over more than anything," he had told me over lunch, "are the human rights." His wife had tried to explain the source of resentment: by exposing the country's old wounds, human rights advocates were preventing any healing from taking place. And what really pissed him off, he had added, was the way these foreigners came criticizing this country that they don't really know.

So what did *he* know about Sacuchum, I wondered now as I prepared to visit the community. If he didn't know what had happened there, how could he criticize the ignorance of "the human rights"? And if he *did* know, well, might that not be even worse?

IV

Fabián Ramos met me in the central square of San Pedro one Thursday afternoon. He was a small, quiet, busy-looking man, although he seemed more at ease here than he had been in the capital the week before. He had with him a hundredweight nylon sack, which he flung over his shoulder after shaking my hand, and stooping under its weight, he led me to the bus stop.

Thursday was market day in San Pedro, and the streets around the market filled with people coming and going like bees around a hive. San Pedro was the twin city of San Marcos. At least they looked like twins on the map — though, in fact, the two towns were separated by a lot more than the little creek that ran between them. San Marcos was the political center of the department; San Pedro was the commercial one. San Marcos was a Ladino town; San Pedro was an Indian one — or had been until Justo Rufino Barrios declared its residents Ladino by presidential decree. Few people in San Pedro still spoke Mam; few women still wore *traje*. But whether or not they considered themselves Indian, they took pride in at least one thing: they weren't from San Marcos. On the other side of the creek, the feeling was mutual.

The bus bound for Sacuchum was overflowing with people and their cargo. Sacks and crates were stuffed under seats and into overhead racks and piled on top of the roof. People stood outside, waiting for the driver's signal to cram themselves in with their things.

The majority of families in Sacuchum lived off commerce, Fabián explained to me as we waited. Every Thursday they came down to the San Pedro market, bought bulk quantities of vegetables and grains grown in the surrounding highlands, and brought them up to Sacuchum. Then during the weekend they fanned out over the other side of the mountain, selling their merchandise in the plantations and setting up stalls in the Sunday markets in La Igualdad and the three other towns. Sacuchum, it turned out, was the commercial hub of the mountain, the primary grocer in the subsistence economy of the plantation workforce. And in addition to agricultural products, it supplied lumber and the homemade liquor known as *"cusha."* The forest around the mountaintop provided the wood, and it also hid their clandestine distilleries.

The women waiting around us wore *traje* — the green and gold pattern that few people in San Pedro still wore. But no one spoke Mam, and Fabián told me that few of the people in Sacuchum still did.

I asked about the name of the town. "Los Dolores" came from the Virgen de los Dolores. And "Sacuchum" was Mam for "dry throat." Why that name? He guessed that it might be because, in the old days, before there were cars, people would carry their cargo up the mountain on their backs and arrive in town with their breath short and their throats dry.

⚜

The overloaded bus lumbered out of town, south toward the mountain, and began to climb. I expected the dirt road to deteriorate, but to my surprise it didn't. In fact, the farther we climbed, the better it seemed to become. The ground was packed solid and smooth, without all the rocks and furrows that plagued the roads below on the piedmont.

The slope soon became too steep to take head-on, and the road swung eastward, climbing at an angle up the mountainside. Down to the left now were the twins, Marcos and Pedro, facing off against each other, a thousand feet below. As the bus made its way around to the eastern side of the mountain, they disappeared behind us. Now we could see the road to La Igualdad, three thousand feet below, and the ravine carved by the Naranjo River dropping another thousand feet farther. The mountainside alternated between sheer rock face, steep slopes blanketed with thick forest, and patches — wherever the ground was even remotely level — that were planted with rows of corn.

Climbing further, we were enveloped by clouds. The distances suddenly vanished. The ground below us disappeared. And we were left with only the hum of the engine. We might have been in an airplane. A cow floated by outside. We kept climbing. The cloud thinned around us and disappeared. And the bus pushed over one final ridge and slowed to a stop. We were at the top.

Below us was a small valley, walled in by steep ridges, like a crudely formed bowl with a jagged rim. The rim was broken in places. A gaping hole on the western side gave way to a thick tumble of clouds. A smaller break, directly across the valley, opened out onto blue sky and the top of a cloud that was climbing the mountainside above La Igualdad.

In the valley there was a little town. A white church with a small belfry overlooked an open square; two box-shaped buildings faced it on the other side, presumably the school and the town hall; a soccer field stretched behind them; a loose grid of paths extended outward, past small houses surrounded by corn and pasture land.

The mountain — eight thousand feet of rock, clay, and ash rising up from the coastal plain — culminated in this: a quiet hamlet, cradled within wooded ridges, held up to the sky like an offering.

⁂

Fabián left me sitting alone on a cot in one room of his two-room house. The pale light of late afternoon filtered in through a single window that opened onto a row of green corn stalks. We hadn't had a moment alone since we met below in San Pedro. I hadn't asked how we would arrange our interviews, and he hadn't raised the topic himself. I assumed he would be taking me to talk to a select few people in their homes. I imagined hushed conversations behind closed doors. If people in La Igualdad had been reluctant to tell me about the violence, I figured people would be even more so here, where things had supposedly been so much worse. The interviews would take time. And night was approaching. We would have to get started soon.

Fabián came back after a few minutes and said, "The meeting is at eight."

I looked at him. "What meeting?"

"To talk about the massacre."

"Oh, good. Who will we be talking with?"

"Everyone."

"Everyone who lost relatives?"

"Everyone who lost relatives and everyone else who wants to come."

This was a surprise. A large meeting meant no anonymity, I thought. And it also meant anyone could find out what I was investigating. "You don't think it might be better to meet just with a few individuals?"

"No," he said. "And everyone already knows about it."

"How do they know?"

"We sent a car around yesterday with a megaphone to announce it."

"Oh really? And what did you say?"

"That an important person was coming to investigate the massacre."

The clouds rolled over the ridges and sealed in the valley like a heavy lid. It began to rain. We got wet as we made our way through the darkness to the center of town. A dozen or so figures huddled under strips of plastic outside the town hall. The door was locked, and Fabián left to go look for someone with a key. I stood alone listening to the rain and wondering whether I had been a bit rash coming here with this person I barely knew. After the *robachicos* scare on that island two years earlier, I had promised myself never to get stuck alone in an unfamiliar community again. But here I was, on top of a mountain, surrounded by strangers, and with no way out until the next bus left in the morning. What's more, the whole town knew I was here to investigate what might be the worst atrocity committed by the army in the region.

Fabián returned with a man he introduced as Apolinario. Apolinario opened the door and I followed him into a single large room with a table at one end and a series of benches facing it. Fabián and Apolinario led me to the table. The people outside filed in, others followed them, and soon the room was packed with some forty people. The two front rows of benches filled with old women in *traje*. The other rows filled with older men, and others stood at the back. The room was cold, and the faces looked ghostly in the pale light of a naked neon bulb. They gazed toward the front in silence, somber and impassive, waiting, as if before a mass.

Fabián spoke first. "It is a great honor to have with us tonight in our community of Sacuchum, this *señor* who has come to document what occurred in the massacre of 1982 . . ." I was sitting on the table with my notebook in my lap. And as Fabián spoke, I looked around the room, trying to read the crowd. I had no idea what they were thinking. What this meeting meant to them. What they expected of me. Fabián was describing me again as an "important person." And it made me feel like an impostor. There was nothing important about me. I was here only to get some background information that would help me understand the history of La Igualdad. I tried to think of what to say: I wanted to dispel any illusions about my "importance," but I also didn't want to disappoint them. I wanted to hear about the massacre, but I didn't want to impose upon them — I was so used to people being afraid to talk about the war, even in private, that I couldn't imagine anyone wanting to talk about it in public. I wanted to make people feel comfortable, but I myself was scared. I saw some young men standing in the far doorway and looked to see if any of them had military haircuts.

When Fabián finished, all eyes focused on me. I cleared my throat and spoke slowly, first thanking Fabián for inviting me here. I said I couldn't offer the community anything other than to record what they told me and try to let people know about it. I said that my aim wasn't to create any problems for anybody — neither the victims nor the perpetrators — but only to find out what had happened.

I stopped talking, and the room was silent, but for the pattering of the rain on the roof above. I opened my notebook. "So to begin . . ." I thought a moment, *how should I begin?* and opted for a specific question. "When exactly did the army arrive in town?"

Again there was silence. I looked around at the unfamiliar faces. They looked back at me. The question hung in the cold air between us. I glanced over at Fabián, but it didn't appear that he was going to answer it. I saw one of the young men in the back step out the door into the rain, and I imagined he was off to report what I had said. My eyes wandered the room, and my mind searched for a way to wrap up this meeting as quickly as possible.

Then I saw an arm rise in the far corner of the room and a shadow of a man step forward. I nodded to him, and he began to speak.

"It was the first of January 1982, a Friday . . ."

⬇

There had been a battle in the woods below, and all day long they had listened to the army bombing the mountainside. Then on Saturday the soldiers came up the mountain from all sides and surrounded the valley. The people had no idea what the army intended to do. So they waited. And on Sunday morning the soldiers came down into the town.

"That wasn't the first time we'd had trouble, you know," the man said, hesitating as if unsure whether it was okay to backtrack. I nodded for him to go on. "Earlier in the year, four of us were stopped by soldiers when we were returning from La Igualdad. They kicked us hundreds of times, all over." He put his hands now on his chest and stomach, as if massaging old wounds. "I was sick for four years after that. After beating us, they tied our arms to boards and made us walk uphill, like we were carrying crosses."

Again there was silence. I had never heard anyone in Guatemala talk like this in public. I looked around the room to see if others would join him. But no one spoke. So I threw out another question: "How many soldiers came into town that day?"

This time it was Apolinario who answered. "There was an enormous number of them — a few hundred soldiers. And more in the hills around town. And there were helicopters — three helicopters — that circled overhead. The soldiers ordered everyone into the center of town. And they dragged people out of their houses."

The man in the corner said, "They dragged some by their hair. They knocked people to the ground as they walked."

Now an older man who was sitting in one of the back rows spoke up: "And they went into the homes and took whatever they wanted. They took radios, clothes, money, whatever they could find."

From the corner: "And they raped the women."

Silence again. I imagined the scene: soldiers swarming up over the mountaintop and down into the valley. What I couldn't conjure up was what had gone on in the houses — the images that must have been playing back now in those eyes that were watching me.

"How many people were raped?"

"About twenty," Apolinario said.

No one elaborated, so I moved on. "And what happened next?"

The man in the corner spoke: "They gathered us into the plaza in front of the church. And there a captain spoke to us from the belfry. 'Today you will be punished,' he told us. 'It's known that you are bad, that the guerrillas have been here, that they're here because they're fed by you. They wouldn't be here if it weren't for your support.' And he said, 'Fish only live where there is water. You here are the water. When the pond dries up, the fish dies. We're going to take care of you, so that the fish will die.' Someone in the crowd spoke up: 'Please, señor, God does not permit this.' The captain yelled at him: 'Here there is no God! Here there is only the Devil!'"

The soldiers then herded the people out to the soccer field and made them form a line and present themselves, one at time, before a group of officials who stood with a civilian wearing a hood. The officials had a list of names and occasionally they would ask the hooded person: "Is it this one?" The people who appeared on the list were taken by the soldiers. The rest were ordered to return to their houses. There were to be no lights or fires, and anyone who ventured outside would be shot.

The older man said: "People couldn't cook. They couldn't sleep. They passed the night worrying, waiting for their relatives who had been taken away."

I looked at the women who sat in the front row like a silent chorus. It occurred to me now that they weren't as old as I had first thought. Yet there was something that made them appear prematurely aged. Their faces had that parched look you see in people who are perennially exposed to the sun in the Andes and other high places. Which was strange since this mountain wasn't *that* high, and the other people in the room didn't have it.

The women gazed back at me, and when our eyes met they didn't look away, as they probably would have under other circumstances. It was as if our gazes never really met, as if it wasn't me they were looking at, but something I represented — something that, for some reason, was in fact important.

Apolinario spoke: "The soldiers left town on Monday morning. Before going, they announced that the people were not to leave their homes for the rest of the day or they would be killed. But as soon as the soldiers left, some of us went out."

"Weren't you scared?" I asked.

The man in the corner answered, "They said they'd kill us if we went out. But I didn't care. I just wanted to find out where my brothers were. I was ready to die if I had to."

Apolinario said, "Some people had seen the soldiers leading the prisoners into the woods. So we went to investigate, climbing up the ridge and down the other side. It was around ten in the morning that we found the first bodies. They were half-buried, in ditches, five or six people in each ditch."

"There were my brothers. They had their throats slit."

"Many of them had their throats cut. Like animals."

"Some had been strangled. They put a cord around their neck, tied it to a stick, and turned the stick until they were choked."

"Forty-four people had been killed. And no bullets had been fired."

There was a moment of silence while I scribbled in my notebook. Then a new voice spoke. A woman's voice. I looked up and saw her *traje*, and it suddenly dawned on me: *of course, these must be the widows.* Her chin was thrust forward, and her eyes were fixed intently upon me — first on my face and then on my notebook, as if she wanted to make sure I wrote down her words. I did write them, and I kept writing as the other people around her began to speak. Later I would remember the look on her face — determined and defiant — as if she were standing at a floodgate and, having just pulled the lever, was bracing herself for the deluge. And it came, from all around her, new voices, with new details, about throats and fingers and skin, but none so horrifying to me as what she had said: "They cut out their tongues."

⇓

When the voices subsided and I was able to look up again from my notebook, I saw that the place had been transformed. The room seemed somehow smaller. There was color in people's faces. And moisture in their eyes. And warmth in the air between us.

"What did you do after you found them?"

Apolinario described how some people went to San Pedro and spoke to the justice of the peace, who then sent the firemen to collect the bodies and bring them down to the morgue in San Marcos. How half the families went to collect the bodies and bury them in Sacuchum, while the other half — too scared to go — left their dead to be buried in a common grave in the San Marcos cemetery. How the army returned to the town regularly for the next few months. How eight more men were abducted. How the townspeople were prohibited from traveling to the piedmont to do business. "Those were months of fear and hunger and sorrow. There were fifty-two widows and more than one hundred orphans. Many of them got sick with fear."

I asked, "Could you denounce the killing to the authorities?"

"No, there was no one we could denounce it to," Apolinario said. "And the newspapers and radio said that the dead were all guerrillas who had died in combat."

"Were you ever able to tell the true story?"

"This is the first time."

⬇

I had just one more question, I said. "After all this happened, how were people in the community able to get on with their lives?"

Apolinario answered, "We needed a lot of time. Each person has had to deal with this in his own way. As they say, the suffering of each is his own sentence. Some have suffered more than others, especially the widows. As a community we had to move ahead. We've worked on projects to improve the town."

"What sorts of projects?"

"Building the road, for instance. We built it with help from the government. It took us twelve years."

I nodded. "It's an impressive road. I noticed when I came up today. I've been in many communities in this country, and the truth is I've never seen such a nice road."

I now saw smiles around the room, like the first rays of sun peeking through the clouds after a storm. Someone said, "Just like the roads in New York, right?" And now people laughed.

"Well, almost!" I said. "Just needs some asphalt."

They laughed again.

"So what other projects?"

"We have a health center, a school, this community hall. We brought electricity, potable water. In this way we've improved ourselves a lot. Even though you never forget, you have to live always with the memory, but we have come together as a community."

·⋔·

Fabián closed the meeting with a short speech thanking me for coming to hear what they had to say. He called for applause. It came loudly and didn't stop. Yes, I could see now, they were applauding an important person: the first outsider who listened to their story. It could have been anyone; it happened to be me.

When the applause finally petered out, one of the widows spoke up. She gave another speech thanking me for listening. Someone in the back called for more applause. And again, it was loud and long. When it died out, the people got up to leave. A widow who had been sitting in the front row, who had remained silent through the meeting, came up to me and offered a warm smile. "*Gracias*," she said and walked away.

I left the meeting feeling more certain than ever that the history of the violence on this mountain needed to be told — and, at the same time, more perplexed about its impact on the plantations below. How could the owners have possibly kept themselves oblivious to events as horrific as these? And why were the workers more reluctant than the people here to talk about what they had suffered?

V

One afternoon, the middle-aged son of a wealthy cattle rancher gave me a ride from Coatepeque east on the coastal highway. The day was clear, and the crown of Sacuchum was silhouetted against the blue sky above us to the north. He drove a large American car, and he drove it fast, around sixty-five, which wouldn't have seemed like much on another country's highways, but Guatemala's roads were not made for such speeds. This "highway" was really just a two-lane road with no divider and not much of a shoulder. The pavement was pocked with potholes. The holes forced most drivers to slow down. But they turned this one into a slalom racer. The only thing that slowed him down was the one-lane wooden ramp that spanned the space where a bridge had recently been blown up by the guerrillas.

"What are we to do with all those *inditos* blowing up bridges?" his seventy-something mother had complained to me earlier. "You foreigners don't understand that human rights is one thing, but governing a country is something else."

His brother, a businessman, had expanded on their mother's comment "Guatemala isn't ready for democracy," echoing a line I'd heard from the coffee exporter. "It doesn't have culture. It needs *mano dura*," the iron fist. "You know how the father of *la Menchú* was burned in the embassy?" He was referring to the father of Nobel laureate Rigoberta Menchú, who, in 1980, had occupied the Spanish embassy with a group of indigenous activists and demanded an end to human rights violations in their communities. The government responded by firebombing the embassy and killing the protesters. "He was burned because if he hadn't been, this country would have gone to hell."

I suggested to him that the reason Menchú's group had occupied the embassy was because they thought things were already pretty bad. "It's true," the brother conceded, "that there are landowners who treat their workers terribly. I always tell others that they shouldn't flaunt their wealth. They shouldn't wear expensive clothes around peasants in rags. They shouldn't arrive at the plantation in expensive cars or planes."

And what about trying to do something for them, like what the Arbenz government did with the Agrarian Reform? I asked this now to the brother who was driving, and he shook his head. "If we parceled up the land, this country would go to hell. Guatemalan peasants are lazy. They don't like to work."

He began to talk about the virtues of hard work. He told me proudly of his daughter, who was studying to be an architect. In this world, a woman needed to be able to fend for herself. She shouldn't have to rely on any man. "Life is difficult," he said, "life is difficult for everybody." Then he began to tell me about his wife. She had cancer. She had been operated on once. Now they could only wait to see if the tumors would return.

He sped around a curve onto a stretch of road that was more populated than the rest. There were small cement houses and wooden huts

thirty feet back from the asphalt, and people were going about thei
ness by the roadside. My right foot was instinctively pressing th
where the brake would have been if it were the driver's side. His foot was
on the accelerator. Up ahead a rooster stepped into the road. It was a
large bird, two and half feet of muscle and magnificent plumage. It strut-
ted to the center of the lane and stopped, surveying the asphalt as if it
owned the place. When it noticed the car, it cocked its head to the side,
started to strut in one direction, then panicked and darted back the other
way. Too late.

His foot came off the accelerator. But he did not brake. There was a
dull thud, and the bird disappeared under the front of the car.

We sailed ahead in silence, his foot hovering in the air. Then he
shrugged. "What could I do?" He pressed down again on the gas and continued telling me about his family. Then he told me about a business venture he was hoping to undertake. He would import a chemical from Europe that could be mixed with asphalt to provide a more durable filling
for potholes. With so many potholes to be fixed on Guatemala's highways,
there would be ample business.

VI

History wouldn't be kind to that business venture. In December
1996, the Guatemalan government and guerrillas signed a peace ac-
cord, bringing an end to the thirty-six-year war. The government then
cashed in its "peace dividend" — hundreds of millions of dollars from
its wealthy trading partners — and bought asphalt. Asphalt flooded the
country, filling the major highways and spilling over onto back roads that
had never seen it (maybe even Sacuchum got some after all). Guatemala
soon looked like a different country. The potholes were gone.

I had gone back to the United States and enrolled in law school, thinking that maybe I should get my life back on the course it had been on before I visited La Igualdad. But as I sat in those classrooms, listening as the
smart young lawyers-in-the-making sought to outdo one another with the
language of "slippery slopes" and "inefficient outcomes," my mind would
drift back to Guatemala, to that mountaintop valley, to that widow releasing the floodgates of memory. Unable to concentrate on torts and con-

tracts, I applied for another fellowship, took a leave of absence, and in the fall of 1997 headed south.

Cajolá had shown me how much people could hide. Sacuchum had shown me how much they might want to tell — if they only had the right opportunity. And now, more than ever, I felt driven to find out what was hidden in La Igualdad and to find a way for the people who wanted to tell their history to do so.

Millions from that "peace dividend" had also gone to the formation of a truth commission — known as the Commission for Historical Clarification — which the government had reluctantly signed off on in the peace accords. Once back in Guatemala City, I met the commission's head investigator. The investigation had been under way for several months now, and they had already collected testimony from thousands of people throughout the highlands and in the cities. I asked him if they had been able to get as much in the coffee region on the piedmont.

"No," he said. "We're getting *nothing* from the plantations."

I said maybe I could help a little — at least in one community in San Marcos. He told me that the help would be appreciated and gave me the phone number of their regional office.

Before I called that number and before I returned to La Igualdad, I went to pay a visit to the people who had just emerged from the shadow world of the war — the former guerrillas now returning to civilian life. Perhaps they would know who in La Igualdad could arrange the sort of meeting that I had had in Sacuchum. And perhaps they could tell me themselves how their war had transformed the region.

THE GUERRILLAS

I

JAVIER HAD BEEN a child of the revolution. Conceived in early 1954 when his parents were landowners in the Agrarian Community of La Independencia, born the following October when they were once again landless peasants, Javier would grow up hearing his mother lament, "How is it possible that we've come to suffer like this again?"

You wouldn't guess that Javier had ever been a coffee worker himself. He looked much too strong. He was only a little taller than average, but he had a muscular build, and a way of carrying it, that set him apart from the people who had once been his peers. Coffee workers tend to be strong, but it is a task-specific strength — machete strength, hundred-pound-sack-on-your-back strength. Javier had the all-around strength of a boxer. A bit past his prime perhaps, but still able to pack a punch.

Then there was the way he himself looked at people. His gaze was steady. His eyes expressive. When he looked, he saw — just as when he listened, he heard — which, of course, is what most people do, but not everyone shows it, especially not in La Igualdad. In front of a foreigner, he didn't assume the pose of the happy servant, abject and smiling, anxiously waiting to step aside or fall back or jump to. Javier didn't nod unless he agreed with what was said. He didn't laugh unless he was amused. You could tell that, if challenged, he would stand his ground — and, if necessary, push back. It wasn't that he was belligerent, or even unfriendly. It was just that he had stopped being *para servirle* a long time ago.

What really set Javier apart was the way he spoke. This I discovered when I first met him. It was at the entrance to a small government housing complex at the outskirts of Xela, where, I'd been told, former guerrillas who had been "demobilized" at war's end were being housed until they could arrange something more permanent. I went there hoping to find someone who could provide me new contacts in La Igualdad. And the first person I encountered, standing at the front gate with a notebook in his hand, was Javier.

I wasn't sure if I had come to the right place, and as I opened my mouth to ask, I hesitated. I had learned my Spanish in Guatemala, where years of violence had made a minefield of the language. At the height of the war, certain combinations of words could prove explosive — costing you your job or even your life. Some words you just didn't use in public, and even when the danger subsided, the caution lingered. You wouldn't talk about "guerrillas" with a stranger — or if you absolutely had to, you'd use a slang term like *canche.* The social function of slang was reversed: to refer to something by its actual name was somehow vulgar, even disrespectful.

"Is this where the ex- . . . uh . . ." I was about to say "combatants," but instead settled for what seemed like a less jarring word, "the ex-militants of the URNG are?"

Javier smiled at my hesitation. And that's when I knew he was different. "Ex-*combatants,*" he corrected me. "Militants, we still are."

Javier gave direct answers to my questions. I asked him if there were any ex-combatants from La Igualdad. He told me that he himself had grown up in La Independencia. I asked if he had any advice on how the Truth Commission might collect testimonies there. He told me that he knew just the person who could help and would arrange for me to meet him. I asked if, in the meantime, he could tell me how he became a guerrilla. He said sure.

⬇

"I grew up in La Independencia," he told me. "My father's parents were Indians from a community in Huehuetenango. My mother's parents were from San Pedro. They were Ladinos thanks to General Barrios, who tried to trick the people into thinking they weren't Indians. No one wanted to be an Indian. The workers all looked down on the Indians who came from the highlands during the harvest season. And within La

Igualdad, the people in the town looked down on the people in the hamlets, and the people in the hamlets looked down on the people in the plantations. Even between the plantations, there were differences. The workers in La Independencia used to call the workers in El Progreso 'those Indians.'

"We were poor. Sometimes all we ate was tortillas and salt. Sometimes we had to eat the maize before it was dry because there wasn't enough to last. And when it ran out, we made tamales out of green bananas. I began school when I was seven. We wrote on slates because we didn't have notebooks. I began working at age ten. I worked in the morning and studied in the afternoon. Then, when I was twelve, I stopped studying and looked for work. I worked in La Patria, El Progreso, La Serena. When the administrator in La Independencia saw that I was strong, they hired me there as a temporary worker. The plantation suspended work every now and then so we wouldn't be permanent workers and they wouldn't have to pay us full benefits.

"I was a hard worker. And always very respectful. So Don Mariano, the administrator, treated me well. And his wife liked me. We lived near their home, and sometimes the kids would gather in the window to watch their television. Because his wife liked me, she would invite me inside. There I saw things other people didn't see. For example, many families wanted Mariano and his wife to be their *compadres,* or godparents of their children, and they would give them tamales. But Mariano and his wife didn't eat them. When the people left they threw them away. It was 'Indian food,' they said.

"It was when I was fourteen or fifteen that I began to see how things really were. Don Mariano was robbing the workers, not paying them the full amount they were owed for what they harvested. He also tricked the owner by adding workers to the payroll who didn't exist. Since the foremen were illiterate, they wouldn't know it when he added names. And like many plantations, La Independencia had military policemen whose job was to patrol and intimidate the people so they worked harder and didn't complain.

"Sometimes I worked with a man named Cayo Ochoa, who had been one of the revolutionary leaders in the time of Arbenz. Don Cayo taught me how to work better, and he talked to me about how things had been before. And my parents also told me about how for a short time we had been able to live with dignity.

"People say that before the fighting we had peace. But what do you call peace? The war begins at the psychological level, in the plantations, where every day we were dying a little bit, every day we were consuming ourselves."

II

As General Gramajo had pointed out in our first interview, "there are some things that do not seem normal in one place, but are normal somewhere else." By the time Javier became a guerrilla in 1979, armed struggle was already a "normal" way to pursue political change in Guatemala. The decision to take up arms — the decision to kill people — had been made by others before him. To understand that decision is to understand how Guatemala's war began.

One of the first to make it — the very first guerrilla leader in the mountains of San Marcos — was a young man named Leonardo Castillo Johnson. Nayito, as he was known among his peers, had inherited his revolutionary outlook from his father, Leonardo Castillo Flores, who had been one of the key players in national politics during the Agrarian Reform. Born to a *campesino* family in the country's mostly Ladino *oriente*, Castillo Flores had managed to go to school and become a schoolteacher. After he helped a group of peasants obtain some land from the government, others sought him out, and before long he was leading thousands of *oriente* men, dressed all in white with sandals, sombreros, and machetes, as they marched on the capital. He joined the PAR, won a seat in Congress, and threw himself into the frenzy of union and party politics. Then he founded the National Peasant Confederation and spent the next few years organizing peasant unions as far away as San Marcos. He became the country's "first national peasant leader," according to José Manuel Fortuny, who considered him "a bit ignorant, but a man with a good heart," and key to the success of the agrarian reform. Since most peasants in Guatemala had little or no experience in the sort of organized political activity envisioned by the reformers, they would need assistance, someone to explain the law, help them form committees and file petitions. It was the role that Rafael Zamora played in La Patria. And Castillo Flores would play it on a national level. By 1954, his organization had over 150,000 members, and when the invasion began, some 15,000 of them gathered in a field on the outskirts of Guatemala City, waiting for arms from the government so they could fight to save their revolution. The arms would never come. And after Arbenz left the country, Castillo Flores followed, joining the exodus of revolutionaries to Mexico, where he would soon become a member of the PGT — the only leftist political organization to survive the coup.

Ironically, while the 1954 coup had succeeded in driving the communists out of the Guatemalan government, it also drove many reform-minded Guatemalans like Castillo Flores to join the PGT, whose revolutionary program now appeared to them to represent the only viable alternative to a U.S.-sponsored dictatorship. In the coming years, with the help of these former noncommunists, the party set about rebuilding itself in Guatemala, forming clandestine cells among students and workers in the cities, and sending organizers out to the plantations, where they would arrive under the cover of night and be welcomed by large gatherings of peasants who were eager to reclaim what had become theirs during the agrarian reform.

It was difficult and dangerous and slow work, and by 1960 they had made only modest progress. But they were confident that history was on their side. In a report their leaders drafted that year, they wrote: "The economic structure of Guatemala is afflicted with a disease which the reactionary classes and imperialism cannot cure but only aggravate." The "disease" was economic underdevelopment, and its primary symptom was a recession that had come to "heat the boiler." The government "doesn't open the escape valves, but rather . . . closes them" and, in so doing, it was sealing its own fate.

An explosion was coming. And the party's task was to ready the "revolutionary forces" to make the most of it. They would first need "to organize the masses" — by which they meant workers and peasants. Then they would set out to "unite the country's democratic forces" — by which they meant forging alliances with other sectors of Guatemalan society that also wanted to modernize the country. Their aim at the time was *not* to destroy the existing political system, but rather to reinsert themselves into it. They stressed the need to "defend the democratic liberties" that were necessary to allow them to participate — secretly at first, then openly — in the political system. Through that participation they would return to power and renew the reform process that had been aborted in 1954. This program was known as the "peaceful road to socialism."

◆

Nayito's friends came of age in the aftermath of 1954, and even before reaching adulthood they knew firsthand the risks that came with working against a repressive regime. When students took to the streets to protest Castillo Armas in 1956, they were met with bullets. Five were killed and many more wounded. As they worked to rebuild the PGT in the coming years, they faced harassment and intimidation. Some were thrown in jail, others driven out of the country. Given the hardships they faced, it's hardly surprising that they began to question the path chosen by their safely exiled elders. The question that emerged wasn't *is it worth it?*, but rather, *isn't there a better way?*

One of those who advocated another way was a young man known as el Patojo (the Kid). In 1953, el Patojo had befriended a twenty-five-year-old Argentine doctor who came to Guatemala wondering what he could do to address Latin America's social ills and found his answer watching the Arbenz government fall the following year: make war against U.S. imperialism. The future "Che" Guevara joined the exodus into Mexico, where he met the exiled Fidel Castro and threw himself into the struggle that would culminate on January 1, 1959, when they marched triumphantly into Havana.

The Cuban Revolution captured the imagination of nationalistic young people throughout the hemisphere — and nowhere was its appeal stronger than in Guatemala, where the anger and humiliation caused by the 1954 coup were still fresh. When el Patojo returned with tales of glory from Cuba, where he had lived for a time in Che Guevara's house, he found a welcome audience among his peers.

The first to take up arms weren't the students, however, but rather a group of young military officers who were upset when their government gave the United States permission to train for the Bay of Pigs invasion on Guatemalan soil. They staged a barracks revolt, which was quickly crushed, and then fled the country. In exile, they established ties with the PGT and launched Guatemala's first guerrilla movement, installing three small guerrilla fronts in the eastern part of the country — two led by veterans of the officers' rebellion and another led by student leaders. They called themselves the Rebel Armed Forces, or simply the FAR.

The PGT leadership at this time believed that the guerrillas might play a useful role in the coming revolution. But it would be a secondary role. Real political change, they insisted, would come "not by way of armed combat but rather through intensive propaganda, education, and organizing." So they focused their energies on extending their clandestine political network throughout the country.

Yet they became concerned when they saw their young militants grow increasingly excited about the armed struggle. Anxious to maintain their authority over the nascent guerrilla movement, the PGT hastily organized its own guerrilla front. The result was a disaster: twenty men marched into the mountains with old guns, overloaded backpacks, and minimal training, only to succumb to an army ambush that left over half of the would-be guerrillas dead and the survivors in jail or exile. Among the dead was el Patojo.

Meanwhile, the years of clandestine political work seemed to be bearing fruit. In March 1962, street protests broke out after the apparently fraudulent outcome of congressional elections. Students were joined by workers and teachers who demanded the resignation of the president. As the daily marches grew in size and a general strike paralyzed the city, it seemed to the PGT that the triumphant culmination of years of organizing was at hand. But once again, police bullets ended the protests, leaving dozens of protesters dead and many more wounded. None of their demands were met. And afterward the student movement radicalized further.

Nayito and his friends began organizing "military units" in the secondary schools of the capital. They conducted "training" sessions behind their houses, setting off strings of firecrackers to mask the sound of shooting practice with the old guns they acquired. They went on "marches" — hiking trips in the mountains outside the city.

And then came the trips to Cuba. Dozens of young revolutionaries traveled to the island to receive military training, political education, moral encouragement, and sometimes financial support. The lucky ones even got, as a memento from Fidel himself, their own personal machine guns. Many of the PGT leaders and other veterans of the Arbenz government (including Arbenz himself) also spent time in Cuba, but they weren't treated with such generosity. Instead, they were subject to the humiliation of hearing the Cubans publicly deride the "errors of Guatemala" that had led to the 1954 coup — errors that the Cubans insisted they would not be so naive as to repeat.

The Cuban influence exacerbated the rift that was beginning to emerge within the ranks of the Guatemalan left. A friend of Nayito, already active in the FAR, remembers it as a "confrontation between the *viejos* and the *jóvenes*," the old generation and the new generation. "The PGT leaders believed that politics should still be the principal form of struggle and that military action was a form of pressure. We in the FAR were only thinking about the armed struggle. We thought that the political forms of struggle were used up."

⬇

Nayito's principal enemy was the United States. He knew that it was the U.S. government that had destroyed all that his father's generation had built. For although the Eisenhower administration presented the coup to the world as a popular insurrection carried out "by the Guatemalans themselves," that pretense was not maintained in Guatemala. In fact, since the coup had relied on the threat of American intervention, the United States had flaunted its role there. While Guatemalans couldn't see the CIA operatives choreographing the invasion, they did see the American planes dropping the bombs. And while they didn't see the U.S. ambassador telling the army officers to accept Castillo Armas as their new leader, they did see the "Liberator" make his triumphant entrance into the capital in the ambassador's private plane rather than at the head of an insurrectionary force. And several months later, after being forced to ratify the ambassador's pick through a plebiscite in which the "vote" consisted of telling election officials whether they approved of the Castillo Armas presidency (485,531 said "yes" and 393 said "no"), they heard the Eisenhower administration announcing to the world that Guatemala had become the region's "showcase for democracy."

The Guatemalans' next taste of this new sort of "democracy" came with the 1958 presidential election, in which leftist parties were excluded from participating and Arbenz's old rival Manuel Ydígoras Fuentes was elected. Ydígoras soon proved to be authoritarian and corrupt and, it seemed to many, a pawn of the United States — especially after he allowed the CIA to use Guatemala as a training ground for the Bay of Pigs invasion. When the group of nationalistic officers rose up in protest, it was once again U.S. planes that did the bombing and helped squash the rebellion.

When the next major election rolled around in 1963, the country was set abuzz by rumors that Juan José Arévalo intended to return from exile, run for president, and restore the old democracy. Nayito and his peers wouldn't know (as we do now from declassified documents) that the U.S. government was sending instructions "to discourage by all available means Juan José Arévalo from returning to Guatemala or running for President," or "[f]ailing in this, exert every effort to preclude and prevent his attaining that office." And they wouldn't know that the U.S. embassy received word from the Guatemalan defense minister that "he had reluctantly come to the conclusion that the only way to stop Arévalo from becoming president would be for the army to force Ydígoras out now" and that "before acting, [he] would want some kind of assurance from the U.S. that we would not look askance." All they would know was that the day after Arévalo did arrive in Guatemala, Ydígoras awoke to find an American-made tank with its turret pointed at his front door. His generals deposed him and took power. The elections were called off, and in the coming months, U.S. military assistance to Guatemala increased five-fold.

Nayito's decision to take up arms had come at the beginning of the decade. Whatever doubts he and his peers may still have had about this course of action would be laid to rest after the next presidential election, in March 1966.

The PGT had decided to throw its support behind the only civilian candidate, Julio César Méndez Montenegro, who promised to continue the reforms that Arévalo and Arbenz had begun. Two months before election day, they corralled the guerrillas into endorsing their efforts on behalf of his candidacy. But the support was half-hearted. One FAR leader voiced his doubts publicly from Cuba: "Many people remain who still naively expect something from the electoral game. So there will be elections. But let it be clear that when we are strong enough, and when the awareness of our people has better grasped the hollowness of elections with a reactionary government in power, we shall forcibly prevent this vile deceit of the people from continuing."

The PGT leadership worried that it was losing control of the younger generation of militants. It circulated a statement warning that "[i]n the future, radicalizing attitudes, positions and ultra-leftist theories will constitute the greatest danger for the revolutionary movement."

And then, just before the election, a group of party leaders, including Leonardo Castillo Flores, sneaked into Guatemala to meet with the *jóvenes* there. Their immediate aim was to make sure that the young militants would not disrupt the election. Their broader aim was to convince them that political struggle should be the primary focus of the revolutionary movement. The first goal would be accomplished: the election went smoothly and Mendez Montenegro won. But the second would prove beyond their powers, and the course of the revolutionary movement would be decided, once and for all, in their absence.

Or rather it would be decided *by* their absence. For on the eve of the election, Castillo Flores and his peers vanished. Word quickly spread that twenty-eight party leaders had been picked up in a series of lightning strikes by the police. In the weeks following the election, the student association demanded that the government release them. But the newly elected president assured the public that the missing people were not in police custody and that the government had no idea where they were.

It would be many months before two former police agents would reveal to the students what the U.S. government knew at the time. In their first major operation since receiving "counter-terror" training from a U.S. military officer, the national police had rounded up some thirty people, tortured and killed them, and then disposed of the bodies, dumping some from a plane into the Pacific Ocean. It was the first large-scale use of a tactic that would be employed by U.S. allies throughout the hemisphere in the coming decades — what would come to be called "disappearing" people.

It was around this time that the French apostle of guerrilla warfare in Latin America, Régis Debray, published a tract that would become required reading for leftist revolutionaries throughout the continent. In it, he observed that "whoever persists in playing at revolution . . . within the rules of constitutional legality, plays a strange game, in which there is only a choice between two ways of losing. Either the player is sent to prison, exile or the grave . . . or he is put in power as an armed demagogue, charged with sending revolutionaries to prison, exile or the grave." Guatemala had seen both of these outcomes. Arbenz had ended up in exile, and Mendez Montenegro had become the figurehead of a highly repressive military regime. The PGT had proven what Debray called "a supreme irony of history": the so-called peaceful road to socialism was, in fact, "the surest road to a future of blood and tears."

What further proof was needed? The *viejos* had been wrong and had paid the ultimate price for their error. Over the next year the young militants threw themselves wholeheartedly into the armed struggle — Nayito traveling to San Marcos to build a guerrilla movement out of the network of contacts that his father had developed during the Agrarian Reform. And in January 1968, the FAR's commanders signed a declaration in which they severed their ties with the party. Where the PGT's 1960 report had advocated a "peaceful road to socialism" and ended with the rallying cry "Viva la Paz!" the FAR's slogan was "Everyone to war now!"

⬇

Nayito's girlfriend was known to be one of the most beautiful women in Guatemala. And she was also one of the most controversial. As a teenager, Rogelia Cruz had competed in the Miss Universe contest in the United States. Beauty pageants were a big deal in Guatemala, where towns, villages, and even plantations regularly elected young women to serve as their "queens" at major public events. And, being Miss Guatemala, Cruz would have been seen as the representative of the nation and the embodiment of its most conservative and patriarchal values. Yet Cruz was from a new generation, and in addition to being a beauty, she was a student. She studied architecture at the public university and became an activist, openly espousing leftist views and creating a small scandal when she was briefly held by police on a weapons possession charge.

The day after the FAR issued its declaration of war, Rogelia Cruz disappeared. While hardly the first abduction in Guatemala, this case was unprecedented in certain respects. One was that she was a woman, and most political violence had, until then, been directed against men. And this wasn't any woman, it was the former Miss Guatemala, a national icon. So her disappearance attracted more media attention than others before it. But while the newspapers reported that she had last been seen in police custody, they didn't suggest that the police had harmed her in any way — not even when they reported, several days later, that her corpse had appeared half-naked under a bridge outside the capital. Only reading between the lines was it possible to discern the story that quickly spread as rumor throughout the country: Cruz had been tortured, gang-raped, and strangled by police officers under the direction of the national police chief. The newspapers did report — with no apparent irony — that President Mendez Montenegro had ordered his police chief to do everything possible to identify the culprits.

Nayito was devastated. The disappearance of his father had proven the futility of nonviolent struggle; now the brutal murder of his girlfriend seemed to have pushed him to new levels of violence. He went in search of vengeance. And three days later he found it on a street in Guatemala City when he gunned down the two top U.S. military officers in the country, Colonel John Webber and Major Ernest Munro. Nayito also died in the shoot-out. He was twenty-three years old.

III

In La Igualdad, the young Javier heard about the killings in the capital. He heard the rumors of guerrillas assaulting plantations in other parts of the coast. When his father bought a short-wave radio, he listened to Radio Havana and Radio Moscow and heard analyses of the political unrest that made more sense than what appeared in the Guatemalan press. He read the FAR pamphlets that occasionally appeared scattered on the roads, and once he even helped a friend scatter some.

But in those days his main passion in life wasn't politics. It was soccer. This was the golden era of plantation soccer that I had heard about from César's friends. And La Independencia had one of the region's best teams, in part because the administrator stocked it with players brought from outside, paying them salaries with the money he stole from the workers and the *patrón*.

Since Javier and his friends were excluded from playing on this team full of outsiders, they decided to form their own team. They raised money from the workers in the plantation to buy uniforms. "And when we played Mariano's team, all the people rooted for us. They yelled at Mariano's players: 'thieves!'"

The memory brought a smile to Javier's face.

"That first year, we were the best team in La Igualdad. We presented our trophy to Don David, the owner of La Independencia. 'That makes me very happy, *vos*,' he said to me. And then he gave us money to buy new uniforms."

The next year the team qualified for a regional tournament, and Javier went to visit the owner in the capital to ask for help paying the team's expenses. The owner agreed to do so. "Then I asked him something else: 'Don David, why don't you pay us the minimum wage?' And Don David said, 'Look kid, you guys don't do the same work as the adults.'"

It was true that they didn't do the *same* work, Javier told me, "but we did work just as hard." And even when they did become adults, the plantation kept them on only as temporary workers and continued to pay them less than the minimum wage.

The players on the team decided to do something about this. They wrote a petition and, after collecting signatures from over eighty temporary workers, took it to a government labor inspector and brought the inspector to the plantation. "When we arrived in La Independencia, the guards pulled their guns on the inspector. But Mariano called them off. He came to me and asked, 'How much do you want?' He thought he could buy me off and get rid of the inspector. But I told him, 'I won't answer that question.'

"We won compensation for a year and a half of wages. I didn't get any of it myself though." One of the guards who was a friend came and warned him that he was in serious danger. So he left the plantation and went to live in the capital.

Javier's rebelliousness had caught the attention of some other people as well. And when he returned during Easter week the following year, they sought him out. "I was there in La Independencia one night, watching the dances, when a friend approached me and said that some men wanted to talk to me. He wouldn't say what it was about. So I followed him down below the chapel, along a path through the coffee grove until we saw a light in a clearing. There were two people from La Igualdad and one I didn't know. They introduced me to him, saying: 'This guy's a real fighter.' The man said it was a pleasure to meet me. And then he talked to me about how they were struggling to change the country. And he asked if I wanted to join them. So the next morning at dawn I packed two blankets in a bag, put on the new boots I had bought in the capital, and headed up into the mountain."

IV

The guerrilla who had met Javier in La Independencia that day was named Lico. One morning Javier and I took a bus down to Coatepeque to meet him. We got off in the "terminal," a cracked and crumbling asphalt lot where fuming buses vied for space, coughed up passengers, packed in more, then nudged and honked their way back out to the highway. We walked quickly through the exhaust and backed-up traffic until we were in a sea of bicycles and scooters and people that occasionally parted around impatient cars. We continued past restaurants and hotels and banks and bars until the street filled with so many vendors that it stopped being a street and became nothing but a market.

The whole town was really nothing but a market. It had grown up as the commercial crossroads connecting the coffee plantations above, and the cattle ranches below, with the highway that ran east to the capital. As the last city before the Mexican border, it was also a gathering point for people heading north, and a receiving point for products coming south. Around the crossroads, shops proliferated: shops that sold things, shops that fixed things, shops that did both — the distinction wasn't so relevant. Market, repair, recycle. That chasm separating the new and the used elsewhere was not maintained here. Recycle, repair, remarket. Warehouses spilled onto shop floors, shop floors onto sidewalks, sidewalks onto streets. Consumers here weren't shielded from the mysteries of production — where the product came from and where it went when you tossed it. The only thing that remotely resembled the American shopping center — with its immaculate counters, ornate showrooms, and dramatic façades — was the Catholic church, and even it looked rather out of place here. In a town like this, you could watch the world economy chugging away, like an engine with its casing off.

I followed Javier through a labyrinth of stalls, ducking to avoid the lines that held up vinyl partitions, until somewhere in the middle we came upon a solid concrete wall. We passed a cavelike opening in which skinned animals hung from metal hooks, and entered another where strips of curled flypaper dangled over wooden stools and tables. At the back stood a short, stocky man swatting at the air with a rolled-up newspaper and, behind him, a woman stirring a large pot of soup.

The man greeted Javier with a warm *"vos"* and then reached out to shake my hand. I noticed that he had lost a finger, but otherwise he looked remarkably hardy for a man who had lived through all that he had lived through. He then introduced me to the woman: his wife, he said, and added with pride: "the first woman combatant in the history of our struggle." He himself was not only an ex-combatant, but also an ex-commander. This was their restaurant.

We sat at one of the two tables, and over hot soup and tortillas Javier and Lico discussed matters that I couldn't quite follow. They had a way of talking about people without mentioning their names. An old habit, I suppose. Later, when we talked about his past, Lico would recall in remarkable detail the names of people and places. Most of those places had since been utterly transformed. And most of those people were dead.

Javier left after lunch, and Lico and I headed across town to a room where we could talk in private. It was an effort to keep up with him as he moved through the labyrinth of stalls. For a moment, I found myself following the wrong person. Where the street became a street again I noticed an ice cream parlor. Elsewhere I had seen a nightclub. But there were no theaters here, no bookstores. There were no landmarks, either. There was little that looked permanent and even less that pretended to be.

⬇

"Before Gaspar arrived, we aren't much of a guerrilla army," Lico told me, recalling the band of young men who participated in the FAR on the San Marcos coast in the late 1960s. "We have some old guns. But we don't really have a political training. Mostly what we do is go after the plantations. We have two types of actions. One is the meat redistribution. We seize a cow from one of the ranches, slaughter it and distribute the meat among the people. The other is executions. We execute two administrators who mistreated their workers. We also execute a landowner couple who were especially abusive. To give you an idea, the wife once made a blind worker stick his hands in an anthill.

"Everything changes when Gaspar arrives." He was referring to Rodrigo Asturias, whose nom de guerre was Gaspar Ilom, the name of the Indian rebel in one of the famous novels of his father, Miguel Angel Asturias. Rodrigo Asturias was a survivor of that ill-fated PGT guerrilla operation that had left el Patojo dead. The young Asturias had been jailed, but President Ydígoras allowed him to leave for exile as a gesture of respect for his father.

"That was May 1971. Gaspar comes from Mexico on his way to meet with the head of the FAR in the Péten. But the contact never shows up. While he's waiting, we have a meeting in the house of one of our *compañeros.* The meeting goes on for several weeks. And when the contact from the FAR finally comes, several months later, Gaspar tells him we have formed our own organization."

Lico spoke with energy and enthusiasm, and with a confidence that even Javier didn't have. It seemed he was used to explaining things to people he didn't know, and he was used to having people actually listen to him.

"With Gaspar we rethink everything. We develop a clearer idea of our purpose. We write up a document outlining our cause. It covers four points. Why do we struggle? How do we struggle? Who do we struggle against? What do we struggle for?"

As he mentioned each one, he counted off with his fingers, and I found myself wondering what he would do when he got to the missing one: skip it or grab the stub?

"*Why?* Because there are injustices. *How?* Through the tactics of guerrilla warfare. *Who against?* The enemies of the people: the government, the army, the rich, the foreign power. *What for . . .?*" He had now reached his missing finger, and instead of skipping it or using the stub, he grabbed the air — or, rather, the ghost of the missing limb, as if it were still there. ". . . A social and political revolution that will bring better education, health and salaries.

"Most of all, we talk about who we are. The first task of the revolutionary is to know yourself. A *pueblo*" — by which he meant a "people" or "community" — "can't struggle if it doesn't have an origin, if it doesn't have roots. If a *pueblo* struggles without knowing its roots, its origins, it's a *pueblo* in the air, without any weight. So we study our origins. We read. We go around with two or three books in our backpacks. And so we get to know ourselves as the *pueblo* that we are. And we realize that it's no longer just a problem of hunger and housing and education and repression. There's something more important — our identity. Before we felt we were alone. But after our ideological formation, we find that we're not alone, that we belong to the *pueblo.* This knowledge of our historical origins is a great force that propels us forward in the struggle.

"And we change our tactics. We stop doing executions and meat redistributions. We become a real guerrilla army. And we head up into the mountains."

⇩

Directly to the north of them was Central America's largest volcano, Tajumulco. To its west, straddling the border with Mexico, was its twin, Tacaná. To the east were the Sacuchum Mountain and the rest of the volcanic chain known as the Sierra Madre. Above the piedmont plantations, the terrain became steep and rugged and forbidding, with cliffs and ravines, volcanic debris, outcroppings and crevices, springs and waterfalls, thick forest and dense underbrush. It was difficult to move around in, especially if you didn't know your way. And finding your way took time, much more time than you would have if you were being shot at, which is why the Sierra Madre was ideal terrain for guerrilla warfare. It deprived a conventional army of the advantages that come from superior numbers and firepower. It gave the upper hand to those who knew its secrets. And it ran like a corridor from the safety of the Mexican border into the heart of the country, right up to the outskirts of the capital.

What's more, this corridor provided easy access both to the plantations on the piedmont below — the backbone of the country's economy — and to the Indian communities in the highlands above.

It was in the foothills of Tajumulco that Nayito had begun building a guerrilla front several years earlier. And now the band led by Gaspar Ilom set out to pick up where he had left off. They managed to find a former union leader who had been a part of Nayito's effort, and they sent a patrol to explore the region with his help. Scouring the mountainside, they found Nayito's old camp (with the marks in the trees where he had hung his hammock), and then discovered a cave they would use for their own first base of operation. In September 1971, the new guerrilla force installed itself on Tajumulco.

They spent several months exploring the terrain, tracking down members of the network Nayito had left behind and expanding it through the plantations around the base of the volcano. Then they headed east to the Sacuchum Mountain, installing themselves in the woods above La Igualdad and exploring the terrain until they knew it as well as the slopes of Tajumulco.

They were now beyond the reach of Nayito's network and would have to start organizing from scratch. From their new camp, they began the slow process of looking for collaborators on the mountainside below, first in the communities on the road to San Marcos, then in the plantations that bordered the woods. While Gaspar Ilom and the light-skinned Ladinos remained in the camp, Lico and those others who could pass for locals would set out, dressed as workers, down the mountainside, avoiding the roads and keeping to the paths that climbed through the coffee groves. When they encountered people, they acted as if they were collecting firewood or hunting. They would strike up conversations. Beginning with innocuous topics like hunting, they would steer the conversation to matters like working conditions in the plantations, to overtly political topics such as the government and the military police. Usually the conversation would go no further than this. But if they thought they detected a kindred spirit, they might push further, ever so cautiously, talking about an organization that was trying to change things, identifying themselves as members of that organization, seeing if the person had any interest in supporting their efforts.

They took great pains to keep the presence of their camp a secret. Yet they soon found that they weren't alone on the mountainside. Every weekend the merchants from Sacuchum carried their merchandise down through the woods to the plantations and towns below. And then there were the *cusheros,* who brewed *cusha* in homemade distilleries hidden in the woods. The guerrillas sometimes ran into them in the night. At first each was distrustful of the other, but they eventually began to interact and realized they had things in common. Both were clandestine. Both used this woods to gain access to the plantation population while remaining hidden from the government authorities. The *cusheros* were the veterans here, and they gave the guerrillas tips about getting around the mountain, pointing out paths and hidden springs. The greatest service they provided, though, was keeping their presence a secret. "The majority of the people in Sacuchum knew where we were," Lico said. "But they never said anything. Sacuchum was the place that guarded the secret of the mountain."

⇓

Lico had found us a room in the second-floor office of a nongovernmental organization, which — judging by the lack of computers, fax machines, and coffeemakers — had not yet found any international sponsors. The room was small and bare, with just two chairs, a table, and a window that looked out at a tangle of telephone lines above a noisy street. Opening the window allowed in some diesel-scented air, but provided no relief from the stifling heat inside.

Lico had been talking for several hours now, and he showed no sign of letting up. He plowed through the seven more years they spent expanding eastward along the volcanic chain, laying the infrastructure that would sustain guerrilla operations when they eventually went to war. The number of combatants slowly grew until there were thirty members, and they divided the group to form two "fronts." By the time they recruited Javier, they had three fronts and a network of collaborators running the length of the Sierra Madre from Chiapas past Lake Atitlán. They still hadn't fought any battles, or even announced their existence to the world.

The fact that they had not had to fight was, Lico pointed out proudly, a testament to the fact that their existence had been kept a secret by the hundreds of people with whom they had come into contact. I began to see that in Lico's world, secrecy had not merely been a necessity, it had been a virtue. And for the first time it occurred to me that people who told me "nothing happened" had actually taken satisfaction in the exercise of that virtue.

It was dark when we decided to stop and continue in the morning. Outside in the street we went separate ways. I headed for a small hotel on the other side of town, checking into a room that — after an afternoon of hearing about caves and forest clearings — seemed luxurious just because it had the basics: a fan, a television, and a remote control. Out the window I could see the dark outline of the mountain that, during all that time I was exploring the foothills, had stood over me like an inscrutable mystery. No longer. I had seen the summit when I visited Sacuchum. And now Lico had filled in the surrounding wilderness with names and events, giving the space a history.

Lico's enthusiasm as he told those stories had been infectious. And now I found his voice still echoing insistently in my head — the way the narrator of a novel you've been reading all day sometimes sticks around after you put it down. But I was tired, and all those people and places he had conjured up wouldn't go away and let me rest. I now felt the stories weighing on me like a burden. What would I do with all of them? I felt compelled to write this history, but who would want to read it? Who really cared about a failed revolution?

Seeking relief, I reached for the remote. I was surprised to hear English come from the television, followed a moment later by the image of a bubbly, bright-eyed gringo giving the local weather forecast for Denver, Colorado. Of course, the hotel had cable. I switched channels. There was ESPN, then CNN in Spanish, then an MTV-like music video channel from Miami. Finally I came to a Guatemalan station. Its newscasters looked stiff compared to their Denver counterparts; their set was drab and lifeless. And I, in need of mind-numbing color, switched back to Miami.

V

"There in the mountain I found my true brothers," Javier said. "Brothers in the sense of the Bible, where it says, 'Watch after your brothers as you would yourself.'" He then listed the names of these "compas," as the guerrillas referred to their co-revolutionaries. Occasionally he added an obituary note: *he fell in San Pablo* or *she fell in Palmar.* Where Lico talked about the organization as a whole, Javier tended to speak of individual members and, above all, his own personal experience.

He recalled the months of training with a nostalgia that reminded me of Franz Endler describing his apprenticeship in El Porvenir. Mornings were spent training for war: learning how to move about on the mountainside; how to walk silently; how to recognize sounds in the forest and observe animals (since animal movement could give away the enemy); how to imitate birdcalls; how to identify footprints. They learned how to move in combat: how to advance, how to retreat, how to evaluate the volume of enemy fire, how to respond to surprise situations. They learned how to fight hand to hand; how to maintain weapons; and when there was rain to muffle the noise, how to fire them.

Afternoons were spent studying: improving reading and writing skills, discussing the history of the country and the nature of its problems, learning how to do political work — to identify sympathetic civilians and recruit them. The reading material included a dense tract on the nature

of inequality in the country (called "Racism"), a series of pamphlets written for barely literate peasants (called "Planting"), and another series for
university students and more sophisticated readers (called "Eruption").

One day word reached camp that an army patrol was approaching
through the woods. They hadn't been planning to begin fighting any
time soon, but now they might have no choice. The commander quickly
instructed them to set up defensive positions, assigning Javier to a
post with a veteran guerrilla named Amílcar. As they settled in, Amílcar
handed Javier a candy and told him he might need it if there was a battle.
As Javier would later learn, a first symptom of battle-induced terror was
an unbearably dry mouth and throat.

They sat in silence. Javier's gun, an old carbine, was ready. But he
wasn't sure he was. "I wasn't that scared of dying," he told me. "After all,
wasn't it better to die like this than die a slave of the plantation? Back
there we had already been dying a slow death." But he kept asking himself, "How can I kill a Christian?" He knew why they were fighting, how,
against whom, for what — but he wasn't sure how to answer this question. He thought about it a while and finally said to himself, "Let God
have the final word."

Javier wouldn't have to kill anyone that day. They heard the soldiers approach and glimpsed them passing through the woods to the east of the camp, heading up the mountain. And half an hour later they saw them pass again, this time on the west, heading back down the mountain.

Javier excelled in his training courses and, after several months, was rewarded for his hard work with a trip to Cuba, where he would spend six months (from the fall of 1979 through the winter of 1980), receiving more extensive training from the Cuban government.

While he was there, revolution was sweeping through Central America. Somoza was toppled in Nicaragua, and news poured in of guerrilla advances in El Salvador and Guatemala. Reports arrived that his own organization had carried out its first operation, occupying a plantation below Quetzaltenango and announcing its existence to the world. They now had a name: the Revolutionary Organization of the People in Arms, or ORPA. More news came several weeks later: ORPA had had its first combat. The army had attacked the camp in the woods above La Igualdad, but the guerrillas had emerged triumphant.

Hearing these reports, Javier was eager to get home and join the fight.

Javier returned to Guatemala at the end of March 1980. Arrangements had been made for him to meet a contact in San Pedro who would lead him back to the front. But the contact didn't show and, with nothing else to do, he decided to travel to La Igualdad to visit his family. It was Holy Week, and he hadn't seen them since he had left for the mountain a year earlier.

One evening he was standing by the road near the workers' quarters in La Independencia, talking with some old friends about soccer, when four armed men came scurrying down an embankment nearby. Three of them were wearing bandannas over their faces. The fourth, with his face exposed, was Lico. He made eye contact with Javier but hurried past him without saying anything. Javier's friends fell silent and watched as the strangers hurried up the road.

"Who are they?" one asked.

"*Saber*," Javier said, intending to keep his affiliation secret. But at that moment he saw a military policeman walking up the road from La

Igualdad, and the reflexes that had been instilled in him during a year of training made him yell: "Enemy at the rearguard!"

The four guerrillas turned around and pointed their guns at the policeman. "Stop! Surrender!" Lico yelled.

The policeman kept coming and defiantly asked, "Who are you?"

"We're the army of the poor. Now surrender!"

But instead of surrendering, the policeman reached for his gun. The four shot him, and he collapsed on the ground, motionless. Then they continued up the road to where other guerrillas were now summoning the workers to a meeting.

Javier stayed behind with his friends, who said nothing but now looked at him strangely. He heard the sound of moaning and saw that the policeman was dragging himself up the road, leaving a dark stain of blood in the dirt behind him. Javier turned and ran up to where the guerrillas were gathering, found a combatant who was also a doctor, and returned with him to the policeman. The doctor checked the policeman's pulse. "He's not going to live." He pulled out a gun and shot the man in the head.

It was the first killing Javier had witnessed. But he didn't dwell on it then. The meeting was beginning above, and the two hurried back to hear their commander address the large crowd of workers.

His speech, Javier told me, went like this: "*Compañeros*, we are the army of the poor! We are fighting to regain what was lost in 1954. We are struggling in this way, because they don't let us do things by legal means, because there are no political spaces, because when we speak of our rights, they kill us. That's why we have turned to the armed struggle. And we want you to join us. A policeman just died down below. It wasn't that we wanted to kill him, but unfortunately he refused to surrender to the army of the people. The plantations have their security forces. And now you have us. You are no longer alone.'"

The workers applauded enthusiastically. "*Que viva ORPA!*" they shouted. They brought out food and drinks for the visitors. They talked to the guerrillas about the ways the plantation cheated them.

Javier joined several guerrillas who were painting graffiti on the walls of the plantation buildings. "We wrote 'ORPA' and next to it we drew a volcano. The volcano was our seal. And we were the eruption."

⬇

The army would be coming to La Igualdad. It always showed up at the places the guerrillas had been — lest the people forget who was really in charge in this country — which gave the guerrillas the opportunity to do what guerrillas do best: ambush.

They set up positions on embankments above the road and waited. Sure enough, a week later, the army came. When the shooting began, Javier was in the commanders' camp further up in the plantation. The commander ordered him and the other combatants who were there to collect the front's provisions and move up the mountain.

As they climbed through the plantation, they listened to the shooting. Occasionally they heard planes roar up from the coast to bomb the area where the fighting was taking place. It took an hour to reach the safety of the woods, and once they were there, the commander sent Javier and an officer named Paco back to retrieve some of the provisions that had been left below. Another hour, and they were back at the deserted camp. They grabbed what remained there and started climbing again, stopping only to hide when they heard planes approaching.

They had gone a little way when a little boy suddenly appeared in their path. "I don't know where he came from, but it was something that I'll never forget. He was the son of Cupertino, a worker in the plantation. He was crying. And because his face was very dirty, his tears left a line of mud on his cheeks. He said to us, 'Why don't you leave us alone? They killed my father. They killed my father because of you. Why'd you have to come here?'

"There was nothing I could say. Paco spoke to him and asked what had happened. He said that the army had killed a group of workers who had been on the road when the fighting broke out. 'How many people died?' Paco asked. 'Eight,' the kid said.

"We continued climbing. We didn't say anything to each other. I couldn't get the kid out of my mind. I thought. 'God, please give him the answer. And if there isn't one, punish us.'"

They lost only one combatant in the battle. After several hours of fighting, their forces had retreated up through the plantation. The front then moved as quickly as it could across the upper face of the mountain and down the western flank to a town called San Rafael.

They sent two combatants, disguised as merchants, to scout out the town. Then Javier was sent with a vanguard force of three combatants led by Paco. The group moved first on the police station, where the two police officers happily surrendered and showed them where their arms were stored.

Javier then went to cut the lines at the telephone office and was warmly welcomed there by the operator, who told him enthusiastically, "I'm a union person!" Outside he ran into three people who greeted him and told him enthusiastically, "We're teachers!"

As the commander was conducting a public meeting in the center of town, a bus rolled into town. The combatants stopped it and made the passengers attend the meeting. Afterward, when they let the bus continue, the ticket collector handed Javier an army uniform, saying that it belonged to his brother but that he wanted to make "a little contribution" to the revolution.

⇊

The front kept moving, downhill now toward the coast. Paco, Javier, and another combatant named Tomás went ahead of the rest of the troops. Heading down a path that ran parallel to the road, they came upon an old peasant standing in front of a hut. "What luck that you passed here!" the man said, and he told them that there were soldiers waiting just down the hill. Paco entered the hut with the man while Javier and Tomás stood guard outside. After a few minutes, Paco came out. "The enemy has set an ambush below," he said and led them back uphill. They broke off branches and used them to sweep away their footprints as they went. After a few minutes, Paco said, "Okay, now we can stop." Javier thought he meant they could stop sweeping. But Paco announced: "*Compañeros, we're going to attack the enemy.*"

When he heard those words, Javier felt fear as he never had before, and his mouth and throat went dry, just as Amílcar had warned him would happen.

They cut through the woods to the road, crossed it, and headed down the other side. Arriving opposite to where the path converged upon the road, they could see a few dozen soldiers a short distance uphill, facing in the other direction.

Paco explained what they were to do: a lightning strike, then a quick getaway. The three then checked their weapons. They waited for a car to pass and then ran across the pavement and up the path. Paco opened fire. The others followed. Javier picked out targets among the scrambling soldiers. Some fell. Some writhed. Some screamed. It was better to wound than to kill — Javier knew from his training — since the screams could demoralize the rest of the troops and distract them from the combat. As he pulled the trigger, Javier felt an enormous release of tension. He was no longer scared.

Paco ordered a retreat. They ran down the path, across the road, and headed back uphill. When they had covered a good distance, Paco said they could rest. "Good work, *compañeros!*" he congratulated them.

Javier felt euphoric.

The front continued to move, now heading eastward again, this time through the foothills, occupying plantations as they went — including La Patria. Everyone now knew who they were. The workers received them warmly. And as they marched through the coffee groves they often heard anonymous cheers echoing through the hills around them: "Qué viva ORPA!"

VI

On the morning of the second day of our interview, I waited for Lico in the tree-lined central plaza of Coatepeque. I watched groups of teenagers passing by in their school uniforms. The older girls had their pleated skirts hiked up over their knees, and the older boys had their hair cut in patterns like the ones I'd seen in the videos from Miami the night before. I wondered if any of the books they carried were history books. And, if so, what they said about this country's twentieth century. Would there be anything about the failed revolution to which Lico had devoted the better part of his life? I wondered if these kids, born at the height of the war, knew much at all about what had happened in those years. Or if they even cared.

My friend César would have cared. His childhood heroes had been Che Guevara and, his local counterpart, a guerrilla named Chano. But then again, he hadn't had access to cable TV growing up.

My reverie was interrupted when a short stocky man approached me with an extended hand, which I shook even before I realized that it belonged to Lico. I looked for the missing finger just to be sure, and it struck me that during all those hours of talking I had forgotten how small he was. I did immediately recognize his voice, affable and energetic and — as soon as we were back in the office — filled with a sense of urgency as if the twenty-year-old events he was describing had happened only yesterday.

He told of ORPA's very first military operation in September 1979. How, after weeks of planning, they occupied a plantation under Santa María, announcing their existence to the world and declaring war on the Guatemalan state. He told of their very first battle two months later. How they fought in the woods above La Igualdad and had their first combat casualty.

He told of how their operations evolved over the next year. How they went from occupying unguarded plantations to moving against plantations that were guarded by military policemen. How they went from occupying unguarded communities to moving against municipalities with military police detachments. And how they were soon ready to attack army posts.

He told of how new recruits began pouring in, mostly from the indigenous communities in the highlands, so that there came a time when several languages were being spoken in camp. He told of how, in a matter of months, the fronts doubled in size, how the three divided and became six. And how the six kept growing.

He told how he was promoted to commander and put in charge of the Ixmatá Front (named in memory of one of ORPA's founders). How he took it over to Quetzaltenango to work on the base of Santa María and adjacent volcanoes, while another veteran, a Ladino from the city named Lucas, took charge of a new front that would operate on the Sacuchum Mountain.

He told of how the army's tactics also evolved. How, once it realized it couldn't outmaneuver the guerrillas in the mountain terrain, it started using more force and entering from multiple directions with the aim of surrounding the guerrillas. "A guerrilla surrounded is a guerrilla annihilated," said Lico, reciting a maxim of guerrilla warfare. But surrounding maneuvers were also difficult on this terrain. And so the guerrillas' main tactic would be to shoot at the army and then depart as quickly as possible. As long as they could avoid being surrounded, they could keep fighting and keep growing.

He talked through the morning and into the afternoon, conjuring up people and places and events in more detail than I would ever be able to reproduce, recreating the flow of history as it accelerated, irreversibly, toward a revolution that would never be.

VII

The rest of the *compas* were hidden among the coffee trees up the mountainside, Javier recalled. He and Paco had climbed down through the grove to take a look at the soldiers resting in the plantation below. He was looking through field glasses, whispering what he saw to Paco, who recorded it in his notebook. A helicopter flew high overhead. They ducked down. When it had passed, they continued with their reconnaissance. Suddenly the branch of a tree exploded above them. They turned and saw that the helicopter was hovering up the hill, between them and the other *compas,* lowering soldiers into the grove. Further above, a *compa* emerged from hiding and sprayed the helicopter with his Thompson. They looked below and saw the soldiers now climbing toward them. They were about to be surrounded. So they ran. He followed Paco as fast as he could, downhill at an angle, across rows of coffee trees, plunging through the branches, intuiting the terrain without being able to see what lay ahead, until he slammed into a pole waiting for him at chest level. One moment he was running full tilt, the next he was on his back, gasping for air. When he was able to breathe, they continued, more slowly now. But the pain in his chest had just begun.

Javier stood alone in camp, exhausted. Two other *compas,* Alex and Pedrito, had just left for sentry duty. Weeks had passed, but the pain was still with him, making it difficult to keep up on their daily marches.

Suddenly there was an explosion, and gunfire erupted all around. Javier fell to the ground and crawled over to a rock — behind or in front of it, he didn't know, since the shooting seemed to come from all over at once. He readied his gun and tried to figure out where the enemy was. Pedrito came running into the clearing, clutching his stomach, and collapsed next to him. The gunfire was deafening. Javier watched Pedrito die.

The gunfire stopped. Javier got to his feet and tried to run. His chest ached. He could manage little more than a jog. He heard something fall to the ground nearby, like fruit from a tree. He glanced over and saw smoke and felt himself lifted into the air.

When he recovered his senses, he was on the ground. His gun was gone. He saw another a few feet away and crawled over to it. The shooting was coming from behind him now. He turned and saw the soldiers. They had filled a shallow bunker that the *compas* had dug at the camp's perimeter. They had their guns pointed over the edge but were shooting blindly, too scared to peer up at their target. He took aim at the tops of their heads and fired. Then he noticed other soldiers running around the side. He was going to be surrounded. Guerrilla surrounded, guerrilla annihilated — he knew the maxim. He got up and pushed himself through the woods. Bullets whistled around him. He came to the edge of a small cliff and, seeing nowhere to go, threw himself over.

He landed hard and lay still. Hours passed. He heard the fighting subside and the soldiers leave. More hours passed. He heard Paco and Tomás talking some distance away. One of them said, "Javier must be dead."

With all the air his battered lungs could muster, he yelled, "Wounded!"

VIII

After taking a late lunch, Lico and I returned to the bare room he had been filling with his stories for the last two days. Evening was approaching, but we wanted to get through the crucial year of 1981 before we broke for the day.

Toward the end of 1981, Lico received orders to move the Ixmatá Front back to the Sacuchum Mountain. And in mid-December he led his force of eighty across the Río Naranjo, where they met a guide who took them across the top of the mountain to a large camp that Lucas had established just below Sacuchum. Lico and Lucas then left their troops and set out with four guards westward to Tajumulco. There, along with the commanders of the other fronts, they would meet with the commander in chief, Gaspar Ilom, who had come from Mexico to explain to them the new direction their war was taking.

And so Lico found himself back on the volcano where they had begun a decade earlier. Spirits were high. After eight years of preparation and two years of war, they were at long last on their way to victory. The fighting had been brutal. They now had *compañeros* buried throughout the Sierra Madre. But they had yet to lose a single battle. And their forces kept growing.

The military government, meanwhile, was floundering. It faced mounting criticism abroad because of its repressive practices. And it was facing dissension within its own ranks because of its inability to mount an effective response to the guerrilla forces that were multiplying throughout the highlands. In addition to ORPA, there were three other guerrilla organizations gaining strength, and talks were under way to unite the four into a single revolutionary army under joint command.

Gaspar briefed them on these promising developments and then announced that they would be merging the six fronts to form three large "columns." With these columns, they would be able to carry out large-scale operations against the army. And, perhaps more important, they would be able to mount a massive display of force that would impress and inspire an already sympathetic public. Lico had seen how that could look when his troops had joined those of Lucas on the Sacuchum Mountain. And what a sight it was! Some 140 combatants, infused with a spirit of camaraderie and confidence like nothing he had seen before.

And there was something else that Lico had never seen before. Lucas had created a fixed camp in the woods just below Sacuchum and was relying almost entirely on that community for food and supplies. Just about every day, townspeople arrived in camp, their mules loaded with provisions. It was an arrangement they wouldn't have attempted in the past, since permanent camps exposed them to easier detection by the enemy, and close contact with a community exposed their collaborators. But the time for caution seemed to have come to an end. The final push was at hand. Support from Sacuchum wasn't anything new, of course. The town's *cusheros* had helped them since they first came to the mountain. But this was different. This was an entire community openly supporting the revolution.

In Sacuchum, Lico thought he saw the future.

The commanders celebrated Christmas together on Tajumulco and, after a week of meetings, headed back to their troops. Lico and Lucas had left two trusted captains, Chilo and Chano (the one who had been César's hero), in charge of the fronts. They didn't expect any trouble from the army. It was Christmas, after all, and even the enemy took vacations.

So it was a big surprise when, as they reached the lower slopes of Tajumulco, they heard the echo of artillery fire coming from the far side of Sacuchum. They found the home of a collaborator and learned, to their horror, that truckloads of soldiers had been seen heading for the

mountain the day before, which meant that somewhere up above, all those combatants they had amassed were now fighting without their commanders. Chilo and Chano were experienced fighters, but they weren't used to commanding such large numbers. And what especially worried Lico was that many of the newer troops in the Ixmatá Front had never operated on this mountain and didn't know the terrain as they should.

They were looking at a possible catastrophe. And though it might be too late to prevent it, the two commanders decided to try to reach their troops. They rested a few hours (they had been hiking all day) and then, at three in the morning, they crossed the road that ran between the mountains, and began to climb up the other side. At the first light of day, they noticed fresh boot prints of soldiers on the path they were climbing. So they left it and began to cut their way through the woods with machetes. Instead of heading directly to the camp, they decided to look for collaborators in the town of Sacuchum who could help them figure out how to avoid the army and find their own troops. They reached the mountaintop on Sunday morning and headed for the home of a collaborator in a wooded area on the outskirts of town.

There they were in for another surprise. The three men they found at the house were astounded to see them. As they talked in agitated voices, it soon became clear why: the army had just occupied the town. There were hundreds of soldiers in the valley and more on the surrounding ridges. Lico and Lucas had just walked into the biggest encircling maneuver ever attempted against them.

"So there we were in the house with these three *compas*," Lico told me, looking astounded himself. "And two of them tell us that they have to go, that the army had summoned everyone to the center of town. Lucas tells them not to go, that the army might kill them. But they say, 'If we don't go, then we'll give ourselves away.' So the two leave, saying they would meet back in the house afterward. But Lucas grabs the other man and begs him not to go.

"So we waited. The whole afternoon. Several times a helicopter circled overhead. All this time, we were thinking that *we* were the principal objective of the military operation. You see, the target of the army's operations had always been the guerrillas. In this case, they had gone after Lucas's camp, and they got my front also.

"At seven o'clock the *compas* still hadn't arrived. Around eight, we left the house and went to hide in the woods nearby. All night the dogs were barking. But the men didn't return. And at dawn, we left to find our troops. We knew the army was all around us in the woods. At one point we even saw the back of a soldier — the last in line passing ahead of us. We arrived at a village in the woods and found an old *compa*. This man was about seventy years old and had been very active supporting us over the years. He was surprised to see us. And he told us that the soldiers had just left moments before. 'What happened?' we asked him. 'They burned all the houses,' he said and told us that our troops had left the area. 'You had better get out of here before they catch you.'

"So we continued down the mountainside, cutting a path through the underbrush and, miraculously, we got through. We reached the plantations and continued to the coast. It took us five days, traveling by night, hiding by day — five days without eating — until finally we arrived in the town of Pajapita and went to the homes of some old collaborators.

"It would be two more weeks before we reestablished contact with the troops and found out what had happened to them. The army had come in with thousands of soldiers. Fortunately, our people saw the attack coming. They set up a series of ambushes a kilometer below the camp and then fought the length of the kilometer. A whole day of combat, and they didn't lose a single combatant!" Lico beamed with pride as he said this. "That night they decided to get down the mountain to the army's rearguard. And they made it through! They had broken the circle!"

Had it ended there, the story would have been a happy one for Lico. But he didn't look happy, and he didn't look surprised by my next question: "And what about Sacuchum?" He gazed out the window, shook his head, and said that it had been several more weeks before they realized that the circle had served another purpose.

⬇

"The people of Sacuchum never imagined what was going to happen. The whole community showed up in the center of town because they were told whoever doesn't show is a guerrilla. But had they known . . ."

Once I had managed to get a former army captain talking about the massacres, and I asked him what might have been going through the minds of the officers who ordered them. "You never see the enemy," he told me. "You may be out there for days being shot at, being ambushed, running into mines. And you never see the combatants trying to kill you. All you see are the people. And you know the people are supporting the guerrillas. You know that without them, there would be no guerrillas. So they are your enemy."

That answer might accurately describe the mental state of the perpetrators, but does it explain why the massacres happened? In this case Lico (like the people in Sacuchum) was convinced that the killing wasn't the impulsive act of frustrated officers. "This wasn't some crazy operation. This was the work of military intelligence. They had put together a list of names beforehand. This was planned."

So why did they do it?

"After two years of combat, we had always come out victorious. They couldn't hurt us. The army decided to give a lesson to the population. That was the only way they could stop the guerrillas. And what was the crime of the people of Sacuchum?"

As he posed this question, his voice faltered and I looked up at his face. We had been talking for two days, and by now he had mentioned dozens of *compañeros* who had died, and even described horrible deaths, like those of the many wounded combatants whose bodies seized up with tetanus. But he always recounted the suffering in a matter-of-fact tone. Not that he was unfeeling, for in fact he conveyed intense feelings as he spoke — enthusiasm about the revolutionary cause, pride in his *compañeros'* commitment to that cause, determination not to succumb to fear. Now, for the first time, I saw pain in his eyes. He took a deep breath, struggling, it seemed, to hold back tears. *It wasn't just a few people dying this time*, I thought. *It was the future of the revolution that he had thought they represented.* But then, as he answered his own question, I reconsidered: *maybe his grief was for the people after all.*

"We would say now, with absolute pride, that they were men who died in order to see profound changes in our country. It was with that hope that the community of Sacuchum gave its blood in that massacre. They died for conviction. How is it that those two *compañeros* died knowing that we — the commanders! — were right there, easy prisoners? Other men would have turned us in. But they didn't. It's an example of how the people of Sacuchum died with the secret. It's an example of the valor of those men. They could have turned us in, but they didn't. They died convinced of their ideas. Of this, for me, Sacuchum will always be an example."

Outside in the street a heavy vehicle rumbled by. Perhaps a truck full of coffee beans headed for the docks. Or one of those four-door pickups weighed down with appliances rolling in from across the border. Or a minibus carrying young men to the threshold of a long journey north. As the radios around the block blared in tinny unison the same canned beat — "*Ay Macarena!*" — the wheels of the world economy churned away, deliberate, unhurried, unrelenting.

THE POLITICIANS

I

IN THOSE DAYS Bartolo Reyes had been municipal secretary. Whenever anyone died in La Igualdad, it had been his job to make the death official. He would first have to *levantar el cadáver*, or "retrieve the corpse," by identifying the body and authorizing the *bomberos* to take it to the morgue in Coatepeque. Then he would record the name, age, and presumed cause of death in the *libro de defunciones,* the "book of deaths."

One of the most memorable corpses Bartolo retrieved was the first ORPA guerrilla to die in combat. It had been in 1979, just after the fall of Somoza in Nicaragua, and the people in La Igualdad, still abuzz with the news of the Sandinista triumph, had been treated to an even greater thrill, the sound of gunfire in the hills above them. The shooting lasted over an hour, and the municipal authorities figured there would be corpses to retrieve, although they waited a week until it seemed safe enough to go look for them.

The expedition left town at dawn. The men climbed quickly through El Progreso and into the woods above. They left the path and hacked their way through the underbrush until their arms grew weary. At last they arrived at the empty guerrilla camp and found, some distance away, the dead guerrilla. He was sprawled on his back, the way they themselves used to fall as kids, playing war in the coffee groves below. His body looked intact, but approaching it they noticed the odor and then saw the worms crawling out of the eye sockets. The back of the man's head was gone.

They managed to tie the stiff arms and legs to a pole and took turns carrying the pole as they climbed down the mountain. The load swung awkwardly from side to side, and by the time they reached El Progreso they could no longer bear its stench. So they buried the guerrilla in an unmarked grave there in the plantation. They returned to town exhausted and still nauseated.

It was only the first of many war dead that Bartolo would retrieve in the coming years. In a way the job got easier with time. The sight of death no longer made him wince. Its smell no longer turned his stomach. But as his knowledge of what bullets can do to a body increased, something else also grew inside of him. And even as the corpses became more manageable, they would continue to feed this something until it became almost unbearable.

⚜

Bartolo was the man who could help the Truth Commission gather testimony in La Igualdad, according to Javier. The two had grown up together in La Independencia. Both had left the plantation as young men, Javier for the mountains, Bartolo for the town hall, where he served as municipal secretary for a decade before being elected mayor in 1988. At the end of his term, he became a justice of the peace and now commuted to work every day at the courthouse in Coatepeque.

Bartolo looked older than Javier at times, and at times he looked younger. His thick hair was graying on the sides, and when I first saw him, following Javier out of the courthouse, he wore the bland but earnest expression of an aging bureaucrat. Away from the crowded doorway his face changed. He flashed a boyish smile, laughing at something Javier was telling him. He spat on the ground and pulled a comb from his back pocket and ran it through his hair like a teenager grooming himself in the schoolyard. He looked like a man who couldn't stop being a boy, or maybe a boy forced too soon to be a man. When Javier introduced us, he changed yet again, reconfiguring the man-boy combination in a way that made me think of a clown. He spoke to me with an exaggerated formality, all the while caressing his slightly bulging belly and spitting absentmindedly at the end of his sentences. Later, as I was adjusting the motorcycle's brakes, I looked over and saw him discussing something with Javier. The clown was gone, replaced by someone entirely new — serious, thoughtful, even dignified. The face of a provincial statesman, I thought, the man who had been mayor.

I guessed this was Bartolo's truest face. But I was never sure. It would be a while before I got another good look at him. The work we did together in the coming weeks could be done only in the tricky light of dawn and dusk, or by the feeble glow of low-wattage electric bulbs, or under the stars. The next time I did see Bartolo at midday, the lines of his face had been redrawn by fear.

⁂

La Igualdad was a different place when I was with Bartolo. Or rather I was a different person — still a stranger in town, but not so strange a presence as before. And though I had already met many individuals in La Igualdad, with Bartolo, for the first time, I felt I was meeting the community.

Everyone knew Bartolo, and just about everyone seemed to like him. Wherever we went, in town and in the plantations, people called out his name, and he responded with theirs. "I know everyone here," he told me. "That's why I got more votes than any mayor in the history of La Igualdad." And though it was years since he had been mayor, the people still stopped him to talk, to tell him their problems. He would listen and nod and spit and dispense advice.

A few days after Javier introduced us, I rode to La Igualdad and waited for him in the Temple, a pub with two tables, a *Happy Days*–era juke box, and a single glossy poster advertising beer with a blonde woman who wore more make-up than clothing. The Temple belonged to the father of Bartolo's *mujer*, Ana, the woman who would have been Bartolo's second wife if he weren't still married to the first.

Bartolo arrived at dusk and led me through a curtained door into the kitchen of the adjoining house, where Ana was making tortillas. We sat for dinner with a quiet, white-haired man, who was Ana's father, and as we ate, I wondered whether it would be okay to bring up our work with the Truth Commission while still at the table.

Bartolo answered the question without my asking it. He pulled out a piece of paper with a list of names and said that these old men could tell me some of the history of the Agrarian Reform. He knew that wasn't the main reason I was here, but I didn't protest. When the old man got up from the table, Bartolo leaned over and said quietly, "I also have another list. But we'll discuss that later."

After dinner we pushed the motorcycle into the pub for the night and walked two blocks across town to Bartolo's other house — the home he had once shared with the wife who now lived in the capital. It was made of cement-block walls and a concrete floor, and had three rooms, which contained two beds, two chairs, a desk, framed photos and diplomas — all of it covered with dust. Bartolo took a broom from the bathroom and killed two roaches and swept them out the front door. Then he closed the door and gave me the key. I could stay here whenever I wanted, he said.

We sat down in the two chairs and he pulled out a folded piece of paper and held it in his hand. "Look, Don Daniel . . ." For the first time he looked me straight in the eyes. "I know that I look like a fool." In the dim light, it was hard to see what he looked like. "But that's what you do here to survive. I've seen lots of things, and I've thought lots of things. Only here it's better not to show that. It's better that they think you're a fool. Do you understand?"

He began to unfold the paper. "I'm telling you these things because you're a friend of Javier and Javier's a friend of mine. A friend for life. When they were in the mountains, I was here, and I always tried to help them. Just as I tried to help the people here. I was able to help because I knew things. That's why knowing things was dangerous."

He spread the piece of paper on his knee and looked up at me again. "Things here were tough. Many people got taken away. As municipal secretary, my job was to retrieve the corpses and record the information. Of course, when there was no corpse, there was nothing to retrieve, nothing to record. According to the government, there was no death. So I kept another list. A list of the people who were abducted. I kept it hidden there behind that diploma." He pointed to a framed high school diploma on the wall behind him. "But there came a time when the risk got to be too much for me. So I burned the list."

He ran his finger over the paper, pressing out the creases. "Since we talked the other day, I've tried to make another list from what I remember. I couldn't remember everything, but I remember a lot. I've put the names and the name of the relatives who can tell the commission what happened."

He passed me the piece of paper. It was typed with a mechanical typewriter. It contained two columns: one listed some forty people who had been killed or disappeared; the other their surviving relatives.

"Will these relatives want to talk to the commission?" I asked.

"They want to talk. Most of them. They've never had a chance to say what happened. But now will they?" He was silent for a moment, staring at the list in my hands. "You see, people here are still scared. Very scared. So if this thing is not done just right" — his eyes now returned to mine, he leaned forward, and, as if for emphasis, he whispered — "the commission won't get a thing."

II

Doing it right meant two things for Bartolo. First and foremost, it meant being discreet. "If the commission people come here and make a lot of noise, that's it, they'll get nothing. The people will clam up. In La Igualdad, no one likes it when you make a lot of noise."

It also meant giving the process of collecting testimony the feel of a public event. "It's better to bring the people together as a group so that they don't feel singled out. So they feel solidarity."

Bartolo had an idea for how to reconcile these two apparently contradictory requirements. We would hold a meeting in a public building where the commission investigators would collect testimonies, but we would only invite the families of victims — and not all of them. There were some people, he said, it would be better not to invite. "The mayor, for example."

"Who's the mayor now?" I asked.

"Alberto Chavez."

"The school principal?" I remembered the bland, soft-spoken man who had given me his father's history book.

"That's right."

"He was tortured by the army, right?"

"That's right. And it affected him in the head. He can't be trusted with things like this."

The meeting would be on a Sunday, market day in La Igualdad, when there was a lot of movement and it was easier for people to move around unnoticed. We would personally invite the people on the list, visiting each one ahead of time and explaining what the meeting entailed. "The advantage I have is that people are used to seeing me walking everywhere in La Igualdad from all the political campaigns I did. So they'll be less suspicious, less afraid."

⬇

The next day I rode up to San Marcos and stopped at the commission's office. The head of the investigation team, a Spanish woman, showed me into an office adorned with maps of the region and posters, now ubiquitous throughout Guatemala, that showed a young indigenous woman in mourning above the words *"Ya es tiempo de decir la verdad"* (it's time now to tell the truth).

The Spanish woman seemed very serious and professional. She accepted Bartolo's plan and seemed to understand the rationale behind it. We set a tentative date to hold the meeting, a Sunday three weeks away. As I got up to leave, she asked for Bartolo's name. I hesitated a moment, unsure whether Bartolo wanted anyone to know about his involvement. But I remembered that confidentiality was rule number one for the commission's investigators. If there was anyone I should be able to tell, it would be her. So I did.

⬇

I spent the next week interviewing Javier and Lico. Then one morning I called the courthouse in Coatepeque and got through to Bartolo. "Is tomorrow still good?" I asked. Without saying what, when, or where, we agreed to meet the following night at the bar in La Igualdad.

As I was getting ready to leave Xela the next morning, the Spanish woman phoned. "Something has come up," she told me. "Something interesting. I think you should come by the office so we can talk about it." She wasn't going to reveal more on the phone.

When I arrived at the San Marcos office two hours later, the Spanish woman had gone out and left one of her investigators with the charge of telling me what the interesting something was. The team had visited La Igualdad the weekend before and met with the local leader of a new leftist political party and told him about the meeting we were planning. When he asked who we were, they gave him Bartolo's name. He then told them that they were making a big mistake, that Bartolo had no credibility in the community, that everyone thought of him as a corrupt politician, that no one would go to a meeting he had organized.

"What ever happened to confidentiality?" I asked, trying to contain my anger.

She offered an excuse: they thought this person was trustworthy because he came recommended by one of their contacts in San Marcos.

I nodded. "So who was this person? Can I ask?"

She hesitated. I had just called them on violating their confidentiality rule, and now I was asking her to break it again. "Was his name Mario?" I asked.

She nodded yes. I guess she felt she owed it to me.

"Chubby guy, health worker?"

She nodded.

"Well," I said, "my sources tell me he's with the military intelligence."

"Oh, no." She looked genuinely alarmed.

"So what did you all decide with Mario?"

They had decided to hold two meetings on the same day, she told me, one organized by Bartolo and me, and the other one organized by him.

There are some things you shouldn't do when you're angry. Riding a motorcycle is one of them, especially on a road like the one from San Marcos to La Igualdad. Roads like these don't tolerate road rage. Twice as I powered my way down the mountain, loose stones nearly knocked the front wheel out from under me.

So much for being discreet. If Mario was with the G-2, he would be telling the army about the meeting. If he wasn't, they would probably find out now anyway. He would be trumpeting it to the world. Perhaps it made no difference what the army knew (eventually news would reach them). The real problem, if Bartolo was right, was that the noise Mario made could scare away the families.

Lurking below my anger was a doubt. What if what Mario had told them about Bartolo *was* actually true? I thought I could trust Bartolo because I thought I could trust Javier. But even after all this time, I realized, my knowledge of this world was limited enough to leave room for large doubts.

III

I arrived in La Igualdad in mid-afternoon, rode through town without stopping, and climbed up to La Patria. That doubt had gotten under my skin, and I needed to find someone to help me get it out. Someone who knew Bartolo and Mario but was beholden to neither.

Everyone in La Igualdad was beholden to somebody else. The trick to finding anything out here was mapping the beholding patterns and working around and through them. In the past I had gone to town to learn more about the plantation, now I would go to the plantation to learn more about the town. The person I had in mind was the head mechanic. He had a secure position in the plantation; he seemed to be doing well, and his doing well didn't depend on anyone in La Igualdad other than Sara.

I found him alone in the processing plant and told him the problem: a team of investigators from the Truth Commission needed someone to arrange a meeting with the families of people killed during the war. Who would do a better job, Bartolo or Mario?

"Bartolo," he said without any hesitation. "Everyone knows him."

"What was he like as a mayor?"

"He was a good mayor. He got along with everyone."

"Did he have problems with corruption?"

"No." He shook his head. "He's an honest man."

"What about Mario?"

"People are scared of Mario. He makes too much noise."

I got corroborating assessments from the cook and one of the drivers, and then headed back down the mountain. I reached the town, crossed to the other side, and, as I slowed to turn a corner, heard someone call out, "Daniel!"

It was Mario. I had been hoping to avoid him until I had conferred with Bartolo. But what could I do now? I let the engine idle and put on a friendly face.

"Where have you been?" he asked. "When are you going to come visit us? I've got lots of interesting things to tell you." I noticed now that he was wearing a T-shirt of a national indigenous rights organization. "We should talk. Where are you staying?"

"With Bartolo."

"Ahh." He smiled. "Bartolo's a friend of mine. Tell him I need to talk to him. It's very important."

⚜

I intended to tell Bartolo right away about what I'd learned in San Marcos. But I needed to talk to him alone, and when he arrived at dusk, there were people in the house. When we went outside, there were people standing near the motorcycle. And as we rode north out of town, the engine was too noisy to permit a conversation. Even when the engine stalled and we came to a stop on a long hill in La Independencia, I put it off again. I knew I had to tell him. He had put his trust in me because of Javier, and now that trust had been blown. But I was worried about how he would take the news. And I didn't feel like breaking it to him on a dark mountain road. Better somewhere where I could see his face and respond more carefully to whatever he said.

Bartolo's plan was to begin with families who lived in the upper reaches of La Igualdad. But the engine kept stalling, and it became clear it wouldn't be able to carry us much farther up the mountain. So we turned around and headed back to town.

We stopped fifty meters before the bust of Justo Rufino Barrios, at an opening in the row of houses. It was the entrance to a street that dropped down into the ravine between the town and a plantation. There were street lamps that created small pools of pale light every forty feet. Most of the street and the houses remained hidden in the dark space in between. The lamps obscured as much of the street as they illuminated.

"This is San Pedrito," Bartolo said as we got off the bike and started down the hill. "This street was hit real hard. They abducted one man one night. And they came back for some others the next, and then more the next, for a whole week."

I was about to tell him about Mario when he stepped up to the door of a house at the edge of one of the first pools of light and rapped his knuckles on the wall. A woman appeared in the doorway, her plastic sandals, long skirt, and T-shirt visible in the light. Her face and shoulders remained in the shadows.

She greeted Bartolo as though he were an old friend, and then added *buenas noches*, apparently to me. Bartolo made no introductions. He simply began to chat with her about her family. She spoke quietly and at first said very little, answering Bartolo's questions about where her sib-

lings were working. Soon, though, Bartolo got her talking about the recent crime wave in La Igualdad. I stood by quietly as she told the story of
a cousin who had recently been assaulted. When she finished, Bartolo
broached the topic that had brought us: "The reason we came by is that
there's this commission now. They call it the commission of the truth.
And what it does is it goes to all the communities so that people can tell
about their relatives who have been kidnapped or killed. Now, they took
your brother from here, right?"

"*Sí pues.*"

"When was it that they took him away?"

"*Pues,* I'd say about fifteen years ago."

"See that's the sort of information that the commission wants."

"*Sí pues.*"

"So we wanted to see if you or your mother wanted to come talk to the
commission?"

She was quiet. Finally she said, "Is this the same thing Mario's doing?"

Damn it, I thought.

"What's Mario doing?" Bartolo asked.

She explained that Mario had come by saying that the United Nations
had asked him to find people to testify about what happened during the
war. "It's nothing bad is it?"

"No, it's nothing bad," Bartolo said and, pointing to me, added, "that's
why we came by here together."

This was my cue. I began to talk, explaining that this Truth Commission
had been created by an agreement between the government and the ex-
guerrillas, and that the idea was to give families like hers a chance to tell
what happened during the war. I said that all the information would be
kept confidential and that the commission had already gathered testimony from thousands of people throughout the country and none of
these people had had any problems. I tried to sound reassuring. But I was
talking to a shadow, and I had no idea what effect my words were having.
When I stopped, there was silence, then her soft voice: "*Sí pues.*"

"Think about it," Bartolo told her. She said she would.

⇓

"There's something I need to tell you," I said as we walked down the
street. But Bartolo asked me to wait and called out to a woman leaning
out a window of a *tienda* across the street. "What a miracle!" she said,

laughing. "Where have you been?" An electric bulb inside lit half her face, so I could see half a smile as she and Bartolo talked about why he hadn't been around lately. "And this one?" she asked him, pointing her chin in my direction.

"He's with me. We came to talk to you about something." His tone became more serious. "See there's this commission that's going to come to La Igualdad . . ."

She interrupted him: "That guy Mario already came by talking about this."

"Really?" Bartolo asked, not looking at all surprised. "What did he say?"

"Something about a commission where people can go say if their family members were taken away during the war."

He nodded. "Yeah, that's it. Are you going to go?"

"You think it's okay?"

"Yeah, it's okay."

"All right then."

Bartolo asked if she could pass the word to other families. She nodded and, pointing her chin to the house we had come from, asked, "Did you talk to them?"

Bartolo told her yes, and she shook her head. "*Pobrecita.* You remember when they brought her brother back? Marched him right past the house. He looked like he was already half dead. She ran out screaming. Tried to grab him but they threw her to the side."

"*Sí pues.*" Bartolo nodded. "And he brought them to your brother, right?"

"*Sí pues.*"

They were both silent for a moment. Then he said, "Things were tough back then."

"*Sí pues,* real tough."

"*Sí pues.* And no one could ever talk about it."

"*Sí pues.*"

They were silent again. Then Bartolo said, "Well, anyway, the meeting will probably be Sunday next week. We'll let you know. And if you have a chance to spread the word to other people who lost family members. We'll try to talk to them, but if you see them, could you also tell them?"

"All right. But you know they're going to be scared."

Bartolo nodded. "But they don't need to be. Not anymore. Things are different now."

⇓

"Bartolo, there's something I need to tell you," I tried again as we continued down the street. "It's about Mario." This time I got through. "Apparently the commission's team in San Marcos came here last week. Did you know that?"

"I was away in the capital. But I heard that there had been a United Nations car here."

"Well, they came and they talked to Mario. They told him what we were doing. And he spoke badly of you to them. He said people in the community didn't trust you and that no one would go to a meeting you organized." I waited for a reaction, but got none, no change of expression, at least none I could see in this light. "I'm really sorry about them mentioning your name like that. I only gave it to them because I assumed everything with them was confidential. That's the way it's supposed to be."

He nodded and spoke in the same even tone he always used. "That's all right. You don't need to worry about it." It didn't sound like *he* was worrying. "I don't think I'll have any problems. If there's a problem, it's for these families."

"Yeah, well, that's the other thing I was worried about. I've heard that Mario worked with military intelligence."

He shook his head slowly. "I don't think so. Maybe before. The problem is something else. The problem is that he wants to do politics. But he doesn't know how. He's not from here, and he doesn't understand the people. The people won't go to the meeting if he organizes it."

Bartolo's equanimity seemed puzzling to me then, but I would come to recognize it as a central aspect of his personality — or at least his public persona. Bartolo never showed anger. And he never criticized anyone. He would point out the adverse effects of people's actions, but without ever speaking ill of the people themselves. His easygoing manner made me trust him more, and it made me feel my own anger was out of place.

I said, "The San Marcos team decided to hold two meetings, one organized by us and one by him."

He shook his head again. "That doesn't make sense. That will just confuse people. It's better we all do it together."

"Well, we could ask the team to reschedule the meetings and do ours a week earlier without telling him?"

"No, we shouldn't fall into the same thing as Mario. That wouldn't be right."

⬇

The next stop was with an older man who wore ragged trousers and a faded T-shirt that was once "Property of Newark Fire Department." Bartolo took a new approach this time, drawing the man first into a discussion about the war. "We're talking with families of people who were disappeared. Like I told this *señor*, things here were really tough, especially here in San Pedrito."

"*Ay Dios!*" The man shook his head and looked at me. "It was real bad, *señor*. At this hour, you couldn't be outside. Everyone kept inside with the lights out. You never knew who Cándido would go after next."

"Cándido?" I asked

"Cándido Juárez," Bartolo explained to me. "He was the military commissioner here. He decided who the military took away."

"A bad person," the old man said. "If it weren't for him, they wouldn't have taken away so many innocent people."

"Well, listen," Bartolo said, ready now to announce our business. "The reason we came by was to let you know that there's a commission now, a commission of truth, so that people can tell the truth about what happened."

The man nodded. "Yeah, I heard about that already. My nephew told me that the doctor, that Mario, came by to get me to talk to some commission."

"And?"

"And, I tell you, when I heard about this at first, I thought it could be a good thing. All these years we haven't been able to say the truth. But then I got to thinking. All day, working out there in the coffee groves, I was thinking about it. And what I thought was, what will stop them from doing to me the same thing that they did to my son?" He looked from Bartolo to me. "You understand? What will stop them?"

"I understand," Bartolo said. "Completely. That's why Don Daniel here and I are going around talking to people so they know they don't have to be scared. This commission has the backing of the whole world, the government of Guatemala, and the governments of other countries."

The man looked me up and down as if he were sizing up the extent of the international support. Bartolo continued: "You see, things are different now. With the peace process and all, and with all the foreigners here now, the government and the army have changed the way they do things."

Still looking at me, the man said: "Maybe you're right. Maybe it's okay now. But my question is, what happens when things change again? What happens when there's another coup?"

"Things can't change the way they used to. The United States won't let there be another coup. If the army tries to take power, the gringos won't let them."

Would they really? I wondered and, for a moment, considered qualifying Bartolo's comment. But I kept silent.

"Well, could be," the man said, shaking his head. "Could be."

Bartolo didn't pressure him. "Think about it. We'll let you know the date."

🔻

I asked Bartolo if he thought the man would go. "Maybe not," he said. We left the last pool of street-lamp light and headed into the darkness below. "It's like I told you. The people here are still scared. That's why you have to handle this sort of thing just right. Otherwise you just scare people more. You make things worse than they already are."

"Do you think Mario will handle it right?"

He spat on the ground, then said, "You should probably talk to him so we can coordinate things better."

I persisted. "And what if, for example, he wants to tell the mayor?"

Bartolo now laughed. "I don't think he'll tell Alberto anything. Actually, they don't get along very well." He then told me of how the mayor had been gathering signatures for a petition asking the army to station troops in La Igualdad in order to fight crime. One day Mario went into the mayor's office to demand that the petition be stopped. He said it violated the peace accords. "Mario had been drinking beforehand, and when Alberto insulted him, he let him have it. He jumped across the desk and began hitting him."

He laughed again and continued. "That was a big mistake. First because a lot of people here actually do want the army to come back. It's not that they like the army. They're still scared of the army. But they're more scared of the criminals. So they're choosing what seems less bad. It's less bad because it's predictable. The robbers rob anyone. The army won't bother you so long as you don't provoke them. And that's Mario's other mistake: going against the army in public. People here don't like that. People learned a lesson during the war: you take on the army, and the whole community will pay for it."

⇓

We turned another corner and continued down the hill. Now there were no street lamps. I wasn't sure if there was even a street. Bartolo switched on a flashlight, but its batteries were dying, and, after trying to shake them to life, he shut it off. All I could see of the world now was silhouettes against the shimmering light of the night sky — Bartolo's figure moving ahead of me, banana trees above us to the left, the mountain climbing up from the ravine to the right. It seemed the universe had been turned inside out. The earth was an empty darkness, while the heavens were filled with shades and textures and shapes. The connecting of dots to make constellations, which seems such a willful stretch of the imagination in urban skies, was unavoidable here.

When my eyes finally adjusted to the darkness, I began to make out the shadows around us. As the imagination populates the stars, it can also give shapes and meanings to the shadows — spooky shapes, menacing meanings. I remembered César and his friends in La Soledad telling me about La Llorona, the phantom woman who haunted these hills, appearing to men in the night and attempting to seduce them with her beauty and her plaintive appeals for solace. When they succumbed, she would lead them to their deaths, over cliffs or into rivers. Every man in the plantation could recall his own encounter with La Llorona. They laughed, though, when they recounted them for me.

They didn't laugh when they told me about the other figures that used to haunt the back roads and paths of the piedmont. These figures would attempt to seduce men with talk of injustice and revolution. The fool who succumbed to their deception, and provided the food or information they asked for, would discover only too late that these men were not guerrillas but army agents in disguise. Their reward would be a painful death.

This is what it must have been like on those nights, I thought as we climbed down into the ravine — the silence, the stillness, the shadows.

⇓

We came to a house with the windows shuttered and only a crack of light visible under the closed door. Bartolo whistled and knocked. "Who's there?" a man's voice asked from inside. Bartolo announced himself, and a shuttered window opened just enough for a man to peer out. As Bartolo told him about the commission, the one eye in the window seemed to stare at me. When Bartolo stopped talking, there was silence. Then the voice said, "This is something political, isn't it?"

"Well, it's something done by both sides," Bartolo said. "And it has backing from all the countries in the United Nations . . ."

"Yeah, this *is* political. I'm sure of it."

IV

Bartolo worked during the day in the Coatepeque courthouse, and almost everyone on our list worked in the plantations — which was why we could only find them at the beginning and end of the day.

We set out each morning in the predawn darkness, riding down the mountain as the eastern sky turned red, passing people walking to work and the morning bus lumbering down to Coatepeque. The air was cool, and the ground was humid. Mist hung in the ravines. Every few minutes Santiaguito coughed up a column of smoke in the distance. When the sun finally peaked above the mountains, it set millions of dew-covered coffee leaves ashimmer. As it climbed skyward, the mist cleared, the air warmed, the ground dried, and the coffee trees began to soak up the light they needed to consume the nutrients their roots harvested from the volcanic soils below.

Bartolo and I would manage visits to one or two people, and I would drop him at the courthouse in Coatepeque as the day's heat was just beginning to bite. Later I would either pick him up at the courthouse or await his arrival in La Igualdad, and we would set out again as the day was ending, the people were returning to their homes, the bus was crawling back up to town, and the sun was dropping over the western horizon.

Some of the people we visited were scared, like the barefoot woman who stood in a ragged blue smock, her fingers fiddling nervously with the loose threads at its seam, her wide eyes fixed on Bartolo's chest as he spoke. "You remember I was the municipal secretary, and I handled the papers for your husband, right?"

"*Sí pues,*" she had nodded.

"You know everyone knows me and I wouldn't be helping this *señor* if there was any danger. "

"*Sí pues.*"

"It used to be dangerous to talk . . ."

"*Sí pues.*"

". . . but now the war is over, and there are lots of foreigners in the country . . ."

"*Sí pues.*"

". . . and lots of people are talking to this commission."

"*Sí pues.*"

"Your husband was killed down below on the road, right?"

"*Sí pues.*"

"Was it the army or the guerrillas who killed him?"

"*Sí pues.*"

⬇

A few were defiant, like the woman in patched-up clothes, surrounded by four half-naked children, who looked me straight in the eye and said, "I don't care if they kill me, I'm not going to lie. It was the army that took my father. They took him away one night and never brought him back. My poor mama was left with nothing. And all us kids to feed. She couldn't get his pension because the government said if there was no corpse, then you can't prove anything. Only recently I went to IGSS to see if after fifteen years they'd accept that he was dead. My brothers tell me to leave it alone, that they'll kill me too if I'm not careful. But I don't care if they kill me. I'm ready to die in the name of my father."

She paused and looked at her kids. "The problem is that my mother wouldn't be able to handle another death in the family. She never got over that one. And then there are my own kids to think about."

⬇

Others weren't about to show how they felt.

One morning we arrived at the center of a small plantation. On one side, a woman stood at the window of a *tienda*. On the other side two brawny men, one with a beeper and the other with a shotgun, stood staring at us. Ahead the road came to a dead end. "This isn't good," Bartolo said over my shoulder as we approached a now inevitable encounter. "That's the woman we're looking for. And that over there is the administrator. He won't like this one bit."

"What do we do?" I asked over my shoulder. We couldn't say we were passing through since there was nowhere to pass through to. And no one would believe that the former mayor, Bartolo, had taken a wrong turn or gotten lost.

"I'll talk to the administrator first."

I pulled up near the men, and Bartolo got off and shook their hands. They clearly knew him, and while their greeting was less than friendly, they were willing to chat until he explained what brought us there. He must have figured he should get as close to the truth as possible, since eventually it would come out in some form or another. He explained that there was a provision of the new peace accords that allowed for the families of people disappeared during the war to begin to collect pensions. That's why we were looking for the woman across the way — to invite her to a meeting where she could learn more about the process.

When the men seemed satisfied, I parked the bike and followed Bartolo over to where the woman was standing. She listened impassively as Bartolo told her about the meeting, out of earshot but under the steady gaze of the two men. She thanked us in a matter-of-fact way, and we left her to ponder the significance of the invitation on her own.

V

As the sun climbed to its midday height, it lost its charm. It got bigger and stronger and seemed to slow down so it could watch the world sweat. All things that could move, moved into the shade. *Campesinos* on the coast went inside for lunch and a siesta. Workers in the plantations lunched under the shade trees. Dogs curled up under cars. Unable to move, the coffee trees had no choice but to soak up the heat and keep working — and working harder, since pouring more sun on them was like throwing more coal in a steam engine.

During the long sluggish stretch of midday, I took care of problems that threatened to interfere with our preparations. One was the motorcycle. After the engine failure that first night, I took it to a shop in

Coatepeque and had a loose valve in the carburetor replaced. But new problems kept sending me back to the shop. Carrying the two of us up and down the mountainside was pushing the old bike past its limit. Yet without the bike, there was no way we could reach all the people on our list.

The other problem was Mario. He no longer worked in the health center, so I dropped by his house late one morning. His wife answered the door and called him. He appeared in a bathrobe and invited me into the kitchen, where his wife served us coffee. He was a little less effusive than he had been in the past — at least he was trying to be less effusive. The effort seemed to strain him, as though he were tightening a belt on a bulging belly.

I told him the commission people had told me about the conversation they had had with him. He nodded and grinned and looked uneasy. "That's right, I'm helping them arrange a meeting."

I said, "Well, you know Bartolo and I are doing the same thing."

He grinned and said nothing.

"And it seems to me that it doesn't make much sense to duplicate each other's efforts. We should work together."

"No, no, of course not," he said, but there was hesitation in his voice. "What does Bartolo say?"

"He says we should all work together on this."

When I said that, he seemed to relax, unbelting his effusive character. "Good," he said. "Good! Why don't you tell him to come by here so we can plan things together."

"Sounds good. How about I bring him by tonight?"

"Very good." He looked pleased.

"One of the things we should talk about is how we go about inviting people to the meeting. My sense from talking to Bartolo and other people is that it's very important that we keep this meeting as discreet as possible." I couldn't tell by his grin how this registered with him. I continued. "So, we should be very careful only to tell people who are trustworthy. People who lost relatives. And not even all of them."

Now he nodded enthusiastically. "Yeah. For example, the mayor, Alberto Chavez. That guy is more a friend of the army than of the people." He then recounted his encounter in the mayor's office, leaving out the part about him being drunk and getting violent.

Having agreed to have a single meeting and be discreet about it, I was ready to leave. But I was curious to hear from his mouth the charges against Bartolo. "The commission people told me there were some allegations that Bartolo had been a corrupt mayor and people didn't trust him."

"No, no, Bartolo isn't corrupt," Mario said quickly.

"Well, the commission people heard from you that he was."

He squirmed a little. "No, I didn't say that, it was other people who were with us." He paused. He seemed to be holding something back. "Alberto's the one who's corrupt. But you know they're from the same party, and Bartolo helped get him elected."

He was still holding back. Then he said, "Look, Daniel, the problem is that we have a power struggle going on here."

He then told me about how he had been working to form a chapter of the URNG — the guerrilla organization turned political party — and how Bartolo and another local politician named Ismael Juárez were angling to take it over. He would be happy if they joined his efforts, but they would have to respect his authority. "After all, I was the one trying to get this party going before the peace accords had been signed. What were they doing then while I was risking my neck?"

I didn't care much about Mario's political ambitions. All I cared about was making sure this loose cannon didn't blow the opportunity for people to give their testimonies to the commission.

When I told Bartolo that Mario wanted us to pay him a visit, he said sure, but another night. The next night, he did the same. And the next. When I finally pushed him to fix a time, he became evasive. And when I said, "Look Bartolo, I told Mario we'd meet with him so we could make sure things go well with the commission," I finally encountered a sharp edge below his amiable exterior.

"I'll meet with him," he said, "but not in his house."

"Why not in his house?"

"Because he would make it look like we were supporting his political campaign."

Exasperated, I said, "So there is a power struggle after all."

Bartolo kept his even temper. "If Mario wants to call it that." He spat on the ground. "But I'm not competing with Mario. I have no desire to be mayor again. I've got a good job that pays well, and I'm not going to give that up."

"So what's the problem then?"

"The problem is that he wants to run for mayor. And he wants our support. Now I've got nothing personal against Mario. But he can't win an election in La Igualdad."

"Why not?"

"He's not from here. He doesn't have roots in the community."

⬇

Ismael Juárez was the other man who, along with Bartolo, was supposedly angling to take charge of the local branch of the URNG. Ismael was a close friend of Bartolo's and had been his predecessor as mayor in the 1980s. The two men had been cut from essentially the same cloth — but under very different circumstances. Ismael was thirty years older and had become involved in politics during the Arbenz years. Both men had worked in the plantations before working in local government, but while it was hard for me to imagine Bartolo ever having wielded a machete, Ismael looked as though he had never stopped being a *campesino*. Both were shrewd politicians. Where Bartolo cloaked his angles in an air of aimless affability, Ismael guarded his behind a wall of formality. Ismael had a way of talking with me that I had encountered often among certain men of his generation, men from modest backgrounds who, during their lifetime, had assumed the voice of authority in the affairs of the world. They weighed their words as carpenters weigh their materials, as if the words themselves possessed some authority, and, if handled properly, this authority would be conveyed upon the speaker.

Speaking this other language, Ismael said many of the same things as Bartolo. "Mario cannot win an election in La Igualdad," for example. "He doesn't know how to do politics."

I asked Ismael how he himself had learned to do politics.

"Everything I know about politics, I learned from a *señor* named Adrián Bautista," he said, beaming with pride as he invoked the name of his mentor. It was the same name that had come up repeatedly in my interviews with the agrarian authorities from the Arbenz years. Ismael now told me about learning how to do political work, mobilizing people to vote, organizing a union, and petitioning for land (in El Progreso) during the Agrarian Reform. He recalled being carted off to jail in 1954. And he recalled how, as they returned to La Igualdad on foot after being released from jail, Adrián Bautista had led the group of newly formed leaders in a discussion of what they could do to stay active in the new era that had come to Guatemala.

"What did you do?" I asked.

"Well, we continued with politics. We ran for local office. We've won every mayoral election since then. Except for the years when the military government appointed the mayor."

"What about the mayor now, Alberto Chavez?" I asked.

Ismael looked at Bartolo, who had just joined our conversation. "He only got elected thanks to us."

Bartolo explained: "It's true. We put him there. It was a mistake. The one before him too. Both were disasters. Very corrupt. And they only won because of us."

"So why did you help them win?" I asked.

Both were silent. Then Ismael said, "Look, Don Daniel, the problem we have today is finding people who are capable of being leaders. There aren't many left."

⬇

No, I wasn't interested in Mario's rivalry with Bartolo and Ismael. But he had raised a question that I had been asking myself: what *were* these men doing when Mario was supposedly "risking his neck"? And what were they doing before, in the 1980s, when Javier and Lico had undoubtedly been risking theirs?

I wasn't interested in this question for the same reason Mario was. I was interested in it because I thought it might help me answer another question. Bartolo's list had now grown to include sixty people who had apparently been killed by the army. Why would the army kill so many people in La Igualdad?

VI

The reason so many people were killed in places like La Igualdad during Guatemala's war was — according to the army's apologists — that tough measures were needed to prevent a leftist revolution. The reason it was necessary to prevent a leftist revolution was — the high-minded among them would continue — that such a revolution threatened the cause of democracy in the region.

This explanation contained a basic contradiction. The first part implied that the victims were themselves revolutionaries: if there were many victims, it followed that there must have been many revolutionaries. Yet the second part implied the opposite: the revolution was anti-democratic. It did *not* have popular support. If the population could freely choose who would govern, it would not choose the revolutionaries.

The easiest way to escape this contradiction was simply to drop the part about democracy. And there were plenty of Guatemalans willing to do just that. But for those who did profess democratic values, the contradiction had to be addressed another way — by questioning the nature of the support that the revolution enjoyed. The revolution had lots of support, but it wasn't *genuine* support.

There were several versions of this explanation. One was the claim that the supporters were being misled and manipulated by outsiders — Cubans and later Nicaraguan Sandinistas. (This view echoed the claim that democracy couldn't work in a country where the people are too ignorant to know when they're being manipulated.) Another was that the support people gave the revolution was coerced by the guerrillas. And a third version was the "between two armies" thesis, which held that it was only in the face of a hostile military state that the population turned to the guerrillas for protection — and that the guerrillas purposefully provoked the state's hostility in order to produce this result.

All these explanations served a political purpose. They shifted the responsibility for the killing from the main killers (the army) to their opponents (the guerrillas).

Were any of them also true? What sort of correlation was there between the killing in La Igualdad and the support for the revolutionary movement? When I asked Bartolo how many of the people killed had been involved with the guerrillas, he pulled out his list. He thought a third of them might have been. A third he thought had not. And a third he had no idea. But it was impossible to know, he said. "No one would talk about their involvement. Except for some drunks who bragged about it, and then you didn't know if they were telling the truth."

It was clear I would need to find another way to gauge guerrilla support in the region. And that is why I was interested in Mario's question. When and how did Ismael and Bartolo support the guerrillas? These men belonged to a network of local leaders who had been able to win every free election since 1954 — which made it difficult to argue that their popularity was not "genuine." It was an imperfect barometer — but it was the best I had. If these leaders had supported the guerrillas, it was likely that many of their own supporters had as well.

Unfortunately, it wouldn't be easy to get a straight answer from them on this. Bartolo was vague about his own involvement. He told me about visiting the guerrilla camps to participate in political workshops, but never said exactly how or how much he helped. Ismael was even more circumspect about his own involvement. I had long ago stopped pushing people for information they didn't want to give. But I was determined to keep an eye out for other people who might answer the question.

One morning, Bartolo and I came upon a man standing near the entrance to the plantation La Serena. He stood motionless, a wraithlike figure in the shadows by the side of the road. I couldn't see his face in the darkness, only the sombrero and white shirt and trousers that hung loosely on his bony frame, as they might on a scarecrow. "Don Cayo!" Bartolo called out and told me to stop.

"Bar-too-loo!" the man answered enthusiastically. And when Bartolo introduced me, he said with a friendly smile, "Cayo Ochoa, *para servirle!*"

From the governmental archives, I knew that he had been one of the most active leaders during the Agrarian Reform in La Igualdad. From Javier, I knew that he had been the future combatant's first mentor, teaching him how to use his machete in the coffee groves and talking to him about agrarian politics. From Bartolo, I knew that he was father of two young men who had been killed by the army.

"Don Cayo," Bartolo said, "do you know there's a commission now, a commission of truth, that is investigating what happened during the war? We're looking for people who want to tell what happened to their family members."

"That's good." His smile was gone, but not his enthusiasm. "Very good. You know they killed my sons."

"*Pues sí.* That's why we wanted to ask if you would like to give your testimony to the commission?"

"Yes, I'd like that. I'd like that very much."

"And you know a lot of the history of the armed conflict here in La Igualdad, don't you?"

"*Ay, Dios!* Here they killed so many! I remember the first one, the very first one, a *señor* named Juan Hernández. He was a worker here in this plantation, and he was a member of the Party."

"Which party?" Bartolo asked.

"The Party of the Workers," he said, apparently referring to the PGT. "It was a clandestine party. We used to meet in the woods."

I asked, "Were there a lot of people in the party?"

"*Sí pues!* All the leaders from those days."

"Like who?" It was Bartolo who asked the question. It seemed he too was curious.

"*Pues,* Artemio Mejía and Adrián Bautista and Armando Tojil and Pedro Díaz . . ." As he listed the names, the rumbling sound of a motor approached from up the hill. Bartolo interrupted him and asked, "Are you taking the bus, Don Cayo?"

He was. He was going to collect his social security payment in Coatepeque. "Don Cayo," I said as the bus rounded the curve above us. "I'd like to hear more about the history of the Workers Party. Is there some time I could interview you?"

"That's fine. Any day you like."

The bus was nearing. Bartolo signaled for it to stop.

"How about next Friday?"

"All right."

"I'll come by your home?"

"All right." We shook hands and he climbed up into the bus.

⬇

One evening, we paid a visit to Artemio Mejía, who had been mayor of La Igualdad in the 1960s and, according to Cayo Ochoa, a member of the clandestine PGT. "Don Artemio helped with all our campaigns," Bartolo told me. "But I haven't talked to him in a while. And I hear he's not doing so well."

Don Artemio had a small plot of land that sloped down from the road a short distance above where we had run into Don Cayo. He sat in a wooden armchair on a landing outside the house. A wooden cane rested at his side, and he gazed out through the coffee grove at the pink and blue swirl of clouds beyond Coatepeque. When he turned his head slowly to see his visitors, he reminded me of Franz Endler on the verandah in Panajachel. When he spoke, he had the mannerisms of Ismael Juárez, and perhaps once he had the same energy. But now his batteries seemed spent. His sentences came slowly, more slowly than Endler's. Some he didn't finish.

He smiled as Bartolo reminded him of the political campaigns they had both worked on. But when he tried to talk, it wasn't clear just how much or what he was actually remembering. His wife, who was younger, brought us coffee and told us about her husband's failing health. She tried to help us decipher what he said, and then offered her own memories of being married to a man who was, she said, as popular among the workers as he was vilified by the landowners. She had become pregnant with his child before they were married, she told us, and when the administrator of El Progreso (where she had grown up) found out who the father was, he ordered her off the plantation. When she refused to leave, he sent workers to remove the house she lived in. They took off the roof, she said, while she was going into labor.

Bartolo knelt down by Don Artemio's side and tried to steer the old man's mind back to the years after 1954. He asked if it were true there had been a clandestine party. But it was to no avail. Don Artemio wasn't dissembling; he was simply senile, his memories forever lost in the fog within his head.

As we got back on the motorcycle, Bartolo said, "It's too bad you can't talk to his sons." He told me that Don Artemio's sons had been good friends of his and also active in politics. He had seen them at the ORPA camp and suspected that they had been active collaborators. One had been abducted by the military and let go after a night of torture that included electrical shocks to his testicles. The other had fled town after being warned he was about to be abducted by the army.

Both lived in the capital now, and Bartolo was certain neither would talk about his family's involvement in revolutionary politics.

One afternoon I arrived at the Coatepeque courthouse to find Bartolo standing outside talking to Lico the ex-commander. A man walked up, wearing cowboy boots and a cowboy hat and a cocky smile. By the way he greeted Bartolo, it was clear they were good friends. *"Canche,"* he greeted me and shook my hand. Then he turned to shake the four-fingered hand of the other *canche.* Lico took him off guard by greeting him informally. "Don't you remember me, *vos?"*

As the man's smile widened, it became less convincing. Lico continued, "We used to visit you in that house by the river."

The man was Ernesto Bautista, the son of Adrián Bautista, the principal leader in La Igualdad during the Agrarian Reform years. I knew from Bartolo that Ernesto had been active in local politics, helping the campaigns of his father and his father's successors. Bartolo said he thought Ernesto had been an active collaborator with the guerrillas, and now Lico seemed to have confirmed this. I also knew from Bartolo that in the 1980s Ernesto had been abducted by the military and appeared several days later, under a bridge down on the coast, wearing nothing but his underwear. He never told anyone what had happened to him, not even his close friends. And, from his reaction to Lico, I could see he wasn't about to tell me whether or not he and his father, Adrián Bautista, the leader from Agrarian Reform years, had supported the guerrillas during the war.

⬇

What connection was there between the political activism of the reform years and the subsequent guerrilla movement? The people who could tell me — the major figures from the reform years — were dead, dying, or unwilling to talk. The only connection I could draw was that their children had, in disproportionate number, been targeted by the army — either killed or traumatized to such an extent that they too were unwilling to talk.

Cayo Ochoa might be the only one left who could tell me what connection there was, if any. On the day we had arranged, I set off to visit him at his home in the plantation La Esperanza. Getting there required traveling through La Serena, one of the largest coffee plantations in the country. Back during the Arbenz years, the plantation had been the hotbed of revolutionary politics. After 1954, it would be the first to see a resurgence of union activity, though that came to an abrupt end when Juan

Hernández, one of the union leaders, was found under the bridge over the Naranjo River with his head blown off. Today, La Serena belonged to a millionaire who had a reputation among La Igualdad's workers for being a heartless *patrón*. Rumor had it that he had recently threatened to deny access to the road through La Serena to another plantation that had begun to pay minimum wage.

My hope was to pass through La Serena unnoticed. But just as I was approaching the plantation center, my back tire went flat. I had not brought the tools I would need to fix it. So I left the bike at the side of the road and walked into the plantation center. The mechanics there would have everything I needed.

I found the plantation office, explained my problem to one of the employees there, and asked if I could bring the bike to the plantation garage. He asked me to wait and went to talk to the administrator. He came back shaking his head. The mechanics were busy in the garage, and they couldn't help me.

As I headed back to the bike, I passed the garage. I poked my head in and found the three mechanics sitting around doing nothing. They were friendly when I greeted them. But when I asked for help they said they would have to consult with the administrator first. One of them headed off. He returned with the same answer I had gotten before. The men stopped being friendly.

I left them and returned to the bike. It would be an hour's walk to Don Cayo's place. But I had already attracted distrustful attention and didn't want to bring it to bear now upon his house. So I headed back to the main road on foot, pushing the bike. It took me nearly an hour, under the midday sun, to reach the intersection. Then I pushed the bike uphill for another fifteen minutes until I arrived at the home of Artemio Mejía. I climbed the embankment and called down. His wife came out the door and walked up. I asked her if I could leave the motorcycle with them overnight. As she said yes, Don Artemio appeared in the doorway, his daughter behind him. He was standing with his torso doubled over, parallel to the ground. Both his gnarled hands clung to the head of a wooden cane. He looked up the hill toward us and then began to climb. He lifted the cane and moved it forward a few inches, then shuffled his legs slowly forward, then lifted the cane. He intended to climb the hill.

"Can I help him?" I asked his wife and started down the path.

"No," she said. "Wait here. He prefers to do it himself."

We stood watching as he climbed. It took him five minutes to reach the embankment. He slowly pushed himself upright, wobbled for a moment, and with his wife's help got his balance. He looked at me and smiled. "*Buenas tardes,* young man!"

VII

We had a problem, Bartolo told me when we met in the evening. The two people who had keys to the building where we had planned to hold the meeting were out of town and wouldn't be back by Sunday. We needed to find another room. He thought we might try the Catholic church. "The priest should help me out," Bartolo said as we walked over there. "I helped him when I was mayor." He knocked on the door of the parish house and added in a whisper: "Even though I haven't been to mass in ages."

The priest was short and pudgy and spoke Spanish with the lisp of a Spaniard. I had visited him once before, two years earlier, when I was first looking for inroads into the community. He had talked to me then of his church and how the Evangelical sects had been drawing away his parishioners in droves. But my questions about the war had produced only vague answers and beads of perspiration above his upper lip.

This evening he seemed more relaxed. He showed us into his small office, and Bartolo had him talking about the war in no time. Horrible years they were, he said, horrible. People lived in constant fear. Especially at night. After eight o'clock no one went outside. Some people were too scared even to go out to their latrines. So they would defecate in their house. "Can you imagine?" he said, looking at me. "And where could they go for comfort? To be a Catholic was dangerous. The military spread the idea that all priests were communists. That was one reason so many people were drawn away by the Evangelicals. Fortunately," he said, looking now at Bartolo, "Cándido never went after me. For some reason he always treated me with respect."

"Yeah, me too," Bartolo said.

The priest remained silent for a moment, remembering. Then he shook his head. "But you know, he always let me see those beans in his hand. It was like some kind of joke for him to play with beans in front of me."

"Beans?" I asked.

"Yes, dry beans. Here some people use them to do magic, or so they say." He laughed, but he didn't really look amused. The memory of Cándido had brought out the perspiration on his upper lip.

Bartolo also forced a laugh. "Yeah, that's the sort of thing he would do. He was a very ignorant person. But very cunning."

⬇

The priest agreed to let us use the parish hall for the meeting. Heading back to Ana's house for dinner, I asked Bartolo, "So were things here really as bad as the priest described them — I mean, people not going out to the bathroom?"

"Of course."

"I wondered because the priest seemed an especially fearful person."

Bartolo chuckled. "The priest didn't like that about the beans, did he?"

"I didn't really understand what that was all about. Cándido did some kind of magic?"

"No one has told you?"

"Told me what?"

"About Cándido."

"What?"

"He was a witch."

⬇

There were two types of witchcraft, Bartolo explained, *espiritismo* and *brujería. Espiritistas* used their powers to do good, to help people solve their problems and bring good fortune. *Brujos* used their powers to do bad, to cause misfortune and illness. Some practiced both. Some only one. It was said that they had no choice. They were born with their power, and if they didn't learn to use it, it would destroy them. As children they were always sick and sometimes suffered bouts of insanity. Their survival depended on another witch recognizing their power, teaching them how to use it, and helping them set up their own "tables," the places where they would practice their craft.

"Do you believe witches really have these powers?" I asked.

He said he didn't, but he seemed to take the question more seriously than I had expected. "I'm not interested in those things," he said. "But, you know, when I was a kid, people thought that I had this thing in my blood." He then explained that he had been a very sickly child and had come close to dying more than once. "Maybe I should have had a table myself. But, see, I took a different path. I chose politics instead."

After a moment he added, "But, you know, I still have a lot of health problems." He rubbed his belly the way he had when I first met him. "Problems with the stomach." I thought maybe he was making a joke, but I wasn't sure.

"My mother-in-law's an *espiritista*. If you want, I'll take you to meet her."

⬇

The gray-haired man standing in the door of the *espiritista's* house greeted us with a friendly smile. It was the father of Bartolo's wife. Bartolo introduced us and told him I wanted to learn about *espiritismo*. The man laughed. I wasn't sure what the laugh meant. "Right now she's with someone. But come inside."

The room we entered was L-shaped, with the back portion hidden by a curtain. Candlelight flickered on the ceiling above the curtain, and the sound of a woman's voice came from behind it. I tried to make out what she was saying but couldn't. The father-in-law flipped a switch, and a single neon tube on the ceiling sputtered alight, giving off a quivering yellow glow. He pulled a bottle out from a cupboard and offered us a drink. "Does the *canche* drink *cusha*?"

"Sure," I said. It had been a long day, and I figured I could use a drink. I accepted the glass he offered me. It had a pungent taste, a bit like fermented cider.

As Bartolo chatted with his father-in-law, I sipped the *cusha* and tried again to make out what the woman was muttering behind the curtain. It wasn't Spanish, I realized. It didn't sound like a Mayan language either. In fact, it didn't sound like any language I'd ever heard. Clearly, though, it meant something to someone. The muttering grew louder. It began to sound like some kind of incantation. It began to give me the creeps.

Then it stopped. A moment later I could hear a quiet conversation taking place in Spanish. Then the curtain parted, and a man came out, his hat in his hands. He greeted Bartolo, nodded to me, and then slipped out the front door. The curtain parted again, and a small woman emerged. Her face brightened when she saw Bartolo, and brightened even more when she saw me. *"Canche!"* she exclaimed, coming over to greet me the way older peasants do, her hand on my elbow. Then she turned back to Bartolo. "Where did you bring him from?"

"He's from the United States. I brought him here because he wants to learn something about *brujos.*"

"Ah, *bueno.*" She smiled again and looked at me. "But you people don't believe in these things, do you?"

I looked at Bartolo. He winked at me. "Well," I said noncommitally, "I don't know anything about them."

"Ah, *canche!*" she said again. She said it affectionately and laughed, tickled apparently by the unexpected treat of having one in her home. "Well, the first thing is that I am not a *bruja.* I'm an *espiritista.* You understand the difference?"

"I explained it to him," Bartolo said. "Tell him how you began to practice."

I sipped the *cusha* and listened as she told me about herself, about how, as a little girl, she had always been sick, always crying, walking in her sleep, some nights wandering out into the yard and hollering at the darkness. Surely she would have died had she not been saved by an *espiritista* who recognized her symptoms and trained her to use her powers, helping her to set up her own table. "Do you want to see my table?"

"Sure," I said.

I downed the rest of the *cusha* and stood up. I felt strangely dizzy. The drink must have been stronger than it tasted. The *espiritista* pulled the curtain back for me. I stepped through into the candlelight on the other side and found myself facing something entirely different from anything I'd seen in all my visits to La Igualdad.

Only once before had I seen something like it. It was years earlier when, wandering the dusty brown streets of a provincial Mexican city, I came across the thick sandstone brick facade of a colonial church and, stepping over the threshold into the cool darkness, I found myself facing a glittering wall of gold that rose, floor to ceiling, above an altar. The contrast to the dusty brown world outside was breathtaking. At first, all I saw was a dazzling display of wealth, and it struck me as grotesque in the midst of such an impoverished land. But then I noticed the people kneeling on the stone floor and, following their enraptured gaze, I saw something else: a portal that connected this world with another. I suppose that's what all altars are supposed to be, but this was the only one where I could see that it was true. And I could see that even if it was only in these people's heads, that other world definitely existed.

Now, in the back of this nondescript house in the middle of La Igualdad, I found myself looking at another such portal. There was no gold here, but the *espiritista*'s table was extravagant in its own way. It stood against the back wall, covered by a black tablecloth and countless candles of all shapes and sizes and colors. There were a dozen portraits of the Virgin Mary and several portraits of saints and a wooden replica of Maximón, the syncretic idol who attracted petitioners and tourists to a town outside of Xela. There were wooden animals and figurines. And there were plastic dolls of Caucasian babies. The dolls were the kind marketed to young girls and designed to look cute and cuddly and in need of maternal protection. In this setting, though, they had lost that cute and cuddly quality. Instead they looked at you like *you* were the one needing the protection.

Countless times I had walked past this house, never imagining anything like this existed inside. I wondered how many of the people I had interviewed knew of this place. How many had been here for consultation?

I stepped closer to the table and saw two color snapshots lying side by side, a young woman and a young man. That was her ex-boyfriend, the *espiritista* explained, and she had come here because she wanted him back in her life. Next to the photos was a piece of paper. It was a list of debts owed by the *señor* who had just left. He didn't know how he was going to pay them off, and he came here for help.

Syncretic capitalism, I said to myself, the joke coming as a defensive reflex to what I was hearing. "What language was that you were speaking with him?" I asked aloud.

"Ay, *saber!* That wasn't me talking. It was one of the spirits talking through me. I don't know what they said."

"What spirits talk through you?"

"Well, sometimes they're saints. Sometimes they're ordinary people who have died."

What sort of people became financial consultants in the afterlife? I asked myself.

"Many times parents of dead children come here to talk to the child," she said.

"They come from where? The plantations?"

"They come from all over. From here, from the capital, some from Mexico. This young woman, for example." She pointed to the snapshot. "She came home all the way from Los Angeles, United States, to consult with me."

I asked if she charged these people for her services. Just a few cents, she said, just enough to put a little more food on the table. But this wasn't a business really. It was something she *had* to do. "You see, if I refused to practice, I would get sick and die."

She was dead serious about this. Bartolo, who had followed us in, winked at me and said, "Why don't you try it?"

"Try what?" Whatever he was suggesting, I knew already I didn't like it.

"Tell her about any problems you have, and she'll consult with the spirits."

My mind groped around for some way to make light of the situation. That joke-making reflex helped me get a grip whenever I felt my perspective on things starting to slip. I felt it slipping now. It was as if the *cusha* and the sun and the stress had loosened something in my head: the valve that helped me keep a proper boundary between what I was hearing and what I believed. For a moment, I half-seriously considered what problem this woman's spirits might help me with. The main problem on my mind lately had been how to document the violence in La Igualdad. *Here's your chance,* I thought, *have her put you in touch with the people on Bartolo's list.* This came to me as a joke. But it only made me shudder. To think I could be put directly in contact with the horrors I had been hearing about . . .

"Maybe another day," I said and headed back to the front of the house.

⯮

Before leaving, I asked about Cándido Juárez. "He was a killer," the husband said.

"Was he an *espiritista* too?" I asked.

"No," the woman answered. "Just a *brujo*. At least he claimed he was."

"More than anything, he just wanted power," the husband said. "But in the end, they made him drink from his own cup. The army cut out his tongue and took out his eyes and as a final reward" — he gestured to his own crotch — "they cut off his *compañero*."

VIII

I walked back to the house alone, still dizzy and feeling a bit spooked. I turned onto the path that dropped down to the house and saw the moon and two planets hovering directly ahead over the horizon. It seemed difficult now to believe that their perfect alignment did *not* portend something. *Damn cusha is making you superstitious*, I told myself. I quickened my pace to get past the shadows and into the house.

Safely inside, I felt ready to collapse. But before I did, I checked to make sure there were no spiders or roaches lurking on the walls around the bed. I had been doing this bug check every night — usually finding one or two little monsters that I didn't want to be sleeping with. Tonight I did the check with special care. Tonight I was ready to believe anything, including the bugphobic's fear that insect brains are capable of malice aforethought. Finding the walls empty, I arranged my boots next to the bed (in case I would need to walk to the bathroom during the night) and stuffed my crumpled socks into them so that nothing could sneak inside. I checked under the covers, turned off the light, and crawled into bed relieved — and unaware that there was one place I had forgotten to check.

In the darkness, I thought about the *espiritista*. I remembered now the story a man in the highlands once told me about his own *brujo* problems. He had been involved in a feud with some neighbors. One neighbor had threatened to kill him. Another had contracted a witch to cause him harm. The man wasn't worried so much about the death threat. ("I can defend myself," he said, "and, if not, my brothers can avenge me.") It was the witchcraft that had unnerved him. He insisted that his family was Catholic and didn't believe in the power of witches. But his wife seemed to have fallen under the witch's spell. She had begun seeing shadows in the middle of the room in the middle of the day. She had begun suffering terrible headaches. And as her fear mounted, any strange occurrence, anything she found out of place, became further evidence of the witch's power over her. She became so terrified that she would weep when he left her alone. He realized he had no choice but to get help from someone who could use "those other powers" to counteract the "bad" the neighbor had done.

I thought now about what he said — about how his wife, once she believed in the *brujo*, became susceptible to his power. That's what had spooked me in the *espiritista*'s house. It had suddenly occurred to me that I might actually believe a little of what she was saying. That by believing it, even just a little, I would be opening a door that I wouldn't be able to close again. This *espiritista* didn't seem at all threatening herself. She only did "good," they said. But if you believed in the power of those who did "good," didn't you also have to believe in that of those who did "bad"? And once you believed, you became vulnerable . . .

A strange sensation cut short my train of thought. Something light had fallen on my neck and was scurrying up my face. And in that instant I knew what I had overlooked: the ceiling. I jumped out of bed, turned on the light, grabbed my boot, found a fat roach scurrying now across the floor, and smashed it. It took another whack to stop its legs from kicking the air. I whacked it a third time just to be sure. I flicked its carcass to the far side of the room and lay back down on the bed, my heart pounding. A moment later I was up again. I opened the front door and swept the dead bug outside, as if to rid the house of its malevolent spirit.

It took me a while, but eventually I slipped into a fitful sleep. I passed through a strange series of unpleasant dreams, which culminated with me in the driver's seat of the car in which I had learned to drive — the old family Volvo, chosen by my parents because its sturdiness could save their teenage children from any reckless mishaps. I was trying to get out from a tight parking space, moving forward and back, getting frustrated, moving back and forward more violently, until I realized that the car itself was doing the moving, banging the vehicles that had trapped it. Then cracks suddenly appeared on the hood and spread throughout the frame, and the whole thing began to crumble around me. As it was crumbling, I was waking to the realization that it wasn't the car moving back and forth but rather the bed. And not just the bed, but rather the whole room. And not just the whole room . . . I jumped up, threw on my pants, started to reach for my boots, and instead ran outside barefoot.

The earth rocked back and forth for another half a minute. Its movement produced an eerie hissing sound in the coffee groves up and down
the mountainside. People poured out of the homes around me. Then the
movement suddenly subsided. People waited, then ventured back into
their houses to survey the damage. Bartolo's house, being essentially bar-
ren, had little to break. The electricity was out, however. And so it was by
the light of my flashlight that I examined the bottom of my foot and
found that what I had felt when I ran outside — but not wanted to believe — was true: the roach had gotten the last laugh. There was no running water, so I used my bottle of drinking water to wash the residue of its
guts from my skin.

It was absurd. Almost funny. But I just couldn't help suspecting the
whole thing had been planned — as if the spirit of that insignificant little
creature could move a continent to work its revenge.

Lying in bed again, I tried to forget about this bizarre evening and
think about something else. My mind drifted back to Friedrich Endler in
1892, waking up with the thought someone was tossing his bed around —
while outside in the night those "savage, ragged creatures" from Cajolá
danced under his electric lights.

IX

When morning came, the people in La Igualdad set about putting their houses back in order. They swept up broken glass, pushed furniture back into place, rehung framed photos and diplomas and religious
images. Electricity returned by midmorning, and the radios reported collapsed houses and crushed families in other parts of the country.

There had been small tremors throughout the night, and they continued through the morning. Each time one began, you could see the fear,
still fresh, flare up in people's eyes. But these tremors also brought relief.
For, as everybody knew, if these small ones didn't come, then there
would be another big one on the way. Some people could tell you why:
once the earth moved one way, it would have to move back the other.

I found someone who was headed to Coatepeque in a pickup truck
and got him to carry my motorcycle to the city. There I fixed the tire and
rode back to La Igualdad, the whole way up thinking about Cándido

Juárez. Bartolo had told me one other interesting fact about him. Ismael Juárez, the former mayor, was his brother.

I had brought copies of the Agrarian Reform petitions from the 1950s in case I wanted to check the names of any people I met while inviting people to the meeting. Now I dug out the petition filed by the agrarian committee of El Progreso. The two Juárez brothers had signed. Ismael's signature was cursive, sloppy but fluid. Cándido's stood out on the page. It was larger than the others, printed with the awkward, shaky hand of a child, and misspelled.

I put the petition away and went to find Ismael.

⟱

"My brother, may his soul rest in peace, was a killer," Ismael Juárez told me with an expression that seemed two parts disgust and one part sorrow.

"Was he a sickly child?"

"No, I don't think so," Ismael said. "Just ignorant. He couldn't read or write."

"But he signed the land petition in 1953, didn't he?"

"He could sign his name, but that was about all he could do."

"So did he know what he was signing?"

"Of course. He wasn't stupid. He just never learned to read. He tried to hide it. But I knew because I was his brother."

"The reason I ask about him being sickly is because people have told me he was a witch. And I was wondering how he became one."

"Cándido *chose* to be a witch. He was already grown up when he did it. One night he went into the cemetery and prayed to the devil. He spent nine nights there, praying to the devil to make him a witch."

"And the devil did?"

"Well, that's what he said. He said he made a pact with the devil, and that gave him his powers. I don't believe in any of that stuff myself."

Cándido had made his living working as a security guard in the plantation El Progreso. He became an assistant to La Igualdad's military commissioner in the mid-1970s. As the level of violence escalated, the commissioner resigned his post, and Cándido asked if he could fill it. They gave him the post because he did what they wanted him to do.

"What did they want him to do?"

"Terrorize the people. And that he did. Everyone was scared of him.

Some people would see him in the street and begin to tremble. He rounded up boys to join the army. So the boys would avoid him in the street. He came to rule this town. He was more powerful than the mayor. He would borrow people's cars whenever he wanted. Who was going to say no? He would tell people they were on the army's list and make them pay him to get them off. When someone was taken away in the night, the relatives would go to him in the morning and beg him to do something. 'I can't do anything,' he'd tell them. But if they offered him money, he would take it and say he'd do what he could. He even denounced me to the army. Me, his own brother!"

"Really? What happened?"

"One night soldiers surrounded my house. They told me to come with them. So I went. But I had my whole family come with me so there would be witnesses to whatever happened to me. They brought me to their captain. Cándido was there with him, and he pointed to me and said, 'This is the individual.' So I said to the captain, 'What is the charge, *mi capitán*?' He wouldn't say. They kept me there overnight. But then they let me go in the morning."

"Why did they let you go?"

"I don't know. Maybe because they saw my whole family there with me. Or maybe Cándido changed his mind."

"Why would Cándido have wanted to denounce you?"

"He wanted to get ahold of my portion of the land we inherited from our father. Like I told you, the man, my brother — may he rest in peace — was a killer. You know he even had a man killed so he could steal his wife."

"And she went with him?"

"What could she do?" he asked back, and a moment later said, "Now, that's someone you should talk to."

⬇

There was nothing unusual about Cándido's house. Nothing sinister in its appearance. Nothing to set it apart from the other houses that lined the street above the cemetery. Nothing, that is, unless you happened to know that this was where people used to come to plead for information about their disappeared children.

As I followed Ismael in through the front door, I felt uneasy, as if I were about to meet the killer himself. Instead, Ismael introduced me to the widow, a small woman with a narrow face and long hair. Nothing sinister about her, either. She was friendly and talkative. She offered me a seat in one corner and sent her daughter to bring me a lemonade. She sat on a cot opposite me, and Ismael, excusing himself, headed out into the street.

This, I thought, would be the closest I could get to the person who served as terror's agent in La Igualdad. I decided to approach the topic by first asking her about her husband, the one Cándido had delivered to the army.

"*Ay Dios!*" she exclaimed. "They took him away. It was a long time ago."

"Who carried him off?"

She sighed and shook her head. "I don't know. I don't remember who they were."

"Do you remember what happened?"

"Well . . . there were five men. They wore white shirts. They came one night, very late." Her expression darkened as she conjured up the memory of that night. "They came into the house with no warning. The door was just a nylon curtain, and they came right through it. I screamed and ran over to the bed where my daughters were." A look of fear came over her face, as if she were reliving the event as she recounted it. "I grabbed my daughters. And the men grabbed my husband. They dragged him to the door. I called out to him. And as they pulled him out of the house he said to me, '*You take care of my daughters!*'"

Her eyes suddenly filled with tears as she repeated his words. "'You take care of my daughters,'" she said again and her cry became a sob. "And I said to him, . . ." she paused for another sob and looked over at the empty doorway, "and I yelled to him, '*Make sure you come back, vos. Come back for your girls!*'"

I sat silently in the corner while she sobbed. The girl returned with my glass of lemonade. She gave it to me and sat down on the cot next to her mother. I guessed she was accustomed to seeing these tears.

After a minute, the widow wiped her eyes and continued with the story. "The other two men stayed and searched the house, throwing everything all over the place. Then they left. I waited until dawn and then I went outside. It was still dark. I went up the hill and stumbled on a man who was lying in the path. He was someone I knew. He was covered with blood, but he was still alive. So I helped him up. Then I went to the mayor. He took down the information about my husband. But he said he couldn't do anything. So I went to Coatepeque, and I went to the military base. They told me they didn't know anything about my husband."

The sobs had passed, leaving only the tearful runoff and the lines of grief that now stood out on her face. I looked at the girl sitting motionless beside her, staring at the ground. She was a handsome child, darker than her mother, though with some of her features. She looked calm, healthy, unmarked by life.

"The next years were difficult," the widow continued with a sigh. "I didn't have anything to give my daughters. The neighbors helped us. They gave us clothing and food. And with that we were able to survive. But it wasn't easy. Some people told me I should give the kids to another family. But I couldn't do that. They were all I had."

"And Cándido?"

"After a time, Cándido began to visit me. He said he wanted a new woman. He said his other woman didn't work hard enough. She didn't wash his clothes right. He said to me, *'You're intelligent. You're a hard worker.'* So he brought me to this house and left his other woman and we lived here."

I had wanted to ask about Cándido's role in the disappearance of her husband. But now I wasn't sure I should. Instead I asked if it was true that Cándido practiced witchcraft. "He had his table right there where you're sitting," she said as matter-of-factly as if it was where he kept a desk and typewriter. "That's where he had the crosses and the images and the beans, where he attended the people who came to him."

I would have liked to ask more about what he did at the table. And about what he did when the families of the disappeared came to him. But just then the widow stroked her daughter's head and said with a tender smile, "This here is Cándido's little girl."

I looked at the girl. She stared back at me. Our eyes locked for a second. I looked away startled, not by what I saw, but what I found myself looking for — some sign that she had Cándido in her blood: the military commissioner, the witch, the killer. Things don't work like that, I told myself. I looked at her again and forced a smile. She just stared until I looked away.

X

On the day before the meeting was to take place, Bartolo and I ate a quick breakfast and set out for Ismael's house, where we would divide up the tasks that remained to be done.

A block away, we ran into Mario. He called to us from across the street. I walked over to him, and Bartolo followed. We had never held that meeting that Mario proposed, though I had visited him several times, hoping to keep tensions at a minimum.

"Everything's set for tomorrow?" Mario asked in a booming voice for all the street to hear.

"Seems like it," I said.

"I've got all my people ready." He said to Bartolo, "You've got yours?"

"Yeah, we're all set," Bartolo answered in a friendly tone. "We just have to make sure people don't get the wrong idea about what we're doing."

Mario nodded enthusiastically. "That's right. We can't invite just anybody."

"No, only the people who were affected," Bartolo said.

"And not even all of those," Mario said. "There are some people you can't trust. Like, for example, that jerk Alberto."

"I'm sure he wouldn't have any problem with this," Bartolo said. "But why don't we talk about it more later? Right now, we've got someone waiting for us."

"All right," Mario said. "Come by my house, and we'll talk."

"Sure, I'll come by."

Bartolo dropped his smile as soon as we had Mario behind us.

⬇

At Ismael's house, we divvied up the list of people who still needed to be tracked down.

My job would be to reach Cayo Ochoa. That meant traveling through La Serena to the plantation where he lived. It was a long way to go to find just one person. But I didn't want Don Cayo to miss the opportunity to give his testimony. The man had lost two sons, after all. And I felt bad about standing him up. *And* I wanted to ask him about the connections between the leaders from Agrarian Reform years and the guerrilla movement in the 1980s.

In order to save time and to avoid attracting as much attention as I had the last time, I decided to take a shortcut that Bartolo had shown me. A quarter mile below the town, I turned off the road onto a wide trail that climbed down into La Serena. I would be able to reach the plantation where he lived on the other side without passing through the plantation's center. It seemed like a good idea. Only as the trail became steeper and more treacherous did it occur to me that I was taking a bigger risk: if the motorcycle had a problem here, I would be in even worse shape than I had been the other day. How would I explain my second appearance in La Serena to the plantation's armed security guards?

I felt some relief when the trail finally let me out on a dirt road. But the relief didn't last long. Standing there at the intersection, waving me down, was a young man. He wore no shirt, and his hair was disheveled. Wanting to make sure I was going in the right direction, I heeded his wave and stopped. "Excuse me," I said, "could you tell me how I get to . . ." As I spoke I noticed the tattoo of a giant black scorpion on his muscular forearm, the word "Kaibil" above it, and a nasty scar above that, and I decided not to say where I was going. ". . . To the center of La Serena."

"I can show you," he said. He looked drunk or crazy or maybe both.

"Thank you," I said, shifting quickly down to first and arching my right hand forward for a quick acceleration. "But I'm in a little bit of a hurry. Could you just tell me?"

"Let's go together." He started toward me.

"No, listen, this bike can't carry two people." That slowed his approach. "Is it this way?"

"*Sí pues.*"

"And at the next intersection, which way do I go?"

"To the right. I'll go with you on foot."

I thanked him and headed down the road. He ran behind me. I wanted to speed away, but the road's wet clay surface made that a dangerous option. If I didn't speed up, he would catch me; if I sped up, I risked a wipeout. For a moment, he did catch up and actually ran alongside me. Maybe he had no intention of doing any harm. But I wasn't going to take chances. As soon as I reached a dry patch, I sped ahead. After a few minutes, I came to an intersection I recognized — the turn off to the left. I went fifty feet down that road, then stopped, turned off the engine, pushed the motorcycle out of sight from the main road and looked back.

Less than a minute later, the shirtless man appeared, still running. He reached the intersection and continued to the right down the other road.

I decided to leave the motorcycle where it was and go the rest of the way on foot. I put a padlock on the wheel and unhooked the tube that brings the gas to the engine. I headed down the path to the Ochoa house.

Just below the house I came upon two young men with beer bottles in their hands. One asked me if I was going to see his father. "Who's your father?" I asked.

"Cayo Ochoa."

He told me his father was out working. "But I thought he was retired," I said. He was, the son explained, but he continued to work off the books. He would be back in a few hours. So I asked him to tell his father that the meeting we had talked about would be tomorrow and he should look for us in the parish hall in town.

He nodded and said, "He was waiting for you the other day. He skipped work and spent the entire day out there by the intersection, just waiting."

I thanked him and retraced my steps up the path to the motorcycle. There would be no shortcuts this time, I decided. I rode quickly through the center of La Serena, ignoring the stares of the people I passed, and made it to the Coatepeque road without encountering the tattooed veteran.

＊

When I reached La Igualdad, I parked the bike in front of Ana's house. This place had begun to feel like home, I realized. It was good to be back. I was looking forward to lunch. I walked through the front room and into the kitchen.

Ana stood by the sink. Bartolo sat at the table. His shirt was rolled up to his chest. He was rubbing his belly with one hand. Ana looked worried. Bartolo too. When he saw me, he tried to put on his usual poker face. But it didn't quite fit this time. It looked like he'd just been dealt a very bad hand. After betting away his house.

"We have a problem," he said.

He rolled down his shirt and offered me a seat. Ana brought a bowl of soup, placed it on the table before me, and stood looking down at him. He stirred his soup and looked at me. He had recovered just enough of his look-like-a-fool look that, for a moment, it was hard for me to take what he said next seriously.

What he said was that someone had threatened to kill us.

XI

Ana had taken the call. The voice on the other end had said, "Tell the gringo son of a bitch and that piece of shit Bartolo that if they hold the meeting, we're going to bomb them!" It was a man's voice, she told me. It sounded like he was sober. It sounded like he meant what he was saying.

I nodded. I stirred my soup. Bartolo stirred his soup. The phone rang.

Ana looked at Bartolo and he nodded for her to answer. She disappeared into the front room. "Hello?" we could hear her say. "Hello? . . . Hello? . . . Who do you want to talk to?" Then there was a yelp, as if the phone had bitten her ear, and the sound of the receiver bouncing off one hard surface and landing on another. Ana appeared in the door. Her eyes were wide and beginning to water. She spoke in a whisper. "It was him. The same voice."

"What did he say?"

"He said, 'Con vos, puta, hija de puta!'"

That means "with you, whore, daughter of a whore." But it meant something else to us right now. It meant that whoever had made the threat definitely wasn't playing games. It meant that this *whoever* wasn't buying the commission's claim that *it was time now to tell the truth.* Bartolo and I had been repeating this claim to families throughout La Igualdad because we believed that they could make it be true. Now, the voice on the phone said: *wrong!*

I watched Bartolo stir his soup some more with one hand, and rub his belly some more with the other. "What are you thinking?" I asked.

"I'm thinking," he said. He put a finger to his lip to silence me and pointed to the wall. The kitchen shared this wall with the neighbors' house. Then he whispered to me, "Let's go talk about it in the next room." And speaking aloud in a cheery voice, he said, "Thanks for lunch."

We left our lunches uneaten and retreated to the one room of the house where no neighbor could overhear us. I leaned against the wall. Bartolo sat on the bed. He wiped his face with his shirtsleeve. He rolled the shirt up over his belly. Then he peeled it off entirely, as if it were a straitjacket he'd been itching to get out of. He lit a cigarette. "I only smoke when I'm scared," he said.

A moment later he added: "I used to smoke a lot."

As the smoke filled the small room, we collected our thoughts. What did we know? We didn't know who made the threat. We didn't know if they had the will or the capacity to carry it out. We didn't know how or what they knew about the meeting. We didn't know how they got the phone number.

Basically, we didn't know much.

What were our options? We could play it safe, cancel the meeting, and betray our conviction that it was truth-telling time. Or we could risk it. The problem was we really didn't know what we were risking. It's the uncertainty that gets you in a situation like this. Uncertainty is the multiplier of terror; it's what can allow just a few bullets to silence a lot of people for a long time.

One thing *was* clear. The malignant force that had confounded my efforts for so long had finally materialized, partially but unmistakably, in human form. And as the initial wave of fear receded, I found it had left something else in its wake, a feeling of vindication. This was the voice that had silenced people. By justifying the fear of telling the truth, it seemed to justify our efforts to have the truth be told — if only to deny it another victory.

"The mistake we made," Bartolo said as he lit his second cigarette, "was when we stopped to talk to Mario in the street. We should have kept on walking. I knew Mario would start talking like that."

"You think someone heard us there?" I asked.

"You know the house we were standing in front of? The guy who lives there is a big supporter of the army. He used to hang out with the army officers who were stationed here. And on top of that, he's a friend of the mayor."

"So when Mario said that about Alberto . . ."

"Exactly."

By the third cigarette, Bartolo had worked over all the variables and come up with a simple equation: "If the call was from someone in town, then it's someone who can't do anything to us. If the call came from the military base, then we're fucked."

A decade earlier, such a distinction would have been meaningless.

Back then, the mechanisms of state terror worked to confound such distinctions. Fresh from their counterinsurgency courses in Fort Benning, Georgia, the army officers had fixated on something Mao once said: the revolutionaries would move through the population like fish through water. To counter this threat, they would need to poison the water. So they let a hundred deadly flowers bloom. A Cándido Juárez in every community to keep the people scared. But things *had* changed. The political cost of repression had become too great to leave it to the locals. The fact that Bartolo could even make this distinction was a measure of progress for the country. Whether it was wishful thinking or not was another matter.

"It seems unlikely that the army would be doing this now," I said. "The commission has already collected testimony in hundreds of communities all over the country. And the army hasn't interfered at all. At least, as far as I know — though maybe we should check with the commission people."

He nodded. "Why don't you give them a call?"

I went to the front room and called. I got the Spanish coordinator on the phone. "Listen, we've got a problem. And we're already *quemados*," which meant we had been discovered, "so there's no point playing with words." I told her about the threat. I told her we were deciding what we should do, and asked if her team would still come under these circumstances. She said that if we decided we still wanted to hold the meeting, she thought they would come, but we should confer again later that afternoon. I asked if she knew of any other cases of commission investigators being threatened like this. She said no, but she would check with her superiors in the capital.

I went back to the bedroom and found Bartolo with his shirt back on and his mind made up. "We've got to do the meeting."

I had already decided that I'd be willing to go ahead with it if he was. I trusted his judgment. What I wasn't sure about, though, was all the other people who were coming. We had assured them that the meeting would entail no risk. Was it right to still have them come when we now knew otherwise?

"That's precisely why we have to do it," Bartolo said. "If we cancel the meeting now, we'll have to explain the reason. And we'll only confirm all their fear. We'll have done more harm than good. After taking a step forward, we'll be taking two steps back."

It was like the witch's power. If you chose to believe in it, then you made it real. If we believed the voice could stop us, then we gave it the power to do so.

Bartolo continued: "The lesson the army taught the people here was, you mess with the army, you're in trouble."

"Well, you *are,* aren't you?"

"Yes, but it's more than that. In those days, you knew that if the guerrillas visited the town, the army would visit next. If you gave the guerrillas information, the army would come looking for you. If you even *acted* like someone who might help the guerrillas, the army might take you away. So you couldn't have one without the other. That's why the people stopped believing in the guerrillas."

Again, it was a fear like the one that had come over me at the *espiritista*'s table: if I let myself believe in the good spirits I would also make myself vulnerable to the bad ones.

"But it wasn't just the guerrillas," Bartolo continued. "They stopped believing in politics. Now there's no war, there's no guerrilla, but the fear hasn't gone away. And you can't ignore that fear. That's why Mario's got it all wrong taking on Alberto. The point now isn't to get people to stand up to the army. The point is to help them recover from their fear."

That's why Bartolo had wanted to have the families come together as a group. There was strength in numbers. Until now, I had thought only in terms of the strength people might need to give testimony to the commission. But it seemed Bartolo was thinking of something more: the strength people needed to regenerate a collective capacity to believe in themselves.

"Now of course," Bartolo said, the wheels in his head still turning, "if one of the people also receives a threat, word of it will spread real quick. And then it will all be over . . ."

XII

It was a few hours later that confirmation came from San Marcos that the meeting was to go forward. There had been no incidents of the army retaliating against people testifying before the commission. And everyone agreed that a "bombing" was highly unlikely.

By now, evening was upon us, and we had one more task to do: the trip that we had kept postponing. We rode out of town and through La Independencia. This time the motorcycle made it. We turned up into La Asunción and climbed for about twenty minutes until we arrived at El Reposo.

Aside from the memories, El Reposo was all that remained of the Agrarian Reform in La Igualdad. The workers of La Asunción had originally acquired this land by making a petition under Decree 900. The owner of the plantation had been a fervent anticommunist. But, according to his son, it was because he was also a devout Catholic that he had decided to let the workers keep the land after the 1954 coup. He was the only landowner to do so in La Igualdad. And that may explain why the people in El Reposo were now better off economically than the workers in the other plantations. Many more of them had their own vehicles and livestock. Many more of their children had gone to study in the city and found better work outside of La Igualdad.

"This community is very well organized," Bartolo said as we rode up through the darkness. "It's the best organized in all La Igualdad. We only have to tell one of them, and they'll come to the meeting."

"Are you sure?" I asked. I wasn't. "You don't think it's too late to get them to a meeting tomorrow morning?"

"I'm sure. Tell one and they'll all be there. You'll see."

No one was home at the three houses we tried. A teenage boy explained to Bartolo that the people were at the schoolhouse for a community meeting. We waited in front of one of the houses for twenty minutes. At last people began to pass. An elderly couple came to the house. They greeted Bartolo warmly and invited us into the house. The electricity was down, they apologized, and the room was lit only by a dim kerosene lantern. The man sat with us while his wife prepared coffee. Bartolo told him about the meeting with the commission team.

The man needed no persuasion. He would be there, he said. And so would the others. They would have to go to mass first — two of them were in the church band and another was a catechist — but they would show up afterward.

The man spoke with a voice that was gentle and self-assured. He didn't edit his words like Bartolo, or weigh them like Ismael, or relish them like Mario, or fear them the way so many of the people we had visited seemed to. When Bartolo asked him the date his son had been abducted, he told the whole story in a tone that was as steady as it was sad. January 20, 1982. Around six-thirty in the evening, soldiers arrived in El Reposo and summoned the people to a meeting in front of the schoolhouse. The families did as they were told. Waiting for them there were Cándido Juárez, two army officers, a detachment of soldiers, and a boy with a hood over his head. One of the officers spoke to them. He told them that there were rotten elements within the community and these rotten elements would have to be removed. He told them that tonight they would learn what happens to people who support the subversives. When he finished, he ordered the hooded boy to point out the guilty members of the community. At first the boy would not point to anyone. But then they threatened him, and he began to point. He picked out seven young men, including their son. The seven were taken away in the pickup truck that belonged to El Progreso.

People in La Independencia would later say that they had seen the pickup leave the next morning with large sacks piled in the back. Someone would find — in the woods by the river — the burned remains of clothing and ID cards belonging to the young men. But no one in La Igualdad would ever see them again.

For months afterward, the families had done everything they could think of to find out what had happened to their sons. They went to the military base repeatedly and pleaded for information. They got none. They went to Guatemala City, and, with the help of the student association at the university, they hired a lawyer to file a habeas corpus petition. But the petition got no response, and the lawyer finally urged them not to pursue the case further. There was nothing they could do.

"Nothing we could do." He repeated the words with a sentiment that seemed more pure, more penetrating than anything I had encountered before in La Igualdad: a boundless sorrow, untainted by fear or guilt.

"For years we kept hoping," he said. "Even now, fifteen years later. Of course, it's clear what happened to those boys. We know it. But there's always that doubt. The doubt won't go away. The doubt is what kills us."

⬇

A thick fog had come down the mountain, enveloping El Reposo and the plantations below. As we headed back downhill, the bike's headlight projected a narrow tunnel of light, which bounced off the damp ground immediately before us and disappeared into the gray nothingness above. There were still people out on the road at this hour, but we saw only the yellow glow of flashlights or occasionally a shadowy figure scurrying out of our tunnel of light. On a long slope just above town, the twin beams of a car's headlights raced uphill toward us. I pulled off the road to give it room to pass, and as I slowed to a stop, the bike's engine sputtered and died, as it sometimes did when it was cold and tired. Our headlight went off with the engine. We sat in the darkness as the twin beams pushed toward us through the fog, like a hungry searchlight, and then sailed right past without finding us. We continued on our way.

When we arrived at the house, the door was closed, and there was broken glass lying on the pavement before it. Inside, Ana looked as frightened as she had at lunchtime. A pickup truck had just come by, she told us. It had stopped right out in front. Gunshots had been fired into the air. A bottle had been smashed against the door of the house. And then the car had raced away up the street toward La Independencia.

Earlier in the day, the bottle and bullets might have shaken our resolve. Now they merely reinforced it. For up in El Reposo we had regained the strength of our conviction. The gentle manner of that elderly man had soothed our own frayed nerves. His self-assurance had rubbed off. It was as if he possessed a special power — culled perhaps from his own sorrow — which could counteract the forces of fear.

We briefly considered whether I should stay the night in the house with Ana's family, rather than by myself across town. I decided not to bother making the change. I'd go across town. Nothing would happen to me, I was sure. And I was determined now not to concede anything to fear — not even a good night's sleep.

As I waited for the sleep to come, I thought about Cayo Ochoa, out at the intersection, waiting all day so he could tell his story.

XIII

I woke up tired. It must have been a bad night after all. The bed looked as though a storm had hit. The sheet was tangled around my feet. The blanket and pillow lay strewn on the dirty floor. I closed my eyes and wished I were somewhere else. Somewhere where I could get the caffeine I needed to face this day like a human being. Here, surrounded by a sea of coffee and not a decent cup anywhere to be had, I felt like a thirsty sailor in the middle of the ocean with no drinking water, the butt of some cosmic joke.

I lay in bed a few minutes and reluctantly allowed it all to come back to me: the meeting, the broken bottle, the ringing telephone. I forced myself up, into my clothes and out the door. Already the streets above were crowded with market-day stalls selling vegetables from the highlands and secondhand clothing from the United States. I made my way through the maze of tables and nylon partitions. I felt as alien as I ever had in La Igualdad. I now knew many of the faces I was passing — but did I really have any idea what they were thinking? Which of them knew about the meeting? The phone call? The gunshots and the bottle? I picked up my pace and kept my head low, hoping to reach Bartolo's place without having to answer any questions.

I should have recognized the woman immediately. But the way she approached me — suddenly, without a word, closing in from my side — is not the way people approach you in La Igualdad, unless they're drunk, or perhaps carrying a weapon. I assumed she was drunk and made to pass her with a polite *"buenos días."*

"Señor, that thing today isn't anything bad, is it?"

I stopped. I looked at her. My groggy mind lurched clumsily into action. *Who is she? How does she know about the meeting?* "Uh, uh, no, no," I stammered, searching her face for a recognizable feature, some detail that matched one of the blurry images my memory was dragging from the archives of the recent past. She seemed to notice my mental effort. Maybe she thought I looked nervous. Maybe I was nervous. Her eyes widened. And, as they did, I made a connection, a tentative one, which I immediately doubted because the woman before me wore a clean white dress and sandals, and the one in my mind stood barefoot in a ragged blue smock, her fingers fiddling with the loose threads at its seam as she listened to Bartolo say:

Your husband was killed down there below the coffee grove, right?

Sí pues.

Was it the army or the guerrillas who killed him?

Sí pues.

"No," I repeated, regaining my composure, still unsure if this was that widow or another, but wanting to sound like I knew her and felt comfortable answering her question in front of the people at the nearby stalls, who were pretending they weren't listening. "It's nothing bad. It's nothing political."

Too late. I had lost her. My hesitation had rekindled that fear I had seen in her eyes the other day. Sure I recognized her now. I knew her by her fear. And as she hurried away, I cursed myself for having been so slow to recognize it.

I continued up the street. One block left. And turning the corner onto the home stretch, I came face to face with the last person I wanted to see right now, Alberto Chavez. For a moment I hoped he would pass me silently, the way he had always done before. But this wasn't the same deflated school principal I had met three years earlier. Now he was the mayor. He had harnessed the winds of provincial power, and his sails were full of bluster. *"Hola,* mister!" he greeted me loudly. *"Hola, canche!"* He cackled and shook my hand. "How's your investigation going?"

Now it's possible he was only referring to the interviews I had done with him and his father three years ago. Or he could have been referring to common knowledge that Bartolo and I had been talking to people lately. But, then again, he might have been referring to today's meeting. And if he was referring to the meeting, he might have known only that we had planned something without sharing our plans with the mayor. Or maybe he knew the meeting was for victims of political violence and that he had been excluded for some reason. Maybe the reason Mario had given in the street had reached his ears. Maybe he knew who was threatening to kill us. Maybe it was him.

"Just fine," I said.

"I'm glad," he said.

In the past, I would have asked him about his father, and I would have plied him for information about La Igualdad. Now I wanted to steer clear of any lines of discussion that could lead to today's meeting. "You haven't had any problems in La Igualdad?" he asked. The tables had turned. Now it was he who would ask the questions. And he asked them as if he were simply the good mayor concerned that all who visited his municipality had a pleasant stay. But the subtext of his interrogation was clear: *this here's my territory you're in.*

"And the motorcycle? Is it running okay?"

He smiled. I smiled. There was no affection in those smiles. I was intensely aware of all the eyes watching us. I wanted to shrink away and disappear. I did the closest thing, disappearing behind empty words and gestures, trying to make my existence seem as insignificant as possible, smiling a dopey smile and saying dopey things. Looking back now, I realize I was attempting the part that Bartolo had perfected, the part of the clown.

⇊

Bartolo stood in his doorway looking a lot better than I felt. He even reminded me of that earnest aging bureaucrat I had seen a few weeks earlier — though perhaps more aged now than earnest. Behind him was Ana, also looking better than the night before — nervous, but still smiling. As I sat down to breakfast, Bartolo left to find the priest and open the parish hall. I ate the eggs put before me, drank the diluted coffee, and headed back outside. I walked up to the northern entrance of town to wait for the Truth Commission.

I stopped at the bust of Justo Rufino Barrios and, nodding my respects to the general, took a seat at his side. Together we gazed up the road where his band of rebels had come on their way to getting this whole mess of a coffee nation going. Today the road would bring a car full of international investigators to document the atrocities committed by the army he had forged. What sort of truth would they get? What effect would their getting it have on anyone's life? I really didn't know. The old general didn't look too worried, though. And I guess I wasn't either. This morning's dose of fear had worn off. Now all I felt was hate.

The hate I felt wasn't directed at anybody in particular. I didn't hate Chavez, for instance, even if he had made me act like an idiot, or the *whoever* whose voice had made the death threat. This was a different sort of hate, an impersonal hate, a hate that had been welling up in me for some time, the hate that had drawn me back to this place year after year. It was the sort of hate that, a century ago, on another continent, drove the fictional truth-seeker Marlow on his famous quest into the "heart of darkness." Marlow hated lies. He hated lies, he said, not because he was holier than the next guy, but because they possessed a "taint of death," which made him sick, the way biting something rotten would do.

Of course the meeting today was "political." Telling history is always a political act. Why did I say otherwise to that scared woman? I could have told her it wasn't "bad" and left it at that. But I went further, saying it wasn't "bad" because it wasn't "political." In my moment of confusion and fear, I had succumbed to the language of a world in which the people — at least the ones who picked the coffee — knew that engaging in something *political* meant engaging in something *bad.*

I had told *their* lie, I thought, staring up the empty road, hoping the commission's car would round the corner and save me from thinking about that other lie I'd told, the one that was really bothering me, the one that mattered.

The road stayed empty. And as I stared at its emptiness I could still see the scared woman asking her question. She hadn't been asking me what *I* thought about the meeting. She had been asking what the people who might harm her thought of it. She had been asking, Is it dangerous? A more honest answer might have been, I'm not sure. Or we've received a threat but don't think it will be carried out. Or even I'm a little scared myself. Instead I told the lie that Bartolo and I had been telling all along. We told the people that they no longer needed to be afraid — that meetings like this were now worth whatever risk they entailed. But we didn't tell them what the risk actually was. We didn't tell them about the voice on the phone or the bottle shards at the door because we didn't think they could handle it.

It was for their own good, I tried to reassure myself. Maybe we were being as patronizing as any *patrón* in his plantation, but it *was* for their own good. That's right, ours was a good lie. And if the people showed up today, it might become true.

Looking back now, I imagine President Barrios laughing over my shoulder: *That's what we used to say! "Tell those capitalists their money is safe in Guatemala and it just might become true." Remember el señor presidente? His problem wasn't the volcano, it was the way the investors would overreact if he canceled his party. So he did what any responsible person would do: he lied.*

And I can see him adding, with a devilish grin: *Your problem is you're just a bad liar.*

Maybe that was a problem. Maybe we did have to lie so the people in La Igualdad could tell the truth. Maybe we did have to patronize them in order to free them from their fear. And maybe I just needed to learn to stomach what was rotten — since, after all, some of that rot was my own.

THE TERRORISTS

I

THERE WOULD BE no bombs that day. No more gunshots. No more broken bottles. And it would seem to us — at least at first — that the risk had paid off.

By the time the commission's car rolled into town, there were around twenty people waiting in the parish hall. It wasn't everyone we had invited, but it was more than we had expected to come. Even the woman I thought I'd scared away would slip in quietly and join the group.

Mario was nowhere to be seen. And when two of the four investigators who had come in the car set off for his house, it became clear that they had never abandoned their plan of holding two simultaneous meetings, despite what they had told us. The deception wouldn't do them much good (they would only find two people waiting with Mario to give them testimonies). And though it felt like a betrayal, it didn't really bother me now. I guess they hadn't been sure whom they could trust. And I guess I couldn't entirely blame them. They knew even less about this place than I did.

Bartolo introduced the two remaining investigators to the group inside the room, and then he joined me at the doorway. Together we stepped out onto the sidewalk. Our job was just about done: La Igualdad would have its day with the Truth Commission. All that remained for us was to guard the door so that no one crashed the meeting and to let the investigators do their work inside.

It wasn't long before Bartolo had struck up a conversation with some people in the street. I glanced back into the room. The investigators had set up chairs in two corners, giving themselves some semblance of privacy as they conducted one-on-one interviews, while the people waited their turn in the middle. My gaze wandered back outside, past the chatting Bartolo, over the rooftops across the street, up through El Progreso to the woods where the guerrillas had set out to launch their revolution.

Now, in the room behind me, the people of La Igualdad were recounting what the war had brought them instead. I already knew, more or less, the stories that each would tell. And piecing them together, I could begin to explain how that revolution got buried.

One way to tell the history of the war in La Igualdad would be to chart the course of the killing on a map. In the 1960s and 1970s, the violence had been sporadic and scattered, but after 1981 a pattern emerged.

It began at the top of the mountain in the first week of 1982 with the massacre in Sacuchum. It reached the top of La Igualdad several weeks later when seven young men were disappeared from El Reposo. The next mass killing occurred at the end of the year, halfway down the mountain, when seven people were disappeared from San Pedrito. Finally, a year later, a similar chain of disappearances took another nine lives, this time in the lower reaches of the municipality.

In La Igualdad, it seems, death ran downhill. And in this sense, the war did produce something that resembled an eruption. Only, it wasn't the one that the guerrillas had dreamed of.

Another way to tell the history is to categorize the victims according to what caused their demise. The stories I had heard with Bartolo fell into several categories.

There were the people who were denounced by army informants (as happened in El Reposo) and those who were denounced by neighbors who had themselves been abducted and gave the names under torture (in sort of a plea bargain arrangement, where the only "bargain" available was a coup de grace).

There were the people who appear to have been denounced by plantations (the first of these being Juan Hernández, who attempted to form a union in La Serena and was found with his head blown off under the bridge over the Naranjo River).

There were those who, in effect, denounced themselves by talking too much (drunks, usually, with the bad habit of speaking their minds in public or, worse, boasting of guerrilla affiliations, real or imagined).

Many were targeted because of their conduct: people who ignored the army's prohibition on selling food anywhere but in town (like the itinerant merchant who kept peddling his wares and was found partially buried at the side of a back road); people who failed to comply with army orders in a timely fashion (like the administrator of one plantation who was disappeared when he didn't get around to clearing the underbrush out of a part of the plantation as instructed by an officer); and people who failed to pass information to the army. One young man had the misfortune of living on the road where an army tank was destroyed in a guerrilla ambush, and he compounded it by making two mistakes: not alerting the army of the guerrilla presence and not showing sufficient remorse when he told other people about what had happened. He was shot in the head after having his eyeballs extracted and his tongue cut off.

And then there were many people who died when others used the war to resolve their own personal disputes. Some of these disputes involved land (like the man disappeared after his own daughters denounced him because they were eager to inherit his property); others involved adultery (like the man who denounced his neighbor, a long-time friend and fellow PGT militant, who was cheating with his wife).

Finally, there were cases of people who died because of their love for others. Such was the case of the two sisters, sixteen and seventeen, who refused to be separated from their father when soldiers came for him one night. The girls grabbed hold of him as he was dragged from their house and, unable to separate them, the soldiers took all three. The neighbors realized they weren't coming back when they saw the officer who had taken them return, alone, in civilian clothes, and lay flowers at the door of the now deserted home. From a safe distance, they watched him weep, alone and inconsolable. Under the circumstances, who would dare to console him?

⬇

The simplest way to tell this part of the history is with a list of La Igualdad's dead and disappeared. Here's what Bartolo's list looked like:

Juan Hernández	Hilario Jiménez
Juan Barrios	Abel Noé Alvarado
Herminia Santos	Dagoberto Ramírez
Emilio Ochoa	Joaquín Pu
Ernesto López	Lico López Hernández
Bernardino Orozco Martínez	Calixto Agustín
Porfirio Ochoa Ramírez	Patricio Castañón
Juan Agustín Barrios	Tranquilino Moreno
Julio Rojas	Basilio Orozco
Eusebio Ramos	Melecio Pérez
Fausto Hernández	Cándido Juárez
Gregorio Miranda Navarro	Fermín Cifuentes
Everardo López	Anival González
Heriberto Orozco	Cayetano Ambrocio
Domingo Arreaga Soto	Efraín Gómez
Baudilio Zapeta	Hija de Efraín Gómez
German Pérez Reyes	Segunda hija de Efraín Gómez
Modesto Sandoval	Armando García
Angel Girón	Saturnino Fuentes
Justo Fuentes	Rubilio Hernández
Vicente Arreaga	Manuel Cupertino Matul
Toribio Bamaca	Gerardo Yoc
Carlos Ortega	Wenceslao Mejía
Felipa López	Felix Moreno
Miguel Angel Hernández	Rosalinda Fuentes
Pedro Zacarías López	Cristóbal Fuentes
Clemente Ortíz Hernández	Pedro Velazquez
Marcos López Chivalan	Santiago Cabrera
Teodoro Agpop	Ismael Chivalan
Umberto Bravo	Horacio Carreto
Santos Gabriel López	Margarito Castillo
Braulio Bamaca	Mauricio Barrios
Guadalupe Morales	Carlos González
Marco Antonio Cardona	Edwin Matías
Absalon Morales	Elvidio Calmo
Rolando Martínez	Diego Gabriel
Salvador Lopéz García	Rosalío Yoc Méndez

That's seventy-four people killed during the war (and doesn't include Sacuchum or the other communities on the mountainside). One or possibly two of them were killed by the guerrillas. The rest were killed by the army. None of them were combatants.

A similar history for the entire country of Guatemala would, according to the Truth Commission, list some two hundred thousand names. That list would be three thousand times as long as this one.

II

General Héctor Gramajo summed up the history of the war like this: in 1981 the army had been worried the guerrillas might triumph; in 1982 they took care of the EGP (in the central and western highlands); in 1983 they took care of ORPA; in 1984 they stopped worrying.

Gramajo had been in charge of the 1983 campaign against ORPA. And sitting in his office, with a tourist map of the country opened on his desk and a pencil in his hand, he explained how the campaign worked. "It isn't exactly a sweep. It's not lining up and going into battle. Rather it's establishing military bases to take charge of the area." He drew dots representing the military bases. "You see, the population doesn't care about the — to use the key word — 'paradigm' of the subversives. They don't care because it's really a question of power. The one who influences them is the one with the power. So I imagine that the population is ambivalent because when you're present, you have power. When you're absent, you don't have power, and the others who are present have power. The population is between two fires. So they don't have a clear definition."

Gramajo often referred to the guerrillas as "terrorists," and when I asked him if this were just a rhetorical preference, he explained the distinction. "What is a 'guerrilla'? I am armed and I live in the village. The village gives me food. The village gives me informers. The village gives me its children to become combatants. I am a guerrilla. The quality that makes me a guerrilla is that I'm sustained by the population. In other words, it's the population that goes to war. But if I have an armed band and I hide from the soldiers, I hide from the village, I hide from everybody, then I'm not a guerrilla, right? So that's what happened. ORPA was a guerrilla army. But they drop down a category and become terrorists. The food doesn't come from the village. Now they send the food in trucks, or rob it on the highway. They come down from the mountain and do terrorism — destruction of the symbols of power, such as the house of the landowner. It no longer matters what the population wants. Now it's just terrorism."

Lico, the former ORPA commander, told me how the guerrillas experienced Gramajo's campaign. "In 1983, the army came in with greater force," he recalled. "They began bombing us in January. And then they launched a large offensive with tanks and helicopters. Within six or seven months, the operational situation had completely changed. But the problem wasn't the military confrontation. We didn't lose that many in battle, and in '82–3 we received large numbers of *compañeros*."

"The problem was food. During the stage of preparation, it had been fairly easy to get food in the communities. In the stage of fighting, it was more difficult, but still possible. There were many people who were happy to help us. The main difficulty then was just that the people were poor.

"In the year before the massacre in Sacuchum, Lucas had moved the camp up close to the town. After the massacre, we had to move back down to the woods just above the plantations. We had to change our form of supplying food, sending out small patrols to get a little here, a little there.

"Then the killings and disappearances began in the plantations. The army took drastic measures, controlling commerce and markets and products, and killing vendors. We couldn't buy from anyone. So we had our collaborators make the purchases, and our patrols would later collect from them. But it was very dangerous work. There were two lines of operation. The first was from the woods to the towns. We worked there first because it was closest to the woods. But when the killings started in this area, we had to move to the second line — from the towns down to the highway."

That would explain why the repression appeared to move downhill. Each time the army destroyed one group of collaborators, the guerrillas moved farther down the mountain to work with another. And when none were left, they were forced to turn to other measures, such as having large quantities of food brought in by cars from outside (which apparently is what Armando Tojil's son was doing when he was caught and killed by the army).

"But it still wasn't enough. A guerrilla force can't grow if it doesn't have the social base to sustain it. And the nucleus of people we had left wasn't sufficient for our growth. The triumph of the revolution escaped us. We missed the grand opportunity, the moment of popular upsurge in 1981 — all the people who we awoke in the first phase, so many people who collaborated, so many people who applauded, so many beautiful people!

"We weren't able to channel this sympathy. And we couldn't expect a massive uprising due to the people's sympathy. What we had was spontaneous support, not organized support. Spontaneous support can't withstand repression. We needed better organizing work. But we failed. It wasn't that the work was intentionally neglected. The organizing work cost many lives. The organizers in the communities were basically wiped out. So the commanders of the fronts had to take charge. And they were already too busy with their military tasks, with leading a large force, to be able to carry out the difficult work of organizing support within the communities.

"As a result, the organization became unbalanced. It grew in one area and not in the other. The military force kept growing, while the popular support diminished. We had a flood of combatants, even as the tide was already receding in the political work. Many times, due to lack of rations, we had to say, '*Stop! no more recruits for now.*'"

In the end, it wasn't only a matter of food, however. "A major part of the army's campaign was to blame the guerrillas. So that people hated us, so that they erased us from their minds. And that's why they promoted the Evangelical churches. The Evangelicals reject everything that's political. They have a vertical relation with God — '*el Señor* and me' — and nothing about the community. Many Evangelical churches appeared after the massacres. The preachers took advantage of people's fear. They called the guerrilla the devil. They needled the pain of the people when they should have been more compassionate, more understanding.

"The cold reaction of the people affected our morale. When you're up there in the mountains under the rain, under the bombardment, and you go into the community and people are too scared to talk to you. . . ." He shook his head and left the sentence hanging, as if he were unwilling or unable to finish it.

⬇

"The strategy in '83 is to restore normal life," Gramajo told me. "Since there's a military government, it's possible to take administrative measures. We're going to make normal life return. So we're going to have fairs and football championships and concerts." He seems especially proud of "Pana Rock" — a rock music festival held in the tourist town of Panajachel.

It was reminiscent of the Minerva celebrations Estrada Cabrera had mounted to cover up the political and economic turmoil that was plaguing the country. And as with Estrada Cabrera, the effort wasn't only cosmetic. The government also took special measures to stimulate the coffee economy. "We tell the landowners: you have to attend to your plantations. Don't abandon the place. Pay attention to your plantation, make life normal. And we're going to stimulate the export of coffee. There are no import taxes. We're going to get rid of the taxes on fertilizers. We're going to help make life normal.

"So there's lots of work that doesn't involve direct combat with the subversion. They continue looking for combat." But, he pointed out, laughing, "now they are terrorists!"

III

The biggest step toward "restoring normal life" — and thereby ending the war — was restoring civilian rule. The military government held general elections in 1985, and the centrist Christian Democrats won at the national and local levels.

In La Igualdad, Ismael Juárez was elected mayor. And the authority of his brother, the military commissioner, began to wane. One day Cándido tried to bully Ismael in public, and Ismael put him in his place. "Here we govern by the law," Ismael told him. "You're not in charge here anymore . . ." and, revealing Cándido's humiliating secret, he added, ". . . you illiterate."

Cándido's problems ran far deeper than a sibling rivalry, however. One day a colonel showed up in town with his guards, and when he saw Cándido in the town square, he yelled for all to hear: "You're still alive, you bastard son of a bitch?" He then warned Cándido that he'd better start doing his job better or he would regret it.

"The poor man wasn't well," Cándido's widow told me. "He didn't want to work anymore." It was not clear which work she was referring to — security guard, commissioner, or witch. "He was sick all the time. He was already sixty-five years old. But he needed money. El Progreso refused to give him his pension. He started to drink. He got drunk, and he cried for his daughter. He had a difficult relationship with her. He was always worried about his kids. He wanted them to get an education. He said he would make sure his son got a good job. He wanted him to be a marimba player and then a soldier."

But he would never see that happen. For in July 1988, Cándido met his maker — so to speak. He was summoned to the military base in Coatepeque, and when he ignored the summons, an army jeep came looking for him.

Rumors circulated afterward about why they came for him that day. Some said he had been seen talking to the guerrillas in El Progreso, which probably meant he was selling information to ORPA (no one suspected him of collaborating out of conviction). Others that the owner of El Progreso had denounced him to the military after he had tried to extort the pension money that the plantation was refusing to pay him.

A condition of Cándido's pact with the devil had been that if he ever stopped practicing witchcraft, he would die. Whether or not Cándido ever gave up being a witch, it seems he had stopped serving his other two masters — the army and the plantation — and that was enough to seal his fate.

When Cándido saw the army car enter town, he ducked into the cemetery, hoping to disappear in the place where he made his Satanic pact and where many of his victims were now buried. But the soldiers found him, dragged him out to the street, threw him in the jeep, and headed back down to the coast. His body appeared several days later on the side of a road near Coatepeque. His throat had been cut.

It is often said that history is written by the winners. But as Cándido Juárez discovered, not everyone on the winning side ends up being a winner.

One of the first people to write a history of Guatemala's war was General Héctor Gramajo. At the time the army retired Cándido Juárez, Gramajo was the minister of defense and actively working to clean up the army's image abroad. He would soon be rewarded for his efforts with a chance to study at Harvard. And there, at the Kennedy School of Government, he would begin his writing.

The hero of Gramajo's history was Gramajo. He was the figure of moderation in a country of extremes, a professional soldier who had inherited a conflict between rich and poor, white and Indian, which dated back to the Spanish Conquest. As minister of defense, Gramajo had shared this notion of historical inheritance with his officers when he wrote the *Thesis of National Stability,* the military's blueprint for the country for the late 1980s. In the opening paragraph he told them: "The current social and economic reality of Guatemala derives from the imposition of the Spanish culture upon the indigenous culture as a result of the conquest, . . . producing the formation of a semi-feudal socio-economic structure . . . and the exploitation of indigenous labor. This basic framework changes little with the passage of time due to the appearance of . . . marginalized minorities that had to make great efforts to survive." These marginalized minorities were, of course, the "Ladinos."

The general had grown up a Ladino in the predominately indigenous town of San Juan Ostuncalco, just south of Cajolá in the Quetzaltenango Valley. As a child, Gramajo told me, he used to visit the surrounding communities to watch the Dance of the Conquest performed on festival days. In this ritualized dance, elaborately costumed indigenous men re-enacted the 1524 battle in which the Spanish conquistadors defeated their Mayan ancestors. "I always wanted to play the part of the Ajis," Gramajo recalled. "The Ajis is the funny red monkey. He's not Spanish. He's not indigenous. He's the one who pesters everyone." And, judging from Gramajo's laugh, the one who entertained the crowd in the process.

It is true that the Ajis played the role of intermediary between the K'iche' warriors and the Spanish conquistadors. His role was actually a bit more complicated — though it basically boiled down to this: he went where the power was. And he was not a monkey. He was a man. And not just any man. He was a witch.

⬇

The dancers in Cajolá would probably not have assigned Gramajo a neutral role in their version of the history. His grandparents were from one of the Ladino towns that had made off with Cajolá's lands in the 1880s. Numerous family members had served in the national militia that enforced the various systems of coerced labor. And Gramajo's father, while tempo-

rarily discharged from the army in the 1930s, had worked as a labor con-
tractor drafting workers by indebting them to the plantations. The men
in Cajolá told me that the general's father had also been their foreman
when they did the roadwork under Ubico, and they still remembered the
severe beatings he used to give villagers who slacked off during the
twelve-hour workday.

But if Gramajo's professed neutrality seemed dubious, his sense of being marginalized in the middle was less so. Provincial Ladinos were no
more welcome within the social circles of the mostly white elite than they
were among the Indian communities, which was why many of them, like
Gramajo, turned to a career in the army. "I entered the army because I
wanted a quality education. The army gives opportunity without being
from the elite. Entering the army, you advance socially. If you don't enter
the army, you can study but your position is always low." In the army, "you
can rise above what is your level."

During the years of army rule, the army's top brass did rise far above
their previous "level," becoming men of considerable wealth and power.
But all their money couldn't buy them entrance into high society. "Take,
for example, Arana," Gramajo told me, referring to General Carlos
Arana, who was president in the 1970s. "Arana has a lot of money. He has
a yacht, he has a plantation, he has horses. And he lives in Zone 14. Everyone in Zone 14 has a lot of money. So Arana lives in Zone 14. But he
doesn't have friends. No one visits him."

Héctor Gramajo also liked to see himself as the "product of a U.S. education." The first lesson he learned from the United States — long before
studying military tactics or public management — was about power.

In 1954, the fourteen-year-old Gramajo had stood by his father in an
army bunker and waited for the American planes to begin bombing.
Gramajo shook his head recalling the day. "It was a conflict," he said, referring to the dilemma faced by officers like his father who, on the one
hand, were wary of the direction in which Arbenz seemed to be taking
the country, and on the other hand shared the president's strong sense of
nationalism. In the crucial moment, Gramajo recalled, it wasn't ideology
or nationalism that decided the day. "What the army did was defend the
army. That is, they forgot about the country, they forgot about commu-

nism, and they thought about the army." (This was basically what the Ajis does in the Dance of the Conquest: abandon his former allegiances in order to save his own skin.)

"I have *never* thought that the United States is good one hundred percent," Gramajo insisted. But that was where the power lay, and the career of an ambitious Guatemalan military officer invariably involved U.S. training. Gramajo would study in the United States five times during his rise through the ranks of the Guatemalan army, three times at the School of the Americas in Fort Benning, once at the Command and General Staff College in Fort Leavenworth, and finally at the Inter-American Defense College in Washington, D.C.

In the Guatemalan military academy he had received "indoctrination of service to the country and all that." Then in the United States he was trained "to think in the political terms of democracy versus totalitarianism, United States versus Soviet Union." He and his fellow officers were immersed in the principles of the National Security Doctrine, which taught them to see local conflicts within the context of the global struggle against the Soviet Bloc.

After 1954, according to Gramajo, the National Security Doctrine of the United States was adopted as the governing philosophy of the Guatemalan military, which would directly or indirectly control the government for the next three decades. The 1956 constitution explicitly outlawed the Communist Party and declared that "all political opposition to the government" constituted a "threat to the state." Consequently, Gramajo observed in his book, "political exclusion" came to be "regarded as a constitutional mandate."

The history Gramajo told did not detail his own participation in the mechanisms of political exclusion. It focused instead on his role in reforming them.

Gramajo had become the country's most powerful reformer when, in 1986, Vinicio Cerezo, the first civilian president since Mendez Montenegro, appointed him to be army chief of staff and, several months later, made him minister of defense. Gramajo was now in charge of the show, at least the military aspect of it, and he set about turning the army into a more professional and politically savvy institution. "When I'm chief of staff, I implement civil affairs, which means less repression, you know more . . . more . . . see how the tensions work themselves out and not repress the tensions."

Gramajo's insight into Guatemalan history was simple: political repression produces instability and violence. Or, as the PGT had put it metaphorically in its 1960 report, when a government "closes the escape valves" on a heated "boiler," it is likely to produce an eruption.

This was "vanguard thinking for Guatemala," Gramajo told me proudly, and it had produced a hostile reaction from the most conservative elements of the economic elite. "The oligarchy is not pleased."

In 1987 Gramajo had bluntly told a group of business leaders that the military's role in Guatemala had changed: "'We the military are no longer your concubines. We are professional soldiers.'" He explained that comment to me: "The oligarchy always wants done the things that favor them. And the army begins to think that not only the things which benefit them are good for Guatemala. They use us like a dirty rag. A dirty rag is for doing dirty work. Never again the dirty rag!"

What was their response? "'Gramajo is a communist.'" He laughed and explained that he appeared along with the archbishop on a death list. "They only think in black and white."

After making his speech, Gramajo withstood two coup attempts that, if successful, would most likely have aborted the Cerezo presidency and returned Guatemala to an overt military dictatorship. The first of these, in 1987, was sponsored by cattle ranchers whom Gramajo called "agents of extreme and radical conservatism." The coup attempt was triggered by the major tax reform law proposed by President Cerezo. "The new tax law is a demonstration of new relations of power that frighten the oligarchy. They say that if today we accept these relations of power, if we subject ourselves to a tax reform, tomorrow it's *agrarian* reform."

The second coup attempt, which came a year later, was a rebellion within the military institution itself. Gramajo's wife and children were held hostage, but the minister of defense refused to give in to the conspirators. In the end, he was able to rally the loyalty of the army and defeat the coup. The perpetrators were jailed temporarily and then discharged from the military.

Motivating the rebellion, Gramajo told me, was the "fear of losing power and small privileges, because democracy removes small privileges.

Abuse of authority and impunity are small privileges." After the coup attempts, Gramajo stepped up his efforts to teach them "democratic thinking." In a public address on Army Day, he warned that "radical ultraconservative groups" posed as much of a danger to Guatemala's security as Marxist guerrillas, because they supported "theories and dogmas that do not respect the people's right to choose their own government." And he led retreats and seminars for his officers where they read and discussed the *Thesis of National Stability*, Gramajo's treatise on why the democratic opening made sense from a military point of view.

It was not an easy lesson to teach officers who felt they had won the war against the guerrillas. "This war was rough on all of us. And you could say we won. So if we won, why are we going to make concessions?" Gramajo answered, "Because wars are not ended by killing everyone. Wars always end politically. There's still struggle, and there are still victims. Political struggle is part of the war."

It was perhaps at this point that Gramajo had come closest to resembling *his* notion of the Ajis — the monkey in the middle pestering *both* sides of the conflict.

⇓

Then it was on to Harvard. "Imagine, one month I was General Gramajo, minister of defense." Gramajo thrust out his chest and assumed his fierce military face. Then he relaxed in his chair and laughed: "And the next month there I am in Cambridge living in Harvard housing by myself, doing my own laundry, cooking my own food!" He described — almost gleefully — what it was like to be a student after years of war — to travel without a chauffeur, without security guards, alone on the "T," to walk around Cambridge in sneakers and jeans with a backpack over his shoulder. "I even let my hair grow a bit long! Imagine Gramajo with long hair!"

In the seminar rooms of the Kennedy School of Government, Gramajo was able to expound upon his version of Guatemala's history, and in a seminar paper, he was able to begin writing it. After two semesters of course work, he had earned his Harvard degree. It was a long way to come for a soldier from San Juan Ostuncalco, and, donning his cap and gown that June, he must have been as thrilled as the rest of his classmates to commence his new life with his new title.

But, unfortunately for him, there were people in the Kennedy School courtyard that day who knew how he had gotten there. And as he was waiting for his diploma, these strangers approached him and handed him something else: a court summons for a civil suit filed by eight indigenous Guatemalans whose families had been tortured and killed in 1982.

The strangers were lawyers from the Center for Constitutional Rights in New York who, in the 1980s, had dusted off an eighteenth-century law, originally written to allow suits against pirates for damages inflicted on the high seas. With the help of international human rights conventions, these lawyers had turned the old law into a tool for suing foreign dictators in U.S. courts. In order for the courts to obtain jurisdiction, the defendants had to receive a summons while in the United States, which is why the lawyers looked for him where they were sure to find him: graduation.

Gramajo stuck around Cambridge for two weeks after graduation to get legal advice on how to handle the case. This was just enough time for the lawyers at the Center for Constitutional Rights to put together a second suit on behalf of an American nun who said she had been tortured and raped by Guatemalan intelligence officers in 1989. This time they went to serve the summons at Gramajo's apartment in Harvard's Peabody Terrace.

It was Gramajo who, during our first interview, had cautioned me that some things that seem abnormal in one place are quite normal in another. It seems that Gramajo himself had become disoriented during his last days in Cambridge, temporarily losing track of which place was which. When he saw strangers waiting in a strange car in front of his home, he apparently became anxious. Such anxiety would have been a "normal" reaction in Guatemala during the years that many people who saw strange cars outside their home had known they were about to be tortured and killed. And what Gramajo then did was a "normal" response for someone in the United States who thinks his life is in danger: he called 911.

When the Cambridge police arrived, an officer let the lawyers explain why they were there and then accompanied them as they presented the summons to the former general.

⬇

Gramajo decided to ignore the summons and return to Guatemala. There he spent the next four years preparing to run for president, appearing on television talk shows, participating in public forums, giving interviews, and completing his history of the war. In February 1995, he published his book. And in May, he completed the constitutional requirement of five years outside of military service that would make him eligible to run for president in November.

But just as he was about to launch his campaign, the U.S. District Court in Boston issued two default judgments against him and ordered him to pay the plaintiffs $47 million in damages.

"Forty-seven million dollars?" an indignant Gramajo said to the local and international press the next day. "I don't even have forty-seven million centavos!" And he dismissed the ruling as hypocrisy on the part of the U.S. government. When I spoke with him, he elaborated on this charge: "If I pay $47 million, how much is Secretary McNamara going to pay for what *his* troops did in Vietnam. Me in *my* country, him in *another* country! How much is Secretary Cheney going to pay for what *his* troops did in Panama?" He was now at the edge of his seat, livid. "In Panama there was a very sophisticated bombardment . . . RRRRRR!!! . . . ," he imitated the sound of the bombers descending, ". . . right on top of the barracks. There was a barracks in the middle of a neighborhood of Panama City, and they killed the entire barracks — three or four thousand people! And civilians as well. But no one sues them!

"This is not a question of law," he concluded, sitting back in his chair. "It's a question of power."

What angered him most perhaps wasn't the judge's ruling, however. It was the reaction of the U.S. army, which publicly revoked his invitation to an annual symposium for American militaries. "They said, 'We're going to tell Gramajo not to come because we don't want to get involved with people like Gramajo.' And before they had said many good things about me." The general did not disguise his bitterness. "They always cover their ass. It's a political thing. 'We have nothing to do with that one.' Right? It's a demonstration of the United States' character. They're not allies for ideology, rather they're allies because of their interests. Now that the interests have passed, 'We dispose of them. We have no friends. We just have mutual interests, not friendships.'"

Gramajo was hurt, but he wasn't entirely surprised. He had already caught a glimpse of the "character" of his former "friends" while he was in Boston. "On July Fourth, my wife was visiting, and we went to the Boston Esplanade for the celebration. And we're walking along amidst all those people, and I see someone coming my way who I know. But I can't quite figure out who it is, because he's wearing shorts and a T-shirt and he hasn't shaved. But I know him! And he sees me and looks the other way trying to avoid me I think. But it's too late. I recognize him. It's the general who had been in charge of Southern Command. So I go and greet him. And he says, 'Hello Héctor, I never expected to run into you here.'" It was evident from Gramajo's impersonation that the man had not been thrilled to see him. "And I tell him, 'Well it just goes to show, old generals don't die, they just fade away into the crowd at the Esplanade.'"

Gramajo didn't laugh as he repeated this joke to me. For, after all, he had not really wanted to fade away.

⚜

"So what do people think of Gramajo?" the presidential candidate asked me when we met one last time, a few months before the 1995 election.

I told him that the wealthy people with whom I had spoken intended to vote for the candidate from the neoliberal PAN party. None of them spoke of voting for Gramajo. (I didn't tell him about the Harvard alumnus who said he wouldn't be invited for dinner, or the other landowners who made fun of the general for thinking that he could pass himself off as something more than a soldier just because he had a Harvard degree.)

Gramajo didn't look surprised. "Well, now in this particular time it's because the chips are down, right? The army is under pressure. So the people distance themselves from the army."

Then I told him that the rest of the country, with the exception of people on the left, did not seem to be very interested in any of the candidates, not even in Gramajo. I had found a considerable amount of apathy regarding the elections.

"This apathy is provoked. It's deliberate," Gramajo responded, now looking a bit piqued. He told me that it resulted from a conspiracy of the "oligarchy" to delegitimize politicians so that few people would vote and their own candidate could carry the election.

Finally, I ventured to tell him about the view on the left. Leftists were certainly not apathetic, but they had no intention of voting for a military person. While some gave Gramajo credit for having sustained civilian rule, they said he had done very little to redress the abuses that the army had committed against the civilian population.

Now Gramajo became angry: "The Guatemalan army is the victim right now, and nobody recognizes that it was the army that allowed the democratic opening. Here, the population did not win the opening. There was not enough, you know, opposition. No, it's deliberate. If you like, it's a *strategic* democracy. But it's there!"

He paused a moment to let this sink in.

"A lot of people want to fix Guatemala's five hundred years of problems. They want to make up for their country's 1954 mistake!" Looking up, I realized that he was directing his comment at me. "And so they say, 'They don't do enough.' *Puta!*" He cursed. His arms flailed. "The expectations are so large! The gringos come, and they say why did I only do this much? *Puta!* In the context, this is enormous. It takes a lot of courage. What is it, in the context, to purge the people who don't have a democratic perspective? Is that worth nothing? Ha, *puta!* How are you going to judge that?"

Later that day I asked a taxi driver about Gramajo's candidacy. He laughed. "No one believes in the military," he told me. An office secretary said the same and then added: "No one believes in anyone anymore."

IV

Did General Gramajo have any good reason to feel betrayed by the United States? Had the U.S. government really encouraged him to do the things for which the federal court had found him liable?

Well, consider the memorandum written in 1968 — just after the death of Leonardo "Nayito" Castillo Johnson — by the second-ranking official in the U.S. embassy, Viron Vaky. The Guatemalan security forces "are guilty of atrocities," he wrote. "Interrogations are brutal, torture is used and bodies are mutilated. Many believe that the very brutal way the ex-beauty queen was killed, obviously tortured and mutilated, provoked the FAR to murder Colonel Webber in retaliation. If true, how tragic that the tactics of 'our side' would in any way be responsible for that event! But the point is that this is a serious practical political problem as well as a moral one: Because of the evidence of this brutality, the government is, in the eyes of many Guatemalans, a cruel government, and therefore righteous outrage, emotion and viciousness have been sucked into the whole political situation. . . . In the minds of many Latin Americans, and, tragically, especially in the sensitive, articulate youth, we are believed to have condoned these tactics, if not actually to have encouraged them. . . .

"This leads to an aspect I personally find the most disturbing of all — that we have not been honest with ourselves. We *have* condoned counter-terror; we may even in effect have encouraged or blessed it. We have been so obsessed with the fear of insurgency that we have rationalized away our qualms and uneasiness. This is not only because we have concluded we cannot do anything about it, for we never really tried. Rather we suspected that maybe it is a good tactic, and that as long as Communists are being killed it is all right. Murder, torture and mutilation are all right if our side is doing it and the victims are Communists. After all hasn't man been a savage from the beginning of time so let us not be too queasy about terror. I have literally heard these arguments from our people.

"Have our values been so twisted by our adversary concept of politics in the hemisphere? Is it conceivable that we are so obsessed with insurgency that we are prepared to rationalize murder as an acceptable counter-insurgency weapon? Is it possible that a nation which so reveres the principle of due process of law has so easily acquiesced in this sort of terror tactic?"

Vaky didn't answer these questions. Nor, apparently, did his colleagues. When the document was declassified three decades later and a journalist asked if it had had any repercussions at the time, Vaky laughed and said, "No one read what I wrote."

Vaky had composed the memo as he was wrapping up his tenure in Guatemala, and he lamented, with hindsight, "My deepest regret is that I did not fight harder within Embassy councils when I was there to press these views. I can in any case understand quite well how easy it is to be complacent or rationalize things."

At the end of his memo, Vaky wrote: "The record must be made clearer that the United States Government opposes the concept and questions the wisdom of counter-terror; the record must be made clearer that we have made this known unambiguously to the Guatemalans; otherwise we will stand before history unable to answer the accusations that we encouraged the Guatemalan Army to do these things."

Or consider the cable sent to Washington by the U.S. embassy just after the massacre in Sacuchum in 1982: "Village in San Marcos Department Reportedly Terrorized, Leaving At Least 38 Dead." The cable noted that "reports of torture and strangulation (and possible incidents of rape) suggest the modus operandi of the extreme right." It then speculated that the guerrillas might in fact have been responsible, which "would suggest a new level of savagery on their part, with possible overtones of the 'racial war' long feared by the right." That speculation, while off base, is nonetheless revealing: the embassy knew that this "savagery" would be "new" for the guerrillas, but was already the "modus operandi" of the "extreme right" (which could only have meant government forces and army-run death squads).

And consider what the State Department did with its knowledge. It told the world, in its annual report on Guatemala published shortly afterward: "The level and nature of the violence is such that one cannot definitively attribute the killing to one group or another." In July 1981, Deputy Assistant Secretary of State Stephen Bosworth had told a congressional committee that leftists were primarily responsible for the violence in Guatemala and that there had been "positive developments" in terms of government forces "taking care to protect innocent bystanders." A year later, Bosworth again testified before Congress, acknowledging now that the Guatemalan government *had* committed abuses the year before, but saying, "I cannot emphasize strongly enough the favorable contrast between the current human rights situation in Guatemala and the situation last December." He told another congressional committee in August 1982: "The government has reduced political violence," and pointed out that "No specific charges of government torture have been brought to our attention." That same month, Ambassador Frederick Chapin told members of Congress: "Over the past three months, most of the killings in the rural areas have been done by insurgents." And when asked about army massacres he said, "Those incidents simply haven't taken place."

Now contrast these public statements with the classified memo that Bosworth wrote in November 1982, reporting that "the military continues to engage in massacres of civilians in the countryside," that the "embassy recently informed us of a new, apparently well-founded allegation of a large-scale killing of Indian men, women and children in a remote area by the army," and that the president, General Efraín Ríos Montt, "seems either unwilling or unable to control this indiscriminate killing." Or consider this one written by Ambassador Chapin the following February: "I am firmly convinced that the violence . . . is Government of Guatemala ordered and directed" and "executions [were] ordered by armed service officers close to President Ríos Montt."

Consider also what Ronald Reagan had to say about Ríos Montt after the two presidents met in Honduras on December 5, 1982. Ríos Montt had come to power eight months earlier in a coup that ousted the previous president, General Romeo Lucas García. In addition to being a retired general, Ríos Montt was an Evangelical preacher, known for using colorful language, as he did at the meeting with Reagan when reporters asked him about the government's "scorched-earth" policy. "We have no scorched-earth policy," he told them. "We have a policy of scorched Communists."

In the months since the army struck Sacuchum, that policy had entailed hundreds of massacres and what the Truth Commission would later call "acts of genocide." In fact, even as the two presidents were exchanging pleasantries, a platoon of elite Kaibil troops was on its way to a community named Las Dos Erres with orders from the high command to commit yet another mass killing. Years later, a forensic team would exhume the remains of "at least" 162 people, including 67 children, and some of the soldiers would tell the Truth Commission what they had done there — how they had killed the younger children by grabbing hold of their legs and swinging them so their heads smashed against a wall, and how they had killed almost everyone else by making them kneel at the edge of a well and, with a blow of a sledge hammer to the head, sending them plunging into the mass of dead and dying bodies piling up inside. They would recount how they had spread the killing over three days and saved for last a group of women and girls whom they raped repeatedly up till the end, and how they forced several pregnant women to miscarry by beating on their stomachs. One would recount how, as they filled in the top of the body-packed well with dirt, they could hear the cries of some of those who were still alive below. The only human remains that visitors would find inside the town afterward were blood on the walls and placenta and umbilical cords on the ground. Among those visitors would be U.S. embassy officers who would report in a confidential memo to Washington that the army had committed yet another massacre.

"Well, I learned a lot," the ever-affable Reagan told reporters on Air Force One as they left Central America that day. "You'd be surprised. They're all individual countries." As for Ríos Montt, Reagan praised the general as "a man of great personal integrity" who was "totally dedicated to democracy," but unfortunately was "faced with a challenge from guerrillas armed and supported from those outside Guatemala." And he dismissed the charges of widespread human rights abuses as simply "a bum rap."

The next day, as Ríos Montt's troops raped and killed the residents of Las Dos Erres, the U.S. news cycle was devoted largely to the question of whether or not the president had known before his trip that Central America consisted of "individual countries." It would seem that Ronald Reagan, while at the pinnacle of the world political order, may have had one thing in common with the Guatemalan peasants at the bottom: a mastery of the strategic use of professed ignorance.

The purpose of the Reagan–Ríos Montt meeting had been to pave the way for renewed U.S. military aid to Guatemala. The obstacle to that aid was Guatemala's human rights record, which had prompted Congress to cut off aid in 1978 after the Carter administration had done something highly unprecedented: told the truth about its ally's repressive practices.

Ever since that cutoff, the State Department had been looking for ways to renew direct military aid (even under Carter). Unable to make Congress budge, U.S. officials helped the Guatemalan army find ways to get what Congress intended to deny them. One technique was to classify such equipment as helicopters that would be used in combat as "nonmilitary" supplies. Another was arranging for U.S. allies to fill in the breach. (Israel in particular provided guns and other equipment, and sent advisers to help the Guatemalan government build its own munitions plant.) And U.S. cash continued to flow to the Guatemalan government, earmarked for nonmilitary purposes — essentially an accounting fiction that freed other money in the government budget to be devoted to the military. In short, the Guatemalan army never really stopped receiving assistance from the United States.

But even though the Guatemalan army continued to obtain weapons and supplies, they still wanted more. And the Reagan administration wanted to give it to them.

Ríos Montt had arrived at the meeting with maps and diagrams and figures to show President Reagan how the human rights situation had improved. But it wasn't Reagan who needed convincing. (And, in fact, declassified documents suggest that the administration was never really convinced.) It was the people in Congress who held the purse strings, and assuaging their concerns required hiding from them what the administration knew.

But there was a problem: information was reaching Congress from another source.

⬇

Reagan called it a bum rap. His men called it something more insidious: "a conspiracy." What they were talking about were the efforts by human rights organizations to document the atrocities being committed in Guatemala. And they set out to discredit these organizations.

Consider now the memo that the U.S. embassy circulated within the State Department in October 1982, accusing Amnesty International and other human rights organizations of "conducting a calculated program of disinformation which originated from Managua, Nicaragua and is part of the worldwide communist conspiracy."

According to the memo, "The campaign's object is simple: to deny the Guatemalan Army the weapons and equipment needed from the U.S. to defeat the guerrillas. Thus, the groups backing the guerrillas intend to win the war against the [Guatemalan government] by making the U.S. Congress the battlefield. It is the old but effective strategy of 'divide and conquer.'"

Assistant Secretary of State Thomas Enders used this memo as a basis for his efforts to publicly discredit an Amnesty International report on Guatemala. In a letter to Amnesty that the State Department publicized in the United States and Guatemala, Enders claimed that many of the violations listed in the Amnesty report could not be corroborated and that others had, in fact, been perpetrated by the guerrillas. He dismissed the rest as being based on sources "closely aligned with, if not largely under the influence of, the guerrilla groups attempting to overthrow the Guatemalan government."

Among the most prominent critics of human rights groups was Elliot Abrams. As assistant secretary of state for human rights, in 1984, he wrote an op-ed in the *New York Times* in which he criticized human rights advocates as being "ill-informed and self-righteous" and suggested that "the people they claim to champion frequently resent the activists' shrill and uninformed criticisms of their country." Although he claimed to find their "strong feelings" about human rights abuses "moving," he argued that "too often . . . the depth of their analysis does not match the depth of their emotion."

Abrams would eventually plead guilty to having illegally withheld information from Congress after the Iran-Contra investigation uncovered the elaborate measures that he and his colleagues had undertaken to arm the Nicaraguan Contras in violation of a congressional ban. One of those measures entailed having a Guatemalan general sign false documents to show that $8 million of weapons sent to the Contras had actually gone to Guatemala. The general who lent his signature may well have been Gramajo — and, if not, it was certainly one of his close associates — which may explain why he might have harbored illusions about friendship with the U.S. government.

We don't know which Guatemalan general helped the Reagan administration with the false documents. That detail was kept secret, along with many other more significant ones. And we can't know the full nature of Gramajo's relationship with the U.S. government, since many of his most important dealings would have been with the CIA, as it continued pouring resources into Guatemala during the years assistance was cut off, retaining top army officers as paid assets.

There was a moment in the 1990s when it appeared that the secret history of U.S. involvement in Central America would at last be shared with the American public. Two successive CIA chiefs promised that the Agency would release previously classified documents from its cold war covert activities. With the cold war over, they said, this was something they could and *should* do. But in 1998, a new director, George J. Tenet, reneged on that promise, announcing a halt to the release of documents.

The reason Tenet gave for his decision was that the Agency did not have the resources necessary to sort through the files. But he had already made clear that the period of CIA openness was over. "I would turn our gaze from the past," he had testified before the Senate during his confirmation hearing. "It is dangerous, frankly, to keep looking over our shoulders."

⚜

But even if we did have more access to secret documents, and if they actually revealed something resembling a bond of friendship, we would have to wonder why Gramajo would have taken it seriously. Why would he expect the U.S. army to be any more faithful to him than his army had been to Cándido Juárez, the military commissioner in La Igualdad? Why would he — who wrote the likes of Juárez out of his own history — expect his U.S. patrons to keep alive the memory of a "friendship" with him?

"You could be burying me in the morning and they'd be burying you that same afternoon." That was how one worker in La Patria had described the epidemic that followed the 1902 eruption — so contagious that those burying the dead would soon follow them to the grave. Something similar might have been said about Juárez and Gramajo, who found themselves contaminated by the casualties of their counterinsurgency. For even in death, their victims could still pose a dangerous question: *How can your power be legitimate if you had to kill us to sustain it?* One way to avoid this question was, in effect, to bury the burial itself. In some cases, that meant eliminating people like Cándido Juárez who had done the dirty work. In others, it meant suppressing information about one's collaboration with them.

By the time Tenet brought a halt to the CIA's release of documents, only two percent of the available files on Guatemala had been released — a smattering of documents with words, lines, and whole paragraphs blacked out, that told us a great deal about what the U.S. government had known, but little about what it had actually done. In the official language of the Agency, these cleaned-up documents had been not "censored," but rather "sanitized."

Perhaps the most eloquent page out of the "sanitized" history of Guatemala can be found in a declassified CIA cable from 1981 that describes an army massacre. The page I have in mind is not the one that says soldiers have just killed "many civilians" in a highland village and points out, matter-of-factly, that "many of them undoubtedly were non-combatants." Rather it is the next, and last, page, which says almost nothing. Its text has been obliterated by a censor's ink, leaving row upon row of blacked-out sentences, lined up likes furrows in a field, inviting one to wonder what information lies buried beneath. What could be worse than what the document had already revealed? What could be so bad that it still needed to remain secret after nearly two decades? Who exactly was implicated? Only two words of the text have survived. They appear in the upper left corner and complete the sentence that begins on the previous page: "The authorities point out, however, that the [guerrillas] appeared to completely control the village, and enjoyed the full support of the. . . ."

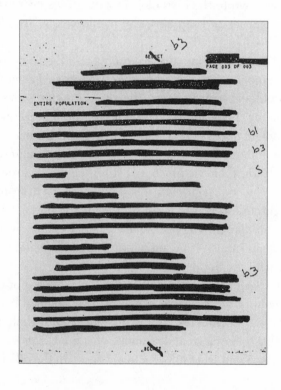

V

On December 29, 1983, two years after the massacre in Sacuchum, guerrillas from the Ixmatá Front burned down the house in La Patria. The burning didn't bring them any closer to a revolution. All it did was cause the *patrón*, Franz Endler, to abandon the plantation.

He was not the only *patrón* to call it quits at the height of the war. "When the guerrillas came along," another coffee grower told me, "the plantations lost their enchantment." For decades, he said, the plantation had been more than a business to them. It had been a part of the families' identity, with those living in the capital visiting on weekends and during holidays. That changed with the violence. Although the guerrillas generally did little more than "burn the symbols of power, like the *casa patronal*, people were still scared to visit. They stopped bringing their families. They stopped going themselves. And they stopped sending their money, because no one likes to invest in something he can't see."

A central part of the army's "normalcy" campaign, according to Gramajo, had been to get capital flowing back to the plantations. The tax incentives they provided may have helped. But what proved decisive was a hike in the world price of coffee in 1986, due to a drought in Brazil. "The 1986 drought is what saved this country," one exporter told me.

As prices rose, and the violence subsided, owners began to return to their plantations. But most would never go back to being the *patrones* they once had been. The patronage system had not survived the war. And while the violence and resulting "disenchantment" may have struck the final blow, the system was probably already doomed.

When Sara Endler took over La Patria, she was determined to run it differently from the way her father had. She would pay minimum wage. She would pay women the same as men. She would not use child labor. She would not participate in the blacklisting of workers by other plantations. She would not treat her workers as dependent children, but rather as adult employees. Sara was determined to have a more humane plantation.

But there was a problem. The population of workers in La Patria had doubled since the 1950s, when her father already had more workers than he needed. If she kept them all, she would not be able to afford to pay minimum wage. And, in fact, even if she paid less, employing them all would probably bankrupt her. She saw only one solution: fire them all, give them plots of land in Las Cruces as severance pay, and then rehire as many as she needed.

The only way to have a more humane plantation, she had decided, was to get rid of the workers.

⁂

Sara wasn't the only one to get rid of her workers. In fact, most of the plantations in the region were doing the same, ending the patronage system by giving their workers small plots of land and turning to the labor market to supply their workforce.

Ironically, it was as if the Agrarian Reform were happening all over again. (In fact, if Decree 900 had been applied now, the outcome would have been essentially the same, since most plantations now used all their land for coffee.) Only this time it was the plantations seeking the freedom of the marketplace. By getting the workers off their land, they could shed the obligations that had come with maintaining a dependent workforce — namely, the obligation to hire them, or at least to provide for their subsistence. Now they could hire whomever they wanted, whenever they wanted, at the wages that the market dictated.

Many, like Sara, justified this transformation in terms of ending the degrading aspects of paternalism inherent in the old system. But few shared her commitment to more decent treatment of the workers they then hired. Many continued to pay below minimum wage, pay women less, and hire people only on a temporary basis in order to avoid the obligation to provide legally mandated benefits.

History repeats itself, Marx once observed, first as tragedy, then as farce. Guatemala's plantation workers had at last been "freed" from the plantations. And now the plantation owners were celebrating this "freedom," using the rhetoric of neoliberalism, the economic paradigm that had emerged triumphant in the wake of the cold war. Free markets, unhindered by social obligations, were better for the economy and therefore ultimately better for everyone participating in it.

Perhaps. But we may ask why it took a century of forced labor, debt peonage, and then patronage, before the plantation owners came to see the virtue of a free market for labor. It can be no coincidence that it also took a century of population growth to provide an excess labor supply where once there was virtually none.

⩓

The most effective way to bury a revolutionary movement is to render it irrelevant. And this was perhaps the ultimate blow that the guerrillas in San Marcos would suffer: the reality they had fought so many years to change ceased to exist. When the guerrillas had shown up on the plantations in 1980, they had not talked so much about a utopian future as about an unjust past. Specifically, they talked about reclaiming what had been taken away in 1954. More generally, they talked about what the plantation owed the workers and why the workers were right to demand justice.

What they said had made sense to the workers. After all, it was these workers' grandparents or great-grandparents who had built the plantation. Their parents had owned — or come close to owning — a part of it during the Agrarian Reform. They had worked there all their lives and probably knew the land better than the owner did. The history of the plantation was the history of their own families, and vice versa. They were a part of the plantation, and the plantation was, in some sense, theirs.

By the end of the war, this sort of talk would not resonate the same way. Workers no longer lived on the plantation their forebears built. Often they no longer even worked on it. Rather, they were hired by several different plantations over the course of a year, and only on a temporary basis. They could no longer claim benefits or privileges because of past work, or feel a sense that the plantation where they were working was also theirs. All they had claim to was the day's wages.

These changes were not unique to the coffee plantations in Guatemala. Rather, they paralleled a shift in employment practices that swept the globe at the end of the twentieth century. The push for more "flexible" workforces, at all levels of the economy, brought an end to lifetime employment with a single employer, in which the employer accrued obligations to the worker with the passage of time. In the new economy, as one prominent French sociologist once observed, "the worker's unremitting commitment is obtained by sweeping away all temporal guarantees."

The terms of the employment relationship had no past and no future, only a fleeting present.

Today young people in La Igualdad no longer see a future in the plantations — and therefore care little about the plantations' past. They face chronic unemployment and poverty, and these hardships are only compounded by the fact that, like the plantation owners, their expectations and tastes are increasingly shaped by what is being marketed from the world's metropolitan centers. Even if they can find work in coffee, they aspire to better things. And so they set out to expand their horizons in the sweatshops and burgeoning shantytowns of Guatemala City, while the more ambitious among them head off to carry the bricks, vacuum the offices, and mow the lawns of the great White Cities to the north.

THE DEFEATED

L EAVING LA IGUALDAD after the Truth Commission meeting, I thought I was done. The people had gotten a chance to tell the commission what they had kept silent all these years, and I had gotten a chance to find out what had silenced them.

I traveled up to the highlands and, reaching the outskirts of Xela, decided to pay Javier, the ex-guerrilla, a visit. I stopped in the government complex where he had been staying, and found only a veteran named Silverio — a small man, shorter than Lico, whom I'd seen watching me from a distance the other times I'd been here. He told me that Javier had just moved to the coffee plantation that the government had bought for the ex-combatants as part of the peace settlement.

I thanked him and turned to go. But it seemed that he wanted to keep talking. "Can *I* help you with something?" he asked.

I said no thanks, but he persisted. "You've been doing the interviews, right?"

I said yes.

"Well, maybe I could tell you some things."

I didn't want to hear any more things. I'd heard enough. More than enough. More than I could ever possibly record . . . And yet, there was *one thing* I had never found out. The one thing that Javier and Lico had refused to talk about — not refused, so much as evaded, saying they hadn't been around when it happened and didn't know who was.

"Do you know anything about the burning of La Patria?"

"*Sí pues.*" He nodded, enthusiastically. "I did it."

"*You* did it?"

"I was in charge of the operation."

We agreed to meet the following day for an interview, and I continued on my way to my apartment in the center of Xela.

⁂

As I entered my apartment, all the fear that I'd bottled away the last few days seemed to rush out and fill the room before me. Shattered glass and loose dirt covered the floor. Books lay open with their leaves exposed to a breeze where there should have been none. *They found me,* I thought and stood paralyzed as an adrenaline bomb exploded in my chest, coursed through my body, and after a few moments, receded just enough for me to hear the voice of reason at the back of my head: *Maybe it was the earthquake.* I looked at the missing window pane, at the furniture that had inched away from the walls, and thought, *Of course, the earthquake.* I walked into the room — *the earthquake, idiot* — and forced a laugh. The more I looked, the more I was sure: the mess was not man-made. My fear settled back in its bottle.

But not for long. Glancing out the window I saw a man standing on the sidewalk below next to my motorcycle. He was just standing there, doing nothing. And as I watched him I felt the fear burst out again. *They know the motorcycle. You shouldn't have left it in front of the house.* The man looked up, and I jumped away from the window. I waited a few moments and peeked out again. He was still there, now gazing down the street. I set about cleaning the apartment, my mind racing. I swept. I stopped and paced. I swept some more. I returned to the window. The man was still there. I swept. I paced. *Still there.* I lay down on the bed, my head spinning like a drunk's. *Calm, calm, calm.* And, still spinning, I dozed off.

When I woke up, the fear had lifted the way a headache might. I went to the window. The man was gone. Once again, my anxiety seemed laughable. And worse, pathetic. How could I let myself be so melodramatic? As if my little scare in La Igualdad was anything compared to what others here had endured.

⁂

I met Silverio in the park and brought him back to my apartment. He entered and, without glancing around, took a seat at the table in the front room. He stared at me with the wide eyes of a man who has seen too much. When I offered to take his windbreaker, he didn't seem to hear me. I sat opposite him, opened my notebook, and asked how he had become a guerrilla. He moved to the edge of his seat and began to talk. Then he stood up, still talking. A moment later he leaned forward on the table. Then he sat down. He seemed unable to stay still, as if he had something burning inside him and didn't know how to put it out. He stood up again and stayed standing, his fingers fumbling with the buttons of his windbreaker, then kneading the edge of the table. And as he talked about some shrapnel that was still lodged in his chest, it dawned on me that the man was unhinged. Unhinged *and* in my home. *Better to get through this quickly,* I thought. *Don't need all these stories. Just that one thing.*

"If we could skip ahead a little, I wanted to ask you about the burning in La Patria. What was the, uh, reason you all decided to do that?"

He didn't pause to think, as Javier and Lico had done when I had asked them this question. The words just tumbled right out: "A *compañero* had been killed there. By the army. The army was camped there. The owner had been collaborating with the army. We had warned him. But he was with the army. So they sent me with a group to burn the plantation."

"And what happened?"

"The first time it didn't work, so we went back a second time and burned it."

"Why didn't it work the first time?"

"The workers wouldn't let us."

So it was true, I thought, surprised. Like César, I had been skeptical of this part of the story Sara told. "They wouldn't let you?"

"That's right. They wanted to defend the plantation. With machetes and stones they attacked us. They yelled at us: 'Thieves! Tools of Havana!' Real aggressive, they were. And we told them, 'Why are you defending the *patrón?*' We said, 'The patrón will never defend you!'"

You could hear the anger as he spoke — both his and that of the people in the plantation. I recalled Lico telling of the cold reaction from the people who had once welcomed them as heroes: "When you're up there in the mountains under the rain, under the bombardment, and you go in the community . . ." And I imagined Gramajo laughing: ". . . and now they were terrorists!"

It was just as Sara had told it: the guerrillas had actually been stopped once by the workers and had returned a week later with more force so they couldn't be stopped again. "And is it true," I asked, "that the workers got drunk on the *patrón*'s liquor and looted the house?"

"That's not true!" Silverio said. "We'd never permit that. No alcohol during an operation." He almost seemed offended, as if the presence of booze would be a gross impropriety while committing arson.

And I believed him. In a way I believed him more than the others. Not because I thought Javier and Lico had deceived me. But it seemed that they had been able to digest their experiences and were turning them into stories. What Silverio said sounded more like raw, unprocessed material. As if he hadn't digested it. As if he just wanted to get it all out of his system.

"And what did you do then?"

"Just waited while it burned."

"And after?"

"We left."

He fell quiet for the first time. I leaned back in my chair and told myself, *Now you know, now you're done.*

But he wasn't. "It was sad to watch," he said. His expression had softened. The anger was gone from his voice. "I mean that house. The way it burned. Such beauty. Such architecture. Such science!"

I looked at him and wondered how different this might have sounded had they won — if not the war itself, then the enduring support of the people in the plantation. Perhaps then the destruction could be justified by having cleared the way for something better. Instead it stood merely as a testament to their defeat. They had been reduced to burning houses and bullying the people they were supposedly fighting for. It brought to my mind a bit of poetry that I had once read:

> *History to the defeated*
> *May say Alas but cannot help or pardon.*

I closed my notebook.

"Well, uh, listen," I said, "I want to thank you for agreeing to talk with me . . ." And with these words I began the process of ushering him out the door.

But he didn't budge. And ignoring my thanks, he said, "There's something bothering me."

"Oh?"

And he began talking. At first I couldn't understand what he was saying. His sentences came disjointed. But I could tell that, in his rambling roundabout way, he was trying to get at something that mattered a great deal to him. He was talking about writing, and then about how all he's ever known is the struggle, and then he was on to family — and now his words became even more roundabout, his fidgeting fingers seemed ready to bore a hole into the wood of the table — and he was saying how he hasn't been able to have a family, that being up in the mountains, it's not so easy to, you know, find a partner, and again about it's all he's known, and about wanting there to be something, something to remember, and then it was back to writing. Someone from the Catholic church had talked to them about writing their history, but this person had never returned, and so Silverio had tried it on his own, since he didn't have anything else, but when he sat down to write he found he couldn't do it, he couldn't get all that stuff out, there were just too many threads, and he didn't know which one to grab. And when he did grab one and got started, he would get this thing in his throat, like a knot, a knot in his throat, and he couldn't bear it, so he would go outside, find some *compañeros*, and talk about other things.

"What produces this thing in your throat?"

He'd be remembering an operation, and then he'd think of one of the *compas* who's no longer here, and then it came, the knot. So many *compañeros*. For example, someone recently came by with a photo of Chano, and when he saw the photo, to see his friend's face again after all these years . . .

And as he talked on, I thought: *Well, Sara, I found out who burned La Patria. He's a little, lonely, nervous man with shrapnel in his chest and a knot in his throat. He wants to write his history, but can't.*

I opened my notebook. I asked him to tell me more, and this time I listened. He told of carrying sticks of dynamite in his backpack, always scared they might blow. He told of using a claymore mine to fill a truck full of soldiers with shrapnel. He told of attacking a lone army post three times before blowing it up with a bazooka. He told of *compañeros* dying and how the survivors kept on moving — up, down, and around the mountains — always ahead of the army, always too quick to be surrounded. *And not realizing,* I thought, *that all the while the army was surrounding them with something much more powerful than its troops: anguish, fear, anger.*

His stories were grim. He didn't embellish. He didn't glorify. And yet what he said seemed to be infused with a glow. Or rather an afterglow, the way stories of heartbreak sometimes radiate a love already lost.

There was one moment of joy in Silverio's history. Back in 1979, after finishing a course in Cuba, he had volunteered to fight in Nicaragua and was with the Sandinistas the day they marched triumphantly into Managua after the fall of the Somoza dictatorship. Thousands upon thousands of people filled the street to welcome them, singing revolutionary songs as the bells in the church towers rang throughout the city.

Now when I remember Silverio, there's a different poem that comes to my mind. "History says, *Don't hope on this side of the grave.*"

> *But then once in a lifetime*
> *The longed-for tidal wave*
> *Of justice can rise up,*
> *And hope and history rhyme.*

Silverio thought he heard them rhyme in Managua that day. He returned to Guatemala and spent the next decade killing people and seeing his friends be killed, always with the hope that he would hear the rhyme again.

Maybe he wasn't anxious to put out a fire. Maybe he was desperate to keep one alive.

⬇

I called Bartolo at the courthouse in Coatepeque to see how he was doing. "Fine," he said in a cheerful voice that was meant for anyone overhearing him, "but I think there are some problems."

"Serious problems?" I asked in the same lighthearted tone.

"I'd say so."

"Problems for who? For me? For you? For some people over there?"

"I'd say maybe for the people. For me. For you."

So I headed out on the bike one last time, through Xela, past the Temple of Minerva, across the valley under Santa María's steady gaze, through the indigenous town where General Gramajo had grown up, through fields that were still white with the ash from 1902, down the steep curves where Silverio had fired a claymore mine into a truckload of soldiers, past the plantation where ORPA first declared war on the Guatemalan state, down to the coastal highway and into Coatepeque.

Bartolo was transformed. He looked as though he hadn't slept in a few days. There had been more threats, he told me as we stood in the shade outside the courthouse. And the army had come by the house asking what we had been up to. As he said this, one of his eyes twitched — a tick I'd never seen before. "I'm not scared of those assholes," he said unconvincingly. "If I faced them back when things were really serious, why not now?"

We stood there a long time talking. I listened as he fleshed out possible scenarios, sorting through the tangle of rivalries within the community and speculating about the perceptions and misperceptions of the officers in the local army base. The only good news was that there had been no reports of other people being harassed.

There wasn't much I could do to help. And he wasn't asking for my help. He had handled situations like this before, he said, his eye twitching. But this would be the last. "From now on, I stay out of politics. It's just not worth it."

⚜

As I rode out of Coatepeque, I wondered whether Bartolo would really abandon politics. It was his calling, after all — or as he put it half jokingly, what he had chosen as the alternative to developing his powers as a witch. And I wondered whether he could stop practicing it, even if he really wanted to.

The larger purpose of the meeting, for him, had been to help make real politics possible again in La Igualdad. Obviously it would take more than one meeting to undo the impact of four decades of terror. Ismael Juárez had impressed this upon me as we stood on the sidewalk, at the entrance to the room where the meeting was taking place. "Here they killed the spirit of the people," he said.

"How?" I asked, curious to hear how he would sum up what took place in the 1980s.

But he went back even further, answering simply, "With what they did to Juan Hernández." He was referring to the union activist assassinated back in the early 1960s.

Yet if the spirit was killed with that first victim, how do we explain a man like Ismael Juárez — a man who had remained active in politics, both open and clandestine, ever since then, a man who faced down his brother Cándido Juárez in public, a man who was terrified by the threats we'd been receiving (according to Bartolo, who had alerted him) and yet still spent the morning tracking down people and now stood guarding the front door for all the world to see?

And how to explain a man like Cayo Ochoa who, despite his eighty-one years, had hiked several miles up the mountain so that he could tell his story to the Truth Commission? When I asked him why he was still working at his age, he explained that he and his wife couldn't live off the meager pension they received, and the plantation where he had worked for twenty-six years refused to pay the severance pay it owed him for his time. This former agrarian leader and PGT militant had had two sons killed by the army because, he said with evident pride, "they were revolutionaries." He told me of the first times the guerrillas showed up and about how his family collaborated with them over the years. He had no regrets, he said. "I gave myself completely to the armed struggle."

Here was another man whose spirit seemed unbroken. However, as he himself pointed out, it was now succumbing to age. "I can't do much anymore because I'm tired," he told me. "Sometimes I think my time has come to die."

Speeding down the newly paved highway, I imagined Ismael Juárez and Cayo Ochoa and the other union leaders back in 1954, walking home to La Igualdad after being released from the San Marcos jail. As they hiked down the mountainside, they had talked about the future, about how they would work to restore the gains of the revolution.

Another way to tell the history of Guatemala's war is this: it took four decades of violence to stamp out what the Agrarian Reform had created — the commitment to the future that those men had shared, the belief that they could transform their nation.

Turning off the coastal highway and onto the road that climbed up to Xela, I decided I'd pay Javier a visit in his new home.

The last time I had seen him was when we traveled together to Chiapas in search of another native of La Igualdad, an elderly man who I thought just might be able to bring all the loose ends of this history to-gether. This veteran of the Agrarian Reform had been the guerrillas' first connection to the network of PGT members in the area and then served as a messenger throughout the war, carrying instructions and information between the fronts, their collaborators, and the high command in Mex-ico. When I first heard Javier describe him, I had been reminded of the pot fixer who César had said would be an ideal source during my very first trip to the region. Just as that pot fixer would know every pot in every home in the region, the veteran in Chiapas would know every collabora-tor in every plantation and would be able to tell how the revolutionary movement grew, changed, and diminished during the course of the war.

We had left Xela in the darkness of night and reached the border shortly after dawn. As we stepped out onto the bridge connecting the two countries, a rising sun cast our shadows ahead of us toward Mexico. Over to our right, we could see the waters from Tajumulco and Tacaná, swollen with the runoff of a hundred plantations and towns, come slowly round a large bend, glide toward the bridge, and, passing beneath, continue on their way to the ocean. Women stood knee deep by the grassy banks, scrubbing clothes as their naked children splashed around them. A man stood on a raft — wooden boards lashed over inner tubes — and pushed his way across the river with a bamboo pole. Farther upstream, more rafts made the crossing.

It was the way Javier had crossed in 1981, when his deteriorating health made it impossible for him to keep fighting. And it was how tens of thousands of Guatemalans would cross in the following years, fleeing the scorched-earth campaign, swelling the refugee camps on the other side, and living among the people who would soon take up arms against their own government.

At the far end of the bridge, we passed through customs and into Chiapas, a state that had been part of Guatemala until the local elite de-cided they'd rather be "the tail of a lion than the head of a rat" and se-ceded to Mexico. People on this side of the river looked the same as those on the other, but the world they lived in was quite different. Everything here seemed bigger, faster and, above all, newer. We traveled all morn-ing, taking a bus inland to a town, riding from there in the back of a truck on a dirt road, jumping off at a dusty crossroads surrounded by coffee trees, walking another half hour on a smaller road, then turning onto a path through a rubber plantation, and at last arriving at our destination: a small clearing with a sagging wooden shack.

But the man was not home. There were some roaming chickens and a pig tied to a tree, but no one to tell us where he might be. So we turned around.

Javier and I had been talking the whole way there, and we kept talking the whole way back. I felt a friendship growing between us, and at one point I stopped calling him *usted* — the form of "you" that Guatemalans use for their bosses, their elders, and most strangers — and tried using the more familiar *vos*. I was hoping he would do the same. But I was disappointed, as I always had been when I tried this with people in the Guatemalan countryside. Javier kept calling me *usted,* preferring to keep the distance between us, or maybe just recognizing its inevitability.

We arrived again at the border, passed through Mexican customs, and walked out onto the bridge. Now a setting sun cast our shadows back toward Guatemala. For Javier, crossing to home would have once meant entering enemy territory. He would have had to move on back roads, following a clandestine network of collaborators, knowing always that detection by the army (or its extensive network of civilian snitches) would mean a trip to the military base, where his captors would keep him alive only long enough for him to map out that clandestine network for them. There would be no hope of holding out long against well-trained torturers; the most anyone could expect of him was that he resist long enough to let his contacts save themselves by making his map obsolete. And then he would disappear. Just like that: gone from the face of the earth. Forever.

The traffic on the river was heavier now than it had been in the morning. Makeshift rafts ferried people from one grassy bank to another. The danger for many of them now lay on the Mexican side. The stakes for them were nothing like what the revolutionaries once faced. But they weren't small either. Poor people were paying thousands of dollars to strangers to smuggle them north, and there would be no refund if they didn't make it. Once outside the law — and desperate to stay there — they became easy prey to the corrupt police and common criminals who circled around the vulnerable the way vultures circle around the dying. Migrants had also been known to disappear.

So this was the border and there were two ways across it: one made of concrete and steel, the other of wood and rubber; one printed on maps, the other spoken in whispers. Many times people in Cajolá and La Igualdad had sought my advice on how to get to the United States and how to find work once they got there. And I always had to tell them I didn't know. They'd get better advice from a Guatemalan who'd already made the trip. For whether it was at this border or another, in their mountains or my cities, we would always be traveling different routes in pursuit of different destinations. And wherever we might meet, in their country or my own, we would forever be foreigners in one another's world.

⬇

I found the ex-guerrillas' new home on a dirt road not far from Barillas's old plantation, La Libertad. I parked by the workers' quarters, a series of small wooden shacks with rusted roofs and open doorways. Looking around, I could see that the prior owner had let the place fall into disrepair. The processing plant looked as run-down as a worker's house. Weeds climbed over the edge of the drying patio. The ordered layout of the coffee groves had begun to break down. The shade trees had spread their branches to capture all the sun they pleased. The coffee plants had grown big and bushy as if they too were going native — which was, in fact, impossible, since they were transplants, strangers to this land, and left a few more years would succumb to the vegetation that, after being suppressed for a century, was now closing in around them.

I found Javier as he returned from a day's work on his new land. He was in good spirits and gave me a tour of the place, explaining the steps they were taking to revive it. Back at the patio, I told him about the commission's visit to La Igualdad and the worries of his old friend, Bartolo. And then I mentioned Silverio.

"He told me about the burning in La Patria." I looked for Javier to react but he said nothing. "He seemed very tense, very anxious. Is he always like that?"

Javier nodded. "Yeah, he has that problem. Something with the nerves. He never sleeps. He'll get up five, six times during the night and go outside."

I thought about this and thought about what Javier had previously told me about his own injuries. After four months of treating his bruised chest in a guerrilla "hospital" in Chiapas, he had rejoined the front in Guatemala, only to find that he still wasn't well enough to fight, and so he returned to Chiapas indefinitely. "You know when you told me that you didn't recover, was the problem with your chest?"

"No, it was my whole body. I would get cold and start sweating for no reason. And I couldn't stand being in bed at night. I'd have to get up and walk around. And when I did sleep, I'd have to ask people not to wake me up suddenly. If I had to be woken up, they should do it by tapping a stick lightly against the wall, but not with loud sounds."

I then asked about Paco, the guerrilla officer who had appeared in a number of his stories.

"I never saw him again," he answered. "But I heard he had a problem with his temper. He would shout at people for no good reason. It seems like his nerves failed him."

I watched some other men returning from the groves and wondered how many of them were still suffering the effects of the war.

"Silverio said the workers in La Patria tried to stop them from burning the house. Why do you think they would have done that?"

He thought a moment and then said, "It's like San Pedro." At first I thought he was talking about the town where his mother was from, the Indian town that Barrios made Ladino. But then I realized he was referring to the biblical story of Saint Peter. "They rejected the guerrillas in order to protect themselves. Before they supported us. When we passed through, they would yell, '*Qué viva ORPA!*' It's easy to say the words, but it's difficult to withstand the reprisals. The people didn't withstand 1983" (the year Gramajo's forces set out to neutralize ORPA).

"Do you think the people there still reject you?"

He shook his head and told me about his first visit to La Igualdad after the war ended. He had walked around San Pedrito, the neighborhood where most of the workers from La Independencia now lived, and the people had come out to greet him. Some had insisted on giving him money, he said, as a token of appreciation. "They told me that they had been praying for me. Whenever they heard fighting in the mountain, they would pray for me." After a moment he added, "They said they prayed for both sides."

"Why don't you go back to live there?"

"It's not the same. The plantation has changed. The children of the revolutionaries are gone. The resistance has been cleaned out."

"But you could try to change that, couldn't you?" Bartolo and Ismael had both told me that Javier would be a very popular politician in La Igualdad and they had tried to convince him to return and run for mayor.

He was quiet for a moment. Then he said, "It doesn't feel like home to me anymore. The people there are so poor. The people in the plantations are really the poorest people in the country. Their appearance might be better than the people in the highlands. They dress well. But inside they're wounded. As they say, 'Candil en la calle, oscuridad en la casa'" (if the lantern is hung out in the street, there will be darkness inside the house). "It's a cultural poverty. They want to say that they're already civilized, that they're superior to the Indians. They don't want to say where they're from. But they can't get rid of their roots."

His hope now was to build a new community in this run-down plantation. It would be something like what his parents had known briefly in La Independencia before the 1954 coup: a plantation without a *patrón.*

It wouldn't be easy though. Javier and many of the others knew as much about growing coffee as the typical *patrón.* But it took more than knowledge to make their plantation work. They would also need cash — cash to refurbish the processing plant, to purchase fertilizers, insecticides, and essential equipment. They would have to go into debt. And it's not easy to get out of debt in the coffee business. Coffee prices go up, coffee prices go down. Lately, they had been down. Plantations throughout the country were going bankrupt. Only those landowners with large cash reserves or alternative sources of income could be certain to survive the cycle. The future of Javier's new community would depend — as other plantations did, as the country itself had for the last century — on their ability to find trusting creditors. It was Guatemala's perennial problem.

THE STORYTELLERS

I F GUATEMALA REMAINED STUCK on the wrong side of the world economy, the options available to Guatemalans seeking to improve their situation had changed in important ways.

For one thing, the cold war was over. The Soviet Union was gone and Castro's Cuba bankrupt, which meant Guatemalans could no longer seek — or be accused of obtaining — support from those totalitarian regimes. The struggle to contain communism could no longer provide a pretext for political repression. And with the specter of communism out of the way, a new menace could take center stage: terrorism.

In the 1990s, terrorism had become public enemy number one in Washington, and in 2001 fighting it became the focus of American foreign policy. After the carnage of September 11, President George W. Bush declared a war on terrorism that would divide the world in two, as the cold war had before it. On one side would be those who opposed terrorism, on the other those who supported it.

There was a key difference between the old enemy and the new: communism was an ideology; terrorism a method. The distinction would become obscured somewhat in the weeks following the president's declaration, as America's public commentators set out to find a definition of "terrorism" that could guide the war effort. What they came up with were, for the most part, convoluted and — by their own accounts — unsatisfying variations on what people used to say about obscenity: you know it when you see it. Those willing to acknowledge that political preferences might influence their "knowing it" dragged out the cliché about one man's terrorist being another man's freedom fighter.

But if a precise definition of terrorism would prove elusive, the basic elements were clear: a terrorist is someone who uses violence to terrorize a population in order to achieve an end — whatever that end might be. What sets terrorism apart from other forms of violence is that its principal objective is to generate fear. Where the standard assassin kills a person to have that person dead, the terrorist's bullet is aimed at scaring the people who survive. Whereas the conventional army, adhering to the laws of war, seeks to overpower its military opponents, the terrorist targets civilians in order to scare them into submission.

Guatemala, during the cold war, became a breeding ground for terrorism. The burning of La Patria was just one small example. Silverio may have been fighting for the welfare of Guatemala's poor when he set the house on fire. Yet, to the extent that this act of violence was intended to terrify the landowners in the region, it should be considered an act of terrorism. Of course one man's terrorist may be another man's freedom fighter — but that doesn't make the person less of a terrorist.

General Gramajo claimed that his army had turned the guerrillas in San Marcos into terrorists. Before his 1983 campaign, he said, they had been something else: an armed organization that was sustained by the civilian population. Their military actions were designed to generate popular support for their effort to topple the government. They were, essentially, a political force. Gramajo's distinction is helpful: politics is about mobilizing supporters; terrorism about intimidating opponents. Politics is about hope; terrorism about fear. The Guatemalan army made the guerrillas turn to acts of terror by making it impossible for them to do politics.

How did the army do this? They did it through the sort of killing that took place in La Igualdad, which is to say, not by killing guerrillas, but by killing their supporters and potential supporters within the civilian population, and by doing so in such an arbitrary and vicious fashion that people in the region came to feel an intense and overwhelming fear, not merely of supporting the guerrillas, but of doing anything that might suggest they sympathized with the guerrillas' cause — such as denouncing the army's methods or giving voice to their own fear. The army did it, in other words, through an extremely effective campaign of terror.

One difficulty with a straightforward definition of terrorism is how readily it can be applied to our own allies. During the cold war, the U.S. government supported regimes in Latin America and other parts of the world whose practices fit the dictionary definition of terrorism. In places like Guatemala, U.S. officials condoned acts of violence that terrorized the civilian population, and the United States even provided material and political support to those who carried them out. They did so in the name of fighting communism. They called it *realpolitik:* you have to be realistic about how power works in the world and do what you can to preserve your own. And they dismissed their critics as wooly-headed liberals who were out of touch with that reality.

The irony, of course, is that the practitioners of *realpolitik* were the ones who felt compelled to pull the wool over the public's eyes time and time again, misrepresenting the "reality" of their policies in Latin America, from the 1954 overthrow of Arbenz through to the Iran-Contra affair in the 1980s. They argued that communism needed to be fought at all costs, but then refused to acknowledge what those costs actually were.

In Guatemala, the cost was some 200,000 lives. And that's just counting the dead. As always with terrorism, a full tally would have to include the impact that the violence had upon the living. It's not something that is easy to gauge, especially for those who have never known the climate of fear and silence it produces.

On September 11, the United States got a taste of that fear. We were fortunate, however, to escape the silence. We were able to denounce the killing, honor the dead, support the bereaved, mobilize to rebuild, and, in the process, overcome our fear. If we didn't do these things, we told ourselves, then terrorism would have won. We repeated this mantra until it became something we could laugh about. But if we stop to imagine how it actually *would* have been — recall those moments of raw fear when our buildings or subway stops were evacuated, recall dreading what we might hear on the evening news, recall what it was like to be staring out an office window or riding an elevator or reading a newspaper and feel a sudden urge to cry, and then imagine the danger being so immediate that we couldn't even talk about it, and imagine that the people doing this to us were proclaiming their own righteousness to the world, and imagine living like this day after day, year after year, until the most we could hope for was to be left alone. If we do this, we may begin to grasp what hundreds of thousands of Guatemalans experienced during their war. For Guatemala was a place where terrorism did, in fact, win.

In the future, it may be more difficult for terrorists to score such victories. At the very least, repressive governments will no longer be able to use the threat of communism to justify their methods and obtain allies in Washington. Some will surely seek to use the war on terrorism as a pretext for their own acts of terror. But maybe — just maybe — they will now find themselves denounced by the same superpower that, in the context of the cold war, might have once called them freedom fighters.

⬇

In addition to the end of the cold war, there was another change taking place that would make it more difficult for governments to hide the costs of political repression, whatever their justification might be.

It was perhaps the only good to come of the dirty wars in Latin America: a human rights movement, which had been in its infancy at the beginning of the 1980s, would mobilize to expose the atrocities being committed in the region and, in the process, build a worldwide network linking local rights advocates to international organizations that had the resources — and media savvy — necessary to publicize human rights abuses around the globe.

Such networks had been built before. There had been the movement to end slavery in Britain and the United States in the nineteenth century, for example, and the movement to end it in King Leopold's Congo at the turn of the twentieth. But those earlier networks, as powerful as they had been in their day, could never have publicized abuses as quickly and effectively as human rights advocates were now able to using the tools of mass communication and, more recently, the Internet.

When the people of Sacuchum were massacred in 1982, the survivors were unable to tell the outside world what had happened. Fifteen years later, when a similar massacre occurred a hundred miles away in a Mexican village named Acteal, the victims' story was broadcast around the world within hours by the major news media and, for months to come, through e-mail lists and Websites.

If you know terrorism when you see it, the odds are now better that people everywhere will see it. Of course, seeing it doesn't always mean stopping it. The genocides of the 1990s in Rwanda and the former Yugoslavia — which were carried out with the world watching — showed us that increased international awareness doesn't necessarily prevent atrocities from taking place. What it *does* mean, however, is that powerful governments find it more difficult to engage in the sort of *realpolitik* that entails hiding the "real" costs of their policies from their own people.

Globalization — the economic interconnectedness and constant communication between places like Guatemala and the wealthier nations to the north — is nothing new. A century ago, Guatemalan presidents and businessmen were actively engaged in cultivating their country's image abroad. What *is* different is that the access to foreign audiences has, in recent years, extended down the social hierarchy to include workers on plantations and peasants in some of the most remote villages.

The implications of this increased access extend far beyond human rights and the struggle against terrorism. For in addition to allowing people to denounce their government's abusive practices, globalization presents them with new ways of pressing their government to address their needs — which is to say, new ways of doing politics.

This change was already becoming apparent when I first arrived in Guatemala in 1993. And among the groups pioneering the uncharted territory of the new globalized politics were the people of Cajolá — that indigenous community whose land was taken in the 1880s, whose mayor was shot after he protested, and who ended up working in La Libertad, the plantation where Friedrich Endler began his life in Guatemala.

One hundred years after Friedrich Endler marveled at the "savage, ragged creatures" dancing their "fantastic dances" under his electric light, the people of Cajolá would be seen putting on another show. The stage this time wasn't a president's private coffee patio, but rather the central plaza of Guatemala City, in front of the National Palace, where the community's leaders had presented a list of demands to the president's personal secretary. The show consisted of holding banners and chanting slogans and telling journalists that the people of Cajolá had lost their land and that the government hadn't fulfilled a promise to help them get it back. When the government responded by sending riot police with clubs and tear gas to drive them from the plaza, the sight — caught on film — caused a national uproar that echoed overseas.

The year was 1992, and once again Columbus's crossing was being commemorated. This time, however, the focus of international attention had shifted from the material progress of Europeans in the New World

to the fate of those people who — since Columbus's fateful miscalcula-
tion — had been called "Indians."

The crackdown in the plaza was hardly a novel sight in Guatemala.
But, because of the context, it seemed to represent something much
larger to many Guatemalans and foreigners — including me when I
showed up in Guatemala a year later with my traveling fellowship. After a
few weeks in Xela, I visited Cajolá and was so captivated by the stories
the community's leaders told that I stayed to piece together the history of
their efforts to reclaim their land.

The protest before the National Palace had been the culmination of a
three-year struggle — they told me — which had begun after they had
found an old property title and, with the authorization of government officials, had occupied the land to which it gave them ownership — part of
a cattle ranch south of Coatepeque.

The rancher, who shared an extension of some five thousand acres
with just his cattle, claimed that the invaders were violating his property
rights. Other ranchers rallied behind him, waging a political campaign on
his behalf, placing paid ads in newspapers that declared they would
"never allow the existence of Private Property to be jeopardized" and that
called upon the government to reestablish "the Sovereignty of the Law"
by evicting the peasants.

It wasn't difficult to see, as I would after a little research, that the law
was indeed on the rancher's side. Like most countries, Guatemala placed
a time limit on reclaiming usurped land. In Guatemala, the limit was ten
years. The rancher had been using this land for over thirty. Only after I
had known the Cajolá leaders for over a year would one of them concede
to me that their title was legally worthless. At first, though, they told me
the same thing they had told the press and the people who supported
their cause: they were simple peasants, they didn't speak Spanish very
well, and they couldn't be expected to understand the intricacies of property law. At the time, I took what they said at face value. Only later would
I realize that it was a strategic obfuscation, an elaborate version of what
would become for me an all-too-familiar refrain: *saber.*

Of course, *saber* wouldn't stand up in a court of law, certainly not against
a wealthy rancher and his lawyers. An eviction order was issued, and the
people of Cajolá were removed from the ranch. But rather than return to
the highlands, they camped on the dirt road that ran its perimeter and set

about drawing public attention to their plight. Living on the road hadn't been easy — they would tell the press — especially not during the dry season when the dirt road became a dust bowl. I saw what this dust was like when I traveled with some of them on another nearby road and a single passing car kicked up enough to cover us all with a thick yellow film. "Look, Daniel," one man yelled, "we're all *canches* now!" And while they all laughed at the idea that they had become "blonds," I could see how difficult it must have been to live with this dust filling the air around them, settling in their food and in their lungs. Over a dozen children had died there from pulmonary complications caused by the dust. Later, when asked why they had come to protest in the capital, the people of Cajolá would say they had been compelled to come by their suffering. And they would talk about the dust, a bit like the way older people in La Igualdad talked to me about the ash.

Outraged that, despite his solid legal claim, he seemed to be losing the public relations war, the rancher took a drastic step. He announced to the press that the people who had invaded the plantation were "heavily armed young people, directed by bearded, white men." He was using the unmistakable code language of a right wing that had always encouraged the idea that the guerrillas were led by foreign agitators. He was calling them blonds — *canches* — guerrillas.

A few years earlier, this charge might have gotten them killed. But this time the defense minister, General Gramajo — who was then brushing up his English and getting together his application to Harvard — chose to ignore the rancher's appeals for army intervention.

The Cajolá leaders denied the charge to the press at the time — and continued to do so when I asked them about it a year later. Or at least I thought they were denying it. Looking back now, I know they were telling me things that I couldn't hear at the time. One afternoon, for instance, after listening to one leader describe how the suffering caused by the dust in the road had radicalized the community, I asked him if there was any truth to the rancher's accusation: *were* they in fact guerrillas? I had expected a flat-out denial. Instead I got something more playful, more poetic; something that, if I had understood it at the time, might have made me realize sooner what good storytellers they were. "Look, Daniel," he said with a grin, "the only thing that made us *canches* was the dust."

At first I thought he was repeating the joke I'd heard before: *the dust had made them blond.* Only later did I see the double meaning that made him smile: *their suffering had driven them to join the guerrillas.* Perhaps if I had picked up on the clue he was offering me and shown him I understood his code language — that I too knew how to speak through silences — then he would have allowed me to know what I would only learn years later: that the leaders of Cajolá had been guerrillas.

By the time I figured that out, I would also know that their involvement with the guerrillas had been only one stage in a struggle to regain their land that went back over a century. During the liberal era at the end of the nineteenth century, they had appealed to the beneficence of the dictator-presidents, couching their appeals in the liberals' own rhetoric of property rights and national progress. During the Arbenz years, they had formed a "peasant union" and briefly acquired land through a petition under Decree 900, only to lose it after the 1954 coup. And during the war years, they had joined the guerrillas, who promised the possibility of another agrarian reform. Each time they had told a different story about who they were and why they deserved the land. But only in 1992 did they hit upon one that worked.

Encuentro de dos mundos, 1492–1992 © 2002 Daniel Hernández-Salazar

After the crackdown in the plaza, the families of Cajolá found shelter in a nearby campus of the university, where they were soon receiving daily visits from student activists like César Sánchez who came — often with foreigners from their language schools in Xela — to show their support for the community. The people of Cajolá listened as these visitors told them about the importance of their cause, about the glorious past of the Mayan people — a label that had, in recent years, come to be used by many Guatemalans as a respectful replacement for "Indian" — and about how, before the Spanish came, all the land had belonged to their ancestors, who had shared it among themselves in harmony. In private, they laughed at the idea — which they found absurd — that their ancestors hadn't known how to divide the land into individually owned plots. But in public they adopted the story. They changed the name of their movement from "Pro-Land" to "Pro-Ethnicity," and began to talk about themselves as "Mayans." The community soon became the poster child for the cause of "indigenous rights" in Guatemala. A photo of them facing off against the riot police appeared on a postcard, with the caption "The Clash of Two Worlds, 1492–1992" and was sold in tourist shops throughout the country to foreigners who, in turn, sent it to their homes around the world. Joined now by the voices of these strangers, the sound of their protests grew louder and louder until, several months after the crackdown in the plaza, they were able to wrest from the government one of the largest land grants in Guatemala since the Agrarian Reform.

⚡

The key to Cajolá's victory was not their new story so much as the audience it attracted. The community had been able to access people like me, from the rich and powerful countries of the world, people who could not be silenced the way they themselves had been in the past. We were the true *canches*. We came to Guatemala in the 1990s to work with human rights groups, dig up clandestine cemeteries, and, eventually, fill the ranks of a Truth Commission that gave people throughout the country an opportunity to denounce the abuses they had suffered over the years. Sometimes — as our critics argued — we didn't entirely know what we were talking about. But on balance, our presence contributed to a more honest discussion of Guatemala's violent history. And when the Truth Commission published its findings in 1999, it put that history on the front pages of newspapers around the world and prompted Bill Clinton to do something that would have been unthinkable for a U.S. president during the cold war: issue a formal apology for the U.S. government's past support of abusive regimes in Guatemala.

There were limits, of course, to what could be achieved through the new globalized politics. In the decade after Cajolá's 1992 victory, the people of Sacuchum and several other Mayan communities would launch similar campaigns to obtain land. But none would succeed in generating the same level of international attention, nor in winning comparable concessions from the government. The leaders of these communities would therefore have to resort to more traditional forms of politics. Working with Mayan activists in the capital, they were able to build a national indigenous rights organization that was stronger than anything Guatemala had seen since before the counterinsurgency crushed all forms of political opposition in the 1980s — an organization with financing from European donors and technical support from a new cadre of Guatemalan intellectuals like César Sánchez.

The last time I saw César, he was helping them draft a proposal for reforming the agricultural sector. The proposal was more modest than the agrarian reform that he and his peers had once dreamed of — and, unlike that one, it contained measures addressing the needs of plantation owners as well. It was too early to tell what success this proposal might have — whether the indigenous rights organization would be able to exact meaningful concessions from the owners or, better yet, actually find a way to work with them to address their common problems.

César did not expect these problems to disappear anytime soon. Nor did Sara Endler. Nor did anyone familiar with Guatemala's history. Poverty would continue to consume the country's poor. Violence would continue to haunt its political life. But, at the very least, there was reason to hope that the silence of the last century would remain a thing of the past.

LIST OF NAMES

The following are the names of people who make multiple appearances in the book. The numbers indicate the page where each is described for the first time. The names are organized alphabetically by first *or* last name, depending upon which I have used to identify the person in the text — a choice that reflects the context in which I knew the person.

In rural Latin America, it is customary to refer to people by their first names, adding the prefix *Don* or *Doña* to express deference. (So, for instance, César Sánchez might be known as Don César in the countryside and Señor Sánchez in Guatemala City.) The noms de guerre of guerrillas usually consist of a single name. In contexts where people are known by their last name, some choose to use their second (or matrilineal) last name in addition to their first.

NOTE ON SOURCES

The research for this book consisted primarily of personal interviews — those re-counted in the text and many others that were not. In addition to the interviews, I con-sulted and, in several passages, drew key information from a wide range of primary documents and secondary sources.

II. Ashes Fell

The Liberal Reforms and the origins of the coffee economy:

For my discussion of the Liberal Era, I relied extensively on David McCreery's comprehensive and richly detailed history, *Rural Guatemala, 1760–1940,* as well as his essays, "State Power, Indigenous Communities, and Land in Nineteenth-Century Gua-temala, 1820–1920," and "Wage Labor, Free Labor, and Vagrancy Law. The Transition to Capitalism in Guatemala, 1920–1945." The examples of coerced labor on page 44 were drawn from *Rural Guatemala* (p. 266). The quotation of the American visitor on page 46 is from Helen Sanborn, *A Winter in Central America and Mexico* (Boston: 1886; cited by McCreery in *Rural Guatemala,* p. 176). The quotation of the Guatema-lan government official ("It is necessary to make the Indian work . . .") on page 76 is also from *Rural Guatemala* (p. 175). The quotation of a foreigner describing the labor contractors' work in the highlands on page 76 is from Robert Burkitt, "Explorations in the Highlands of Western Guatemala," *The Museum Journal* (University of Pennsylva-nia) 21, no. 1 (1930), cited by McCreery in *Rural Guatemala* (p. 176). Regina Wagner's *Los Alemanes en Guatemala* provided much of the information on the history of the German community in Guatemala, as well as on the economic and political crises faced by President Manuel Estrada Cabrera at the turn of the century.

Other texts I consulted on the history of the Liberal Era include Greg Grandin's work, *The Blood of Guatemalans: A History of Race and Nation,* Robert Williams's *States and Social Evolution: Coffee and the Rise of National Governments in Central America,* Paul Burgess's *Justo Rufino Barrios: Una Biografía,* and Julio C. Cambranes's *Café y campesinos en Guatemala, 1853–1897.*

For the story of Estrada Cabrera's 1902 decree being read in Quetzaltenango, I relied on Rafael Arévalo Martínez's *Ecce Pericles!: La tiranía de Manuel Estrada Cabrera en Guatemala* and Eduardo Galeano's *Memory of Fire: Century of the Wind.*

Ethnic identity:
    My discussion of ethnic identity in Guatemala was informed by the scholarly works of Richard N. Adams, Greg Grandin, Diane N. Nelson, and Arturo Taracena, as well as two Guatemalan research institutions, the Asociación para el Avance de las Ciencias Sociales en Guatemala (AVANCSO) and the Centro de Investigaciones Regionales de Mesoamérica (CIRMA). The quotation on page 47 ("My dad always . . .") was taken from Valentín Solórzano Fernández's *El Relato de Juan Tayun: La Vida de un Indio Guatemalteco* (p. 19).

Travel narratives:
    The quotation that opens Part II (and appears again in the chapter "Decree") is from William Tufts Brigham's *Guatemala: The Land of the Quetzal* (1887). Other travel narratives I consulted include John L. Stephens's *Incidents of Travel in the Central America, Chiapas, and Yucatan* (1841), Lindesay Brine's *Travels Amongst American Indians, Their Ancient Earthworks and Temples; Including a Journey in Guatemala, Mexico and Yucatan. . . .* (1894), and Aldous Huxley's *Beyond the Mexique Bay* (1934).

III. A Future Was Buried

The October Revolution and the Agrarian Reform:
    I drew upon Jim Handy's *Revolution in the Countryside: Rural Conflict and Agrarian Reform in Guatemala, 1944–54,* Guillermo Paz Cárcamo's *Guatemala: Reforma Agraria,* Stephen C. Schlesinger and Stephen Kinzer's *Bitter Fruit: The Untold Story of the American Coup in Guatemala,* Piero Gleijeses' *Shattered Hope: The Guatemalan Revolution and the United States, 1944–1954,* Cindy Forster's *The Time of Freedom: Campesino Workers in Guatemala's October Revolution,* Neale J. Pearson's unpublished thesis, "The Confederación Nacional Campesina de Guatemala (CNCG) and Peasant Unionism in Guatemala, 1944–1954," and Gustavo Porras's essay, "Análisis estructural y recomposición clasista de la sociedad guatemalteca de 1954–1980."

The United States and the 1954 coup:
    For the U.S. government's role in the 1954 coup, I relied heavily upon the CIA's internal history, *Operation PBSUCCESS: The United States and Guatemala, 1952–1954,* which was written by Nicholas Cullather in 1994 and declassified in 1997. (The declassified text has since been published as Nicholas Cullather, *Secret History. The CIA's Classified Account of Its Operations in Guatemala, 1952–1954.* Stanford: Stanford University Press, 1999.)
    I also relied on other declassified U.S. government documents obtained by the National Security Archive (NSA) in Washington, D.C. Most of these documents can be found on the NSA's Web page (www.gwu.edu/~nsarchiv) in its *Electronic Briefing Book No. 4,* "CIA and Assassinations. The Guatemala 1954 Documents," edited by Kate Doyle and Peter Kornbluh. For evidence of the CIA's assassination plans see Document 1, "CIA and Guatemala Assassination Proposals, 1952–1954," CIA History Staff Analysis by Gerald K. Haines, June 1995; Document 2, "A Study of Assassination," un-

signed, undated; Document 3, "Selection of individuals for disposal by Junta Group," March 31, 1954; Document 4, "Guatemalan Communist Personnel to be disposed of during Military Operations of Calligeris," origin deleted, undated.

Finally, I drew upon accounts of the coup in the books of Schlesinger and Kinzer, Handy, and Gleijeses, as well as a series of articles run by the *New York Times* in 1997, which included "C.I.A. Plotted Killing of 58 In Guatemala" and the "Role of C.I.A. in Guatemala Told in Files of Publisher" by Tim Weiner.

IV. And They Were the Eruption

The Chicago World's Columbian Exposition:
I relied upon Reid Badger's *The Great American Fair,* Robert W. Rydell's *All the World's a Fair: Visions of Empire at American International Expositions, 1876–1916,* and Alan Trachtenberg's *The Incorporation of America: Culture and Society in the Gilded Age.* Some of the information on the Guatemalan exhibit came from the 1893 publication *A Descriptive Account of the Republic of Guatemala Central America.*

Oral history from Cajolá:
The story of how the people of Cajolá prevented foreigners from mining their hills can be found in *Nab'ab'l Qtanam: La memoria colectiva del pueblo mam de Quetzaltenango,* compiled by Rainer Hostnig and Luis Vásquez Vicente.

The Cuban Revolution and the Latin American Left:
I referred to Jon Lee Anderson's *Che: A Revolutionary Life,* Jorge G. Castañeda's *Utopia Unarmed: The Latin American Left After the Cold War,* and Richard Gott's *Guerrilla Movements in Latin America,* among others. The quotation from Regis Débray on page 226 came from his book *Revolution in the Revolution? Armed Struggle and Political Struggle in Latin America* (p. 147).

Political repression, civil war, and civilian casualties in Guatemala:
The most comprehensive and authoritative account of the violence and its impact on Guatemalan society is the twelve-volume report *Guatemala: Memoria del silencio,* published by the Comisión de Esclarecimiento Histórico (or "Truth Commission") in February 1999. Another detailed and comprehensive report was published by the Archbishop's Human Rights Office (Oficina de Derechos Humanos del Arzobispado de Guatemala, or ODHA), *Guatemala, Nunca más.*

The account of the massacre in Las Dos Erres on page 327 was based on the Truth Commission's findings. (See "Caso ilustrativo No. 31, Masacre de las Dos Erres," *Guatemala: Memoria del silencio,* Tomo VI, p. 397.)

Gramajo and the Guatemalan army:
For the history of General Héctor Gramajo and the Guatemalan military, I drew upon Gramajo's *Tesis de la estabilidad nacional* and *De la guerra . . . a la guerra: la difícil transición política en Guatemala.* I also referred to Jennifer Schirmer's *The Guatemalan Military Project: A Violence Called Democracy.*

The United States and Guatemalan counterinsurgency:
For the history of U.S. support for the Guatemalan military since the 1954 coup, I drew upon Greg Grandin's introduction to *Denegado en Su Totalidad: Documentos estadounidenses liberados,* as well as *The American Connection,* vol 2., *State Terror and Popular Resistance in Guatemala,* by Michael McClintock, and *With Friends Like These: The Americas Watch Report on Human Rights and U.S. Policy in Latin America,* edited by Cynthia Brown.

Again, I relied on declassified documents obtained by the National Security Archive. Most of these are available on the NSA Web site in *Electronic Briefing Book No. 11,* "The Guatemalan Military. What the U.S. Files Reveal," edited by Kate Doyle. For evidence that the United States government knew about the abduction and execution of Leonardo Castillo Flores and his PGT colleagues, see Document 1, "U.S. Counter-Terror Assistance to Guatemalan Security Forces," Agency for International Development, secret cable, January 4, 1966; Document 2, "Interrogation and Execution of Five Prisoners," CIA, secret cable, March 1966; Document 3, "Death List," CIA, secret cable, March 1966. Evidence that the perpetrators of the 1966 mass disappearance employed "counter-terror" techniques learned from the United States came from a declassified document *not* available on the NSA Web page. It is a "Public Safety Monthly Report" sent by the U.S. embassy in Guatemala in March of 1966. Paragraph 4 of the document notes that the Guatemalan security forces "apparently did score a considerable success when they captured a number of leading Communists, including Victor Manuel Gutierrez, Leonardo Castillo Flores, and Francisco Amado." Later in the report, the embassy points out the effectiveness of the "counter-terror" training the United States had recently provided Guatemala's security forces, in which they taught, among other things, how to implement a method of carrying out mass detentions called the "frozen area plan." "The police in Guatemala City have conducted 80 raids during the past month using the 'frozen area plan.' The raids have been productive in apprehensions (see paragraph 4)."

Other documents on the NSA Web site include Viron Vaky's 1968 memo, Document 8, "Guatemala and Counter-terror," Department of State, secret memorandum, March 29, 1968; Ambassador Chapin's comment ("I am firmly convinced . . ."); Document 23, "[Ríos Montt Gives Carte Blanche to Archivos to Deal with Insurgency]," CIA, secret cable, February 1983; the memo accusing international human rights organizations of participating in a "worldwide communist conspiracy"; Document 16, "Analysis of Human Rights Reports on Guatemala by Amnesty International, WOLA/ NISGUA, and Guatemala Human Rights Commission," Department of State, confidential cable, October 22, 1982; the censored report of the 1981 massacre reprinted on page 332, Document 17, "[Guatemalan Soldiers Kill Civilians in Cocob]," CIA, secret cable, April 1981.

One declassified document that does not appear on the NSA Web site is the cable reporting the Sacuchum massacre: "Village in San Marcos Department Reportedly Terrorized, Leaving at Least 38 Dead," January 1982.

The public statements made by U.S. and Guatemalan government officials were taken mostly from major U.S. newspapers. For Vaky's comment on his 1968 memo, see Douglas Farah, "'We've Not Been Honest'; '68 Memo Assails U.S. Role in Guatemalan War," *Washington Post,* March 12, 1999, p. A25. For Efraín Ríos Montt's comment about the "scorched Communist" policy on page 327, see "Guatemalan Vows to Aid

Democracy," *New York Times,* December 6, 1982, p. A14. For Ronald Reagan's "bum rap" comment on page 328, see Steven R. Weisman, "Reagan Denounces Threats to Peace in Latin America," *New York Times,* December 5, 1982, sec. 1, p. 1. For the debate over whether Reagan had previously known that Central America consisted of "individual countries" on page 328, see John M. Goshko, "Reagan Remarks Draw Explications," *Washington Post,* December 7, 1982, p. A1. The op-ed by Elliot Abrams cited on page 330 was "The Myopia of Human Rights Advocates," *New York Times,* August 10, 1984, p. A25.

The public statements made by Deputy Assistant Secretary of State Stephen Bosworth on pages 326–27 were taken from Americas Watch ("positive developments," p. 5; "I cannot emphasize strongly enough . . . ," p. 7; "The government has reduced political violence . . ." p. 12). The public statement of Ambassador Frederick Chapin on page 326 ("Over the past three months. . .") also came from Americas Watch (p. 12); as did the excerpt from the 1981 State Department Country Report on page 326 ("The level and nature of the violence. . . . ," p. 6).

For a discussion of the multiple ways the congressional ban on military aid to Guatemala was evaded, see Tanya Broder and Bernard D. Lambek, "Military Aid to Guatemala. The Failure of U.S. Human Rights Legislation," 13, *Yale Journal of International Law* 129–31 (1988). See also Richard J. Meislin, "U.S. Military Aid for Guatemala Continuing Despite Official Curbs," *New York Times,* December 19, 1982, p. 1. For the Carter administration's efforts to renew direct military aid to Guatemala, see John M. Goshko, "Controversy Looms Over Bid to Aid Guatemala," *Washington Post,* March 11, 1979, p. A4. For how the Reagan administration was able to renew direct military aid, see Bernard Gwertzman, "U.S. Lifts Embargo on Military Sales to Guatemalans," *New York Times,* January 8, 1983, p. 1, and "U.S. Agrees to Sell Helicopter Parts to Guatemalans," *New York Times,* January 30, 1984, p. A1.

The information on the CIA's decision not to continue releasing documents came from Tim Weiner, "C.I.A.'s Openness Derided as a 'Snow Job,'" *New York Times,* May 20, 1997, p. A16; "Committee Says C.I.A.'s Secrecy Threatens to Make History a Lie," *New York Times,* April 9, 1998, p. A22; and "C.I.A., Breaking Promises, Puts Off Release of Cold War Files," *New York Times,* July 15, 1998, p. A13. George J. Tenet's testimony (cited on p. 331) was given before the Senate Intelligence Committee during the Confirmation Hearing on the Selection of the Director of Central Intelligence on May 6, 1997.

Other sources of information include Stephen Engelberg, "The White House Crisis. The Contras," *New York Times,* February 26, 1987, p. A1, on the assistance a Guatemalan general gave U.S. government officials in their unlawful efforts to arm the Contras); David Johnston, "Poindexter Wins Iran-Contra Case in Appeals Court," *New York Times,* November 16, 1991, p. 1, which reports on Elliot Abrams's guilty plea on misdemeanor charges; and John M. Broder, "Clinton Offers His Apologies to Guatemala," *New York Times,* March 11, 1999, p. A1, on President Clinton's apology in Guatemala.

SELECTED BIBLIOGRAPHY

Archives

Archivo General de Centro América, Guatemala City.
Archivo de Gobernación, Quetzaltenango.
Archivo Histórico de Quetzaltenango.
Centro de Investigaciones Regionales de Mesoamérica's Photograph Archive (CIRMA), Antigua.
Instituto Nacional de Transformación Agraria (which holds the records of the Departamento Agrario Nacional).
Segundo Registro de Propiedad, Quetzaltenango.

Primary Sources

Comisión de Esclarecimiento Histórico. *Guatemala: Memoria del silencio.* Guatemala City, 1999.
Comisión Guatemalteca de la Exposición de Chicago. "Instructiones Generales para los Expositores de Guatemala." May 12, 1892.
Dirección General de Estadística. *Censo general de la república de Guatemala.* Guatemala City: Tipografía Nacional, 1894.
Fuerzas Armadas Rebeldes (FAR). "Declaración de la Sierra de las Minas." January 10, 1968.
Government of Guatemala. *A Descriptive Account of the Republic of Guatemala Central America.* Chicago: The Department of Public Works, 1893.
Oficina de Derechos Humanos del Arzobispado de Guatemala. *Guatemala: Nunca más.* Guatemala City: Oficina de Derechos Humanos del Arzobispado de Guatemala, 1988.
Organización Revolucionaria del Pueblo en Armas (ORPA). *La verdadera magnitud del racismo (Racismo II).* 1978.
Partido Guatemalteco de Trabajo (PGT). "Informe del Comité Central al III Congreso." Guatemala City, 1960.

Secondary Sources

Adams, Richard N. *Crucifixion by Power: Essays on Capitalist National Social Structure, 1944–1966.* Austin: University of Texas Press, 1970.

————. "Conclusions. What Can We Know about the Harvest of Violence?" In *The Harvest of Violence: The Maya Indians and the Guatemalan Crisis,* edited by Robert Carmack. Norman: University of Oklahoma Press, 1988.

————. *Etnias en evolución social: Estudios de Guatemala y Centroamérica.* Mexico: Universidad Autónoma Metropolitana, 1995.

Americas Watch. *Guatemala: The Group for Mutual Support.* New York: Americas Watch Committee, 1985.

————. *Guatemala Revised: How the Reagan Administration Finds "Improvements" in Human Rights in Guatemala.* New York: Americas Watch Committee, 1985.

Anderson, Jon Lee. *Che: A Revolutionary Life.* New York: Grove Press, 1997.

Arévalo Martínez, Rafael. *Ecce Pericles! La tiranía de Manuel Estrada Cabrera en Guatemala.* San José, Costa Rica: EDUCA, 1983.

Arias, Arturo. "Changing Indian Ethnicity. Guatemala's Violent Transition to Modernity." In *Guatemalan Indians and the State, 1540–1988,* edited by Carol A. Smith. Austin: University of Texas Press, 1990.

Asturias, Miguel Angel. *El señor presidente.* Translated by Frances Partridge. New York: Atheneum, 1983.

Badger, Reid. *The Great American Fair.* Chicago: Nelson Hall, 1979.

Bastos, Santiago, and Manuela Camus. *Quebrando el silencio: Organizaciones del pueblo maya y sus demandas.* Guatemala City: Facultad Latinoamerica de Ciencas Sociales (FLACSO), 1992.

Black, George. *The Good Neighbor: How the United States Wrote the History of Central America and the Caribbean.* New York: Pantheon Books, 1988.

Bourdieu, Pierre. *Acts of Resistance: Against the Tyranny of the Market.* New York: New Press, 1998.

Brigham, William Tufts. *Guatemala: The Land of the Quetzal.* New York: C. Scribner's Sons, 1887.

Brine, Lindesay. *Travels Amongst American Indians: Their Ancient Earthworks and Temples; Including a Journey in Guatemala, Mexico and Yucatan . . . .* London: Sampson Low, Marston & Company, 1894.

Brown, Cynthia, ed. *With Friends Like These: The Americas Watch Report on Human Rights and U.S. Policy in Latin America.* New York: Pantheon Books, 1985.

Burgess, Paul. *Justo Rufino Barrios: Una Biografía.* Translated by Francis Gall. Guatemala City: Publicación Especial No. 17 de la Sociedad de Geografía e Historía de Guatemala, 1971.

Cambranes, Julio C. *Café y campesinos en Guatemala, 1853–1897.* Guatemala: Editorial Universitaria, 1985.

Carr, Barry, and Steve Ellner. *The Latin American Left: From the Fall of Allende to Perestroika.* San Francisco: Westview Press, 1993.

Casaus Arzú, Marta. *Guatemala: Linaje y Racismo.* Guatemala City: Facultad Latinoamerica de Ciencas Sociales (FLACSO), 1995.

Castañeda, Jorge G. *Utopia Unarmed: The Latin American Left After the Cold War.* New York: Vintage, 1993.

The Chicago Record's History of the World's Fair. Chicago: Chicago Daily News Co., 1893.

Cojtí, Demetrio Cuxil. *El Movimiento Maya (en Guatemala).* Guatemala City: Editorial Cholsamaj, 1997.

Cullather, Nicholas. *Operation PBSUCCESS: The United States and Guatemala, 1952–1954.* Washington D.C.: Center for the Study of Intelligence, Central Intelligence Agency, 1994 (declassified in 1997).

Davis, Shelton. "Introduction. Sowing the Seeds of Violence." In *The Harvest of Violence: The Maya Indians and the Guatemalan Crisis,* edited by Robert Carmack. Norman: University of Oklahoma Press, 1988.

Debray, Regis. *Revolution in the Revolution? Armed Struggle and Political Struggle in Latin America.* New York: Monthly Review Press, 1967.

Dicum, Gregory, and Nina Luttinger. *The Coffee Book: Anatomy of an Industry from Crop to the Last Drop.* New York: New Press, 1999.

Falla, Ricardo. *Masacres de la selva: Ixcán, Guatemala 1975–1982.* Guatemala City: Editorial Universitaria, 1993.

Figueroa Ibarra, Carlos. *El recuso del miedo: Ensayo sobre el Estado y el terror en Guatemala.* San José, Costa Rica: EDUCA, 1991.

Forster, Cindy. *The Time of Freedom: Campesino Workers in Guatemala's October Revolution.* Pittsburgh: University of Pittsburgh Press, 2001.

Galeano, Eduardo. *Memory of Fire: Century of the Wind.* New York: Pantheon Books, 1988.

Gleijeses, Piero. *Shattered Hope: The Guatemalan Revolution and the United States, 1944–1954.* Princeton: Princeton University Press, 1991.

Goldman, Francisco. *The Long Night of White Chickens.* New York: Atlantic Monthly Press, 1992.

González, Matilde. "La historia oral, una vía para la reconfiguración del sentido." Guatemala City: Asociación para el Avance de las Ciencias Sociales en Guatemala (AVANCSO), 1998.

Gott, Richard. *Guerrilla Movements in Latin America.* London: Nelson, 1970.

Gramajo Morales, Héctor Alejandro. *De la guerra . . . a la guerra: la difícil transición política en Guatemala.* Guatemala City: Fondo de Cultura Editorial, 1995.

———. *Tesis de la estabilidad nacional.* Guatemala City: EDE, 1989.

Grandin, Greg. *The Blood of Guatemalans: A History of Race and Nation.* Durham: Duke University Press, 2000.

———, ed. *Denegado en Su Totalidad: Documentos estadounidenses liberados.* Guatemala City: Asociación para el Avance de las Ciencias Sociales en Guatemala (AVANCSO), 2001.

Handy, Jim. *Gift of the Devil.* Boston: South End Press, 1984.

———. *Revolution in the Countryside: Rural Conflict and Agrarian Reform in Guatemala, 1944–54.* Chapel Hill: University of North Carolina Press, 1994.

Harbury, Jennifer. *Bridge of Courage.* Monroe, Maine: Common Courage Press, 1994.

Hostnig, Rainer, and Luis Vásquez Vicente. *Nab'ab'l Qtanam: La memoria colectiva del pueblo mam de Quetzaltenango.* Guatemala City: CCIC, 1994.

Huxley, Aldous. *Beyond the Mexique Bay.* New York: Harper & Brothers Publishers, 1934.

Jiménez, Michael F. "'From Plantation to Cup.' Coffee and Capitalism in the United

States, 1830–1930." In *Coffee, Society, and Power in Latin America*. Edited by William Roseberry, Lowell Gudmundson, and Mario Samper Kutschbach. Baltimore: Johns Hopkins University Press, 1995.

Jonas, Susanne. *The Battle for Guatemala: Rebels, Death Squads, and U.S. Power.* Boulder, Colo.: Westview Press, 1991.

LaFeber, Walter. *Inevitable Revolutions: The United States in Central America.* New York: W. W. Norton, 1993.

Le Bot, Yvon. *La Guerra en tierras mayas: Comunidad, violencia y modernidad en Guatemala (1970–1992).* México, D.F.: Fondo de Cultura Económica, 1992.

Levenson-Estrada, Deborah. *Trade Unionists Against Terror: Guatemala City, 1954–1985.* Chapel Hill: University of North Carolina Press, 1994.

Martínez Peláez, Severo. *La patria del criollo: Ensayo de interpretación de la realidad colonial guatemalteca.* 4th ed. Guatemala City: Editorial Universitaria, 1976.

McAllister, Carlota. "Authenticity and Guatemala's Maya Queen." In *Beauty Queens on the Global Stage: Gender, Contests, and Power,* edited by Collen Ballerino Cohen et al. New York: Routledge, 1996.

McClintock, Michael. *The American Connection.* Vol. 2, *State Terror and Popular Resistance in Guatemala.* London: Zed Books, 1985.

McCreery, David. "State Power, Indigenous Communities, and Land in Nineteenth-Century Guatemala, 1820–1920." In *Guatemalan Indians and the State, 1540–1988,* edited by Carol A. Smith. Austin: University of Texas Press, 1990.

———. *Rural Guatemala, 1760–1940.* Stanford: Stanford University Press, 1994.

———. "Wage Labor, Free Labor, and Vagrancy Law. The Transition to Capitalism in Guatemala, 1920–1945." In *Coffee, Society, and Power in Latin America,* edited by William Roseberry, Lowell Gudmundson, and Mario Samper Kutschbach. Baltimore: Johns Hopkins University Press, 1995.

Menchú, Rigoberta. *I, Rigoberta Menchú: An Indian Woman in Guatemala.* Edited by Elisabeth Burgos-Débray, translated by Ann Wright. New York: Verso, 1984.

———. *Trenzando el futuro: Luchas campesinas en la historia reciente de Guatemala.* Madrid: Tercera Prensa-Hirugarren Prentsa, S.L., 1992.

Nelson, Diane. *A Finger in the Wound: Body Politics in Quincentennial Guatemala.* Berkeley: University of California Press, 1999.

Oglesby, Elizabeth. "Desde los Cuadernos de Myrna Mack. Reflections sobre la violencia, la memoria y la investigación social." In *De la memoria a la reconstrucción histórica.* Guatemala City:. Asociación para el Avance de las Ciencias Sociales en Guatemala (AVANCSO), 1999.

Paige, Jeffery M. *Coffee and Power: Revolution and the Rise of Democracy in Central America.* Cambridge: Harvard University Press, 1997.

Payeras, Mario. *Los pueblos indígenas y la revolución guatemalteca.* Guatemala City: Luna y Sol, 1997.

Paz Cárcamo, Guillermo. *Guatemala: Reforma Agraria.* 3rd ed. Guatemala City: Facultad Latinoamerica de Ciencas Sociales (FLACSO), 1997.

Pearson, Neale J. "The *Confederación Nacional Campesina de Guatemala* (CNCG) and Peasant Unionism in Guatemala, 1944–1954." Master's thesis, Georgetown University, 1964.

Porras, Gustavo. "Análisis estructural y recomposición clasista de la sociedad guatemalteca de 1954–1980." In *Seminario Estado, Clases Sociales y Cuestión*

Etnico-Nacional, edited by Centro de Estudios Integrados de Desarrollo Comunal. Mexico City: Editorial Praxis, 1992.

Rodríguez Elizondo, José. *Crisis y Renovación de las Izquierdas: De la revolución cubana a Chiapas, pasando por "el caso chileno."* Santiago de Chile: Editorial Andres Bello, 1995.

Rydell, Robert W. *All the World's a Fair: Visions of Empire at American International Expositions, 1876–1916.* Chicago: University of Chicago Press, 1984.

Schirmer, Jennifer. *The Guatemalan Military Project: A Violence Called Democracy.* Philadelphia: University of Pennsylvania Press, 1998.

Schlesinger, Stephen C., and Stephen Kinzer. *Bitter Fruit: The Untold Story of the American Coup in Guatemala.* New York: Doubleday, 1982.

Solórzano Fernández, Valentín. *El Relato de Juan Tayun: La Vida de un Indio Guatemalteco.* México, D.F. Costa-Amic, 1985.

Stephens, John L. *Incidents of Travel in the Central America, Chiapas, and Yucatan.* 2 vols. New York. Harper & Brothers, 1841.

Stoll, David. *Between Two Armies in the Ixil Towns of Guatemala.* New York: Columbia University Press, 1993.

———. *Rigoberta Menchú and the Story of All Poor Guatemalans.* Boulder, Colo.: Westview Press, 1999.

Taracena Arriola, Arturo. *Invención criolla, sueño ladino, pesadilla indígena: Los Altos de Guatemala, de región a Estado, 1740–1850.* Antigua: Centro de Investigaciones Regionales de Mesoamérica, 1997.

Trachtenberg, Alan. *The Incorporation of America: Culture and Society in the Gilded Age.* New York: Hill and Wang, 1982.

Wagner, Regina. *Los Alemanes en Guatemala.* Guatemala City: Editorial IDEA, 1991.

Wickham-Crowley, Timothy P. *Guerrillas and Revolution in Latin America: A Comparative Study of Insurgents and Regimes since 1956.* Princeton: Princeton University Press, 1992.

Williams, Robert. *States and Social Evolution. Coffee and the Rise of National Governments in Central America.* Chapel Hill: University of North Carolina Press, 1994.

ACKNOWLEDGMENTS

I am indebted above all to the many Guatemalans who entrusted me with their stories. Two in particular deserve credit for making this book possible. Sara Endler initially opened a door into the coffee world and then allowed me free rein to examine her plantation's troubled past. She really did have "nothing to hide" — not because of what she did or did not know, but because of her unflagging commitment to open, honest discussion of her country's history. The other is César Sánchez, who provided as good a guide to plantation life as one could hope for, combining the most compelling and enduring ideals of his generation — the power to analyze and the courage to criticize — with a remarkably open mind and a deep empathy for the experience of all people.

I'm also very grateful to the many other friends who helped me find my way in Guatemala. Among these were Tani Adams, Marcie Mersky, Juan Carlos Longo, Jude Sunderland, Debbie Arthur, Matilde Gonzalez, Liz Oglesby, Karin Coc, Violeta Contreras, Federico Velázquez, Manuela Méndez, Aaron Pollack, Virginia Scott, Juventino Vail, John Pauly, and especially Sonia Alvarez and Erwin Rabanales. Many thanks go to Rick and Betty Adams for their hospitality, wisdom, and good cheer. Special thanks also to Crescencio and Cristina Vail for giving this *Xq'an* a place in their home.

I would probably never have met any of these people if not for the Michael C. Rockefeller Fellowship Program. In addition to providing the money that got me to Guatemala, the fellowship gave me the courage I needed to step off the beaten path once I was there. For that, I am grateful to the fellowship committee and to the Rockefeller family. Thanks also to the Fulbright Program for its support, which allowed me to finish my investigation.

I was extremely fortunate to be able to work with an agent as talented as Tina Bennett. Many thanks to her for the enthusiasm and good sense she brought to this project. Many thanks also to Anton Mueller, an awesome editor who saw exactly what I was trying to do and showed me how to do it better. It's been an honor to work with him. Many thanks also to his colleagues at Houghton Mifflin: Erica Avery, Liz Duvall, Jay Boggis, and Gracie Doyle.

Before I had a real editor, I relied on a wide circle of friends for editorial feedback and other advice. These include Richard Buery, Amy Chazkel, Wei Cui, Alex Demir, David Gartner, Paul Kobrak, Dan Lehman, Tim Lytton, Lexy Mayers, Phil McBlain, Sharon McBlain, Corey Robin, Caroline Sadlowski, Tico Taussig, Mark Weiner, Robert Wheeler, and Andrew Wilson. At Yale, I received generous support from some great teachers, including Owen Fiss, Gil Joseph, Emilia Viotti da Costa, Harlon Dalton, and the late Joseph Goldstein. At Human Rights Watch, I received invaluable support during the book's final stages from a phenomenal group of colleagues, including Carroll Bogert, Joanne Csete, Maureen Langloss, Joanne Mariner, Veronica Matushaj, Ken Roth, and José Miguel Vivanco.

Very special thanks to Frank Goldman, good friend and master storyteller (*Guatemala sí existe, vos*). And to Greg Grandin, pioneer in his field and, before that, partner in crime during the Xela years — thanks for everything (especially the cinnamon rolls). Thanks also to my family: my parents, John and Virginia Wilkinson, for their constant support; my sister, Marie, for her insightful comments and a memorable visit; and especially my brother, Patrick, the most generous and thoughtful reader of them all. Many thanks to the people who, at critical moments along the way, saved me from myself: Wei, Emilia, Greg, and — above all — Patricia Mathews Salazar, to whom this book is dedicated. And, last, thanks to Martín, who sampled pages of the manuscript weeks before he was really ready for solid foods. As a Guatemalan poet once observed, there are few things more beautiful than reimagining the world through the eyes of a child — and as Martín has shown me, there are few things that are more fun.

INDEX

Daniel Wilkinson, a graduate of Harvard College and Yale Law School, works with Human Rights Watch and lives in New York City.

$x > 1$

$y > 0$

$x = 2$

$y = 0.5$ $y = 1$

y^x y^{x+1}

$\left(\frac{1}{2}\right)^2$ $\left(\frac{1}{2}\right)^{2+1}$

$\left(\frac{1}{2}\right)^2$ $\left(\frac{1}{2}\right)^3$

$\frac{1}{2} \times \frac{1}{2} \times$ $\frac{1}{2} \times \frac{1}{2} \times \frac{1}{2}$

$\left(\frac{1}{4}\right) > \frac{1}{8}$

1^2 2 1^3 x.

$(x^3)^2$ $2a + b = 17$ $2a = 17 - b$

$(2^3)^2$ $b - 3 = 2$ $b = 5$

$a = 6 \Rightarrow b = 5$ $2a = 17 - 5$

$2 \times 2 \times 2$ $8^2 = 64$ $2a = 12$

$2 \times 2 \times 2$ $a = \frac{12}{2} = 6$

$2 \times 16 \times 2$ $32 < 64$.

Essay One - Wilkinson Silence on the Mountain

(Due - Next Thursday)

This essay will be a short (c. 3 pages) summary of one specific dimension of Wilkinson's efforts to represent the task of "truth telling" or learning to listen to silences. Pick a specific piece of the book where he probes the accessibility of the truth to explain his position on the public act of telling the truth through speaking, writing, or other forms. Take a tiny part of his work to try to summarize and explain clearly, precisely and fairly. This might mean doing an intensive textual representation of a single point in the text as the first step towards doing an in-depth analysis. In presenting the specific point please use the text itself as evidence and then use the text to shed light on what the author might mean by what they say. Obviously, this means that you should **not** paraphrase Wilkinson, rather try to present what he is saying. You should try to develop an approach which incorporates you as an active narrator while keeping the author present as well. "Wilkinson presents the idea that the silence he encountered was product of repression and fear" or "He argues that the signing of the peace in 1996 had few effects on who held power in la Igualdad" are examples of the tone I would like you to develop in this essay. Put in its most simple form I want you to constantly remind the reader that you are talking about an argument, an author, and a chapter/section.